strike!

by Jeremy Brecher

The Book Division of Rolling Stone

Grateful acknowledgement is made for permission to quote the
following material in this book: excerpts from *My America*
by Louis Adamic. Copyright © 1938 by Louis Adamic. By
permission of Harper & Row Publishers, Inc./ *The Many and
the Few* by Henry Kraus, published by Plantin Press, 1948.
Reprinted by permission/ *Industrial Valley* by Ruth McKenney,
published by Harcourt Brace. Copyright © 1939 by Ruth
McKenney. Reprinted by permission of Curtis Brown Ltd./
"The Trade Union as a Wage-Fixing Institution" by E.A. Ross,
from *American Economic Review*, September 1947. Reprinted
by permission/ *The American City* by Charles Rumford Walker.
Copyright © 1965 by Charles Rumford Walker. Reprinted by
permission of Holt, Rinehart and Winston Inc./ "Counter-
Planning on the Shop Floor" by Bill Watson, from *Radical
America*. Reprinted by permission.

First Printing

STRAIGHT ARROW BOOKS
The Book Division of Rolling Stone
625 Third Street
San Francisco, CA 94107

Library of Congress Catalog Card Number: 79/181709
SBN 0/87932/018/4 (paperbound)
SBN 0/87932/011/7 (hardcover)

Distributed by the World Publishing Company
Printed by: Edwards Brothers, Ann Arbor

Cover Picture
The Sixth Maryland Regiment marching through Baltimore

The Baltimore and Ohio Railroad employees strike against a 10% pay
reduction. 150 soldiers marched to Camden station to protect R.R.
property. The employees engaged them in a battle during which 9 civilians were killed, 17 wounded and 24 soldiers wounded.

Engraving from a photograph by Bendann from Harper's Weekly,
August 11, 1877.
Historical Pictures Service

Contents

Acknowledgements

Even so personal a project as writing a book is only made possible by the help of many other people. I would like to thank here those who have been of the most immediate help. Almost all have disagreed at one point or another; responsibility for errors of fact or interpretation remains completely my own.

Much of the initial work on this book was done at the Institute for Policy Studies in Washington, D.C. The Fellows, students, staff, and hangers-on of the Institute have contributed much to my education over the past six years. It was Marcus Raskin there who gave me the necessary encouragement to stop talking and start writing.

My colleagues on *Root & Branch* have contributed much individually and together to my understanding of the matters dealt with herein.

Edward M. Brecher not only made available an ideal place to prepare the manuscript, but gave me the benefit of his writing experience by painstakingly blue-penciling the first draft.

Sharon Hammer, printer and artist, skillfully prepared the final manuscript. She was also the first to appreciate the humor of the book.

A grant from the Louis M. Rabinowitz Foundation helped finance my research.

James H. Williams, Catherine Roraback, and Joel and Jeanne Stein lent me materials which otherwise would have been difficult to obtain.

A number of others have been extremely generous with their time in reading and commenting on the manuscript before final revision. I would like to thank especially Stanley Aronowitz, William Earl Brecher, Fred Gardner, Dorothy Lee, Staughton Lynd, Paul Mattick, Jr., David Montgomery, Alan Rinzler, Steve Sapolsky, and Arthur Waskow.

Foreword

As I grew up in the 1950's and 1960's, two facts about my personal future haunted me. The first was the likelihood that I, my family and friends would sooner or later be killed in a nuclear war we felt powerless to prevent. The second was that even if we escaped this fate, we would probably have to spend most of our lives tied to jobs we found onerous, boring, and stunting; working not for ourselves but for someone else; doing work which, far from meeting real needs, would likely be useless if not positively harmful; wasting our lives away, angry, frustrated, and unable to do much of anything about it.

Like many of my contemporaries, I wanted to understand and change the situation in which I found myself. But American history as we were taught it was worse than useless for that purpose. The history of our country, we were told, was the story of continuing progress toward ever-greater freedom, well-being and perfection. And throughout that history, ordinary Americans wanted nothing else but to go along for the ride.

This view makes the problems we face today incomprehensible. For if American history is such a success story, why are we in such a mess? Further, this view allows us no alternatives to our present predicament—alternatives rooted in our own past. For if ordinary people throughout American history merely went along with the course set by the powerful and were incapable of acting on their own, where can we look for alternatives?

But gradually I discovered that we have been told anything but the whole truth about American history. The reality of the American past is quite different. Looking back, we can see the roots of our current problems developing through the years. And equally important, we can see that ordinary Americans have *not* acquiesced in that development.

This book is the story of repeated, massive, and often violent revolts by ordinary working people in America. It gives a picture far different from the usual high school or college history course. The story includes virtual nation-wide general strikes, the seizure of vast industrial establishments, guerrilla warfare, and armed battles with artillery and aircraft. I was myself amazed as I gradually uncovered the various strands of the story.

The main actors in the story are ordinary working people. Most historians, whether radical or conservative, tend to consider ordinary workers a mere "rank and file," controlled and directed by unions and labor leaders. Strikes are presumably the work of these organizations and leaders. I have found, on the contrary, that far from fomenting strikes and rebellions, unions and labor leaders have most often striven to prevent or contain them, while the drive to extend them has generally come from a most undocile "rank and file." Indeed, the most important lesson I learned in preparing this book is the extent to which ordinary working people, acting on their own, have through the decades thought, planned, drawn lessons from their own experiences, organized themselves, and taken action in common. Much of the time these abilities have had no chance for expression; they were suppressed in a society which believed ordinary people should distrust one another and obey their superiors. But when "looking out for number one" and "getting along by going along" no longer worked, people discovered that together they had powers they never suspected.

This is important because the greatest problem we face today is our powerlessness. It underlies every particular problem we face: war, pollution, racism, brutality, injustice, insecurity, and the feeling of being trapped, our lives wasting away, pushed around by forces beyond our control. The source of all these problems is not some cruel decree of fate; every one of them results from the fact that we do not control the life of our own society. The fundamental problem we face — and the key to solving the more particular problems — is to transform society so that ordinary people control it.

Most people feel powerless to affect what goes on in our society. The official channels through which they are supposed to be able to do so — elections, pressure groups, unions, public discussion — appear more and more useless. And yet ordinary people — together — have potentially the greatest power of all. For it is their activity which makes up society. If they refuse to work, the country stops. If they take control of their own activity, their own work, they thereby take control of society.

Of course, the kind of power which would result if they did so would be far different from that with which we are familiar now. Today, power means the power of some people to tell others what to do. The power we see rising in this book is the power of people directing their own action cooperatively toward common purposes. Ordinary people can only have power over social life when power as we have known it — power of some people over others — is dissolved completely.

This book shows ordinary people developing such a new form of power. Needless to say, it has so far only been expressed in partial, limited forms. But even from these we can learn a great deal that is helpful in solving our own problem of powerlessness. We can see the real forces blocking the transformation of our society. We can grasp the process by which people discover how to rely on each other and not on their superiors. And we can see the results of different forms of organization and action.

All historical writing is a matter of selecting a limited number of significant facts from an infinity of others. In this book, far from trying to present a general history of labor in the United States, I have deliberately focused on those aspects of the story which can help us in the tasks we face today.

The Prologue of this book gives the background of how ordinary people came to be so powerless. Part I, Chapters One through Six present six peak periods of strikes and related actions— what I have called periods of mass strike. In Part II, Chapter Seven analyzes the significance of these events and the factors that have limited them. Chapter Eight discusses the situation we face today and the actions working people are taking right now. Chapter Nine tries to project these actions beyond the limits they have reached so far, to see how they could lead to a transformation of society.

The actions recounted in this book grew out of the daily problems of ordinary people. What happens when we go to work or school, make a home, shop, try to make a life, may seem at first glance far removed from making history. But in trying to solve the problems of their daily lives, people sometimes find they must act in ways which also challenge the whole organization of society. I started work on this book in response to problems in my own life— problems most of us share. The book is dedicated to those who would likewise share in the solutions.

Jeremy Brecher
February, 1972

Part I
The History of
American Strikes

Prologue

Visiting the United States in 1831, the French traveller Alexis de Tocqueville was impressed above all by the equality which marked life in America. The great majority of Americans were farmers working their own land, primarily for their own needs. Most of the rest were self-employed artisans, merchants, traders, and professionals. Other classes—employees and industrialists in the North, slaves and planters in the South—were relatively small. The great majority of Americans were independent and free from anybody's command.

Yet the forces that were to undermine this equality—and to produce the mass strikes which are the subject of this book—were already visible. With sadness, Tocqueville noted "small aristocratic societies that are formed by some manufacturers in the midst of the immense democracy of our age."[1] Like the aristocratic societies of former ages, this one tended to divide men into classes, made up of "some men who are very opulent and a multitude who are wretchedly poor,"[2] with few means of escaping their condition.

Further, Tocqueville saw that production tended to become more and more centralized, for "when a workman is engaged every day upon the same details, the whole commodity is produced with greater ease, speed, and economy."[3] Thus, "the cost of production of manufactured goods is diminished by the extent of the establishment in which they are made and by the amount of capital employed."[4] The large, centralized companies naturally won out.

This process shaped both the worker and the employer. "When a workman is unceasingly and exclusively engaged in the fabrication of one thing, he ultimately does his work with singular dexterity; but at the same time he loses the general faculty of applying his mind to the direction of the work."[5] Thus, "in proportion as the workman improves, the man is degraded . . . he no longer belongs to himself, but to the calling that he has chosen."[6] But, Tocqueville argued, while "the science of manufacture lowers the class of workmen, it raises the class of masters,"[7] until the employer more and more resembles the administrator of a vast empire.

Tocqueville believed that "the manufacturing aristocracy which is growing up under our eyes is one of the harshest that ever existed in the world."[8] And he concluded that "if ever a permanent inequality of conditions and aristocracy again penetrates into the world, it may be predicted that this is the gate by which they will enter." [9]

Tocqueville's dire predictions soon proved all too true. Industry grew at an incredible rate. In the fifty years following the start of the Civil War, investment in manufacturing grew twelve-fold. Railroad mileage grew from 30,000 miles to more than 200,000. By the turn of the century, more than three-fourths of manufactured products came from factories owned by corporations and other associations of stockholders. In 1860, only one-sixth of the American people lived in cities of 8,000 or more; by 1900 it was one-third. The number of wage-earners, meanwhile, grew from 1.5 million to 5.5 million.

Looking back on how these changes had affected workers during his lifetime, a labor leader wrote in 1889 —

With the introduction of machinery, large manufacturing establishments were erected in the cities and towns. Articles that were formerly made by hand, were turned out in large quantities by machinery; prices were lowered, and those who worked by hand found themselves competing with something that could withstand hunger and cold and not suffer in the least. The village blacksmith shop was abandoned, the road-side shoe shop was deserted, the tailor left his bench, and all together these mechanics [workers] turned away from their country homes and wended their way to the cities wherein the large factories had been erected. The gates were unlocked in the morning to allow them to enter, and after their daily task was done the gates were closed after them in the evening.

Silently and thoughtfully, these men went to their homes. They no longer carried the keys of the workshop, for workshop, tools and keys belonged not to them, but to their master. Thrown together in this way, in these large hives of industry, men became acquainted with each other, and frequently discussed the question of labor's rights and wrongs. [10]

Out of this experience, out of these discussions, workers concluded that they were no longer free and equal citizens; more and more they felt like wage slaves, able to live only by working for someone else, left to walk the streets unemployed when no employer would hire them. No longer possessing the keys to the workshop, they were left virtually helpless. Yet they possessed one weapon which gave them power — the strike. For without their labor, all the factories and offices, railroads and mines could produce nothing.

Strikes seem to have occurred ever since some people were forced to work for others; there are records of strikes by workers on the Great Pyramids of Egypt thousands of years ago. But until the end of the Civil War, strikes were relatively small in the United States. The great majority of workers were self-employed. They might protest by voting, by demonstrating, by rioting, even from time to time by armed rebellion, but they could not strike.

Thus our story starts a dozen years after the Civil War, with the Great Upheaval of 1877—the first event to bring to the country's attention the vast new class of workers who possessed neither workshops nor farms, and thus had to work for those who did, the new class of industrial capitalists.

From the time of the Civil War, the U.S. government followed policies of immense benefit to the rising industrialists. Four key measures passed during the war set the pattern. In 1862, Congress gave a vast grant of land and loans to a group of promoters to build the first transcontinental railroad. The next year, Congress passed a national banking act which undermined the local banks and established a national banking system—essential to the new corporate order. By 1864, the tariff on foreign manufactured goods —designed to protect American producers from competition— reached forty-seven percent, and remained so high in the following decades that the government was often embarrassed to find itself running a budget surplus. Also in 1864, Congress authorized employers to import foreign workers under contracts which forced them to work for the employer who imported them until their passage was paid off. Immigration provided a cheap labor force for industry; 28.5 million immigrants came to the United States from 1860 to 1920. It is little wonder that many contemporaries—and historians—have felt it was the industrial capitalists who really emerged the victors from the Civil War.

Railroads, factories and farms grew at breakneck speed in the years following the Civil War. The frontier moved steadily westward as one after another territory was opened to homesteaders— and land speculators. The railroads bribed Congressmen and received land grants the size of whole countries. The attention of the nation turned away from politics and toward the astonishing advance of industry. It seemed a "Gilded Age," and the magnates who amassed great fortunes and vast enterprises were widely viewed as the conquering heroes of a new industrial civilization.

The government established the conditions for economic growth but did little to cope with the consequences. Chaos resulted when private enterprisers used their control of the nation's resources to increase their own fortunes by any means necessary. The result was an unorganized, disorderly society. The social institutions which today try to moderate social conflict, ease distress, and defuse discontent were virtually non-existent. Only those on whose backs the industrialists rode to power considered them not knights in armor but "robber barons."

Then the bubble burst. In September, 1873, the leading American banking house, Jay Cooke and Company, suddenly declared

XIV itself bankrupt. The stock market tumbled, and by the end of the month the Stock Exchange itself had closed its doors. In 1873 alone, 5,183 businesses worth over $200 million failed.

Depressions had been a regular feature of capitalist society since its start. But by 1877, depression had lasted longer than any time before in American history. For workers, conditions were quite desperate. Wages throughout industry had been cut more than twenty-five percent, below subsistence in many cases, while an estimated one million industrial workers were unemployed. Large numbers of the unemployed hit the road looking for work, often travelling in bands of what became known as "tramps."

The wealthier classes observed these conditions and trembled. Only six years before, the workers of Paris had arisen, taken over the city by armed force, and established the famous Paris Commune. Now it was not only Europe that was haunted by the "spectre of communism"; a Workingman's Party, dedicated to the overthrow of capitalism, had arisen in America as well. Perhaps even more terrifying were the sallow, sullen faces of men, women and children, walking the streets with little in their stomachs and hardly a place to lay their heads. An English visitor found wealthy Americans "pervaded by an uneasy feeling that they were living over a mine of social and industrial discontent with which the power of the government, under American institutions, was wholly inadequate to deal: and that some day this mine would explode and blow society into the air." [11]

That explosion came with the Great Upheaval of 1877.

Prologue: Footnotes

1. Alexis de Tocqueville, *Democracy in America* & (N.Y.: Vintage Edition) Vol. II, p. 170.
2. *Ibid.,* p. 170.
3. *Ibid.,* p. 168.
4. *Ibid., p. 168.*
5. *Ibid.,* p. 168.
6. *Ibid.,* p. 168-9.
7. *Ibid.,* p. 169.
8. *Ibid.,* p. 171.
9. *Ibid.,* p. 171.
10. Terence V. Powderly, *Thirty Years of Labor 1859-1889* (Columbus, Ohio: Excelsior Publishing House, 1889), pp. 26-7.
11. Goldwin Smith, "The Labour War in the United States," in *The Contemporary Review,* XXX (September 1877), p. 537, cited in Robert V. Bruce, *1877: Year of Violence* (N.Y.: Bobbs-Merrill Co., Inc., 1959), p. 26.

Chapter I
The Great Upheaval

In the centers of many American cities are positioned huge armories, grim nineteenth-century edifices of brick or stone. They are fortresses, complete with massive walls and loopholes for guns. You may have wondered why they are there, but it has probably never occurred to you that they were built to protect America, not against invasion from abroad, but against popular revolt at home. Their erection was a monument to the Great Upheaval of 1877.

July, 1877, does not appear in many history books as a memorable date, yet it marks the first great American mass strike, a movement which was viewed at the time as a violent rebellion. Strikers stopped and seized the nation's most important industry, the railroads, and crowds defeated or won over first the police, then the state militias, and in some cases even the Federal troops. General strikes stopped all activity in a dozen major cities, and strikers took over social authority in communities across the nation.

It all began on Monday, July 16th, 1877, in the little railroad town of Martinsburg, West Virginia. On that day, the Baltimore and Ohio Railroad cut wages ten percent, the second cut in eight months. [1] In Martinsburg, men gathered around the railroad yards, talking, waiting through the day. Toward evening the crew of a cattle train, fed up, abandoned the train, and other trainmen refused to replace them.

As a crowd gathered, the strikers uncoupled the engines, ran them into the roundhouse, and announced to B&O officials that no trains would leave Martinsburg till the pay cut was rescinded. The Mayor arrived and conferred with railroad officials. He tried to soothe the crowd and was booed; when he ordered the arrest of the strike leaders they just laughed at him, backed up in their resistance by the angry crowd. The Mayor's police were helpless against the population of the town. No railroad workers could be found willing to take out a train, so the police withdrew and by midnight the yard was occupied only by a guard of strikers left to enforce the blockade. [2]

That night, B&O officials in Wheeling went to see Governor Matthews, took him to their company telegraph office, and waited while he wired Col. Charles Faulkner, Jr., at Martinsburg, to have his Berkeley Light Guards preserve the peace "if necessary, . . . prevent any interference by rioters with the men at work, and also

2   prevent the obstruction of the trains." [3]

Next morning, when the Martinsburg Master of Transportation ordered the cattle train out again, the strikers' guard swooped down on it and ordered the engineer to stop or be killed. He stopped. By now, hundreds of strikers and townspeople had gathered, and the next train out hardly moved before it was boarded, uncoupled, and run into the roundhouse.

About 9:00 a.m., the Berkeley Light Guards arrived to the sound of a fife and drum; the crowd cheered them. Most of the militiamen were themselves railroaders. [4] Now the cattle train came out once more, this time covered with militiamen, their rifles loaded with ball cartridges. As the train pulled through the yelling crowd, a striker named William Vandergriff turned a switch to derail the train and guarded it with a pistol. A soldier jumped off the train to reset the switch; Vandergriff shot him and in turn was fatally shot himself. [5]

At this, the attempt to break the blockade at Martinsburg was abandoned. The strikebreaking engineer and fireman climbed down from the engine and departed. Col. Faulkner called in vain for volunteers to run the train, announced that the Governor's orders had been fulfilled, dismissed his men, and telegraphed the governor that he was helpless to control the situation.

With this confrontation began the Great Upheaval of 1877, a spontaneous, nationwide, virtually general strike. The pattern of Martinsburg — a railroad strike in response to a pay cut, an attempt by the companies to run trains with the support of military forces, the defeat or dissolution of those forces by amassed crowds representing general popular support — became that same week the pattern for the nation.

With news of success at Martinsburg, the strike spread to all divisions of the B&O, with engineers, brakemen, and conductors joining with the firemen who gave the initial impetus. Freight traffic was stopped all along the line, while the men continued to run passenger and mail cars without interference. Seventy engines and six hundred freight cars were soon piled up in the Martinsburg yards.

The Governor, resolved to break the strike, promised to send a company "in which there are no men unwilling to suppress the riots and execute the law." He sent his only available military force, sixty Light Guards from Wheeling. But the Guards were hardly reliable, for sentiment in Wheeling supported the strike strongly. They marched out of town surrounded by an excited crowd, who, a reporter noted, "all expressed sympathy with the strikers;" [7] box and can makers in Wheeling were already on strike and soon people would be discussing a general strike of all labor. When the Guards' train arrived in Martinsburg, it was met by a large, orderly crowd. The militia's commander conferred with railroad and town officials, but dared not use the troops, lest they "further exasperate the strikers."[8] Instead, he marched them away to the courthouse.

At this point the strike was virtually won. But hardly had the strike broken out when the president of B&O began pressing for the use of the U.S. Army against the strikers in West Virginia. "The loss of an hour would most seriously affect us and imperil vast interests," he wrote. With Federal troops, "the rioters could be dispersed and there would be no difficulty in the movement of trains." The road's vice-president wired his Washington agent, saying that the Governor might soon call for Federal troops, and telling him "to see the Secretary of War and inform him of the serious situation of affairs, that he may be ready to send the necessary force to the scene of action at once."[10] Although a newspaperman on the scene of action at Martinsburg reported "perfect order,"[11] and other correspondents were unable to find violence to report, the Colonel of the Guards wired the Governor:

> The feeling here is most intense, and the rioters are largely cooperated with by civilians. . . . The disaffection has become so general that no employee could now be found to run an engine even under certain protection. I am satisfied that Faulkner's experiment of yesterday was thorough and that any repetition of it today would precipitate a bloody conflict, with the odds largely against our small force. . . .[12]

On the basis of this report, the Governor in turn wired the President:

To His Excellency, R.B. Hayes,
President of the U.S.
Washington, D.C.:

> Owing to unlawful combinations and domestic violence now existing at Martinsburg and at other points along the line of the Baltimore and Ohio Railroad, it is impossible with any force at my command to execute the laws of the State. I therefore call upon your Excellency for the assistance of the United States military to protect the law abiding people of the State against domestic violence, and to maintain supremacy of the law.[13]

The president of the B&O added his appeal, wiring the President that West Virginia had done all it could "to suppress this insurrection" and warning that "this great national highway [the B&O] can only be restored for public use by the interposition of U.S. forces."[14] In response, President Hayes sent 300 Federal troops to suppress what his Secretary of War was already referring

4   to publicly as "an insurrection." [15]

This "insurrection" was spontaneous and unplanned, but it grew out of the social conditions of the time and the recent experience of the workers. The tactics of the railroad strikers had been developed in a series of local strikes, mostly without trade union support, that occurred in 1873 and 1874. In December, 1873, for example, engineers and firemen on the Pennsylvania Railroad system struck in Chicago, Pittsburgh, Cincinnati, Louisville, Columbus, Indianapolis, and various smaller towns, in what the *Portsmouth* [Ohio] *Tribune* called "the greatest railroad strike" in the nation's history. [16] Huge crowds gathered in depot yards and supported the strikers against attempts to run the trains. State troops were sent into Dennison, Ohio, and Logansport, Indiana, to break strike strongholds. [17] At Susquehanna Depot, Pennsylvania, three months later, shop and repair workers struck. After electing a "Workingmen's Committee," they seized control of the repair shops; within twenty minutes the entire works was reported "under complete control of the men." [18] The strike was finally broken when 1,800 Philadelphia soldiers with thirty pieces of cannon es-

Fight for control of a tunnel near Harpersville on the Albany and Susquehanna Railroad.

The strikes were generally unsuccessful; but, as Herbert Gutman wrote, they "revealed the power of the railroad workers to disrupt traffic on many roads." [20] The employers learned that "they had a rather tenuous hold on the loyalties of their men. Something was radically wrong if workers could successfully stop trains for from two or three days to as much as a week, destroy property, and even 'manage' it as if it were their own." [21] And, Gutman continued, " . . . the same essential patterns of behavior that were widespread in 1877 were found in the 1873-1874 strikes. Three and a half years of severe depression ignited a series of local brush fires into a national conflagration . . . " [22]

The more immediate background of the 1877 railroad strike also helps explain why it took the form of virtual insurrection, for this struggle grew out of the failure of other, less violent forms of action.

The wage cut on the B&O was part of a general pattern which had started June 1st on the Pennsylvania Railroad. When the leaders of the Brotherhoods of Engineers, Conductors, and Firemen made no effort to combat the cut, the railroad workers on the Pennsylvania system took action themselves. A week before the cut went into effect, the Newark, New Jersey division of the Engineers held an angry protest meeting against the cut. The Jersey City lodge met the next day, voted for a strike, and put out feelers to other workers; by the day the cut took effect, engineers' and firemen's locals throughout the Pennsylvania system had chosen delegates to a joint grievance committee, ignoring the leadership of their national union. Nor was the wage cut their only grievance; the committee proposed what amounted to a complete reorganization of work. They opposed the system of assigning trains, in which the first crew into town was the first crew out, leaving them no time to rest or see their families; they wanted regular runs to stabilize pay and working days; they wanted passes home in case of long layovers; they wanted the system of "classification" of workers by length of service and efficiency—used to keep wages down—abolished. [23]

But the grievance committee delegates were easily intimidated and cajoled by Tom Scott, the masterful ruler of the Pennsylvania Railroad, who talked them into accepting the cut without consulting those who elected them. A majority of brakemen, many conductors, and some engineers wanted to repudiate the committee's action; but, their unity broken, the locals decided not to strike. [24]

Since the railroad brotherhoods had clearly failed, the work-

6 ers' next step was to create a new, secret organization, the Trainmen's Union. It was started by workers on the Pittsburgh, Fort Wayne and Chicago. Within three weeks, lodges had sprung up from Baltimore to Chicago, with thousands of members on many different lines. The Trainmen's Union recognized that the privileged engineers "generally patched things up for themselves," [25] so it included conductors, firemen, brakemen, switchmen, and others besides engineers. The union also realized that the various railroad managements were cooperating against the workers, one railroad after another imitating the Pennsylvania with a ten percent wage cut. The union's strategy was to organize at least three-quarters of the trainmen on each trunk line, then strike against the cuts and other grievances. When a strike came, firemen would not take engineers' jobs, and men on non-striking roads would not handle struck equipment. [26]

But the union was full of spies. On one railroad the firing of members began only four days after the union was formed, and others followed suit: "Determined to stamp it out," as one railroad official put it, the company has issued orders to discharge all men belonging to "the Brotherhood or Union." [27] Nonetheless, on June 24th, forty men fanned out over the railroads to call a general railroad strike for the following week. The railroads learned about the strike through their spies, fired the strike committee in a body, and thus panicked part of the leadership into spreading false word that the strike was off. Local lodges, unprepared to act on their own, flooded the union headquarters with telegrams asking what to do. Union officials were denied use of railroad telegraphs to reply, the companies ran their trains, and the strike failed utterly. [28]

Thus, the Martinsburg strike broke out because the B&O workers had discovered that they had no alternative but to act completely on their own. Not only were their wages being cut, but, as one newspaper reported, the men felt they were "treated just as the rolling stock or locomotives"—squeezed for every drop of profit. Reduced crews were forced to handle extra cars, with lowered pay classifications, and extra pay for overtime eliminated. [29]

A similar spontaneous strike developed that same day in Baltimore in response to the B&O wage cut, but the railroad had simply put strikebreakers on the trains and used local police to disperse the crowds of strikers. [30] What made Martinsburg different? The key to the strike, according to historian Robert Bruce, was that "a conventional strike would last only until strikebreakers could be summoned." To succeed, the strikers had to "beat off strikebreakers by force, seize trains, yards, roundhouses . . . " [31] This was possible in Martinsburg because the people of the town so passionately supported the railroad workers that they amassed and resisted the state militia. It was now the support of others elsewhere which allowed the strikers to resist the Federal troops as well.

On Thursday, 300 Federal troops arrived in Martinsburg to quell the "insurrection" and bivouacked in the roundhouse. With militiamen and U.S. soldiers guarding the yards, the company was able to get a few trains loaded with regulars through the town. When 100 armed strikers tried to stop a train, the Sheriff and the militia marched to the scene and arrested the leader. No one in Martinsburg would take out another train, but with the military in control, strikebreakers from Baltimore were able to run freights through unimpeded. The strike seemed broken.

But the population of the surrounding area also now rallied behind the railroad workers. Hundreds of unemployed and striking boatmen on the Chesapeake and Ohio Canal lay in ambush at Sir John's Run, where they stoned the freight that had broken the Martinsburg blockade, forced it to stop, and then hid when the U.S. regulars attacked. The movement soon spread into Maryland, where at Cumberland a crowd of boatmen, railroaders, and others swarmed around the train and uncoupled the cars. When the train finally got away, a mob at Keyser, West Virginia, ran it onto a side track and took the crew off by force—while the U.S. troops stood helplessly by. [22] Just before midnight, the miners of the area met at Piedmont, four miles from Keyser, and resolved to go to Keyser in the morning and help stop trains. Coal miners and others—"a motley crowd, white and black"—halted a train guarded by fifty U.S. regulars after it pulled out of Martinsburg. [23] At Piedmont a handbill was printed warning the B&O that 15,000 miners, the united citizenry of local communities, and "the working classes of every state in the Union" would support the strikers. "Therefore let the clashing of arms be heard . . . in view of the rights and in the defense of our families we shall conquer, or we shall die." [34]

The result was that most of the trains sent west from Martinsburg never even reached Keyser. All but one, which was under heavy military escort, were stopped by a crowd of unemployed rolling-mill men, migrant workers, boatmen, and young boys at Cumberland, Maryland, and even on the one that went through a trainman was wounded by a gunshot. When two leaders of the crowd were arrested, a great throng went to the Mayor's house, demanded the release of the prisoners, and carried them off on their shoulders.

Faced with the spread of the strike through Maryland, the president of the B&O now persuaded Governor Carrol of Maryland to call up the National Guard in Baltimore and send it to Cumber-

8   land. They did not reckon, however, on the reaction of Baltimore to the strike. "The working people everywhere are with us," said a leader of the railroad strikers in Baltimore. "They know what it is to bring up a family on ninety cents a day, to live on beans and corn meal week in and week out, to run in debt at the stores until you cannot get trusted any longer, to see the wife breaking down under privation and distress, and the children growing up sharp and fierce like wolves day after day because they don't get enough to eat." [35]

The bells rang in Baltimore for the militia to assemble just as the factories were letting out for the evening, and a vast crowd assembled as well. At first they cheered the troops, but severely stoned them as they started to march. The crowd was described as "a rough element eager for disturbance; a proportion of mechanics [workers] either out of work or upon inadequate pay, whose sullen hearts rankled; and muttering and murmuring gangs of boys, almost outlaws, and ripe for any sort of disturbance." [36] As the 250 men of the first regiment marched out, 25 of them were injured by the stoning of the crowd, but this was only a love-tap. The second regiment was unable even to leave its own armory for a time. Then, when the order was given to march anyway, the crowd stoned them so severely that the troops panicked and opened fire. In the bloody march that followed, the militia killed ten and seriously wounded more than twenty of the crowd, but the crowd continued to resist, and one by one the troops dropped out and went home, and changed into civilian clothing. By the time they reached the station, only 59 of the original 120 men remained in line. [37] Even after they reached the depot, the remaining troops were unable to leave for Cumberland, for a crowd of about 200 drove away the engineer and firemen of the waiting troop train and beat back a squad of policemen who tried to restore control. The militia charged the growing crowd, but were driven back by brickbats and pistol fire. It was at that stage that Governor Carrol, himself bottled up in the depot by the crowd of 15,000, in desperation wired President Hayes to send

By 1877, railroad workers had found they could only make strikes effective if they used force to prevent passage of the trains.

Like the railroad workers, others joined the "insurrection" out of frustration with other means of struggle. Over the previous years they had experimented with one means of resistance after another, each more radical than the last. First to prove their failure had been the trade unions. In 1870, there were about thirty-three national unions enrolling perhaps five percent of non-farm workers; by 1877, only about nine were left. Total membership plummeted from 300,000 in 1870 to 50,000 in 1876. [38] Under depression conditions, they were simply unable to withstand the organized attack levied by lockouts and blacklisting. Unemployment demonstrations in New York had been ruthlessly broken up by police. Then the first major industrial union in the United States, the Workingmen's Benevolent Association of the anthracite miners, led a strike which was finally broken by the companies, one of which claimed the conflict had cost it $4 million. Next the Molly Maguires—a secret terrorist organization the Irish miners developed to fight the coal operators—were infiltrated and destroyed by agents from the Pinkerton Detective Agency, which specialized in providing spies, agents provocateurs, and private armed forces for employers combatting labor organizations. [39] Thus, by the summer of 1877 it had become clear that no single group of workers—whether through peaceful demonstration, tightly-knit trade unions, armed terrorism, or surprise strikes—could stand against the power of the companies, their armed guards, the Pinkertons, and the armed forces of the Government.

Indeed, the Great Upheaval had been preceded by a seeming quiescence on the part of workers. The general manager of one railroad wrote, June 21st: "The experiment of reducing the salaries has been successfully carried out by all the Roads that have tried it of late, and I have no fear of any trouble with our employees if it is done with a proper show of firmness on our part and they see that they must accept it cheerfully or leave." [40] The very day the strike was breaking out at Martinsburg, Governor Hartranft of Pennsylvania was agreeing with his Adjutant General that the state was enjoying such a calm as it had not known for several years. [41] In less than a week, it would be the center of the insurrection.

Three days after Governor Hartranft's assessment, the Pennsylvania Railroad ordered that all freights eastward from Pittsburgh be run as "double-headers"—with two engines and twice as many cars. This meant in effect a speed-up—more work and increased danger of accidents and layoffs. The trains were likely to break and the sections collide, sending fifty or sixty men out of

10   work. Then Pennsylvania trainmen were sitting in the Pittsburgh roundhouse listening to a fireman read them news of the strike elsewhere when the order came to take out a "double-header." At the last minute a flagman named Augustus Harris, acting on his own initiative, refused to obey the order. The conductor appealed to the rest of the crew, but they too refused to move the train. When the company sent for replacements, twenty-five brakemen and conductors refused to take out the train and were fined on the spot. When the dispatcher finally found three yard brakemen to take out the train, a crowd of twenty angry strikers refused to let the train go through. One of them threw a link at a scab, whereupon the volunteer yardmen gave up and went away. Said flagman Andrew Hice, "It's a question of bread or blood, and we're going to resist." [42]

Freight crews joined the strike as their trains came in and were stopped, and a crowd of mill workers, tramps, and boys began to gather at the crossings, preventing freight trains from running while letting passenger trains go through. The company asked the Mayor for police, but since the city was nearly bankrupt the force had been cut in half, and only eight men were available. Further, the Mayor was elected by the strong working-class vote of the city, and shared the city's upper crust's hatred for the Pennsylvania Railroad and its rate discrimination against Pittsburgh. At most the railroad got seventeen police, whom it had to pay itself. [43]

As elsewhere, the Trainmen's Union had nothing to do with the start of the strike. Its top leader, Robert Ammon, had left Pittsburgh to take a job elsewhere, and the president of the Pittsburgh Division didn't even know that trouble was at hand; he slept late that morning, didn't hear about the strike until nearly noon—his first comment was "Impossible!"—and he busied himself primarily at trying to persuade his colleagues to go home and keep out of trouble. [44]

The Trainmen's Union did, however, provide a nucleus for a meeting of the strikers and representatives of such groups as the rolling-mill workers. "We're with you," said one rolling-mill man, pledging the railroaders support from the rest of Pittsburgh labor. "We're in the same boat. I heard a reduction of ten percent hinted at in our mill this morning. I won't call employers despots, I won't call them tyrants, but the term capitalists is sort of synonymous and will do as well." [45] The meeting called on "all workingmen to make common cause with their brethren on the railroad." [46]

In Pittsburgh, railroad officials picked up the ailing Sheriff, waited while he gave the crowd a *pro forma* order to disperse, and then persuaded him to appeal for state troops. That night state offi-

cials ordered the militia called up in Pittsburgh but only part of the
troops called arrived. Some were held up by the strikers, others
simply failed to show up. Two-thirds of one regiment made it; in
another regiment not one man appeared. [47] Nor were the troops reliable. As one officer reported to his superior, "You can place little
dependence on the troops of your division; some have thrown down
their arms, and others have left, and I fear the situation very
much." [48] Another officer explained why the troops were unreliable. "Meeting an enemy on the field of battle, you go there to kill.
The more you kill, and the quicker you do it, the better. But here
you had men with fathers and brothers and relatives mingled in the
crowd of rioters. The sympathy of the people, the sympathy of the
troops, my own sympathy, was with the strikers proper. We all felt
that those men were not receiving enough wages." [49] Indeed, by
Saturday morning the militiamen had stacked their arms and were
chatting with the crowd, eating hardtack with them, and walking
up and down the streets with them, behaving, as a regular army
lieutenant put it, "as though they were going to have a party." [50]
"You may be called upon to clear the tracks down there," said a
lawyer to a soldier. "They may call on me," the soldier replied,
"and they may call pretty damn loud before they will clear the
tracks." [51]

The *Pittsburgh Leader* came out with an editorial warning of
"The Talk of the Desperate" and purporting to quote a "representative workingman": " 'This may be the beginning of a great civil
war in this country, between labor and capital. It only needs that
the strikers . . . should boldly attack and rout the troops sent to
quell them — and they could easily do it if they tried. . . . The workingmen everywhere would all join and help . . . The laboring people, who mostly constitute the militia, will not take up arms to put
down their brethren. Will capital, then, rely on the United States
Army? Pshaw! These ten or fifteen thousand available men would
be swept from our path like leaves in the whirlwind. The workingmen of this country can capture and hold it if they will only stick
together. . . . Even if so-called law and order should beat them
down in blood . . . we would, at least, have our revenge on the men
who have coined our sweat and muscles into millions for themselves, while they think dip is good enough butter for us.' " [52]

All day Friday, the crowds controlled the switches and the officer commanding the Pittsburgh militia refused to clear the crossing with artillery because of the slaughter that would result. People
swarmed aboard passenger trains and rode through the city free of
charge. [53] The Sheriff warned the women and children to leave
lest they be hurt when the army came, but the women replied that

12   they were there to urge the men on. "Why are you acting this way, and why is this crowd here?" the Sheriff asked one young man who had come to Pittsburgh from Eastern Pennsylvania for the strike. "The Pennsylvania has two ends," he replied, "one in Philadelphia and one in Pittsburgh. In Philadelphia they have a strong police force, and they're with the railroad. But in Pittsburgh they have a weak force, and it's a mining and manufacturing district, and we can get all the help we want from the laboring elements, and we've determined to make the strike here." "Are you a railroader?" the Sheriff asked. "No, I'm a laboring man," came the reply. [54]

Railroad and National Guard officials, realizing that the local Pittsburgh militia units were completely unreliable, sent for 600 fresh troops from its commercial rival, Philadelphia. A Pittsburgh steel manufacturer came to warn railroad officials not to send the troops out until workingmen were back in their factories. "I think I know the temper of our men pretty well, and you would be wise not to do anything until Monday. . . . If there's going to be firing, you ought to have at least ten thousand men, and I doubt if even that many could quell the mob that would be brought down on us." [55] These words were prophetic. But, remembering the 2,000 freight cars and locomotives lying idle in the yards, and the still-effective blockade, the railroad official replied, "We must have our property." He looked at his watch and said, "We have now lost an hour and a half's time." He had confidently predicted that "the Philadelphia regiment won't fire over the heads of the mob." [56] Now the massacre he counted on—and the city's retaliation—was at hand.

As the imported troops marched toward the 28th Street railroad crossing, a crowd of 6,000 gathered, mostly spectators. The troops began clearing the tracks with fixed bayonets and the crowd replied with a furious barrage of stones, bricks, coal, and possibly revolver fire. Without orders, the Philadelphia militia began firing as fast as they could, killing twenty people in five minutes as the crowd scattered. [57] Meanwhile, the local Pittsburgh militia stood on the hillside at carry arms and broke for cover when they saw the Philadelphians' Gatling gun come forward. Soon they went home or joined the mob. [58]

With the crossing cleared, the railroad fired up a dozen doubleheaders, but even trainmen who had previously declined to join the strike now refused to run them, and the strike remained unbroken. Their efforts in vain, the Philadelphia militia retired to the roundhouse.

Meanwhile, the entire city mobilized in a fury against the troops who had conducted the massacre and against the Pennsylvania Railroad. Workers rushed home from their factories for pistols, muskets and butcher knives. A delegation of 600 workingmen from nearby Temperanceville marched in with a full band and colors. In some cases the crowd organized itself into crude armed military units, marching together with drums. Civil authority collapsed in the face of the crowd; the Mayor refused to send police or even to try to quiet the crowd himself.

The crowd peppered the troops in the roundhouse with pistol and musket fire, but finally decided, as one member put it, "We'll

JW Alexander/Library of Congress

When soldiers fired into a crowd in Pittsburgh during the Great Upheaval, killing twenty, the population of the town retaliated by burning the railroad yards. The locomotives and cars destroyed would have made a train 11.5 miles long.

have them out if we have to roast them out."[59] Oil, coke, and whiskey cars were set alight and pushed downhill toward the roundhouse. A few men began systematically to burn the yards, despite rifle fire from the soldiers, while the crowd held off fire trucks at gunpoint. Sunday morning, the roundhouse caught fire and the Philadelphia militia were forced to evacuate. As they marched along the street they were peppered with fire by the crowd and, according to the troops' own testimony, by Pittsburgh policemen as well.[60] Most of the troops were marched out of town and found refuge a dozen miles away. The few left to guard ammunition found civilian clothes, sneaked away, and hid until the crisis was over. By Saturday night, the last remaining regiment of Pittsburgh militia was disbanded. The crowd had completely routed the army.

Sunday morning, hundreds of people broke into the freight cars in the yards and distributed the goods to the crowds below — on

14   occasion with assistance from police. Burning of cars continued. (According to Carroll D. Wright, first U.S. Commissioner of Labor, "A great many old freight cars which must soon have been replaced by new, were pushed into the fire by agents of the railroad company," to be added to the claims against the country. [61]) The crowd prevented firemen from saving a grain elevator, though it was not owned by the railroad, saying "it's a monopoly, and we're tired of it," [62] but workers pitched in to prevent the spread of the fire to nearby tenements. [63] By Monday, 104 locomotives, more than 2,000 cars, and all of the railroad buildings had been destroyed.

Across the river from Pittsburgh, in the railroad town of Allegheny, a remarkable transfer of authority took place. Using the pretext that the Governor was out of the state, the strikers maintained that the state militia was without legal authority, and therefore proposed to treat them as no more than a mob. The strikers armed themselves — by breaking into the local armory, according to the Mayor — dug rifle pits and trenches outside the Allegheny depot, set up patrols, and warned civilians away from the probable line of fire. The strikers took possession of the telegraph and sent messages up and down the road. They took over management of the railroad, running passenger trains smoothly, moving the freight cars out of the yards, and posting regular armed guards over them. Economic management and political power had in effect been taken over by the strikers. Of course, this kind of transfer of power was not universally understood or approved of, even by those who supported the strike. For example, a meeting of rolling-mill men in Columbus, Ohio, endorsed the railroad strikers, urged labor to combine politically and legislate justice, but rejected "mobbism" as apt to destroy "the best form of republican government." [64]

The strike spread almost as fast as word of it, and with it the conflict with the military. In Columbia, Meadville, and Chenago, Pennsylvania, strikers seized the railroads, occupied the roundhouses, and stopped troop trains. In Buffalo, New York, the militia was stoned on Sunday but scattered the crowd by threatening to shoot. Next morning a crowd armed with knives and cudgels stormed into the railroad shops, brushed aside militia guards and forced shopmen to quit work. They seized the Erie roundhouse and barricaded it. When a militia company marched out to recapture the property, a thousand people blocked and drove them back. By Monday evening, all the major U.S. roads had given up trying to move anything but local passenger trains out of Buffalo. Court testimony later gave a good picture of how the strike spread to Reading, Pennsylvania. At a meeting of workers on the Reading Rail-

road, the chairman suggested that it would not be a bad idea to do
what had been done on the B&O. "While it is hot we can keep the
ball rolling," someone chimed in. After some discussion, men volunteered to head off incoming trains. [65] Next day a crowd of 2,000
assembled while twenty-five or fifty men, their faces blackened
with coal dust, tore up track, fired trains, and burned a railroad
bridge. That evening seven companies of the National Guard arrived. As they marched through a tenement district to clear the
tracks, the people of the neighborhood severely stoned them,
wounding twenty with missiles and pistol shots. The soldiers opened fire without orders and killed eleven. [66] As in Pittsburgh, the
population grew furious over the killings. They plundered freight
cars, tore up tracks, and broke into an arsenal, taking sixty rifles.
Next day the companies which had conducted the massacre marched down the track together with newly arrived troops; the crowd
stoned the former and fraternized with the latter. When the hated
Grays turned menacingly toward the crowd, the new troops announced that they would not fire on the people, turned some of
their ammunition over to the crowd, and told the Grays, "If you
fire at the mob, we'll fire at you." [67]

Such fraternization between troops and the crowd was common. When the Governor sent 170 troops to Newark, Ohio, they
were so unpopular that the county commissioners refused to provide
their rations. Thereupon the strikers themselves volunteered to
feed them. By the end of the day strikers and soldiers were frater-
nizing in high good humor. Similarly, when the Governor of New
York sent 600 troops to the railroad center of Hornellsville, in response to the strike on the Erie, the troops and strikers fraternized,
making commanders doubtful of their power to act. When the entire Pennsylvania National Guard was called up in response to the
Pittsburgh uprising, a company in Lebanon, Pennsylvania, mutinied and marched through town amidst great excitement. In Al-
toona, a crowd captured a westbound train carrying 500 militiamen. The troops gave up their arms with the best of will and fraternized with the crowd. The crowd refused to let them proceed, but
was glad to let them go home — which one full company and parts of
the others proceeded to do. A Philadelphia militia unit straggling
home decided to march to Harrisburg and surrender. They entered
jovially, shook hands all around, and gave up their guns to the
crowd.

Persuasion worked likewise against would-be strikebreakers.
When a volunteer started to take a freight train out of Newark,
Ohio, a striking fireman held up his hand, three fingers of which
had been cut off by a railroad accident. "This is the man whose

16   place you are taking," shouted another striker. "This is the man
who works with a hand and a half to earn a dollar and a half a day,
three days in the week, for his wife and children. Are you going to
take the bread out of his mouth and theirs?" [68] The strikebreaker
jumped down amidst cheers.

By now, the movement was no longer simply a railroad strike.
With the battles between soldiers and crowds drawn from all parts
of the working population, it was increasingly perceived as a struggle between workers as a whole and employers as a whole. This
was now reflected in the rapid development of general strikes. After the burning of the railroad yards in Pittsburgh, a general strike
movement swept through the area. At nearby McKeesport, workers of the National Tube Works gathered early Monday morning
and marched all over town to martial music, calling fellow workers
from their houses. From the tube workers the strike spread first to
a rolling mill, then a car works, then a planing mill. In mid-morn-
ing, 1,000 McKeesport strikers marched with a brass band to Andrew Carnegie's great steel works, calling out planing-mill and tin-
mill workers as they went. By mid-afternoon the Carnegie workers
and the Braddocks car workers joined the strike. At Castle Shan-
non, 500 miners struck. On the South Side, laborers struck at Jones
and Laughlin and at the Evans, Dalzell & Co. pipe works. [69]

In Buffalo, New York, crowds roamed the city trying to bring
about a general strike. They effectively stopped operations at planing mills, tanneries, car works, a bolt and nut factory, hog yards,
coal yards, and canal works. In Harrisburg, Pennsylvania, factories
and shops throughout the city were closed by strikes and crowd
action. In Zanesville, Ohio, 300 unemployed men halted construction on a hotel, then moved through town shutting down nearly
every factory and foundry and sending horse-cars to the barns.
Next morning a meeting of workingmen drew up a schedule of acceptable wages. In Columbus, a crowd growing from 300 to 2,000
went through town spreading a general strike, successfully calling
out workers at a rolling mill, pipe works, fire clay works, pot
works, and planing mill. "Shut up or burn up" was the mob's slogan. [80] An offshoot of a rally to support the railroad workers in Toledo, Ohio, resolved to call a general strike for a minimum wage of
$1.50 a day. Next morning a large crowd of laborers, grain trim-
mers, stevedores, and others assembled and created a committee
of safety composed of one member from every trade represented
in the movement. Three hundred men formed a procession four
abreast while a committee called on the management of each factory; workers of those not meeting the demands joined in the strike.

In Chicago, the movement began with a series of mass rallies called by the Workingman's Party, the main radical party of the day, and a strike by forty switchmen on the Michigan Central Railroad. The switchmen roamed through the railroad property with a crowd of 500 others, including strikers from the East who had ridden in to spread the strike, calling out other workers and closing down those railroads that were still running. Next the crowd called out the workers at the stockyards and several packinghouses. Smaller crowds spread out to broaden the strike; one group, for example, called out 500 planing-mill workers, and with them marched down Canal Street and Blue Island Avenue closing down factories. Crews on several lake vessels struck. With transportation dead, the North Chicago rolling mill and many other industries closed for lack of coke and other supplies. Next day the strike spread still further: streetcars, wagons and buggies were stopped; tanneries, stoneworks, clothing factories, lumber yards, brickyards, furniture factories, and a large distillery were closed in response to roving crowds. One day more and the crowds forced officials at the stockyards and gasworks to sign promises to raise wages to $2.00 a day, while more dock and lumber yard workers struck. [71] In the midst of this, the Workingman's Party proclaimed: "Fellow Workers . . . Under any circumstances keep quiet until we have given the present crisis a due consideration." [72]

The general strikes spread even into the South, often starting with black workers and spreading to whites. Texas and Pacific Railroad workers at Marshall, Texas, struck against the pay cut. In response, black longshoremen in nearby Galveston struck for and won pay equal to that of their white fellow workers. Fifty black workers marched down the Strand in Galveston, persuading construction men, track layers and others to strike for $2.00 a day. The next day committees circulated supporting the strike. White workers joined in. The movement was victorious, and $2.00 a day became the going wage for Galveston. In Louisville, Kentucky, black workers made the round of sewers under construction, urging a strike for $1.50 a day. At noon, sewer workers had quit everywhere in town. On Tuesday night a march of 500 stoned the depot of the Louisville and Nashville Railroad, which was refusing a wage increase for laborers. By Wednesday, most of Louisville's factories were shut down by roving crowds, and Thursday brought further strikes by coopers, textile and plow factory workers, brickmakers, and cabinetworkers.

The day the railroad strike reached East St. Louis, the St. Louis Workingman's Party marched 500 strong across the river to join a meeting of 1,000 railroad workers and residents. Said one of the speakers, "All you have to do, gentlemen, for you have the

18   numbers, is to unite on one idea—that the workingmen shall rule the country. What man makes, belongs to him, and the working-men made this country." [72] The St. Louis General Strike, the peak of the Great Upheaval, for a time nearly realized that goal.

The railroad workers at that meeting voted for a strike, set up a committee of one man from each railroad, and occupied the Relay Depot as their headquarters. The committee promptly posted General Order No. 1, forbidding freight trains from leaving any yard.

That night, across the river in St. Louis, the Workingman's Party called a mass meeting, with crowds so large that three separate speakers' stands were set up simultaneously. "The working-men," said one speaker, "intend now to assert their rights, even if the result is shedding of blood. . . . They are ready to take up arms at any moment." [74]

Next morning, workers from different shops and plants began to appear at the party headquarters, requesting that committees be sent around to "notify them to stop work and join the other work-ingmen, that they might have a reason for doing so." [75] The party began to send such committees around, with unexpected results. The coopers struck, marching from shop to shop with a fife and drum shouting, "Come out, come out! No barrels less than nine cents." [76] Newsboys, gasworkers, boatmen, and engineers struck as well. Railroadmen arrived from East St. Louis on engines and flatcars they had commandeered, moving through the yards enforcing General Order No. 1 and closing a wire works.

That day, an "Executive Committee" formed, based at the Workingman's Party headquarters, to coordinate the strike. As one historian wrote, "Nobody ever knew who that executive commit-tee really was; it seems to have been a rather loose body composed of whomsoever chanced to come in and take part in its delibera-tions." [77]

In the evening, 1,500 men, mostly molders and mechanics,

U.S. Regulars "giving the butt" to crowd during the Pullman strike of 1894.

armed themselves with lathes and clubs and marched to the evening's rally. To a crowd of 10,000 the first speaker, a cooper, began, "There was a time in the history of France when the poor found themselves oppressed to such an extent that forbearance ceased to be a virtue, and hundreds of heads tumbled into the basket. That time may have arrived with us." [78] Another speaker called upon the workingmen to organize into companies of ten, twenty, and a hundred, to establish patrols to protect property, and to "organize force to meet force." Someone suggested that "the colored men should have a chance." A black steamboatman spoke for the roustabouts and levee workers. He asked the crowd would they stand behind the levee strikers, regardless of color? "We will!" the crowd shouted back. [79]

The general strike got under way in earnest the next morning. The employees of a beef cannery struck and paraded. The coopers met and discussed their objectives. A force of strikers marched to the levee, where a crowd of steamboatmen and roustabouts "of all colors" [80] forced the captains of boat after boat to sign written promises of fifty percent higher pay. Finally everyone assembled for the day's great march. Six hundred factory workers marched up behind a brass band; a company of railroad strikers came with coupling pins, brake rods, red signal flags and other "irons and implements emblematic of their calling." [81] Strikers' committees went out ahead to call out those still working, and as the march came by, a loaf of bread on a flag-staff for its emblem, workers in foundries, bagging companies, flour mills, bakeries, chemical, zinc and white lead works poured out of their shops and into the crowd. In Carondolet, far on the south side of the city, a similar march developed autonomously, as a crowd of iron workers closed down two zinc works, the Bessemer Steel Works, and other plants. In East St. Louis, there was a parade of women in support of the strike. By sundown, nearly all the manufacturing establishments in the city had been closed. "Business is fairly paralyzed here," said the *Daily Market Reporter*. [82]

But economic activities did not cease completely; some continued under control or by permission of the strikers. The British Consul in St. Louis noted how the railroad strikers had "taken the road into their own hands, running the trains and collecting fares"; "it is to be deplored that a large portion of the general public appear to regard such conduct as a legitimate mode of warfare." [83] It was now the railroad managements which wanted to stop all traffic. One official stated frankly that by stopping all passenger trains, the companies would cut the strikers off from mail facilities and prevent them from sending committees from one point to an-

20   other along the lines. [84] Railroad officials, according to the *St. Louis Times,* saw advantage in stopping passenger trains and thus "incommoding the public so as to produce a revolution in the sentiment which now seems to be in favor of the strikers." [85] From the strikers' point of view, running non-freights allowed them to coordinate the strike and show their social responsibility.

The strikers had apparently decided to allow the manufacture of bread, for they permitted a flour mill to remain open. When the owner of the Belcher Sugar Refinery applied to the Executive Committee for permission to operate his plant for forty-eight hours, lest a large quantity of sugar spoil, the Executive Committee persuaded the refinery workers to go back to work and sent a guard of 200 men to protect the refinery. Concludes one historian of the strike, "the Belcher episode revealed . . . the spectacle of the owner of one of the city's largest industrial enterprises recognizing the *de facto* authority of the Executive Committee." [86]

But the strikers here and elsewhere failed to hold what they had conquered. Having shattered the authority of the status quo for a few short days, they faltered and fell back, unsure of what to do. Meanwhile, the forces of law and order—no longer cowering in the face of overwhelming mass force—began to organize. Chicago was typical: President Hayes authorized the use of Federal regulars; citizens' patrols were organized ward by ward, using Civil War veterans; 5,000 special police were sworn in, freeing the regular police for action; big employers organized their reliable employees into armed companies—many of which were sworn in as special police. At first the crowd successfully out-maneuvered the police in the street fighting that ensued, but after killing at least eighteen people the police finally gained control of the crowd and thus broke the back of the movement. [87]

Behind them stood the Federal government. "This insurrection," said General Hancock, the comander in charge of all Federal troops used in the strike, must be stifled "by all possible means." [88] Not that the Federal troops were strong and reliable. The Army was largely tied down by the rebellion of Nez Perces Indians, led by Chief Joseph. In the words of Lieutenant Philip Sheridan, "The troubles on the Rio Grande border, the Indian outbreak on the western frontier of New Mexico, and the Indian war in the Departments of the Platte and Dakota, have kept the small and inadequate forces in this division in a constant state of activity, almost without rest, night and day." [89] Most of the enlisted men had not been paid for months—for the Congress had refused to pass the Army Appropriations Bill so as to force the withdrawal of Reconstruction troops from the South. Finally, the Army included many workers driven into military service by unemployment. As one union iron molder in the Army wrote, "It does not follow that a change of dress involves a change of principle." [90] No mutinies occurred, however, as the 3,000 available Federal troops were rushed under direction of the War Department from city to city, wherever the movement seemed to grow out of control. "The strikers," President Hayes noted emphatically in his diary, "have been put down by *force.*" [91] More than 100 of them were killed in the process.

The Great Upheaval was an expression of the new economic and social system in America, just as surely as the cities, railroads and factories from which it had sprung. The enormous expansion of industry after the Civil War had transformed millions of people who had grown up as farmers and self-employed artisans and entrepreneurs into employees, growing thousands of whom were concentrated within each of the new corporate empires. They were no longer part of village and town communities with their extended families and stable, unchallenged values, but concentrated in cities, with all their anonymity and freedom; their work was no longer individual and competitive, but group and cooperative; they no longer directed their own work, but worked under control of a boss; they no longer controlled the property on which they worked or its fruits, and therefore could not find fruitful employment unless someone with property agreed to hire them. The Great Upheaval grew out of their intuitive sense that they needed each other, had the support of each other, and together were powerful.

This sense of unity was not embodied in any centralized plan or leadership, but in the feelings and action of each participant. "There was no concert of action at the start," the editor of the *Labor Standard* pointed out. "It spread because the workmen of Pittsburgh felt the same oppression that was felt by the workmen of West Virginia and so with the workmen of Chicago and St. Louis." [92] In Pittsburgh, concludes historian Robert Bruce, "Men like Andrew Hice or Gus Harris or David Davis assumed the lead briefly at one point or another, but only because they happened to be foremost in nerve or vehemence." [93] In Newark, Ohio, "no single individual seemed to command the . . . strikers. They followed the sense of the meeting, as Quakers might say, on such proposals as one or another of them . . . put forward. Yet they proceeded with notable coherence, as though fused by their common adversity." [94]

The Great Upheaval was in the end thoroughly defeated, but the struggle was by no means a total loss. Insofar as it aimed at preventing the continued decline of workers' living standards, it won

22 wage concessions in a number of cases and undoubtedly gave pause to would-be wage-cutters to come, for whom the explosive force of the social dynamite with which they tampered had now been revealed. Insofar as it aimed at a workers' seizure of power, its goal was chimerical, for the workers as yet still formed only a minority in a predominantly farm and middle-class society. But the power of workers to virtually stop society, to counter the forces of repression, and to organize cooperative action on a vast scale was revealed in the most dramatic form.

It was not only upon the workers that the Great Upheaval left its mark. Their opponents began building up their power as well, symbolized by the National Guard Armories whose construction began the following year, to contain upheavals yet to come.

Certain periods, wrote Irving Bernstein, bear a special quality in American labor history. "There occurred at these times strikes and social upheavals of extraordinary importance, drama, and violence which ripped the cloak of civilized decorum from society, leaving exposed naked class conflict." [95] Such periods were analyzed before World War I by Rosa Luxemburg and others under the concept of mass strikes. The mass strike, she wrote, signifies not just a single act but a whole period of class struggle.

> Its use, its effects, its reasons for coming about are in a constant state of flux . . . political and economic strikes, united and partial strikes, defensive strikes and combat strikes, general strikes of individual sections of industry and general strikes of entire cities, peaceful wage strikes and street battles, uprisings with barricades—all run together and run alongside each other, get in each other's way, overlap each other; a perpetually moving and changing sea of phenomena. [96]

The Great Upheaval was the first—but by no means the last—mass strike in American history.

Chapter I: Footnotes

1. *Minute Book Journal,* p. 306, in B&O Archives; cited in Bruce, p. 64.
2. F. Vernon Aler, *Aler's History of Martinsburg and Berkeley County, West Virginia* (Hagerstown, Md., 1888), pp. 301-4, cited in Bruce, p. 76.
3. WPA, *Mathews Papers,* pp. 30-2, cited in Bruce, p. 77.
4. Aler, pp. 308-9, cited in Bruce, p. 77.
5. *Wheeling Register,* July 19, 1877, cited in Bruce, p. 78
6. *Mathews Papers,* p. 34, cited in Bruce, p. 79.
7. *Wheeling Intelligencer,* July 18, 1877, cited in Bruce, p. 80.
8. *Baltimore Sun,* July 19, 1877, cited in Bruce, p. 83.
9. *Mathews Papers,* pp. 36-7, cited in Bruce, p. 80.
10. National Archives, Adjutant General's Office, Letters Received, 1877, No. 8035 (enclosure 80), cited in Bruce, pp. 81-2.
11. *Baltimore Sun,* July 18, 1877, cited in Bruce, p. 82.
12. *Wheeling Register,* July 18, 1877, cited in Bruce, p. 84.

13. *Martinsburg Independent,* July 21, 1877, cited in Bruce, pp. 84-5.
14. *Wheeling Register,* July 18, 1877, cited in Bruce, p. 85.
15. *Wheeling Register,* July 19, 1877, cited in Bruce, pp. 90-1.
16. Herbert G. Gutman, "Trouble on the Railroads in 1873-1874: Prelude to the 1877 Crisis?" in *Labor History,* Vol. II, No. 2 (Spring 1961), p. 221.
17. *Ibid.,* p. 231.
18. *Ibid.,* p. 220.
19. *Ibid.,* p. 232.
20. *Ibid.,* p. 218.
21. *Ibid.,* p. 229.
22. *Ibid.,* p. 235.
23. *Reports of Riots Committee,* p. 925, cited in Bruce, p. 50.
24. *Pittsburgh Post,* June 7, 1877, cited in Bruce, p. 51.
25. *Reports of Riots Committee,* p. 671, cited in Bruce, p. 59.
26. *Ibid.,* pp. 673-4, cited in Bruce, p. 59.
27. *Pittsburgh Post,* June 7, 1877, cited in Bruce, p. 61.
28. *Pittsburgh Chronicle,* June 27, 1877, cited in Bruce, p. 62.
29. *Wheeling Intelligencer,* June 15, 1877, cited in Bruce, p. 65.
30. Clifton K. Yearley, Jr., "The Baltimore and Ohio Railroad Strike of 1877," in *Maryland Historical Magazine, LI* (September 1956), cited in Bruce, p. 75.
31. Aler, pp. 301-4, cited in Bruce, p. 74.
32. *Cumberland Civilian,* July 22, 1877, cited in Bruce, p. 96.
33. *Wheeling Register,* July 21, 1877, cited in Bruce, p. 97.
34. *Wheeling Intelligencer,* July 23, 1877, cited in Bruce, p. 101.
35. *Philadelphia Inquirer,* July 23, 1877, cited in Bruce, p. 101.
36. *Baltimore Evening Bulletin,* July 21, 1877, cited in Bruce, p. 104.
37. *Baltimore Sun,* July 21, 1877, cited in Bruce, p. 108.
38. Bruce, pp. 15, 17.
39. Norman J. Ware, *The Labor Movement in the United States 1860-1890* (N.Y.: Vintage Books, 1964), p. 45.
40. J.N.A. Griswold to R. Harris, July 7, 1877, cited in Bruce, p. 56.
41. *Pittsburgh Post,* July 19, 1877, cited in Bruce, p. 73.
42. Cited in Bruce, p. 119.
43. Bruce, pp. 122-3.
44. *Report of Riots Committee,* cited in Bruce, pp. 124-5.
45. *Railroad Dispatch,* July 20, 1877, cited in Bruce, p. 125.
46. *Ibid.*
47. *Report of Riots Committee,* cited in Bruce, p. 137.
48. Bruce, p. 143.
49. Bruce, p. 143-4.
50. *Report of Riots Committee,* cited in Bruce, p. 140.
51. *Ibid.*
52. *Pittsburgh Leader,* cited in Bruce, pp. 135-6.
53. Bruce, p. 134.
54. *Report of Riots Committee,* cited in Bruce, p. 135.
55. Bruce, p. 141.
56. Bruce, pp. 141-2.
57. *Pittsburgh Commercial Gazette,* July 23, 1877, cited in Bruce, p. 147.
58. *Pittsburgh Commercial Gazette,* July 31, 1877, cited in Bruce, p. 147.
59. *Report of Riots Committee,* cited in Bruce, p. 155.
60. Bruce, pp. 166-7.
61. Carroll D. Wright, *The Battles of Labor* (Phila., 1906), p. 122, cited in Bruce, p. 176.
62. *Report of Riots Committee,* p. 260, cited in Bruce, p. 176.

24   63.   Bruce, pp. 175-6.
64.   *Columbus Dispatch,* July 25, 1877, cited in Bruce, p. 207.
65.   *Reading Eagle,* July 23, 1877, and *New York Times,* Oct. 4, 1877, cited in Bruce, p. 189.
66.   Bruce, pp. 192-3.
67.   Bruce, p. 194.
68.   *Ohio State Journal,* July 20, 1877, cited in Bruce, pp. 127-8.
69.   Bruce, p. 182.
70.   *Ohio State Journal,* July 24, 1877, cited in Bruce, p. 207.
71.   Bruce, p. 250.
72.   *Chicago Times,* July 25, 1877, cited in Bruce, p. 243.
73.   Cited in Bruce, p. 156.
74.   David T. Burbank, *Reign of the Rabble, The St. Louis General Strike of 1877* (N.Y.: Augustus M. Kelley, 1966), p. 61.
75.   *Ibid.,* p. 43.
76.   *Ibid.*
77.   Morris Hillquit, *History of Socialism in the United States* (N.Y., 1910), p. 77, cited in Bruce, p. 260.
78.   Burbank, p. 53.
79.   *Ibid.,* p. 54.
80.   *Ibid.,* p. 70.
81.   *Ibid.,* p. 73.
82.   *Daily Market Reporter,* cited in Burbank, p. 78.
83.   Burbank, pp. 63-4.
84.   *Ibid.,* p. 69.
85.   *St. Louis Times,* July 25, 1877, cited in Bruce, p. 260.
86.   Burbank, p. 112.
87.   Bruce, p. 252.
88.   AGO, Letters Received, 1844, Nos. 4413, 4905 (enclosure 56), cited by Bruce, p. 286.
89.   Major General Philip Sheridan, *Annual Report of the Military Division of the Missouri for 1877,* printed copy in Philip Sheridan Mss., Library of Congress, cited in Bruce, p. 88.
90.   *Iron Molders' Journal* XIII (Mar. 10, 1877), p. 275, cited in Bruce, p. 89.
91.   R.B. Hayes Mss., cited in Bruce, p. 315.
92.   *Labor Standard,* Aug. 11, 1877, cited in Bruce, p. 229.
93.   Bruce, p. 124.
94.   *Columbus [Ohio] Dispatch,* July 20, 1877, cited in Bruce, pp. 128-9.
95.   Irving Bernstein, *Turbulent Years* (Boston: Houghton Mifflin, 1970), p. 217.
96.   Rosa Luxemburg, "Massenstreik, Partei und Gewerkschaften" [The Mass Strike, the Political Party and the Trade Unions], Hamburg, 1906, cited in J.P. Nettl, *Rosa Luxemburg, Vol. II* (London: Oxford University Press, 1966), p. 500.

✊

Chapter 2
May Day

Labor discontent was not long in re-emerging after the suppression of the Great Upheaval. By the mid-1880's, a vast "labor agitation" was coursing from the largest cities to the smallest towns. Perhaps typical were the groups that developed in the obscure railroad town of Sedalia, Missouri, in 1884. Led by a cobbler and a railroad machinist, they would meet night after night, discussing the condition of workers and how to change it, debating various labor philosophies and their promise for immediate action. From these groups came the leaders of future strikes in the area.

The discontent frightened Terence Powderly, the somewhat bumbling head of the Knights of Labor—soon to become the most important labor organization in the land—and in December, 1884, he issued a secret circular, charged with fear that workers might try a "repetition of 1877 on a larger scale." [1]

"A change is slowly but surely coming over the whole country," he wrote. "The discussion of the labor question takes up more of the time and attention of men in all walks of life at the present time than it ever did before. . . . The number of unemployed at the present time is very great, and constantly increasing. Reduction in wages, suspension of men, stoppage of factories and furnaces are of daily occurrence. . . . Under such circumstances as I have pointed out it is but natural for men to grow desperate and restive. The demonstrations in some of our large cities testify to that fact." [2]

Of course, history never repeats the same external events, and the strike wave of 1886—like each subsequent one—developed on a pattern of its own. No other period of mass strike in American history developed quite the character of a national insurrection seen in the Great Upheaval of 1877. Indeed, that character was a result of the extremely undeveloped and disorganized condition of capitalist society at that time. Nonetheless, historians have generally considered the mid-1880's a more revolutionary period, even though it was marked by less insurrectionary violence. As in the Great Upheaval, workers were responding to a general depression that led to unemployment and wage cutting. But they responded with a far higher degree of planning, organization, and thought-out goals.

According to John R. Commons' classic *History of the Labor Movement in the United States,* "all the peculiar characteristics of

26   the dramatic events of 1886 and 1887, the highly feverish pace at which organizations grew, the nationwide wave of strikes, . . . the wide use of the boycott, the obliteration, apparently complete, of all lines that divide the laboring class, whether geographic or trade, the violence and turbulence which accompanied the movement — all of these were the signs of a great movement by the class of the unskilled, which had finally risen in rebellion. This movement, rising as an elemental protest against oppression and degradation, could be but feebly restrained by any considerations of expediency or prudence. . . . The movement bore in every way the aspect of a social war. A frenzied hatred of labour for capital was shown in every important strike. . . . Extreme bitterness toward capital manifested itself in all the actions of the Knights of Labor, and wherever the leaders undertook to hold it within bounds they were generally discarded by their followers, and others who would lead as directed were placed in charge. The feeling of 'give no quarter' is illustrated in the refusal to submit grievances to arbitration when the employees felt that they had the upper hand over their employers." [3]

Two months after Powderly's circular, a five percent wage cut was added to a previous ten percent reduction for shopmen on the Missouri Pacific Railroad, the Missouri, Kansas and Texas, and the Wabash — the lines composing Jay Gould's Southwest System.

The Wabash shopmen struck spontaneously the day after they received their wage cuts, and the strike rapidly spread to the shopmen· on the other Southwest System roads. By the first week of March the strike had spread to all the important shops of the system in Missouri and Texas, involving 10,000 miles of railroad.

Railroad officials tried to move the hundreds of freight cars that piled up, but without success, for the trainmen supported the strike. When an engine was fired up and attached to a train, the engineer was approached by the strikers with the plea: "For the sake of your family and ours, don't take out that engine." [4] Missouri Pacific retracted the cut and agreed to other demands on March 15th.

In the course of the strike, the railroad workers on the Union Pacific Railroad, who were members of the Knights of Labor, sent $30,000 and an organizer to support the strike. As a result, the Southwest System strikers began organizing local assemblies of the Knights of Labor; soon there were thirty locals and thousands of members. The railroads decided to move against the Knights, and began firing shopmen on the Wabash and finally closing the railroad shops altogether, then opening them up again with fifty scabs armed with revolvers and brass knuckles.

In reply, all Knights of Labor on the Wabash struck. The work-

ers on the rest of the Southwest System demanded support from
the leaders of the Knights of Labor, who reluctantly instructed all
members to refuse to handle Wabash rolling stock "and if this order is antagonized by the companies through any of its officials,
your executive committee is hereby ordered to call out all K. of L.
on the above system without any further action." [5]

The Southwest System was controlled by Jay Gould, known as
"The Wizard of Wall Street," and perhaps the most hated of the
robber barons of his day. Faced now with a strike that would equal
the dimensions of the 1877 railroad strike and close down his entire
system, Gould decided instead to come to terms, at least for the
time being. He met with the Executive Board of the Knights of Labor and, according to them, Gould advised the general manager of
the Wabash to agree with their demands. The manager thereupon
agreed to reinstate those fired and promised that "no official shall
discriminate against the K. of L." [6]

John R. Commons' *History of Labor* put well the significance
of the victory: "Here a labor organization for the first time dealt
on an equal footing with the most powerful capitalist in the country. It forced Jay Gould to recognize it as a power equal to himself,
a fact which he amply conceded when he declared his readiness to
arbitrate all labor difficulties that might arise. The oppressed laboring masses finally discovered a champion which could curb the
power of a man stronger even than the government itself. All the
pent-up feeling of bitterness and resentment which had accumulated during the two years of depression, in consequence of the repeated cuts in wages and the intensified domination by employers,
now found vent in a rush to organize under the banner of the
powerful Knights of Labor." [7]

The result of these victories—headlined across the country—
was the sudden explosive growth both of strikes and of the Knights
of Labor. "Every week," wrote a contemporary labor journalist,
"trade unions are turned into local [Knights of Labor] assemblies
or assemblies are organized out of trade unions and every day new
mixed assemblies spring into existence. The numerous strikes East
and West during the past twelve months have added greatly to its
growth." [8] The usual pattern was to "strike first and then join the
Knights of Labor."

The growth of the Knights of Labor was phenomenal. Here are the figures:

July 1, 1884	71,326
July 1, 1885	111,395
July 1, 1886	729,677 [9]

The Knights of Labor had been founded by nine obscure garment cutters in Philadelphia in 1869. It combined the functions of a trade union with an opposition to the wage system as a whole, and originally had a deep religious strain as well. As one of its founders, Uriah Stephens, put it, "Knighthood must base its claims for labor upon higher ground than participation in the profits and emoluments, and a lessening of the hours and fatigues of labor. These are only physical effects and objects of a grosser nature, and, although imperative, are but the stepping-stone to a higher cause, of a nobler nature. The real and ultimate reason must be based upon the more exalted and divine nature of man, his high and noble capability for good. Excessive labor and small pay stints and blunts and degrades those God-like faculties, until the image of God, in which he was created and intended by his great Author to exhibit, are scarcely discernable." [10]

The one great sentiment embodied in the Knights of Labor was the idea of solidarity among all workers, whether white or black, skilled or unskilled, men or women. As historian Norman Ware put it, "The solidarity of labor was fast becoming an economic reality if not a psychological fact . . . The Order tried to teach the American wage-earner that he was a wage-earner first and a bricklayer, carpenter, miner, shoemaker, . . . a Catholic, Protestant, Jew, white, black, Democrat, Republican after." [11] The Order's motto, "An injury to one is the concern of all," captured the popular imagination. This feeling was expressed over and over again by the head of the Order, Grand Master Workman Terence Powderly:

"The belief was prevalent until a short time ago among workingmen, that only the man who was engaged in manual toil could be called a workingman. The man who labored at the bench or anvil, the man who held the throttles of the engine or delved in the everlasting gloom of the coal mine did not believe that the man who made the drawings from which he forged, turned, or dug could be classed as a worker. The draughtsman, the timekeeper, the clerk, the school teacher, the civil engineer, the editor, the reporter, or the worst paid, most abused and illy appreciated of all toilers — women — could not be called a worker. . . . Narrow prejudice, born of the injustice and oppressions of the past, must be overcome, and all who interest themselves in producing for the world's good must be made to understand that their interests are identical." [12]

This sense of class unity developed in opposition of the spirit of the trade unions, which at that time generally represented only the most highly skilled craftsmen, the "aristocracy of labor," and fought to maintain their privileged position. According to Powderly, "The sentiment expressed in the words, 'The condition of one part of our class can not be improved permanently unless *all* are improved *together*,' was not acceptable to trade unionists, who were selfishly bound up in the work of ameliorating the condition of those who belonged to their own particular callings alone." [13]

"The failure which really led to the organization of the Knights of Labor, was the failure of the trade union to grapple, and satisfactorily deal with, the labor question on its broad, far-reaching basic principle: the right of all to have a say in the affairs of one. . . . The rights of the common, every-day laborer were to be considered by the new order," [14] whereas the trade unions' attitude was, "we will not associate with the common, every-day laborers in any organization of labor . . ."

Trade unions also differed from the Knights, Powderly pointed out, in that they accepted the wage system. "Many of the members of these organizations seemed to regard themselves as being hired for life; they were content with demanding and obtaining from their masters better conditions in the regulation of workshops and wages; beyond that they did not think they had a right to venture." [15] The Knights—and workers generally at the time—felt differently. "We are the willing victims of an outrageous system . . . We should not war with men for being what we make them, but strike a powerful, telling blow at the base of the system which makes the laborer the slave of his master. . . . So long as a pernicious system leaves one man at the mercy of another, so long will labor and capital be at war. . . . Far be it from me to say that I can point out the way . . . I can only offer a suggestion that comes to me as a result of experience . . . to abolish the wage system." [16]

Although they had no clear idea of how to put it into practice, the Knights saw a society based on cooperative production as the alternative. "The fundamental principle on which the organization was based was co-operation; not a co-operation of men for the mere purpose of enhancing the value of their combined contributions to any productive enterprise alone, but a co-operation of the various callings and crafts by which men earned the right to remain upon the earth's surface as contributors to the public good." [17] Indeed, the idea of a class of permanent wage workers—so distant from the ideal that every man could become an independent entrepreneur—still seemed positively un-American to the workers of the

30 1880's; as Norman Ware wrote, "The reluctance of the labor movement to accept collective bargaining as its major function was due
largely to the fact that this involved an acceptance of the wage system." [18]

Yet despite their opposition to the wage system, the leaders of
the Knights of Labor opposed strikes and revolutionary activities
even more. "I will never advocate a strike," Powderly wrote, "unless it be a strike at the ballot-box, or such a one as was proclaimed
to the world by the unmistakable sound of the strikers' guns on the
field of Lexington. But the necessity for such a strike as the latter
does not exist at the present. The men who made the name of Lexington famous in the world's history were forced to adopt the bullet
because they did not possess the ballot." [19] Powderly still hoped
that the former position of workers as independent producers could
be restored by creating producers' cooperatives and by controlling
monopoly through the government. He feared that strikes distract-
ed from this task and threatened to generate revolutionary disorder. Much of Powderly's energy, as we shall see, went into forestalling and weakening strikes.

But this opposition to strikes did not stop men who wanted to
strike from joining the Knights. As John Swinton, perhaps the
leading contemporary labor journalist, wrote, "While the order is
opposed to strikes, the first news we are likely to hear after its [a
strike's] close is of the union of the men with the K. of L." [20] Nor
did the Order stop the Knights from striking, for while in theory it
was highly centralized, in practice each local assembly acted on its
own initiative, striking despite disapproval from on high.

During the same years as the Knights' rapid growth, a revolutionary tendency began developing within the labor movement,
generally referred to as anarchism. The anarchists called upon all
"revolutionists and armed workingmen's organizations in the country" to prepare to "offer armed resistance to the invasions by the
capitalistic class and capitalistic legislatures." [21] This development
was a response to the evident failure of political action and trade
unionism in the face of the growing misery of the depression. Indeed, one of the leading anarchists, Albert Parson, had only a few
years before spent his time running for political office in Chicago
and lobbying in Washington for the eight-hour day for Federal employees. The anarchist program, as set forth by a national congress
in 1883, read in part:

By force our ancestors liberated themselves from political oppression,
by force their children will have to liberate themselves from economic
bondage. "It is, therefore, your right, it is your duty," says Jefferson, "to
arm!"

What we would achieve is, therefore, plainly and simply:

First—Destruction of the existing class rule by all means—i.e., by energetic, relentless, revolutionary and international action.

Second—Establishment of a free society based upon co-operative organization of production.

Third—Free exchange of equivalent products by and between the productive organizations without commerce and profit-mongery.

Fourth—Organization of education on a secular, scientific, and equal basis for both sexes.

Fifth—Equal rights for all, without distinction to sex or race.

Sixth—Regulation of all public affairs by free contracts between the autonomous (independent) Communes and associations, resting on a federalistic basis. [22]

In many places the anarchists were only a small sect, but in Chicago a significant section of the workers joined the revolutionary trend. In 1884, a large part of the Chicago cigar makers called for "open rebellion of the robbed class," pulled out of the existing Amalgamated Trades and Labor Assembly, and organized the Central Labor Union along with the German metalworkers, the carpenters and joiners, the cabinetworkers, and the butchers. By the end of 1885 the new Central Labor Union was nearly as large and strong as the old Assembly, and by April, 1886, it included the eleven largest unions in the city.

Eighteen-eighty-six was a year of tumult. One contemporary aptly called it "the year of the great uprising of labor." [23] Historians have called it a "revolutionary year," [24] and the "great upheaval," "more deserving of this title than even the convulsive events of 1887." [25] This movement took a form originally promoted by neither the anarchists nor the Knights of Labor—an enormous strike wave culminating in a virtual nationwide general strike. These statistics suggest what happened:

Year	Strikes	Establishments	No. striking & involved [86]
1881	471	2,928	129,521
1882	454	2,105	154,671
1883	478	2,759	149,763
1884	443	2,367	147,054
1885	645	2,284	242,705
1886	1,411	9,891	499,489

To summarize, the number of strikers in 1886 tripled compared with the average for the previous five years, and the number of establishments struck nearly quadrupled. The strikes were of every

32   trade and in every area.

Further, the character of strikes changed radically. Through the depression years that preceded 1886, strikes had mostly been in resistence to wage cuts. Now, with the beginnings of business recovery, they became above all strikes for power over such issues as the hours of labor, hiring and firing, the organization of work, and the arbitrary power of foremen and superintendents.

The wave began late in 1885 with "spontaneous outbreaks of unorganized masses." [27] Typical was a strike for the ten-hour day in the Saginaw Valley in Michigan. The legislature had passed a ten-hour law which proved unenforceable. In response, with little previous organization, the predominantly Polish and American workers in the lumber and shingle mills struck for an immediate ten-hour day with no reduction in pay. The strikers marched in a body from mill to mill, demanding that the men quit work, and shut down the entire lumber industry, turning off steam and banking fires, including seventeen shingle mills, sixty-one lumber mills, and fifty-eight salt blocks. Although the employers imported more than fifty Pinkerton detectives and a large body of militia was poised to intervene, the strike was won after two months.

The workers on Jay Gould's Southwestern Railroad System exemplified this movement. They had discovered their power in previous strikes and had developed their own organization and coordination. Yet they still were subject to the arbitrary power of their employers, their wages constantly cut or chiseled, arbitrarily transferred from one job to another, harassed by local railroad officials, and beset by grievances on which they could get no answer. When one of their members was fired for attending a union meeting, even though he had been given permission, the strike they had long felt inevitable broke out March 6th, 1886.

A letter from one of the strikers to a contemporary labor journal gives the spirit in which they struck:

"Tell the world that the men of the Gould Southwest System are on strike. We strike for justice to ourselves and our fellowmen everywhere. Fourteen thousand men are out.... I would say to all railroad employees everywhere . . . make your demands to the corporation for the eight-hour day and no reduction of pay. Demand $1.50 per day for all laboring men. Demand that yourselves and your families be carried on all railways for one cent a mile. Bring in all your grievances in one bundle at once, and come out to a man and stay out until they are all settled to your entire satisfaction. Let us demand our rights and compel the exploiters to accede to our demands . . ." [28]

The objective of the strikers, according to Ruth Allen, the historian of the strike, was to be recognized by management as "men equally powerful in and responsible for the conduct of the Gould Southwest System." Recognition, according to the worker whose firing triggered the strike, meant that corporation officials, instead of holding all authority themselves, would "recognize and treat with the committee appointed by the Order to settle by arbitration the difficulties or grievances that might arise." [29] (The term "arbitration" at that time included any settlement reached through negotiation or collective bargaining.) H.M. Hoxie, Gould's top official on the scene, agreed that the time had come "when the question had to be decided whether he should run his own railroad or have the Knights of Labor run it." [30]

When the strike began on the Texas and Pacific Railroad, Joseph Buchanan, one of the most radical leaders of the Knights of Labor, tried to dissuade others on the Southwest System from striking in sympathy. "Let us say the strike is ordered and the shops closed, though the trains are running. You know as well as I do that you cannot defeat a railroad company if the trains continue to run; therefore you will attempt to stop the trains. The police, deputy United States marshals, deputy sheriffs, and constables will swarm in the yards and on the tracks; you must drive them off. You are husky fellows and full of fight, so I'll admit that you can whip the police and deputies. Then the militia of the various states through which the roads run will be called out to oppose you. Who are the militiamen? Only a lot of spindle-legged counter-jumpers, but they are well trained and armed for business. Still, guns are plentiful in your part of the country and most of you are pretty good shooters yourselves; besides, you will be battling for a principle and the welfare of 'Betty and the babies.' If you are brave men and have intelligent leadership, you can clean out the militia. Now what happens? The Federal judges, under whom the roads are being operated, appeal to the President of the United States for assistance, and the regulars are sent to put down what has by this time become an armed revolution—rebellion, in fact." [31] Nonetheless, the shopmen, switchmen, trackmen and telegraph operators, and even coal heavers and miners throughout Missouri, Kansas, Arkansas, Nebraska, and Indian Territory joined the strike.

According to the *New York Times,* the "striking mania" in Missouri had even extended to

a class of laborers who it was supposed would be the last to fall into line. The farm hands of these counties have demanded of their employers an increase from $15 and board to $20 and board per month. The demand was at first refused, when no less than 50 men quit work. The employers have conceded their demands . . . and the projectors hope to have the demand become general throughout the State. [32]

34   The Great Southwest Strike began March 1st, 1886, with an occupation of the shops similar in some ways to the sitdown strikes of later years. When the men walked out, responsible strikers were placed in control of the shops and rolling stock to prevent it from being used and to protect it from violence. But soon the railroads secured dozens of injunctions, bench warrants, and writs of assistance, thus putting the strikers in contempt of court. Special police paid by the railroads and large numbers of extraordinary deputies were sworn in to enforce the orders.

To break the strike, the companies advertised widely for strikebreakers. In one bizarre episode, nine young men were recruited in New Orleans and sent to Marshall, Texas, on the assurance there was no strike in progress. On arrival they were sworn in as deputy United States marshals to protect company property. Next morning they wrote in the local paper that, "After due investigation, and hearing both sides of the question, we found undeniable proof of a strike, and as man to man we could not justifiably go to work and take the bread out of our fellow-workmen's mouths, no matter how much we needed it ourselves." [33] Thereupon the United States Marshal for East Texas arrested the men under a charge of contempt and intimidation and defrauding the company by their refusal to work after accepting transportation from New Orleans, and had them given sentences of three to four months in the Galveston County jail.

The characteristic response of the workers to the attempts to break the strike was the "killing" of engines. This was done by putting out the engine's fire, letting out the water, displacing engine connections, and destroying part of the machinery. The workers also tried to prevent operation by strikebreakers by tampering with the rails and setting fires at terminals, water tanks, and shops. A dispatch from Atchison, Kansas, gave a vivid example:

> At 12:45 this morning the ten men on guard at the Missouri Pacific roundhouse were surprised by the appearance of 35 or 40 masked men. The guards were corralled in the oil room by a detachment of the visitors, who stood guard with pistols . . . drawn, while the rest of them thoroughly disabled 12 locomotives which stood in the stalls. [34]

Another from Dallas, Texas, illustrated the widespread court action against strikers' tactics:

> Charles Wilson, charged with displacing a switch for the purpose of derailing an engine at Denton on March 27, was sentenced to five months' imprisonment in the county jail; C. Bishop, for taking possession of a switch at Forth Worth on April 2, was found guilty and remanded to await sentence; Richard Gordon, striking a switchman with a stone at night, three months' imprisonment in the county jail. [35]

In addition, the railroads relied upon armed force to break the strike. They started in Palestine, Texas, where 300 links, 500 couplings, and 500 "draw-heads" had been removed, and where, of thirty-seven engines, two had been thrown from the track, eight were held by the strikers, and twenty-seven had been "killed." When the strikers gave notice that no trains would be allowed to move, the Sheriff summoned a posse of 200 armed men and cleared the tracks; the first train was sent out guarded by armed men. [36] In Fort Worth, an old-style western gunman (who had once fled arrest in New Mexico because his methods of "freeing the land of 'squatters'" resulted in two deaths) was Acting City Marshal. He engaged in a shoot-out to get a train through in which half a dozen officers and strikers were killed or wounded. Thereupon a vigilante group of 100 was formed in Fort Worth and nearly 300 state militia troops were rushed in. A news dispatch described one scene there:

Lawlessness and disorder have won in Fort Worth. One thousand desperado men have set the law and its executors at defiance, and their sweet will rules. . . . As early as 8:30 o'clock citizens who had been summoned by the Sheriff began to repair to the Missouri Pacific yards. Strikers and Knights of Labor, with sympathizers to the number of at least 400, were already there. Many of them had been there all night. . . . By 9:00 o'clock not less than 3,000 people were gathered in the yards of the road.

At 10:00 o'clock a train was made up on a side track. A Missouri Pacific locomotive left the Texas and Pacific roundhouse, and the strikers yelled "Here she comes." On this locomotive and tender were a dozen officers. . . . About the locomotive was a squad of officers. The strikers surged about the train, but were forced back by the officers. Pistols flashed in the sunlight in an ominous manner.

"Kill the engine, kill the engine!" yelled a striker, and the bulk of the crowd rushed forward to the locomotive.

"Back! I'll kill the first man who touches this engine," cried out the Chief Deputy. The officers stationed along the train left their posts and, throwing the strikers to right and left, gathered about the locomotive. That engine wasn't touched, but the strikers, seeing their opportunity, rushed between the cars, pulled the pins, and even took the nuts out of the draw-heads. Sheriff Maddox ordered the engineer to pull up, but not a car followed the engine, and the strikers yelled themselves hoarse with derision. [37]

This process reached its peak in East St. Louis, where on April 9th a group of deputies fired into a crowd, killing nine and wounding many. The crowd in fury retaliated by burning the shops and yards, destroying $75,000 of railroad property. According to the *New York Times,* it started when one member of a crowd stepped on railroad property. He was arrested, and as part of the crowd

36 surged forward to rescue him,

there was a pistol shot, which in a few seconds was followed by the ringing reports of Winchester rifles. The shrieks and yells that rose from the crowd could be heard on the bridge, a third of a mile away. "Crack, crack" went the deadly rifles. The crowd split into two unequal parts and ran like mad in opposite directions. . . . Terror was king and drove all before him. The deadly ball had been fired at short range against a solid wall of flesh and blood. . . . On the bridge and roadway lay Mrs. John Pfeffer, shot through the spine and mortally wounded; John Bonner, a coal miner, dead; Oscar Washington, a painter, dead; Patrick Driscoll, a Wabash section hand, dead, and Major Rychman, a rolling mill employee, shot in the head and shoulder, mortally wounded.

When the fleeing mob recovered from its terror, and turning saw its assailants in full flight toward the Louisville and Nashville freight house, shouts rose from it of "To arms, to arms," and men who stood over the dead and wounded vowed they would have a terrible revenge. Some of the wildest spirits rushed through the town calling on the strikers and their friends to arm themselves and kill all Deputy Sheriffs on sight. Pale-faced men soon appeared on the streets armed with revolvers and shotguns. Here and there a man could be seen carrying a small coil of rope. The cry of "Hang them" kept pace with that of "Kill them all." [38]

Leaders of the Knights of Labor tried to head off the crowd. One of them addressed the crowd:

"Brothers, I appeal to you, be calm and disperse to your homes. . . . I beg of you please do nothing rash. . . . Don't forget how hard we worked to build up our organization, do not tear it down in ruins by one rash act."

Nonetheless, the *New York Times* reported, a few hours later

. . . the sky was reddened by the burning of the Louisville and Nashville freight house. The mob had begun the work of what it considered retaliation. The fire was not long confined to cars, for at midnight the Cairo Short Line freight depot was in flames. [39]

The Governor responded by sending in 700 National Guardsmen and putting East St. Louis under military law.

The strikers held out for two months in the face of such opposition, but as the company broke their blockade with strikebreakers and armed violence, they eventually were forced to return to work defeated. The final call to end the strike came May 4th, but most of the strikers were refused their jobs, which had been taken by the strikebreakers.

Shorter hours had long been a major objective for labor, both to decrease the burden of toil and to cut unemployment by spreading the work. Ever since the 1830's the 1840's, labor reform societies had pushed for legislation establishing first the ten- and then

the eight-hour day. But even when such legislation passed, it remained a dead letter, unenforced. Some trades likewise had tried to shorten hours by strikes and negotiation, but with limited success, since unless the eight-hour system was adopted everywhere it put those firms which accepted it at a competitive disadvantage.

In 1884, a dying organization, the Federation of Organized Trades and Labor Unions passed a resolution that "eight hours shall constitute a legal day's work from and after May 1, 1886." [40] According to historian Norman J. Ware, "By a stroke of fortune, a resolution passed in the dull times of 1884 reached fruition in the revolutionary year of 1886 and became a rallying point and a battle cry for the aggressive forces of that year. . . . It was little more than a gesture which, because of the changed conditions of 1886, became a revolutionary threat." [41]

As a resolution passed by the Federation in December, 1885, suggests, the idea of a general strike for the eight-hour day developed out of the failure of other methods. The resolution noted that

. . . it would be in vain to expect the introduction of the eight-hour rule through legislative measures, and that a united demand to reduce the hours of labor, supported by a firmly established and determined organization, would be far more effective than a thousand laws, whose execution depends upon the good will of aspiring politicians or syncophantic department officials.

The call for a general strike was based upon the view

That the workmen in their endeavor to reform the prevailing economic conditions must rely upon themselves and their own power exclusively. [42]

The May Day strike movement received little support from existing organizations. The Federation that originally suggested the May 1st deadline was so weak that when it polled its members on the plan only about 2,500 even voted. Powderly, head of the Knights of Labor, opposed the May Day strike from the start. In a secret circular December 15th, 1884, he proposed that instead of striking, each Knights of Labor assembly "have its members write short essays on the eight-hour question." [43] The anarchists at first argued that the eight-hour movement was a compromise with the wage system. Their paper, the *Alarm*, declared that "it is a lost battle, and . . . though the eight-hour system should be established the wage workers would gain nothing." [44]

But the idea of a general strike for the eight-hour day had caught the imagination of tens of thousands of workers. Despite the opposition of national leaders, the movement burgeoned locally across the country. Local Knights of Labor organizers, over protest

38   of the national organization, established new local assemblies
around the eight-hour issue; one formed three new assemblies in
one night, despite a rule that an organizer must attend five weekly meetings before chartering a local. In the one month of February,
1886, 515 new locals were organized. The Knights of Labor Secretary for the Boston District Assembly reported on April 19th, 1886,
that the Order had more than trebled in the previous three months,
and that in the Boston Area District there were four times as many
members as thirteen weeks before. [45]

The leadership was alarmed at the militance of the new members pouring in. Powderly complained that "the majority of the
newcomers were not of the quality the order had sought for in the
past." [46] They suspended organizing of new assemblies for forty
days, but the organizers went on anyway, simply holding back
charter fees until the forty days expired. In an attempt to halt the
growth of their own organization, the Knights of Labor leaders next
refused to approve 300 new organizers' commissions, and finally
suspended all their organizers.

Powderly gives a vivid picture of what was happening locally: "In the early part of 1886 many of the new local assemblies began to pass resolutions favoring the 'action of the General Assembly in fixing the first of May, 1886, as the day on which to strike
for eight hours.' They sent them to the General Master Workman,
who saw at once that a grave danger threatened the Order through
the ignorance of the members who had been so hurriedly gathered
into the assemblies. They were induced to come in by a false statement. Many organizers assisted in keeping up the delusion for the
purpose of making 'big returns.'" [47]

At this point, Powderly tried deliberately to sabotage the
movement. He issued a secret circular to Knights of Labor locals
saying, "The executive officers of the Knights of Labor have never
fixed upon the first of May for a strike of any kind, and they will
not do so. . . . No assembly of the Knights of Labor must strike for
the eight-hour system on May 1st under the impression that they
are obeying orders from headquarters, for such an order was not,
and will not, be given." [48] The movement represented a kind of
class conflict which Powderly abhorred. The opposition of the
Knights of Labor leadership was unable to stop the strike, or even
to stop widespread participation of Knights of Labor locals, but it
did severely disrupt the unity and effectiveness of the movement.

Preparatory agitation for the strike built up to major proportions in March and came to a head in April. A considerable number
of eight-hour strikes broke out ahead of time, the eight-hour demand was injected into labor struggles over other issues, and mas-

The movement centered in the major industrial cities of Chicago, New York, Cincinnati, Baltimore, and Milwaukee, with Boston, Pittsburgh, St. Louis, and Washington affected to a lesser degree. Even before May 1st, almost a quarter of a million workers throughout the country were involved in the eight-hour movement. Some 30,000 had already been granted an eight-hour, or at least a shorter, day. At least 6,000 were on strike during the last week of April. It was estimated in April that not less than 100,000 were prepared to resort to the strike to secure their demand.

Yet the movement in fact proved even bigger than anticipated. By the second week in May, some 340,000 workers had participated, 190,000 of them by striking. [49] Eighty thousand struck in Chicago, 45,000 in New York, 32,000 in Cincinnati, 9,000 in Baltimore, 7,000 in Milwaukee, 4,700 in Boston, 4,250 in Pittsburgh, 3,000 in Detroit, 2,000 in St. Louis, 1,500 in Washington, and 13,000 in other cities. [50] Nearly 200,000 workers, according to *Bradstreet's,* won shorter hours.

Socialist satirist Oscar Ameringer, writing half a century later, described the May Day strike in Cincinnati. He had just arrived from Germany and found a job in a furniture factory — which he found totally different from his father's carpentry shop.

Here everything was done by machine. Our only task was assembling, gluing together, and finishing, at so much a chair or table, the two specialties of the factory. Speed came first, quality of workmanship last . . .

The work was monotonous, the hours of drudgery ten a day, my wages a dollar a day. Also, spring was coming on. Birds and blue hills beckoned. And so, when agitators from the Knights of Labor invaded our sweatshop preaching the divine message of less work for more pay, I became theirs . . . [51]

Ameringer joined a woodworkers' union affiliated with the Knights of Labor. "The membership was almost exclusively German and seasoned with a good sprinkling of anarchists." Before the May Day strike, "there had been groups of older or more militant members manufacturing bombs out of gas pipes. All of us expected violence, I suppose." At the kick-off march, "only red flags were carried . . . the only song we sang was the 'Arbeiters Marseillaise' . . . a workers' battalion of 400 Springfield rifles headed the procession. It was the Lehr und Wehr Verein, the educational and protective society of embattled toil." [52]

Such brigades of armed workers had grown up in a number of cities, largely in response to the use of police and military forces in 1877. By 1886 they existed not only in Cincinnati, but also Detroit, Chicago, St. Louis, Omaha, Newark, New York, San Francisco,

40   Denver, and other cities, adding to the feeling that a bitter conflict was at hand.

In Milwaukee, an enormous labor agitation was launched well in advance of May Day. In February, 1886, the local assemblies of the Knights of Labor, despite the national leadership, organized an Eight Hour League, and in the following month were joined by the local trade unions. A mass meeting of 3,000 built pressure for the change [53]

The Commissioner of Labor and Industrial Statistics reported,

... the agitation permeated our entire social atmosphere. Skilled and unskilled laborers formed unions or assemblies. Men, and even women, contributed money and time to its promulgation. It was *the* topic of conversation in the shop, on the street, at the family table, at the bar, in the counting rooms, and the subject of numerous able sermons from the pulpit. [54]

As May 1st approached, workers in 200 workshops and factories made their demands. On April 29th, the workers at the large John Plankinton & Co. packing house and several hundred workers from the sash and door shops struck for eight hours.

By May 1st, 3,000 brewers, 1,500 carpenters and other construction workers, and large numbers of bakers, cigar-makers, brickyard workers, slaughterhouse workers, laborers, and others had struck—a total of about 8,000. On Sunday, May 2nd, 2,500 workers held a parade through downtown Milwaukee complete with several bands and ending with a picnic. The strike continued to spread on Monday, as workers from smaller shops left their jobs. By the end of the day 14,000 were on strike, and victories began appearing. The master masons and bricklayers granted a twenty percent wage increase and allowed their men to work eight or ten hours, as they preferred; the Filer-Stowell foundry granted eight hours; Best Brewing met the workers' wage and hour demands, but total victory seemed at hand and the workers refused to go back unless the company would fire those workers who had not struck.

The strike now began to spread in the pattern of the General Strikes of 1877. Monday morning, 1,000 striking brewers lined up in front of the Falk Brewery, the only large brewery not on strike, to prevent employees from going to work; the Falk workers quit when the local assembly of the Knights of Labor called them out. That afternoon a crowd of several hundred strikers tried to force 1,400 men at the West Milwaukee Railway shops to quit. Turned away by the police, they marched on the still-running Allis works, where they were dispersed after being doused with streams of water from the mill. Fearing further violence, Allis decided to close the works, charging that "this afternoon a band of Polish laborers

marched from the West Milwaukee shops . . . to my works, and
with brandished clubs endeavored to force an entrance. Although
the mob of men with clubs marched directly before the eyes of the
police at the south side station, who had been notified of their
coming and of their purpose, not a policeman moved to keep them
from attack." [55] The Chicago, Milwaukee, and St. Paul Railroad
shops likewise closed to avoid violence.

The next morning one crowd gathered in the Menomonee
River valley and moved along the river trying to close plants.
Seventy-five policemen were powerless to control the crowd.
Another group of 1,500 workers moved on the Brandt & Co. stove
works and forced the men to quit work. Still another crowd gathered at St. Stanislaus Church in the Polish district and decided to
march to the North Chicago Rolling Mills plant at Bay View, the
largest plant in the city still in operation. When a committee of the
crowd presented the mill officials' explanation that the workers were
paid by the ton not by the hour and asked if they were satisfied
with it, the crowd yelled back "Eight Hours!" They felt that it was
no longer a matter between individual workers and employers, but
rather a test of power between workers and employers as a whole.
As one of the employers they attacked put it, the issue had become
more than hours and wages, it was a question of "my right to run
my works and your right to sell me your time and labor. Our whole
civilization and independence hangs on these . . ." [56]

Alarmed, Governor Rusk of Wisconsin called up the militia and
sent them to Bay View. Three companies arrived by train and
were stoned by the crowd as they marched onto the mill grounds.
About 350 militiamen stayed in the mill overnight.

Next morning at 6:00 a.m., a crowd of 1,500 gathered again at
St. Stanislaus Church to return to the Bay View mills. A *Milwaukee Journal* reporter who spent the night with the rioters reported,
"They have no organization or leaders, and act merely under pressure of momentary excitement." [57] The men assured reporters "that
they had no intention of making an attack on the militia or the company's property, and simply wished to show that they had not been
intimidated by the presence of the militia." [58] They marched to
the mill in orderly fashion, led by a red, white and blue banner
with a clock set at eight o'clock in the middle. They carried clubs,
iron bars, broken scythes, stones, and a few guns. According to
General Charles King of the Wisconsin National Guard, Governor
Rusk was telephoned and gave the order, "Fire on them!" [59]

As the crowd approached the mill, the commander of the
militia gave them an inaudible warning to stop, then ordered the
militia to fire. "As if by a common impulse the entire crowd fell

42 headlong to the ground, and for a minute it appeared as though nearly all had been killed or wounded by the first discharge. When the troops ceased firing, all who were uninjured turned and ran pell mell back to the city, leaving six dead or dying in the dusty road." [60] The shooting broke the back of the eight-hour movement in Milwaukee, and gradually the strikers returned to work, mostly at the old terms.

The eight-hour movement was launched in New York with a rally of 20,000 in Union Square, under a heavy police guard: "About 600 police officers were visible to the naked eye and over 100 more were hidden from view in the buildings surrounding the square. Not many blocks away 200 or 300 more officers might have been quickly called." [61] Nearly 4,000 furniture workers established shorter hours simply by reporting for work at 8:00 and leaving at 5:00. One thousand piano workers, seven hundred fifty furriers, five hundred carriage and wagon makers, two hundred fifty marble workers, to select a few examples, struck for shorter hours. Those winning their demands included:

Eight Hours

Brownstone Cutters	1,600
Cigarmakers and Packers	11,000
Cabinet & other furniture trades	4,000
Piano Makers	3,000
Fresco Painters	700
Furriers	750
Typographers	360
Wagon and Carriage Makers	600
	22,000

Nine Hours

Coopers	1,500
Machinist & Pattern Makers	20,000
Bricklayers & Building Trades	40,000
Metal Workers, including Brass Workers	2,000
Clothing Cutters	1,500
	65,000

"Besides the above trades there are numerous others, such as the bakers and brewers, and salesmen of all kinds that have reduced their hours of labor from fifteen to twelve and ten." [62] The street railway men reduced their working day by as much as five hours to twelve a day.

From Baltimore, *John Swinton's Paper* reported, "the third of May will be remembered in Baltimore as witnessing the largest and most imposing street parades of organized workingmen ever seen in this section. . . . Twenty thousand is the estimated number . . . a monster mass meeting . . . in the eight-hour interest was held at Concordia Opera House. About 10,000 organized workingmen were in line of procession. . . . The streets along the road were a blaze of light, lit up by thousands of torches and lanterns carried by the men in line." [63]

In Pittsburgh, cabinetmakers struck for a twenty percent advance in wages and a reduction from ten to eight hours; the carpenters struck for nine hours and a ten percent increase; stonecutters quickly won nine hours. Bakers closed 120 of 160 bakeries demanding shorter hours in Pittsburgh and Allegheny; coal miners at Imperial, Pennsylvania, struck for an advance of half a cent per bushel; 1,500 colliers won wage increases. "The horseshoers are happy," a labor paper reported. "Hereafter they quit work at 4:00 p.m. Saturdays." [64]

In Troy, New York, 5,000 went out on strike for eight hours, including 2,000 stove molders and all the building trades. Three hundred Italian railroad laborers struck for a wage increase, and "after stopping work they tied red handkerchiefs to their pickaxes and shovels and marched down the track in a body to another place where a second gang was at work and induced them to join the strikers." [65]

In Grand Rapids, several thousand furniture workers held a mass meeting demanding the eight-hour day; manufacturers accepted eight hours only with comparable wage reductions and were struck. In Detroit there were a number of strikes. On May 10th, sixty policemen were drawn up in a line in front of the Michigan Car Works in an attempt to break a strike there.

The street in front of the works was thronged with strikers waiting to see how many of their number would, as had been announced, return to work when the whistle sounded. Several "spotters" were stationed near the gates leading into the works. These closely scrutinized each workman who entered, apparently taking notes for future reference. Every time a man in working garb turned from the sidewalk to pass through the gate, loud cries of "Come out of that," "Coward," "shame," &c., went up from the waiting and watching strikers. . . . The net result of all this effort was that nine-tenths of the men were eventually kept out. [66]

In St. Louis, plumbers and water works employees struck for eight hours without wage cuts; carpenters imposed the eight-hour rule; furniture manufacturers agreed to eight hours, but with no wage adjustment. In Indianapolis, furniture workers struck for

44   eight hours, and wheel works employees were locked out. In Louisville, Kentucky, furniture workers were shut out for demanding
eight hours with adjusted pay. In Washington, D.C., the building
trades decided to impose the eight-hour day, and were soon seen at
quitting time brushing shoulders with the government clerks, who
already had attained it. The tinners of Fort Worth, Texas, adopted
the eight-hour system. Ten thousand miners at Wilkes Barre demonstrated for the eight-hour day. From New Haven, Connecticut,
the *New York Times* reported: "This town has picked up the repu-
tation lately of having more strikes than any other city of its size
in the country. Very likely it deserves it; at any rate the labor problem is in everybody's mouth. There are two societies devoted to its
discussion," drawing hundreds of participants.[64] In Portland,
Maine, cigar makers struck for wage increases.

Of course, in a number of cities the eight-hour movement failed to catch on. From Boston, for example, *John Swinton's Paper*
reported, "Although there have been a great deal of agitation, discussion and argument in this city for the last seven months over the
adoption of the eight-hour day"—indeed, 100 meetings on the question had been held by May 1st—"yet when the third of May arrived only four trades struck for the proposed change . . . the carpenters, plumbers, painters and masons."[68] And from Philadelphia it reported,

> The short hour movement has caused several strikes, most notably
> among the furniture workers and cabinet makers. . . . But the whole move-
> ment is dull as ditch water in Philadelphia."[69]

The heart of the eight-hour movement was in Chicago. Local
Knights of Labor, trade unionists and anarchists—reversing their
previous opposition—all supported the Eight-Hour Association
which agitated for the strike. Through April, a series of huge mass
demonstrations drew upwards of 25,000 people each. "Nearly
everyone was certain that with this display of spirit and the excel-
lent organization of the Chicago workers, the movement would succeed."[70]

The other side prepared as well. The police were readied for
emergency action; the militia was equipped for instant participation in street disorders; and leading businessmen created a committee of the Citizens' Association of Chicago to hold almost continuous sessions "for the purpose of agreeing upon a plan of action
in case the necessities of the situation should demand [its] intervention in any way."[71]

More than a year before, newspapers had reported the formation of military armed bodies by businessmen, who armed their
employees in wholesale houses, and the enlargement of the Na-

tional Guard. "In one large business house alone there is an organization of 150 young men who have been armed with Remington breech-loading rifles and pursue a regular course of drilling. . . . This is by no means an isolated case." [72]

On the eve of the strike, the *Times* reported from Chicago that "within the past forty-eight hours nearly $2,000 has been subscribed by various members of the Commercial Club, with which it is proposed to purchase some sort of a machine gun for the First Infantry, Illinois National Guard. The idea was suggested at the inspection and drill of the regiment Tuesday night and was readily adopted, when it was hinted that in case of a riot such a piece would prove a valuable weapon in the hands of the Guardsmen." [73]

By May Day, the movement in Chicago had already won impressive concessions: 1,000 brewers reduced their hours from sixteen to ten; 1,000 bakers who formerly worked fourteen to eighteen hours, gained a ten-hour day. A good proportion of furniture workers won the eight-hour day with a twenty-five percent increase in hourly wages; 1,600 clothing cutters won ten hours' pay for eight hours' work. Some tobacco, shoe, lard, packing, and other companies likewise reduced hours. A great many more workers, however, were expecting a hard fight to win. Among these were 4,000 bricklayers and stonemasons, 1,500 brickmakers, 1,200 metalworkers, butchers, carpenters, coopers, lathers, shoemakers, upholsterers, and molders.

On May 1st, the *Illinois State Register* reported, "The supreme officers of the police department have ceased in the attempt to smooth over the fears of the last few weeks regarding the labor movement. Their sole idea now is that . . . there will be a great deal of trouble." [74] That day 30,000 struck, including 10,000 lumbermen, 2,500 freight handlers, and 5,000 carpenters and woodworkers. [75] Perhaps twice that number watched or took part in demonstrations. [76] Freight handlers met and made a tour of the railroad freight depots, bringing out their fellows on all but two railroads. About 10,000 Bohemians, Poles, and Germans employed in and about the lumberyards marched through the streets with music and flags. [77] Perhaps because of their overwhelming numbers, there were no violent conflicts with the police.

By May 3rd, more and more groups of workers were joining the strike. A correspondent for *John Swinton's Paper* reported jubilantly, "It is an eight-hour boom, and we are scoring victory after victory. Today the packing houses of the Union Stock Yards all yielded . . . men . . . are wild with joy at the grand victory they have gained." [78]

But that day the police fired on a crowd that was attacking strikebreakers at the McCormack factory, killing four and seriously wounding many. With this the atmosphere turned bitter, and next day repeated street fighting developed between the crowd and police. The anarchists issued an appeal for workers to take up arms, and many labor gatherings were called for that night, including a rally at Haymarket Square to protest police brutality.

Only about 1,200 people attended the Haymarket rally; all but about 300 of them had left as rain began to fall. The last speaker was just saying, "In conclusion . . ." when to everyone's amazement a body of 180 policemen marched in and ordered the meeting to disperse. As the speakers climbed down from their platform, suddenly a dynamite bomb flew through the air and exploded among the police, killing one and wounding almost seventy. The police reformed ranks and fired into the crowd, killing one and wounding many.

Popular hysteria followed. The next day, wrote a Chicago lawyer, "I passed many groups of people . . . whose excited conversations about the events of the preceding night, I could not fail to overhear. Everybody assumed that the speakers at the meeting and other labor agitators were the perpetrators of the horrible crime. 'Hang them first and try them afterwards,' was an expression which I heard repeatedly. . . . The air was charged with anger, fear and hatred." [79] The press throughout the country did everything possible to stir up this feeling. The *New York Times*, for example, wrote, "No disturbance of the peace that has occurred in the United States since the war of the rebellion has excited public sentiment through the Union as it is excited by the Anarchists' murder of policemen in Chicago on Tuesday night. We say murder with the fullest consciousness of what that word means. It is silly to speak of the crime as a riot. All the evidence goes to show that it was concerted, deliberately planned, and cooly executed murder." [80]

The hysteria aroused by the bombing was turned against labor in general. As an anonymous Chicagoan wrote at the time, "the newspapers have taken advantage of the trouble to lump the socialists, anarchists, and strikers all together, making no distinction between them, and the consequence is that the labor cause will have to suffer. There will be a lull, and then a terrible reaction." [81] "The bomb," John Swinton wrote, "was a godsend to the enemies of the labor movement. They have used it as an explosive against all the objects that the working people are bent upon accomplishing, and in defense of all the evils that capital is bent upon maintaining." [82]

The reaction was not long in coming. Mayor Carter Harrison of Chicago issued a proclamation declaring that, since crowds, processions and the like were "dangerous" with conditions as they were, he had ordered the police to break up all such gatherings. An enormous police dragnet was organized, no less than fifty supposed "hang-outs" of radicals were raided within two days, and those under even the slightest suspicion of radical affiliation were arrested. It was reported that "the principal police stations are filled with anarchists and men who were arrested out of the mobs Tuesday night. At Desplaines Street alone there are over fifty, at the Armory nearly seventy-five, and about twenty-five at the Twelfth Street Station." [83] Most of those arrested were taken without warrants, and for some time no specific charges were lodged against them. As a Chicago socialist wrote to William Morris at the time,

> One week ago freedom of speech and of the press was a right unquestioned by the bitterest anti-Socialist. . . . Today all this is changed. . . . Socialists are hunted like wolves. . . . The Chicago papers are loud and unceasing in their demand for the lives of all prominent Socialists. To proclaim one's-self a Socialist in Chicago now is to invite immediate arrest. . . . All the *attaches* of all the Socialist papers have been seized and the papers broken up." [84]

Seven of the anarchists seized were tried and sentenced to death; four were eventually hanged, although there was virtually no evidence connecting them with the bombing.

The Haymarket hysteria gave the signal for the law and order forces throughout the country to act. Oscar Ameringer describes its effects on the eight-hour strike in Cincinnati. At first, it had been a "jolly strike;" victory had seemed certain, for "the forces of the opposition kept in the background, and did not almost everyone belong to the Knights of Labor?" As the strike benefits ran out, however, morale had begun to decline. Then suddenly newsboys were crying "Anarchists bomb-throwers kill one hundred policemen in Haymarket in Chicago . . ."

"The bad news from Chicago," Ameringer wrote, "fell like an exceedingly cold blanket on us strikers. To our erstwhile friends and sympathizers the news was the clarion for speedy evaporation. Some of our weaker Knights broke rank. . . . The police grew more numerous and ill-mannered." [85]

The First Regiment Militia was stationed in the Cincinnati Armory and three regiments from Columbus and Springfield were camped at Carthage, ten miles out, with special trains at hand to bring them into the city in twenty minutes if necessary. Most of the trades had compromised by May 10th on nine hours' pay for eight hours' work. Only the furniture makers remained out; their strike

Sensational accounts spread hysteria after the "Haymarket Riot" in Chicago, May, 1886. In contrast to this "artist's conception," the speakers had stepped down and the crowd was dispersing before the bomb exploded, whereupon police began firing into crowd.

T de Thulstrup / Library of Congress

50   was gradually broken and the men returned to work.

The pattern of demoralization and compromise was the same throughout the country.

The mass strike of 1886 was an attempt by the new class of industrial workers to use their power to gain some control over the conditions of their life and work. The Southwest strike was a direct bid for dual power over the operation of the railroads. The eight-hour strike was both an assertion that the worker was a human being whose life should not be consumed in toil, and an attack on the deliberate policy of keeping hours long and unemployment high in order to get the most work for the least wages.

The movement was met with a fierce wave of reaction, taking the Haymarket hysteria as its starting point and utilizing the techniques that had been developed against the Southwest strikes.

There developed a "tidal wave of formation of employers' associations to check the abuses of unionism, even to crush it."[86] By September, a leading labor journalist was writing that "Since May last, many corporations and Employers' Associations have been resorting to all sorts of unusual expedients to break up the labor organizations whose strength has become so great within the past two or three years."[87]

To take two cases out of scores, the association of shirt manufacturers of Jamesburg, New Jersey, locked out 2,000 employees whom they discovered had joined the Knights of Labor, and the manufacturers of silver goods in New York, Brooklyn, and Providence formed an association and locked out 1,200 workers for the same reason.[88] Thousands were not only fired but blacklisted, and thus kept from getting work elsewhere. The "Iron-Clad Oath" (later known as the "Yellow-Dog Contract"), which forced workers to swear they would not join a labor organization, became widely required for employment. The movement for labor solidarity and power was broken for the time, but it would arise again in less than a decade.

Chapter 2: Footnotes

1. Terence V. Powderly, *Thirty Years of Labor 1859-1889* (Columbus, Ohio: Excelsior Publishing House, 1889), p. 539.
2. *Ibid.*, p. 538.
3. John R. Commons, *History of Labour in the United States,* Vol. II (N.Y.: Macmillan Co., 1918), pp. 373-4.
4. Harry Frumerman, "The Railroad Strikes of 1885-86," in *Marxist Quarterly* (Oct.-Dec. 1937), Vol. I, pp. 394-6.
5. Norman J. Ware, *The Labor Movement in the United States 1860-1895,* A Study in Democracy (N.Y.: Vintage Books, 1964), p. 143.
6. *Proceedings*, 1885 General Assembly, pp. 84-91, quoted in Ware, p. 143.
7. Commons, Vol. II, p. 370.

8. John Swinton, *John Swinton's Paper,* April 12, 1885, cited in Ware, p. 66.
9. Ware, p. 66.
10. Powderly, p. 163.
11. Ware, p. xviii.
12. Powderly, pp. 258-9.
13. *Ibid.,* p. 123.
14. *Ibid.,* p. 156.
15. *Ibid.,* p. 53.
16. Ware, pp. xv-xvi.
17. Powderly, p. 151.
18. Ware, p. 320.
19. Powderly, p. 275.
20. *John Swinton's Paper,* April 12, 1885, cited in Ware, p. 140.
21. Cited in Ware, p. 307.
22. Lucy E. Parsons, *Life of Albert R. Parsons with Brief History of the Labor Movement in America* (Chicago: Lucy E. Parsons, 1889), p. 22.
23. Henry David, *The History of the Haymarket Affair, A Study in the American Social-Revolutionary and Labor Movements* (N.Y.: Collier Books, 1963), p. 21.
24. Ware, p. 302.
25. David, p. 21.
26. *Report of the Commissioner of Labor,* Third Annual Report, 1887, p. 12.
27. Commons, Vol. II, p. 366.
28. *John Swinton's Paper,* March 14, 1886, cited in Ware, p. 146.
29. Ruth Allen
30. *Ibid.,* p. 156.
31. *Ibid.,* pp. 132-3.
32. *New York Times,* March 20, 1886.
33. Allen, pp. 76-7.
34. *New York Times,* March 24, 1886.
35. *New York Times,* April 18, 1886.
36. Allen, pp. 77-8.
37. *New York Times,* April 3, 1886.
38. *New York Times,* April 10, 1886.
39. *Ibid.*
40. *Proceedings,* Federation, 1884, pp. 24-5, cited in Ware, p. 301.
41. Ware, p. 302.
42. *Proceedings,* Federation, 1885, cited in Powderly, pp. 499-500.
43. Powderly, p. 483.
44. Cited in David, p. 148.
45. *New York Times,* April 20, 1886.
46. Powderly, p. 495.
47. *Ibid.*
48. Cited *Ibid.,* p. 496.
49. *Ibid.,* p. 156.
50. Commons, Vol. II, p. 385.
51. Oscar Ameringer, *If You Don't Weaken* (N.Y.: Henry Holt and Co., 1940), p. 44.
52. *Ibid.,* pp. 44-5.
53. Thomas W. Gavett, *Development of the Labor Movement in Milwaukee* (Madison and Milwaukee, Wisc.: The University of Wisconsin Press, 1965), p. 58.
54. Wisconsin Bureau Labor Statistics, *Second Biennial Report,* p. 319, cited in Gavett, p. 59.
55. *Ibid.,* p. 330, cited in Roger Simon, "The Bay View Incident and the People's Party in Milwaukee," unpublished paper, 1967, p. 6.

52 56. *Milwaukee Daily Journal,* May 5, 1886, cited in Simon, p. 9.
57. Cited in Gavett, p. 64.
58. *Milwaukee Daily Journal,* May 5, 1886, cited in Simon, p. 10.
59. Gavett, p. 64.
60. *Milwaukee Daily Journal,* May 5, 1886, cited in Simon, p. 11.
61. *New York Times,* May 2, 1886.
62. *John Swinton's Paper,* May 9, 1886.
63. *John Swinton's Paper,* May 9, 1886.
64. *Ibid.*
65. *New York Times,* May 2, 1886.
66. *New York Times,* May 11, 1886.
67. *New York Times,* May 2, 1886.
68. *John Swinton's Paper,* May 9, 1886.
69. *John Swinton's Paper,* May 9, 1886.
70. David, p. 159.
71. *Ibid.,* p. 161.
72. *Ibid.,* p. 137.
73. *New York Times,* May 1, 1886.
74. *Illinois State Register,* May 1, 1886, cited in David, p. 163.
75. *New York Times,* May 2, 1886.
76. David, p. 163.
77. *New York Times,* May 2, 1886.
78. *John Swinton's Paper,* May 9, 1886.
79. Cited in David, p. 179.
80. *New York Times,* cited in David, p. 183.
81. Cited in David, p. 194.
82. *John Swinton's Paper,* cited in David, p. 186.
83. Cited in David, p. 190.
84. Cited in David, p. 193.
85. Ameringer, p. 46.
86. Clarence E. Bonnett, *History of Employers' Associations in the United States* (N.Y.: Vantage Press, 1956), p. 282.
87. Commons, Vol. II, p. 414.
88. *Ibid.*

Chapter 3
'The Ragged Edge
of Anarchy'

Late in 1892, Henry Clay Frick, the chairman of the Carnegie Steel Company, wrote a letter to Andrew Carnegie. In it he complained, "The mills have never been able to turn out the product they should owing to being held back by the Amalgamated men."[1] The Amalgamated men were a small number of highly-skilled steelworkers who belonged to the Amalgamated Association of Iron and Steel Workers, the strongest trade union the country had ever seen. The Amalgamated was affiliated with the American Federation of Labor, a loose confederation of the exclusive trade unions of highly-skilled workers against which Powderly had inveighed. A hostile historian described the power the skilled steelworkers held over the actual process of production at Carnegie's Homestead Works near Pittsburgh:

The method of apportioning the work, of regulating the turns, of altering the machinery, in short, every detail of working the great plant, was subject to the interference of some busybody representing the Amalgamated Association. . . . The heats of a turn were designated, as were the weights of the various charges constituting a heat. The product per worker was limited; the proportion of scrap that might be used in running a furnace was fixed; the quality of pig-iron was stated; the puddlers' use of brick and fire clay was prohibited; nor might one lend his tools to another.[2]

This power was exercised by committees in each department. When investigator John Fitch inquired years later, he was told by both older workmen and a prominent Carnegie official that the union had actually run the Homestead Works.[3]

In 1889, Carnegie had moved to break the union's power, proposing a twenty-five percent wage reduction and individual contracts for each worker — putting an end to collective bargaining. The workers struck. The company hired detectives and tried to bring in strikebreakers, but was defeated by mass picketing. As Frick described it later:

The posse taken up by the sheriff — something over 100 men — were not permitted to land on our property; were driven off with threats of bodily harm, and it looked as if there was going to be great destruction of life and property.[4]

In the face of sympathetic strike movements against other Carne-

54   gie plants, its subsidiary, the H.C. Frick Coke Company, and the railroads handling Carnegie products, the company backed down and signed a three-year contract with the Amalgamated, to expire in 1892.

The contract, however, was clearly only a truce, for the Carnegie Company grew more determined than ever to eliminate the union. David Brody, in his *Steelworkers in America: The Non-Union Era* points out that the great objective of the steel masters was to drive down costs. "The maximization of labor savings required complete freedom from union interference."[5] As a Carnegie partner put it, "The Amalgamated placed a tax on improvements, therefore the Amalgamated had to go."[6]

In January, 1892, the company proposed a new wage scale that admittedly would reduce Amalgamated men's wages eighteen percent, tipping off the workers that another conflict was approaching. Early in May, Carnegie drafted a statement which read:

These Works having been consolidated with the Edgar Thomson and Duquesne, and other mills, there has been forced upon this Firm the question whether its Works are to be run 'Union' or 'Non-Union.' As the vast majority of our employees are Non-Union, the Firm has decided that the minority must give place to the majority. These works, therefore, will be necessarily Non-Union after the expiration of the present agreement. . . . This action is not taken in any spirit of hostility to labor organizations, but every man will see that the firm cannot run Union and Non-Union."[7]

Frick, however, understood that he could break the union without making this the ostensible issue of the conflict, simply by making impossible demands. A Congressional committee later concluded that Frick was

opposed to the Amalgamated Association and its methods, and hence had no anxiety to contract with his laborers through that organization . . . this is the true reason why he appeared to them as autocratic and uncompromising in his demands.[8]

Following Carnegie's advice, Frick began his preparations for the anticipated strike by stepping up production to record levels. He ordered the construction of a great fence, twelve feet high and three miles long, around the works. Three-inch holes were bored at shoulder height every twenty-five feet, and the fence was topped with three strands of barbed wire. It was quickly dubbed "Fort Frick" and immortalized in verse:

> There stands today with great pretense
> Enclosed within a whitewashed fence
> A wondrous change of great import,
> The mills transformed into a fort.[9]

✊

We will want 300 guards for service at our Homestead mills as a measure of precaution against interference with our plan to start operation of the works July 6th, 1892.

The only trouble we anticipate is that an attempt will be made to prevent such of our men with whom we will by that time have made satisfactory arrangements from going to work, and possibly some demonstration of violence upon the part of those whose places have been filled, or most likely by an element which usually is attracted to such scenes for the purpose of stirring up trouble....

These guards should be assembled at Ashtabula, Ohio, not later than the morning of July 5th, when they may be taken by train to McKee's Rocks, or some other point upon the Ohio River below Pittsburgh, where they can be transferred to boats and landed within the enclosure of our premises at Homestead. We think absolute secrecy essential in the movement of these men.[10]

The Pinkerton Agency was ready, able and willing to provide the men. In the previous decades it had provided its services for management in seventy major labor disputes, and its 2,000 active agents and 30,000 reserves totalled more than the standing army of the nation.[11]

Frick issued an ultimatum that unless the union accepted his terms by June 24th, the company would deal with the men only as individuals. Four days later, the company closed down departments where 800 men worked; by July 2nd it had laid off the entire work force. The battle was on in earnest.

In preparation for the strike, the Amalgamated had formed an "Advisory Committee" of five delegates from each of its eight lodges. Since the Amalgamated Association included only 750 of the 3,800 workers at Homestead, the Advisory Committee called on the rest to support the strike. Three thousand workers packed into the Opera House and voted overwhelmingly that everyone would strike—for the semi-skilled and unskilled feared that their wages would be reduced as well. The Advisory Committee then circulated the following statement:

The Committee has, after mature deliberation, decided to organize their forces on a truly military basis. The force of four thousand men has been divided into three divisions or watches, each of these divisions is to devote eight hours of the twenty-four to the task of watching the plant. The Commanders of these divisions are to have as assistants eight captains composed of one trusted man from each of the eight local lodges. These Captains will report to the Division Commanders, who in turn will receive the orders of the Advisory Committee. During their hours of duty these Captains will have personal charge of the most important posts, i.e., the river front, the water gates and pumps, the railway stations, and the

56   main gates of the plant. The girdle of pickets will file reports to the main headquarters every half hour, and so complete and detailed is the plan of campaign that in ten minutes' time the Committee can communicate with the men at any given point within a radius of five miles. In addition to all this, there will be held in reserve a force of 800 Slavs and Hungarians. The brigade of foreigners will be under the command of two Hungarians and two interpreters.[12]

Military preparations began at once. Frick's plan for a naval landing of Pinkerton men had apparently become known to the Amalgamated men, for they chartered a paddle steamer, the *Edna* fitted with steam whistles to give the alarm. Day and night it cruised the Monongahela, supported by an armada of fifty two-man skiffs. Every road leading to Homestead was blockaded. Armed guards surrounded the railroad depots. Sentries patrolled the waterfront and watched from the peaks of surrounding hills. A communications system was created, using flags, skyrockets and a steam whistle, with the telegraph at the strike headquarters. The picket line grew steadily, until 1,000 men were patrolling ten miles of the river on both sides.

Meanwhile, the Advisory Committee took over authority in the town. It directed the running of the gas, water, and electric stations. It shut the saloons, kept the peace, and issued *ad hoc* laws. When eleven deputy sheriffs arrived to occupy the works, they were surrounded by 1,000 pickets and told, "No deputy will ever go in there alive."[13] The *Edna* then politely ferried the deputies back to Pittsburgh. When Sheriff McCleary of Allegheny County visited himself, the Advisory Committee gave him a guided tour of the plant and suggested that he deputize 500 strikers to guard it and keep out trespassers. He refused. The Advisory Committee offered to let fifty deputies take over the works—fearing the illegality of its own acts. But the Sheriff was unable to raise a posse, for nobody in Allegheny County wanted to fight the Homestead workers. The few men he was able to recruit refused to bear arms, interfere with picketing or escort strikebreakers. The Sheriff was powerless.

By late June, the Homestead workers had been informed by supporters in Chicago and New York that Pinkerton guards were on the way. The guards arrived five miles down river from Pittsburgh on the night of July 5th and boarded the two barges that had been prepared for them. The union was immediately informed by telegraph that several hundred strangers had arrived. As the barges passed Pittsburgh somewhat after 3 a.m., a union lookout wired headquarters, "Watch the river. Steamer with barges left here."[14] The river patrol was intensified, and a union skiff almost run down by the Pinkerton's tug fired revolvers at the barges. A little before 4 a.m., the Advisory Committee pulled the steam whistle with the signal indicating a river landing threatened, and a mounted sentry burst into Homestead shouting, "The Pinkertons are coming!"[15] Workers and their families piled from their beds. By the time the barges approached the landing, the crowd that met them numbered 10,000. Several hundred carried carbines, rifles, shotguns, pistols and revolvers, most of the rest sticks, stones and nailed clubs.

The Pinkertons, armed with Winchester repeaters, threw out a gangplank and began to land. "Don't step off that boat," someone yelled from the jeering crowd. One striker lay down on the gangplank. When the first Pinkerton detective tried to shove him aside, he pulled a revolver and shot the detective through the thigh, knocking him over backward. Gunfire instantly raked the Pinkertons, killing one and wounding five. A force of additional Pinkertons rushed on deck and began firing steadily into the crowd, hitting over thirty and killing at least three. The fire from the crowd quickly drove the Pinkertons back below decks. When they tried again to land a few hours later, four more were shot down instantly and the attempt was abandoned.

The strikers, joined by large numbers of armed supporters from other towns, now tried to find a way to drive the Pinkertons out of the barges. First they built barricades of steel and pig iron from which they could fire with safety on the barges. Skiffs swarmed around the barges, firing at point-blank range. Half-pound sticks of dynamite were hurled onto the barges, blowing

George Scott / Historical Pictures Services

private army of Pinkerton Guards tried to invade the town of Homestead during steel strike of 1892. The strikers, organized and armed, battled them with dynamite, cannon and rifles from boats and steel barricades.

58   holes in the sides but failing to sink them. A twenty-pound brass
cannon used for holiday celebrations and a smaller one residing in
a veterans' hall were wheeled out and trained on the barges. Workers flooded the river around them with oil, but were unable to set
them afire. A flaming raft was floated toward them, but the current
carried it past. A natural gas main was directed toward the barges
and the gas ignited with Fourth of July firecrackers, but only a
small explosion was triggered.

By the end of the day the Pinkertons were faced with a mutiny
of their own men. Most of those on the barges were not regular
company detectives but guards hired under false pretenses, then
shipped to Homestead at gunpoint much against their wills. Many
were wounded; all were terrified; the July heat in the barges was
unbearable; the chance of escape was nil. Under these conditions,
the men voted almost unanimously to surrender. They were marched out, disarmed, and made to run a bloody gauntlet in which all
were injured, many seriously. The crowd, enraged by the deaths it
had suffered, initially demanded that "Not one must escape
alive!"[16] The Advisory Committee, fearing the public reaction to
a massacre, finally persuaded the workers to let the Pinkertons go.

The battle electrified the nation. On the strikers' side, forty
were shot and nine killed. On the Pinkertons', twenty were shot,
seven died, and nearly three hundred were injured running the
gauntlet.[17] Reporters from all over the country—and even other
countries—poured into Homestead. A song, "Father Was Killed by
the Pinkerton Men," became an overnight hit.

For several days, the strikers held the works unchallenged.
The Sheriff, with no effective force of his own, appealed again and
again to Governor Pattison for the militia. Pattison stalled, stating
"I am of the opinion that there would not have been a drop of blood
shed if the proposition had been accepted to let the locked-out men
guard the premises."[18] But pressure on him mounted, and finally
he ordered the militia to Homestead. They arrived July 12th.

In the wake of the Great Upheaval of 1877, the Pennsylvania
militia had been reorganized and brought to a high state of efficiency. By 1892 it included well over 8,000 officers and men, well armed
with Springfield .45's and Gatling guns. The strikers at first wanted to oppose the militia, but the Advisory Committee persuaded
them to welcome it instead. As the troops marched off the train,
they were met by a welcoming committee, complete with band. A
spokesman for the Advisory Committee stepped up and said, "On
the part of the Amalgamated Association, I wish to say that after
suffering an attack of illegal authority, we are glad to have the legal authority of the State here." General George Snowden, in com-

UPI

Defeated by the strikers, the Pinkerton guards mutinied against their own officers and surrendered. They were marched out of the barges, surrendered their arms, and barely escaped with their lives.

60   mand of the troops, replied: "I do not recognize your association, sir. I recognize no one but the citizens of this city. We have come here to restore law and order and they are already restored."[19] The General's conception of law and order soon became apparent. That same day he was asked, "General, is it intended to use your troops for the protection of non-union men?" Snowden answered, "The gates are open and you may enter if the company permits it."[20] Strikers maintained massive armed picket lines around the works, but the company began ferrying in small groups of strikebreakers by barge. The Guard prevented retaliation. At first the militiamen fraternized with the strikers, but Snowden quickly put an end to it by forbidding his men to consort with workers or enter town without an officer. "Pennsylvanians can hardly appreciate the actual communisn of these people. They believe the works are theirs quite as much as Carnegie's," Snowden reported.[21]

In response to the killings and the militia, the strike soon spread to the rest of the Carnegie works in the Pittsburgh area. At the Union Iron Mills the men declared July 14th that they would not return to work until the Homestead dispute was settled. The company gradually resumed production there with strikebreakers. The next day, workers at the Beaver Fall mills refused to work until the company opened negotiations with the Homestead strikers. Frick declared a lockout and the strike continued for four months. Workers at Duquesne joined the Amalgamated and struck a week later, following appeals from the Homestead strikers. The State militia in August escorted repairmen, mechanics, and other strikebreakers into the plant, suppressed a riot, and allowed production to resume.

On July 16th, the company posted a notice giving Homestead workers until July 21st to apply for rehiring:

> It is our desire to retain in our service all of our employees whose past record is satisfactory, and who did not take part in the attempts which have been made to interfere with our right to manage our business.[22]

But not a single one of the locked-out men applied.

The company was forced to other tactics. Its law firm brought warrants for murder against leading Advisory Committee members. At least 160 other strikers were charged with lesser crimes. They were no sooner acquitted than the entire Advisory Committee was re-arrested for treason against the State of Pennsylvania. The Chief Justice of the State personally charged the grand jury:

> . . . when a large number of men arm and organize themselves by divisions and companies, appoint officers, and engage in a common purpose to defy the law, to resist its officers and to deprive any portion of their fellow citizens of the rights to which they are entitled . . . it is a levying of war against

the State, and the offense is treason . . . The men had no further demand upon its property than has a domestic servant upon the household goods of his employer when he is discharged . . . [23]

In the end, no Pittsburgh jury ever found a striker guilty on any charge. But the prosecutions served their purpose nonetheless. They tied up enormous funds in bail and legal costs. After bail money ran out they kept large parts of the strike leadership in jail awaiting trial. And by all accounts they confused and demoralized the strikers at Homestead. The Amalgamated men had considered themselves conservative, patriotic citizens—most were solid Republicans—defending their rights against Frick's private army, the Pinkertons. The trials made them doubt the legitimacy of what they themselves had done. Were they in fact just a murderous, treasonous mob?

The Carnegie Company continued bringing strikebreakers into Homestead, but had great difficulty recruiting the scarce, highly skilled steelworkers most needed to resume operations. In many cases, strikebreakers had to be virtually shanghaied. Fifty-six men hired in Cincinnati, for example, were offered easy work and good pay at another Carnegie steelworks. They boarded a train and only after the doors and windows were locked did the armed guards tell them their real destination. They battled with the guards and forced the doors; only twenty-one remained by the time they reached Homestead. Once there, a strikebreaker reported,

We were made prisoners in the works and guarded like convicts. The more ignorant were told by the foreman that if they ventured outside the union men would shoot them like dogs. . . . At least half of them are sick from heat, bad water and poor food. [24]

A local paper reported that desertions were occurring "at such a lively rate . . . as to threaten to depopulate the mill in a week." [25] Strikers threw pamphlets from a train into the works, promising good treatment and free train fare home for deserting strikebreakers. There followed a grand rush for the exit, and company officials were powerless to stop a large number from leaving. Nonetheless, by September nearly every department of the plant was running, albeit poorly.

The strike held solid for four months. Frick wrote Carnegie, "The firmness with which these strikers hold on is surprising to everyone." [26] But with the company restoring production and winter coming on, morale finally began to decline. On November 18th, the unskilled workers asked to be released from their strike pledge. The Amalgamated agreed, and two days later called off the strike. The men returned to work as individuals—with the leaders blacklisted forever. Frick cabled Carnegie:

62 Strike officially declared off yesterday. Our victory is now complete and most gratifying. Do not think we will ever have any serious labor trouble again. [27]

In the wake of the Homestead defeat, the once-powerful Amalgamated Association was practically driven out of the steel industry. By 1895 it retained but half its pre-Homestead membership, little of it in steel. The steel masters had created a seemingly impenetrable arsenal of weapons against unionism—an arsenal we shall meet again in 1919.

In the final analysis, the strikers were defeated by the new technology of the steel industry. In earlier days, it had been impossible to run the mills without the skilled men of the Amalgamated, and so all that was necessary to defeat an employer was "to withhold our skills from them until such time as they agree." [28] But with the increasing mechanization of the mills, employers could start up with new men and only a nucleus of experienced workers. The new giant corporations with many plants could easily shift work from a struck plant to an unstruck one and thus be relatively unscathed by a strike. Only a movement embracing all steelworkers, skilled and unskilled, and supported by workers in allied industries would have stood a chance against a corporation as powerful as the Carnegie Company. As we shall see, many workers—especially on the railroads—drew this lesson. But the Amalgamated—like the rest of the A.F.L.—refused to adapt to the new realities of industrial America.

The employers made substantial gains from their defeat of unionism in the Homestead strike. They were enabled without resistance to reduce labor costs and introduce new machinery to increase productivity. In 1897 a Carnegie executive reported "a marked reduction in the number of men employed." The Homestead Works "can now be run full with about 2,900 men," a twenty-five percent decrease since 1892. [29] David Brody points out that

In the two decades after 1890, the furnace worker's productivity tripled in exchange for an income rise of one-half; the steelworker's output doubled in exchange for an income rise of one-fifth [much of these wage increases merely compensated for inflation]. At bottom, the remarkable cost reduction of American steel manufacture rested on those figures.

The accomplishment was possible only with a labor force powerless to oppose the decisions of the steel men. [30]

In the depression year of 1893, wages in iron and steel fell an average of twenty-five percent. With the union smashed, the cuts went practically unopposed. A Carnegie official, announcing wage cuts, stated, more successfully than ever before and will probably have a material advantage over many of its competitors in cost sheets. [31]

In the period from 1892 to 1907, the daily earnings of highly skilled plate-mill workers at Homestead shrank by one-fifth, while their hours increased from eight to twelve. [32]

But the most important result of the Homestead strike was its effect on American workers. Secretary of the Treasury Charles Foster, campaigning in Ohio, reported "trouble among laboring men." "They were talking about Homestead, and about Carnegie being too rich, while they were poor." [33] The bloody battle of July 6th stirred a deep sense of identification in workers throughout the country. For example, 90,000 workers in Chicago had celebrated a "Homestead Day" and raised $40,000 for the strikers. Other contributions had poured into Homestead. The defeat of the nation's most powerful trade union at the hands of a private army, the state militia, and the Carnegie company, started workers everywhere on a search for new solutions and a broader solidarity.

Almost simultaneously with Homestead, armed conflict broke out in the Coeur d'Alenes mining district of Idaho. In January, 1892, the companies of the district began closing down their mines; the ostensible reason was to force cheaper railroad rates, but as one mine-owner confided, "such is not the main issue, and you will find when the mines resume operation, wages will be $3.00 per day for shovelers and car men," a fifteen percent reduction. [34] The workers, including the skilled miners whose wages remained uncut, refused to accept the new scale. Soon the owners began bringing in strikebreakers protected by armed detectives, but workers often persuaded incoming strikebreakers to leave. In one case, sympathetic railroad men assigned eighty strikebreakers from California to ride in boxcars, then shipped them 250 miles in the opposite direction.

In May, the Governor was still complimenting union officials on holding their members in check, but this restraint was not to last. Tension built between miners and guards, breaking out in fist fights and peaking June 10th, when the miners gathered with their guns in response to a rumor that the militia was on its way. Early next morning a miner was fired upon by guards at the Frisco mill, and as the miners gathered "a general cry went up to capture the mill." [35] The miners circled the hill, dodging the fire of the guards until they got above them. Then, as the battle raged, they loaded a car with powder and sent it down the hill with a short fuse, demol-

64 ishing the old mill. No one was injured, but the strikebreakers hoisted a white flag and surrendered; they were marched as prisoners down to the union hall. Following this, the strikers peacefully took possession of other mines and plants in the district, taking prisoner the strikebreakers occupying them.

The Governor immediately declared martial law and sent in the militia. When they proved totally inadequate, the President sent in Federal troops at the Governor's request. But the strikers occupied the Bunker Hill and Sullivan concentrator, and threatened to destroy it unless the strikebreakers departed.

Martial law meant military repression of the strike. The Sheriff and Marshal, who had been elected by miners' votes, were removed, and a hated company doctor installed as Sheriff. Four hundred and eighty people were indicted (although none was ever convicted of any crime) and numbers of strikers and sympathizers were arrested and imprisoned in "bull pens"—stockade enclosures. Two mines running with union workers were closed by order of an Army Colonel, ostensibly because union men used them as a meeting place.

The conflict at Coeur d'Alenes erupted again seven years later. When the Governor on that occasion declared an insurrection beyond the power of the state to control, the strike was quelled by the U.S. Army.

The conflicts of 1892 reached far into the South. Early in that year, streetcar drivers in New Orleans had won a reduction in hours from sixteen to twelve. The street railways, however, in an attempt to break the union, quickly discharged sixteen of the workers who had sponsored the twelve-hour movement. The workers struck, and the entire city polarized on the issue. On the side of labor—

Sentiment in favor of a sympathetic strike swept the rank and file of other unions, and was checked only by the conservative leaders who took charge of the car-drivers' fight. [36]

On the side of business, a committee of fifty merchants from the Board of Trade and the commodity and security exchanges—"representing the commercial capital of New Orleans" [37]—came to the aid of the railways, denounced the closed shop, and despite the absence of significant violence, appealed to the Governor to send the militia. The leaders of the strike were arrested on conspiracy charges. The issue stalemated, both sides agreed to arbitration, and the workers were finally granted the preferential closed shop.

In the wake of this victory, workers flooded into the A.F.L.

unions of the city. Thirty new unions were chartered. A Working-men's Amalgamated Council with two delegates elected from each of forty-nine unions was established, representing more than 20,000 workers. Most important was the creation of the "Triple-Alliance" of recently organized Teamsters, Scalesmen, and Packers. These three unions included both white and black members. They were potentially powerful because they performed the manual labor essential to the commerce of the city.

On October 24th, 1892, at the peak of business, the men of the Triple Alliance struck, demanding a ten-hour day, overtime pay, and a preferential closed shop. The Workingmen's Amalgamated Council thereupon appointed a committee of five from the most conservative unions, including one Negro, to direct the strike. Not one member of the committee came from the striking unions.

The strikers faced the unified opposition of all New Orleans employers. The Board of Trade centralized its decision making in a committee of five merchants, backed by the four railway systems entering New Orleans, the cotton, sugar, and rice exchanges, the clearing house, and mechanics' and dealers' exchanges. It raised a defense fund of several thousand dollars, and pushed for intervention by the militia and the courts. For a week it refused to recognize the existence of the Triple Alliance or to enter negotiations.

The stalemate paralyzed the city. The Labor Committee, "moved to action by the indignation of the rank and file," [38] called a general strike. Under this threat, the unity of employers cracked, and those not yet struck pressured the Board of Trade to negotiate. An agreement to resume work pending a final agreement was reached. But the agreement blew up when many workers did not return to work and others were refused their jobs. There was bitterness on both sides. The employers' position hardened, and they refused to consider arbitration until every striker had returned to work.

The Amalgamated Council again ordered a general strike.

. . . The unions polled their members in heated meetings which generally ratified the strike order. Despite such eagerness for a demonstration of strength, the Labor Committee did all in its power to avoid it. [39]

The strike was twice postponed, but on November 8th over 20,000 workers walked out. This was only partly a sympathetic strike; each union on strike demanded recognition, a closed shop, and in many cases wage and hour gains for its own men. The strike was joined by such associations of non-industrial workers as musicians and hat, clothing, and shoe clerks. Gas and water workers, electric light trimmers, and other public utility workers had recently been organized with a full understanding of their critical im-

66 portance. When they joined the strike, the Labor Committee at the behest of the Governor ordered them back, but was twice defied by the workers. Streetcar drivers and printers broke their contracts to join the strike, but the strike was kept from being complete by the continued working of other trades with such agreements. Nevertheless, the strike was highly effective; business came almost to a standstill and bank clearings were cut in half.

Employers moved to break the strike. With the assistance of the railroads, they telegraphed Birmingham, Memphis, Mobile, and Galveston and began bringing in strikebreakers. They pressured the Mayor to call for special deputies, but only fifty-nine citizens responded. They began training their own clerks for riot duty, and offered to pay all the costs of the State militia if the Governor would call it up. Under their pressure, the Governor issued a proclamation ordering citizens not to congregate in crowds, implying that the militia would be called if the strike continued, virtually declaring martial law, and warning labor of possible bloodshed.

The unions, unwilling to stake their existence upon a collision with the militia, decided after three days to bring the strike to an end. An agreement was worked out granting the wage and hour demands of the Triple Alliance, but refusing recognition to the unions. New Orleans continued as an open shop city. Forty-five strike leaders were indicted in Federal court for violating the Sherman Anti-Trust Act.

The New Orleans general strike revealed an extraordinary solidarity. The close cooperation and loyal mutual support of skilled and unskilled, black and white workers suggest that racism was not always unsurmountable, even in the deep South. The strike indicates how widespread was labor insurgency in 1892. And it stands as a monument to lost opportunities in the South.

Meanwhile in Tennessee another little-known struggle was culminating. Throughout much of the South, convicts from the state penitentiaries were leased out to politically powerful employers at extremely low rates. An investigation by the Tennessee legislature reported that the branch prisons were "hell holes of rage, cruelty, despair and vice."[40] A conservative newspaper added —

> Employers of convicts pay so little for their labor that it makes it next to impossible for those who give work to free labor to compete with them in any line of business. As a result, the price paid for labor is based on the price paid convicts.[41]

Colonel Colyar, the Tennessee Democratic leader and general counsel for the Tennessee Coal, Iron and Railroad Company, an employer of convict labor, wrote:

For some years after we began the convict labor system, we found that we were right in calculating that free laborers would be loath to enter upon strikes when they saw that the company was amply provided with convict labor. [42]

In the spring of 1891, miners in Briceville, Anderson County, turned down a contract which would forbid strikes against grievances, give up the right to a checkweightman, and provide pay in "scrip" redeemable only to the company store—the last two were illegal under Tennessee law. On July 5th, the operators imported a carload of forty convicts. The convicts tore down the miners' houses and erected stockades for themselves. Ten days later, the miners decided at a mass meeting to act before the main body of convicts arrived the next day. Just after midnight 300 armed miners advanced on the stockade in a massed line, demanding the release of the convicts. The officers and guards realized that resistance was futile. The miners marched convicts, guards, and officers to the depot at Coal Creek and packed them on the train to Knoxville.

The next day the Governor in person came to Anderson County, at the head of three companies of the militia, with the convicts in tow. After the Governor departed, the miners entertained the soldiers in their homes and slipped food into their barracks. The militia requested leaves of absence and one whole detachment nearly deserted. It was generally doubted that the militiamen would have taken any action against the miners. Similarly, according to the State Superintendent of Prisons, "nearly all the citizens of Anderson County around [the] mines are in sympathy with the mob." [43]

At 6 a.m., on July 20th, miners from the surrounding counties, including some from Kentucky, armed with shotguns, Winchester rifles, and Colt pistols, began pouring into Briceville and Coal Creek, on trains and mules and even on foot. They formed a line and marched on the offending mine, spreading out into the mountain ranges and taking cover behind rocks and trees as they drew close. They sent a committee forward to demand the expulsion of prisoners. When a militia Colonel moved as if to capture the committee, one of its members waved a handkerchief as a signal to the miners, who sprang from cover. The 2,000 armed miners had little difficulty persuading the militia and guards to accompany them to the railroad station with the convicts, and return again to Knoxville. Meanwhile, the Briceville miners marched on another mine and sent guards and convicts packing.

The Governor immediately ordered fourteen companies of militia—600 men—to Anderson County. The miners were talked into accepting a truce if the Governor would call a special session of the legislature to repeal the convict lease law. The session convened, but the leasing companies were too powerful and nothing resulted. The miners then appealed to the courts for relief, but received none. Therefore, they turned again to direct action.

At a mass meeting on October 28th, 1891, the committee which had represented the miners at the legislature resigned, and leadership was taken by men of a more radical tendency. The miners then held a series of secret meetings to prepare their action. On the evening of October 31st, the miners filed up to the stockade and demanded the release of the prisoners. Officials turned the 163 convicts over to the miners, who set them free. The miners then marched to another mine and released 120 more convicts in the same manner. Two nights later, the miners rode on horseback to the stockade at Oliver Springs, battered down the door with a sledge hammer, and quickly released the convicts. In each case, the stockades were burned to the ground.

For a time it looked as if the miners had won. All available miners were hired full time with their own checkweightman; other objectionable features were removed from their contracts as well. "Peace and prosperity had descended upon the entire valley from Coal Creek to Briceville." [44] But in the middle of December, the Governor announced that the convicts would be sent back into the mine stockades at Briceville, Oliver Springs, and Coal Creek. "Fort Anderson," a permanent military camp, was established, with 175 civil and military guards, surrounding trenches, and a Gatling gun overlooking the valley. The miners deeply resented this virtual military occupation.

The climax of the miners' struggle against the convict lease system came in the summer of 1892. In July, an operator in Tracy City, Grundy County, put regular miners on half time and brought in 360 convicts to work full time. The miners began holding secret meetings. On the morning of August 10th, the miners converged on the convict stockade, overpowered the guards, captured the mines, and put the prisoners on the train to Nashville. The miners then marched to the Inman mine and repeated the same maneuvers.

This triggered renewed conflict in Anderson County. On August 15th, 100 miners marched on the convicts' quarters at Oliver Springs and demanded their release. For the first time the guards, instead of submitting, opened fire on the miners, wounding several. In response, miners from the surrounding area poured into Coal Creek, commandeered two freight trains, and ordered the engineers to Oliver Springs at gunpoint. Bands of fifty to one hundred miners continued to arrive and mass into formation. They marched to the stockade, disarmed the guards, burned the blockhouse, and returned guards and convicts to Knoxville. They then laid seige to the militia at Fort Anderson, firing on it from the surrounding hills. Only when an army of 500 soldiers was organized and marched to Anderson County was the seige relieved.

Large numbers of local citizens were arrested and locked up in railroad cars, the school house, and the Methodist church. In the end, nearly all were released by local juries. Although the militia succeeded in crushing the revolt, the convict lease system was thoroughly discredited and was abolished soon thereafter.

The struggles at Homestead, Coeur d'Alenes and Briceville all involved organized, armed resistance by groups of workers to military attack. The New Orleans General Strike revealed an extraordinary solidarity among all races and classes of labor. But these struggles provide only a prelude to the bitterness and unity of the conflicts of 1894. The strikes of 1892 revealed to workers everywhere their own capacity for cooperation and resistance. But 1892 also revealed that struggles by isolated, local groups of workers could be defeated by the superior force of the corporations. In 1894, 750,000 workers struck — more than in any previous year — and half of them did so simultaneously in the overlapping national strikes of miners and railroad workers.

In 1893, the country went into a serious depression. By 1894, *Bradstreet's* estimated there were three million unemployed in the country; the Mayor of Chicago reported 200,000 in that city alone. Wages were slashed throughout the coal districts of the country. In the Pittsburgh district, for example, the scale fell from seventy-nine to fifty cents or less per ton. [45] Miners were cut to part time. Their desperation was indicated by a miner at Minerton, Ohio:

> I have never seen as discouraged a set of men as the miners in this neighborhood have been since the last reduction was made. They know it matters not how steady they work they cannot make enough money to keep a small-sized family in the necessary food, and they have concluded that if they are to starve they prefer doing so at once and not by degrees. [46]

Thus it is not surprising that when the United Mine Workers convention declared a nation-wide "suspension," the *New York Times* reported from one mining field, "the miners are elated by the action taken by their delegates at Columbus in declaring for a general suspension to go into effect on April 21st." [47] The aim of the strike was to end the coal glut, thereby forcing prices up and allowing the operators to raise wages to the old rate. [48]

The United Mine Workers had no more than 20,000 members, but on April 21st, more than 125,000 miners struck. [49] The strike eventually reached from Tacoma, Washington to Birmingham, Ala-

bama, to Springhill, Nova Scotia, including many areas where th
U.M.W. had no organization whatever. Andrew Roy, a miner
union official, reports that even "the general officers were surprise
at the magnitude of the strike . . . " [50] According to the U.M.W., n
more than 24,000 bituminous miners remained at work in the entir
country.

The extent of the strike made the workers optimistic. After te
days, President McBride of the U.M.W., announced:

> Already operators are offering to pay the price asked, and in som
> instances more than has been demanded to get men to resume work, b
> the men are true to the orders issued by the National Convention, and r
> fuse to work at any price until a general settlement has been made. . .
> Your power having once been demonstrated, you are masters of the situ
> tion, and can command anything within reason. [51]

The miners of Thompson Run, Pennsylvania, illustrate what Mc
Bride meant. They were granted an increase of wages and guarde
by deputy sheriffs, but nonetheless went out on strike in sympath
with the rest of the miners. [53]

The miners organized themselves into bands of a few dozen t
many thousands, and engaged in widespread direct action whic
became, at times, virtual guerrilla warfare. They began wit
marches to spread the strike to unaffected areas. Two thousand m
ners from Spring Valley, Illinois, headed by two brass band
marched into La Salle, Illinois, and organized a mass meeting "a

In 1872, nearly 100,000 participated in a strike for the eight-hour day in building an
mechanical trades in New York. The objective was largely won—only to be lost i
the depression that began the following year.

ressed in a dozen languages," to persuade miners there to strike.[53] A delegation of Clearfield, Pennsylvania, miners went to West Virginia to induce their fellows to join the strike. At Pomeroy, Ohio, 500 miners chartered a steamboat and started down the river with a brass band, appealing to the miners along the valley in Ohio and West Virginia to join the strike.[54]

These activities were usually peaceful, until many operators began trying to reopen with strikebreakers, generally under the protection of special deputies. Under these circumstances, the bands of miners developed into what the press called "armies of intimidation." [56] The violence of the miners to strikebreakers is easily understood, for they themselves were making the greatest sacrifices for the strike. The miners "have been on short time for two years, and are in poor condition to stand a long lockout," the New York Times reported on the first day of the strike. It added a week later:

The most alarming feature of the strike at present is the extreme destitution among the strikers. It is estimated that fully one-third or more of the families at the various plants are in destitute circumstances, and do not know where their next meal is to come from. Many of them proclaim their circumstances, and boldly announce that they will either have to go to work or steal.[56]

One center of disturbance was the Connellsville, Pennsylvania, coke region. Strikebreakers were imported early there:

Rainey & Cochran, who own the plants in the Vanderbilt region, say they will work tomorrow, and have asked Sheriff Wilhelm for protection. A large force of deputies was sent to Vanderbilt tonight. Rainey put fifty Italians in his Elm Grove mines yesterday, and will, it is reported, employ Italians at the coke plant if his employees join the strike.[57]

At Scottsdale, Pennsylvania, a crowd of women marched to the coke ovens determined to drive out strikebreakers. A mine official fired a rifle at them. The striking men thereupon rushed the mine and several were shot. They captured and severely beat the official. The strikers who had been shot were subsequently arrested.[58] Another plant was fired up with a large force of men under a strong guard of deputies. An hour later, strikers armed with clubs, stones, and coke forks advanced under cover of darkness and attacked the men at work. The attack was so sudden the deputies were caught by surprise and the strikebreakers fled in terror.[59] A few weeks later, when an agent imported blacks from Virginia to Mount Pleasant, Pennsylvania, to work in Frick's Standard Works, the wives of the strikers caught him and tore out most of his beard.[60]

Conflict in the coke region culminated in a massacre at a mine that was being operated by strikebreakers under guard of more than fifty deputies. Two thousand strikers from mining camps a-

72   long the Monongahela and Youghiogheny Rivers assembled near the mine. The *New York Times* reported them armed with rifles, shotguns, revolvers, and clubs, though this was subsequently denied by strikers.[61] Squads of strikers marched up and down the road to the music of brass bands and fifes and drums. Delegations visited the strikebreakers and deputies with messages such as this:

> We are fully prepared to resist every attempt to start these mines. We know the workmen here would join the strike if they were not intimidated by armed mercenaries. We are heavily armed and will return bullet for bullet if the deputies fire on us. We are American citizens and demand the protection that is afforded the company.[62]

Next morning when the strikebreakers, guarded by deputies, marched to the mines, the strikers yelled to them to go home. The strikebreakers turned around and started back, to the cheers of the strikers. Instantly, the deputies rushed out of the mines and began "escorting" the strikebreakers to the mines. When the strikers moved forward a deputy fired — perhaps in the air. "In a moment bullets were flying in all directions." The strikers fled down the road.

> The deputies followed closely upon them, and continued firing at them. The narrow defile of the road prevented the strikers from scattering or getting away. . . . The deputies neared the surging mass of men, and continued to shoot directly at them.[63]

Four of the strikers were killed outright, an unknown number wounded. Sixty-six strikers were captured, and one hundred fifty were in jail by the next day.[64] The *New York Times* reported from the coke region:

> The prospect of a speedy settlement of the strike by peaceable means has been swept away by the riot at the Washington Run mines. The news of the killing of strikers has caused the men to become very angry. . . . The leaders realize the danger of an outbreak in any part of the region and are doing all in their power to hold the men in check. Numerous appeals were issued from headquarters today to the men to abstain from violence and to keep within the bounds of the law. . . . The leaders themselves now admit their inability to control the angry strikers. . . .[65]

In Spring Valley, Illinois, about 200 striking miners marched on a mine and drove out the strikebreakers. "A battle with clubs and stones ensued." [66] The strikers banked the fires and nailed up the entrances to the mines. Fifty deputies charged the strikers and captured one of the "ringleaders." "The mob followed the deputies to the jail, and, after breaking down the door, liberated their fellow-striker."[67]

At La Salle, Illinois, strikers held a mass meeting, then proceeded to the La Salle mine and engaged in a gun battle with the

Sheriff and his deputies. Running out of ammunition, the deputies fled. Three of them were shot, the rest beaten. Having driven them off, the crowd occupied the town. When they learned that two of their numbers had been taken prisoner they marched on the jail, forcing the Mayor to release them.[68] The Sheriff wired Governor Altgeld for the militia, concluding, "Mob surrounding hotel where I am wounded."[69] A day later troops arrived. They intercepted 250 miners who had captured a railroad train at Ladd and were passing through La Salle on the way to Ottawa to release miners imprisoned there.[70]

At Duquoin, Illinois, 700 miners captured a freight train and forced the engineer to take them to Centralia, where they sabotaged a mine that had begun work there. "The shaft was filled with loose material, the belting on the machinery was cut, and the oil cups knocked from all the shafting."[71] The militia was sent in and at least eighty-eight men were arrested.

The bands of strikers ranged over considerable area. At Coal Bluff, Indiana, 5,000 miners at a mass meeting decided to march en masse to Pana, Illinois, to force miners there to quit. That same day at Grant, Indiana, 1,000 men captured a freight train and took it to Terre Haute, on their way to Pana for the same purpose.

Of course, violence was by no means always necessary to persuade strikebreakers to quit. When the Baltimore and Ohio Railroad ordered its shopmen and its Italian trackmen to replace the striking miners, they refused and were fired.[72] At the Elm Grove mines near Wheeling, West Virginia, the operators imported four lots of strikebreakers, only to have them quit one after another.

Whenever it proved impossible to prevent the mining of coal, the miners turned to blockading coal trains as a way to enforce the suspension. At Oglesby, Illinois, strikers piled rails across the tracks of the Illinois Central Railroad in front of a coal train, causing a wreck.[74] At Minonk, Illinois, miners put ties, bolts and the like across the tracks and forbade the passage of coal cars. Governor Altgeld sent in the militia; he was also appealed to for arms, but reported he had none left.[75] Strikers at Shelburne, Indiana, stopped and examined all trains passing through. "If no coal was found, the trains were allowed to proceed; but when coal was found the cars were sidetracked."[76] At Fontanet, women took over the coal chutes on the Big Four Railroad and refused to let the company fuel its engines.[77] At Lyford, miners climbed on coal cars and set the brakes.[78] Governor Matthews called out the Indiana National Guard to enforce the passage of trains through Cannellsburg.[79] At Jackson, Ohio, 5,000 miners held a mass meeting to decide how to prevent passage of coal. They paraded the town with

74   half-a-dozen bands. "Communications from the various railroads
were read, many of which were to the effect that the railroads will
not haul any more non-union coal."[80] At Martin's Ferry, Ohio,
strikers burned two railroad bridges. "They had prepared a stone
as large as an engine tender at Barton tunnel to drop on a coal train
should it succeed in passing the miners' fort."[81] Striking miners
from Will and Grundy Counties in Illinois burned a bridge near
Carbon "as a warning to the company to stop transferring coal."[82]

Miners at Terre Haute, Indiana, were stopped from blockading coal trains by the arrival of the militia. When the militia moved
to another town, they resumed searching trains. "Their policy now
is to stop the trains whenever the militia is not present, and, if the
militia is sent to where they are, they will congregate at another
point on the road."[83]

At Salineville, Ohio, 500 miners captured a coal train that had
been released by troops earlier in the day. They soaped the tracks
so that the train could get no traction, backed it onto a siding, and
spiked the switch. "Within an hour the coal was scattered all over
the ground and the cars were empty."[84] In the Kanawha Valley of
West Virginia, miners burned a drum house and trestle at a working mine, stopped all traffic on one local railroad, and dynamited a
railroad bridge. Another railroad simply gave up hauling coal.[85]

In all, the militia was called out in at least five states. At Ens-
ley, Alabama, fifteen companies were encamped, but the strikers
found new allies as well: "Several hundred idle mechanics and other laborers in Birmingham contemplate going to the Pratt Mines
and encamping there, so as to be on hand to aid the miners in case
of a conflict with the troops."[86]

But elsewhere the militia was effective in breaking the strikers'
spirit. From Indiana a journalist reported, "The formidable force
of militia has awed the strikers."[87] Another wrote from Maryland—

> The coming of the militia had a most satisfactory effect on the strikers
> at all the mines. The men seem to realize that unless they at once resume
> work new help will be employed to fill their places. At the Eckhart Mine,
> guarded by three companies of the Fifth Regiment, seventy-five men went
> to work this morning. . . . The outlook for the return of all the strikers un-
> der guard of the militia is exceedingly good.[88]

When the strikers interfered with trains, the United States
government entered the fray. On May 28th, a railroad lawyer arrived in Terre Haute with a restraining order from a U.S. Judge
forbidding the blocking of trains. This allowed the U.S. Marshal to
organize a force against the strikers. "The power of the Federal
government being behind the writ, all the force necessary to move
the train will be used."[89] A week later, the U.S. Marshal at Chi-

cago went with a large body of deputies to Coal City and Streator
to enforce an injunction against blockading trains on railroads under Federal receivership.[90]

Coal shortages quickly appeared. By April 28th, for example, the Colebrook furances in Lebanon, Pennsylvania, were banked for want of coal.[91] "It will not be long," McBride remarked April 30th, "until there will not be coal enough left in the general market to boil a tea kettle with."[92] From Bellaire, Ohio, it was reported on May 5th that nine blast furnaces and four steel plants and nail mills in the area were closed for want of coal.[93] The Baltimore and Ohio Railroad Company "seized for the road's use all soft coal in transit to customers." [94] On the Chicago, Burlington and Quincy railroad, many of the engines were reduced to burning wood instead of coal.[95] In Des Moines, Iowa, the water works of the city were shut down for lack of coal to run them.[96] All departments but one of the great Edgar Thomson Steel Works in Braddock, Pennsylvania, closed down for lack of iron and coal.[97] In St. Louis, by May 24th the coal dealers were simply unable to fill orders in many cases; all but five of the city's flour mills were shut down for want of coal, and the five still in operation were burning wood.[99] The Philadelphia and Erie Railroad was forced to switch to anthracite coal. The Missouri River steamers switched to wood. By May 27th, the railroads were reported confiscating "all the coal in sight."[100] In Lincoln, Illinois, the electric streetcars were obliged to stop running,[102] and local coal dealers at Carthage reported that it was almost impossible to get coal.[102]

As the strike kept on week after week, the condition of the miners grew severe. From Minonk, Illinois, the *New York Times* reported on May 30th —

The miners say their wives and children are at the point of starvation. They are subsisting mainly on dandelions, but have no flour, meat or other provisions.[103]

Despite starvation conditions, the workers held out bitterly. When union officials accepted a new scale below the old one, large numbers of miners continued the strike anyway. A mass meeting of miners near Camden, Pennsylvania, on June 13th, voted unanimously that the new rate was unacceptable. From Punxsutawney, Pennsylvania, the miners were reported "indignant at the settlement." At Glenroy, Ohio, 2,000 miners met and decided to continue the strike. At Bellaire, Ohio, the miners said "they will starve before accepting the sixty-cent rate decided on at Columbus." At Spring Valley, Illinois, a mass meeting adopted resolutions "denouncing the action of the convention and calling upon the executive officers to resign." A mass meeting at La Salle resolved to ac-

76   cept nothing less than a return to the previous scale.[104]

But the strikers were defeated in the end by their inability to make the strike universal. As Andrew Roy wrote, "vast train-loads of coal from the anthracite fields of Pennsylvania, the New River and Pocahontas fields of West and Old Virginia (whose miners had not suspended work) were being poured into the markets which the suspension had been inaugurated to deplete."[105] In Fairmont, West Virginia,

The leading mine operators in this section state that over 200% more coal is being mined in the valley between this place and Clarksburg than was ever mined before. Large numbers of miners are flooding in and every pit is being worked to its full capacity. Over 3,500 men are now at work where a month ago there were only about 1,200.[106]

Under such conditions, the strike was finally defeated, and after more than two months the starving miners returned to work.

Simultaneously with the coal suspension, strikes had spread among the metal miners. The iron mines of the Eastern Mesaba Range in Minnesota were closed by strikes on May 2nd. "An armed gang of 300 foreign miners . . . marched through the streets of Iron Mountain . . . forced the miners in the Iron Mountain and Rathbone Mines to stop work and join their ranks, and also stopped work in White & McDevitt's saw mill. The rioters declare that work in all industries must cease. Fifty deputy sheriffs have been sworn in."[107] Two days later, thirty armed miners marched to Iron Mountain and prevented the opening of mines there.[108]

Especially dramatic was the conflict at Cripple Creek, Colorado. Some mine-owners there had tried to lengthen the working day from eight to ten hours; the workers at various mines replied by organizing a union and declaring that all mines would have to adopt eight hours by February 7th, 1894. In response, the largest mines shifted to ten hours, and the men walked out. After a month of quiet, tension began to rise as some of the mines reopened with strikebreakers guarded by armed deputies. The District Court Judge issued an injunction against interfering with the operation of the mines, and the president of the union was arrested for violating the injunction.

The mine-owners now pledged money and arms to the county if it would enroll a large body of deputies to protect the opening of the mines. The county commissioners accepted the offer, and Sheriff Bowers soon recruited and imported an army of 1,200 men.[109]

The strikers in turn organized on a military basis, establishing a headquarters and camp on Bull Hill under direction of a miner with three years' training at West Point. Taking the initiative, the miners marched under the noses of the deputies and cut them off

Polish strikers attack Pennsylvania Coal and Iron Police—called by the miners "the Cossacks"—in the Schuylkill region in 1888. Conflict in the coal fields has been chronic from the Civil War to the present.

78 from a number of the mines. Next they attacked and captured without bloodshed the Strong mine, which was guarded by a squad of deputies, confiscating their arms and ammunition. Early next morning, the strikers tried to raid the deputies' camp to obtain more guns and ammunition; one deputy and one striker were killed in the battle that followed.[110]

Meanwhile, groups of armed men were forming in mining towns throughout Colorado, planning to march to Cripple Creek to support the strikers. At Rico, for instance, a hundred fully armed men seized a train and rode 100 miles toward Cripple Creek before they were stopped. In Colorado Springs, the mine-owners' citadel, rumors were widely believed that the city was about to be attacked.

The Populist Governor of the state finally negotiated a settlement establishing the eight-hour day, but the army of deputies remained in Cripple Creek.[111] Only by sending the militia and interposing them between the strikers and the deputies was a new engagement prevented. Under militia guard, work began again, but it was only a truce. In less than ten years, Cripple Creek and Colorado would again be the center of a bloody mine war.

The wage cuts and layoffs of the depression of the midnineties extended far beyond the miners. An extreme example of the prevalent wage cuts occurred at the works of the Pullman Palace Car Company at Pullman, Illinois. The entire town — land, houses, stores, churches, and all — was owned by George Pullman. Rents were deducted from wages by the company, and were unreduced as wages fell. The result, according to the minister of the Pullman Methodist-Episcopal Church was that

> After deducting rent the men invariably had only from one to six dollars or so on which to live for two weeks. One man has a pay check in his possession of *two* cents after paying rent. . . . He has it framed.[112]

During March and April, 1894, a majority of the workers at Pullman joined a new organization called the American Railway Union, which had started at the beginning of the depression. The Pullman employees, although not railroad workers, were able to join because Pullman owned a few miles of railroad, and anyone who worked for a railroad company — even a coal miner or longshoreman — was eligible. Indeed, the whole purpose of the A.R.U. was to overcome the disunity among railroad workers by uniting them — and eventually all labor — into a single organization. As its president, Eugene Victor Debs, put it,

> The forces of labor must unite. The dividing lines must grow dimmer day by day until they become unperceptible, and then labor's hosts,

marshalled under one conquering banner, shall march together, vote together and fight together, until working men shall receive and enjoy all the fruits of their toil.[113]

(Despite this objective the A.R.U. maintained the railroad brotherhoods' traditional principle of including only white workers, with the consequence that some blacks gladly took railroad jobs during the great strike. That, however, did not prevent Chicago blacks from taking part in the movement to the extent of tipping over railroad cars in their own neighborhoods. [114])

The first major event in which the A.R.U. was involved was a strike on the Great Northern Railroad, controlled by James J. Hill. Three times within a year the Great Northern had cut wages; three times the officers of the railroad brotherhoods had recommended that the men accept the cuts. [115] Disgusted, a number of the men had joined the A.R.U. Under its rules—in contrast to those of the brotherhoods—a strike could be called by a majority of members on the railroad line involved. After the third wage cut, the A.R.U. members on the Great Northern declared a strike, although the A.R.U. was so new that not a single lodge had as yet been organized.[116] The strike was supported not only by A.R.U. members, but by a great many other workers, including even the rank and file of the railroad brotherhoods. Even though brotherhood officials helped the company recruit strikebreakers to run the trains, the strike stopped all freight traffic on the line without recourse to blockade. Within little more than two weeks, the company was forced to accept an arbitration decision that was practically a complete victory for the workers.

The victory over Jim Hill in 1894 had much the same results for the A.R.U. that the victory over Jay Gould had had for the Knights of Labor in 1885. Coming in the midst of rising discontent and a series of defeats, the victory dramatized for workers everywhere the possibility and power of solidarity. Workers flooded into the A.R.U. According to Ray Ginger, Debs' biographer,

The officers were unable to pass out charters fast enough to keep pace with the applications. Entire lodges of the Railway Carmen and the Switchmen transferred to the A.R.U. Firemen, conductors, even engineers, joined the industrial union. But the great majority of recruits came from previously unorganized men who had been unable to meet the high monthly dues of the Brotherhoods. [Indeed, a large proportion of them were not even eligible for membership in the restricted Brotherhoods.] The unskilled workers had been unprotected, underpaid, exploited; now the dikes snapped and a reservoir of bitterness and hope drove men pell-mell into the American Railway Union . . . The officials did not have to coax or persuade; their main job was to sign cards and issue charters.[117]

Within a year, the A.R.U. had 150,000 members, more than

80   all the old brotherhoods together and only 25,000 fewer than the entire A.F.L.[118] The new spirit of unity that imbued the railroad workers was revealed when the auditing clerks on one Western railroad wanted to organize, but were told by the company that any clerk joining the A.R.U. would be fired on the spot. The switchmen called on the manager and warned him not to threaten the clerks. "During a grave depression, when unemployed men stood on every street corner, such action seemed suicidal, but the switchmen made it stick, and for the first time a railroad office was filled with union men."[119] This spirit was what made possible the great Pullman boycott of 1894.

    The workers at Pullman sent a grievance committee to visit the manager. When three members of the committee were fired on May 10th, sentiment for a strike reached a fever pitch. At an all night session of the grievance committee, two top A.R.U. officials strongly advised against a strike and Debs wired caution, but "Howard's oratory, Keliher's ebullient charm, and Debs' influence all went for nothing."[120] The committee voted unanimously to strike. The strikers held open meetings daily at which reports of committees were given and matters of policy decided; a central strike committee with representatives of each local union directed the strike. Three hundred strikers guarded the Pullman works day and night. The strike was a desperation move. As a strike spokesman put it:

> We do not expect the company to concede our demands. We do not know what the outcome will be, and in fact we do not care much. We do know we are working for less wages than will maintain ourselves and our families in the necessaries of life, and on that proposition we absolutely refuse to work any longer.[121]

    A month after the strike began, the American Railway Union held its first regular convention. The workers at Pullman appealed to the convention for aid. For the 400 delegates, many of whom had visited Pullman, the issue became symbolic of everything they hated — the poverty of the workers, the arrogance of George Pullman, and the overwhelming power of the corporation. According to Ginger,

> Debs now used every rein of control in the hands of a chairman. His shrewdness, his eloquence, his influence, were all thrown into battle against headstrong action, and, in the end, they all went for nothing. The entire hall was filled with muffled, bitter comments: George Pullman had gone too far. It was time to show the bloodsucker. The A.R.U. should boycott all Pullman cars, not move a single sleeper until Pullman settled with his workers. . . . Finally one man spoke for dozens of men: A boycott against Pullman cars should be declared immediately. Debs, in his calmest voice, refused to entertain the motion. . . . Above everything else, he

The leadership of the union did everything possible to avoid a sympathetic strike. But when Pullman refused arbitration, saying there was "nothing to arbitrate,"[123] and even to arbitrate whether there was anything to arbitrate, a committee of the A.R.U. convention urged that a boycott of Pullman cars be instituted. When the delegates wired home for instructions they found sentiment overwhelmingly in favor of the plan, and they voted unanimously to apply it.

Of course, it was not solely sympathy for the workers at Pullman that led the railroad workers to such an extraordinary decision. Debs himself put clearly the reasons for this sudden development of solidarity. The railroad employees had lost confidence in the Brotherhoods because they "had failed, in a single instance, to successfully resist" the wage cuts gradually sweeping the country. All of the delegates, therefore, came to the A.R.U. convention expecting to act to—

restore their wages and to protect them in their rights and wages as employees. This is the reason that they were so ripe to espouse the cause of the injured Pullman employees. . . . While the injuries and grievances of the Pullman employees appealed to their sense of justice and to their sense of duty for redress, these further grievances of their own made the matter more binding upon them . . . to do everything in their power to protect the Pullman employees, as well as their constituents. . . . [124]

The testimony of workers from around the country gives a picture of those grievances. At La Salle, 100 miles west of Chicago, the workers had voted to strike even before the Pullman boycott was called, to protest the firing of A.R.U. members.[125] At Des Moines, Iowa, the main grievance was "the radical change in the rules of the company concerning promotion and priority," putting extra workers on the employment rolls and using the surplus to drive down wages and forestall strikes.[126] At Rock Island, "some six or seven . . . men were discharged, which caused a very restless feeling among the men . . . and when it was learned that switchmen on the Rock Island had been discharged as members of the A.R.U., for refusing to handle Pullman cars, they took a vote in the local union and decided to take the same stand the members of the union did in Chicago."[127] On the Grand Trunk railroad one official "would get so drunk he did not know anything and then go around and dictate to men that did know their business . . . " while another would "pry into the affairs of the men and . . . cut the force down to such an extent that a man was dogged around and chased around as though he was not human in order to get the work done." In addition, the Grand Trunk used inexperienced road officials to do

82 switching while laying off regular switchmen.[128] On the B&O, the complaints were "favoritism, pets, and maladministration of some of the petty officers." [129] On the Pittsburgh, Fort Wayne and Chicago, engineers and foremen were deprived of paid dinner hours they had won in a previous agreement.[130] One fireman summarized: "there was a feeling among railroad men in general that I had occasion to meet that there was going to be a reduction of wages on nearly every road throughout the country. . . . In a large number of roads there was a feeling among the employees that they were almost in a helpless condition to stand against the oppression of the petty officials, and the petty officials took advantage of that feeling and deviled the men . . ."[131]

The boycott began on June 26th, 1894, when switchmen on a number of lines out of Chicago refused to switch Pullman cars. They were instantly fired, leading other workers on the lines to walk off in protest. Two days later, four or five Chicago railroads were stopped, with 18,000 men on strike. This was what Debs and the other A.R.U. officials had expected; but they were greatly surprised as committees and groups of railroad workers from all over started appearing at the strike headquarters, announcing that their local unions had decided to strike in support of the Pullman workers.[132] Soon virtually all twenty-six roads out of Chicago were paralyzed, and all transcontinental lines except the Great Northern—which carried no Pullman cars—were stopped. The struggle extended to twenty-seven states and territories. An estimated 260,000 railroad workers, nearly half of them not members of the A.R.U., joined the strike; *Bradstreet's* estimated that 500,000 were out of work because of the strike.

Coming at the same time as the coal strike, the Pullman boycott represented a social crisis of the first order. The *New York Times* saw in it "the greatest battle between labor and capital that has ever been inaugurated in the United States."[133] By July 3rd, the *Chicago Tribune* declared that the strike had attained the "dignity of an insurrection." [134]

Direction of the action moved on two levels. The A.R.U. convention had left the conduct of the strike in charge of its President Eugene Debs and its executive board. They rapidly set up a strike headquarters and threw themselves wholeheartedly into the strike in Chicago. These officials articulated the strikers' position, formulated aims, counciled non-violence, held daily mass meetings in Chicago, and sent out hundreds of telegrams a day encouraging the strikers. Operational control, however, rested in the strike committees that sprang up within each body of strikers. As Debs explained it, "The committees came from all yards and from all roads to confer with us. The switchmen, for instance, would send a committee to us, and we would authorize that committee to act for that yard or for that road, and that committee would then go to that yard and take charge of the affairs." [135] The A.R.U. officials consulted daily with these committees in shaping strike decisions. The committees also served in part to contain the strike within the limits set by the leadership, although this was by no means always the case; for example, when the Mobile and Ohio Railroad offered not to run Pullman cars, the A.R.U. advised the workers there to call off their strike, but they refused because they felt it would weaken the unity of the strike.[136] This informal structure of strike committees allowed the coordination of the strike over a vast area of the country despite the lack of organized preparations.

The conflict rapidly came to be understood as a general struggle between all workers and the corporations as a whole. The General Managers' Association, which represented the twenty-six Chicago railroads, served as a general staff for management, planning strategy, recruiting strikebreakers, and using its enormous power to influence public opinion and the government. As Debs wrote in an appeal to the railroad workers of America to support the strike,

The struggle with the Pullman Company has developed into a contest between the producing classes and the money power of the country. . . . The

The Pullman strike of 1894 showed the power of railroad workers to halt the commerce of the nation. The fear and rage generated by this fact was largely focused on Eugene Victor Debs, here portrayed as "King Debs."

84 fight was between the American Railway Union and the Pullman Company. The American Railway Union resolved that its members would refuse to handle Pullman cars and equipment. Then the railway corporations, through the General Managers' Association, came to the rescue, and in a series of whereases declared to the world that they would go into partnership with Pullman, so to speak, and stand by him in his devilish work of starving his employees to death. The American Railway Union accepted the gage of war, and thus the contest is now on between the railway corporations united solidly upon the one hand and the labor forces on the other. . . . [137]

The strike was effective beyond anyone's expectation. For the week ending June 30th, 1894, ten trunk-line railroads out of Chicago carried 42,892 tons of east-bound freight; for the week ending July 7th they carried only 11,600; the Baltimore and Ohio carried fifty-two tons and the Big Four Railroad carried not one ton. [138] As Debs wrote later, the strike was won as far as beating the railroad companies was concerned; "the combined corporations were paralyzed and helpless." [139] Even John Egan of the General Managers' Association admitted by July 2nd that the railroads had been "fought to a standstill." [140]

But by June 30th the legal committee of the G.M.A. had worked out detailed plans to bring a power against the workers which the A.R.U. had not reckoned on—the United States government. According to Almont Lindsey's careful study, *The Pullman Strike:*

A vital part of the strategy of the association was to draw the United States government into the struggle and then to make it appear that the battle was no longer between the workers and the railroads but between the workers and the government . . . it was the policy of the roads not to alleviate the inconvenience in transportation but rather to aggravate this condition wherever possible, in order to arouse the anger of the travelling public and thus hasten action by the federal authorities. [141]

In line with this policy, John Egan of the G.M.A. on July 2nd called for the use of Federal troops, since there was no "other recourse left." With these troops, "the strike would collapse like a punctured balloon. It is the government's duty to take this business in hand, restore law, suppress the riots, and restore to the public the service it is now deprived of by conspirators and lawless men." [142]

President Cleveland and his Attorney General, Richard Olney, were more than happy to use the force of the U.S. government to crush the strike. Olney, for thirty-five years a railroad lawyer and still a director of several railroads (including one involved in the boycott) considered the strike an attack on railroad property and corporate control. The administration decided to break the strike in Chicago, for, as Olney confided to a trusted agent there, "if the

rights of the United States were vigorously asserted in Chicago, the
origin and center of the demonstration, the result would be to make
it a failure everywhere else and to prevent its spread over the entire
country." [143] Grover Cleveland concurred in this strategy; as he
wrote years later—

> It was from the first anticipated that [Chicago] would be the seat of
> the most serious complications, and the place where the strong arm of the
> law would be needed. In these circumstances, it would have been criminal
> neglect of duty if those charged with the protection of governmental agen-
> cies and the enforcement of orderly obedience and submission to federal
> authority, had been remiss in preparations for an emergency in that quar-
> ter. [144]

Olney's first move was to appoint Edwin Walker, a member
of the G.M.A.'s legal committee and general counsel for one of the
struck railways, a special Federal Attorney in Chicago. His next
was to secure a blanket injunction forbidding all strike activities—
even attempting by persuasion to induce an employee to abandon
his job. [145] Soon such blanket injunctions covered the country from
Michigan to California, putting all strike supporters in contempt of
court. One of the judges issuing the first injunction proudly called
it a "Gatling gun on paper." [146]

As the editor of the *Chicago Times* observed, "the object of
the injunction is not so much to prevent interference with the trains
as to lay a foundation for calling out the United States troops." [147]
On July 2nd, the Federal Marshal in Chicago read the injunction to
a jeering crowd outside Chicago; the crowd responded by dragging
baggage cars across the tracks to prevent the passage of trains. The
next day he wired Olney, warning that a general strike was expected and saying, "I am unable to disperse the mob, clear the tracks,
or arrest the men who were engaged in the acts named, and believe
that no force less than the regular troops of the United States can
procure the passage of the mail trains or enforce the orders of the
court." [148] Over the protest of Governor Altgeld of Illinois, Federal
troops marched into Chicago. Attorney General Olney told reporters, "We have been brought to the ragged edge of anarchy and it is
time to see whether the law is sufficiently strong to prevent this
condition of affairs." [149]

Until Federal troops arrived, the strike in Chicago had been
extraordinarily peaceful. Debs and the other A.R.U. officials had
told the workers that violence would play into the hands of the
companies, and that the strike could be won simply by the refusal
of the railroad workers to work. With the U.S. Army on the scene
to break the strike, however, such a peaceful victory was no longer
possible, and the popular mood shifted rapidly. As an A.R.U. of-

ficial testified later, "the people of America have been treated so unfairly—I do not speak of myself, but from the experience we had in going through the country—that the very sight of a blue coat arouses their anger; they feel it is another instrument of oppression that has come, and they are liable to do things they would not do if the blue coats were kept away." [150] The prevailing atmosphere is suggested by Debs' statement when troops were sent in:

> The first shot fired by the regular soldiers at the mobs here will be the signal for a civil war. I believe this as firmly as I believe in the ultimate success of our course. Bloodshed will follow, and 90% of the people of the U.S. will be arrayed against the other 10%. And I would not care to be arrayed against the laboring people in the contest, or find myself out of the ranks of labor when the struggle ended. I do not say this as an alarmist, but calmly and thoughtfully. [151]

General Nelson Miles, commander of the U.S. troops in Chicago, likewise believed there was danger that the civil government and authority of the United States would be paralyzed, if not overthrown, as a result of the conflict. [152]

Violent confrontation did in fact follow the arrival on July 4th of U.S. troops in Chicago. That night, crowds began to gather on railroad property, overturning boxcars and resisting authority. They were not composed of railroad workers, but of the most depressed part of the working class—immigrants, unemployed, unskilled. Next day the crowds grew, throwing switches, changing signal lights, blocking tracks with toppled boxcars. The largest crowd, numbering 10,000, started at the stockyards and moved slowly eastward all day along the Rock Island Line. The general sentiment was caught by a crowd that marched through railroad yards calling out workers, yelling that it was a "fight between labor and capital, and they must come out." [153] That night a great fire broke out, destroying seven structures at the World's Columbian Exposition, while at many other points railroad cars were fired.

Next morning, a railroad agent on the Illinois Central shot two members of a crowd. The crowd retaliated by burning the yards. The action spread to other lines, peaking that night when the crowd destroyed 700 cars at the Panhandle yards in South Chicago. In one day, the crowds destroyed railroad property valued at $340,000.

The total armed forces occupying Chicago, including Federal troops, state militia, and deputy marshals hired and paid by the railroads, reached 14,000. In the course of the intermittent warfare, thirteen people were killed and fifty-three seriously wounded. Nonetheless, the strike remained firm. The Associated Press reported on July 6th:

Despite the presence of the United States troops and the mobilization of five regiments of state militia; despite threats of martial law and bullet and bayonet, the great strike inaugurated by the American Railway Union holds three-fourths of the roads running out of Chicago in its strong fetters, and last night traffic was more fully paralyzed than at any time since the inception of the tie up. [154]

Meanwhile, the conflict spread across the country.

In Trinidad, Colorado, on July 1st, a large crowd captured and disarmed forty-two deputy marshals coming into town to break the strike on the Santa Fe. Next morning, without even consulting the Populist Governor of the state, the President ordered up five companies of U.S. troops from Fort Logan. The troops cleared the tracks and protected the deputy marshals as they arrested forty-eight "ringleaders" who had made "incendiary speeches" at a meeting of the strikers. The deputy U.S. marshals were instructed to arrest without warrants anyone trying to induce railroad employees to quit, and to ignore opposition from local magistrates and officials, arresting them if they tried to intervene. This, charged Populist Governor David Waite, "allowed the U.S. Marshal to enlist a private army to suppress alleged state troubles . . . waging an active war in Colorado without any declaration thereof by the U.S. . . . and utterly in violation of law." [156]

The center of resistance on the Santa Fe next shifted to Raton, New Mexico, where 500 members of the A.R.U. lodge were supported by the County Sheriff and 300 striking coal miners, many of them armed. The U.S. Marshal and eighty-five deputies entered Raton with instructions to arrest the Sheriff if he interfered. They were met with such hatred in the town that hotel workers quit rather than serve them, and the hotels were thereafter staffed with deputy marshals. Meanwhile, a crowd at the little mining town of Blassburg, three miles above Raton, launched sixteen cars down the grade, crashing in Raton and blocking the tracks. Even after the Tenth Infantry arrived, the railroads were unable to move trains because of insufficient crews.

In California, public hostility toward the railroad monopolies was so great that the special Federal Attorney at Los Angeles warned Olney that he believed open rebellion an imminent possibility. [157] Five companies of California militia assembled at their armory and declared their sympathy for the strike. Troops were ordered into Los Angeles following a coded report from the U.S. Attorney that heavily-armed strike sympathizers were pouring into town, and that in enforcing the injunction the U.S. government might encounter resistance from 5,000 armed men.[158] The strike was finally broken in the Los Angeles vicinity by putting a detachment of troops on each train.

88   Meanwhile, a large number of railroad workers at Sacramento joined the strike, while hundreds more poured in from up and
down the lines — including a large, heavily-armed party aboard a
train they had seized at Dunsmuir. When the U.S. Marshal and his
deputies tried to protect a mail train containing Pullman cars, the
strikers manhandled him and disconnected the train. He then called in two regiments of the state militia, some of whom simply deserted from the ranks in open defiance of orders, while the rest
were unwilling to charge or fire out of sympathy for the strikers.
Finally 542 Federal soldiers were landed in Sacramento by boat,
where they cleared the railroads with fixed bayonets.

        Similarly, at Oakland a large crowd occupied the railroad
yards, "killing" engines and leaving them to block the tracks.
When 370 sailors and marines were landed, the wives and mothers
of the strikers organized a Ladies' Relief Organization and turned
a local hall into a hospital, in anticipation of a battle that never occurred.

        The struggle spread with great popular support throughout the
Western states of Nebraska, Wyoming, Utah, Nevada, and Montana. In Rawling, Wyoming, the city authorities ordered all deputy
marshals combatting the strike out of town. At Ogden, Utah, the
strikers completely controlled the western terminal of the Union
Pacific, uncoupling Pullman cars by force when necessary. They
defied the U.S. Marshal, who was able to raise only a small force
of deputies, and was afraid to make arrests lest he provoke a riot.
When word came that Federal troops were soon to arrive, fires
were set simultaneously in seven different parts of the city. Railroad bridges were burned at Carlin, Nevada. The Great Northern,
which used no Pullman cars, was the only transcontinental railroad not on strike, but when the Army planned to move troops to
Helena, Montana, on it, the workers threatened to strike. The order

To break the Pullman strike, government and railroads recruit special armed deputies nationwide, an armed force to which crowds often responded with direct action.

At Dubuque and Sioux City, Iowa, switches were spiked and tracks obstructed until the Governor sent six militia companies into the latter. At Hammond, Indiana, the strikers sidetracked all Pullman cars despite the resistance of the Sheriff, the Federal Marshal, and their deputies. Large crowds ranged over the tracks attacking strikebreakers, derailing trains, and seizing a telegraph office to prevent an appeal for the militia. On July 8th, State militia and Federal soldiers both arrived in Hammond and cleared the tracks by firing indiscriminately into the crowd. "I would like to know," demanded the Mayor, "by what authority U.S. troops come in here and shoot our citizens without the slightest warning."[159] In Duluth, dock workers struck in sympathy with the Pullman workers.[160] At Spring Valley, Illinois, striking miners provided the resistance; when a crowd stoned a train guarded by Federal soldiers, the troops fired on them, killing two and wounding several. By the end of the Pullman strike, an estimated thirty-four people had been killed, and Federal or state troops had been called out in Nebraska, Iowa, Colorado, Oklahoma, California, and Illinois.[161] General Miles maintained that only Federal troops had saved the country "from a serious rebellion."[162]

Meanwhile, the U.S. government proceeded systematically with its plan to break the strike in Chicago. On July 10th, Debs was arrested for conspiracy. The A.R.U. office was ransacked by Federal Marshals, who seized all books and papers in a manner even the Department of Justice later admitted was illegal. The blockade out of Chicago was finally broken by sending trains, each escorted by forty deputy marshals and a contingent of U.S. troops, along the various lines. The east-bound freight on the ten trunk lines out of Chicago, which had fallen to 4,142 tons for the week ending July 14th, had risen to 29,146 tons by the following week.[163] As the United States Strike Commission which later investigated the conflict wrote,

The action of the courts deprived the A.R.U. of leadership, enabled the General Managers' Association to disintegrate its forces, and to make inroads into its ranks. The mobs had worn out their fury, or had succumbed to the combined corces of the police, the U.S. troops and marshals, and the State militia.[164]

Besides the government, the General Managers' Association had another powerful ally—the old railroad brotherhoods. When 400 engineers had struck on the Wabash, the head of their union denounced them and announced that unemployed engineers would be permitted to serve as strikebreakers. The union head even went so far as to recommend particular men to replace striking engine-

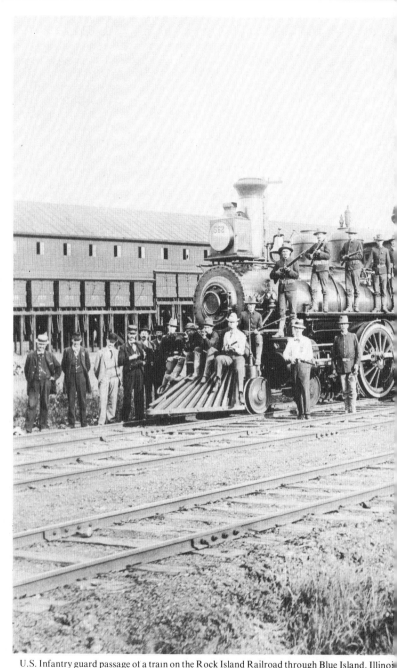
U.S. Infantry guard passage of a train on the Rock Island Railroad through Blue Island, Illinois

man strike. Crowds called out workers, declaring it was "a fight between labor and capital."

92   ers. The chief of the Conductors took the same stand. The Brotherhood of Trainmen instructed its members to "perform their regular duties." [165] Its head declared, "The triumph of this railroad strike would be the triumph of anarchy." [166] It is no surprise that Everett St. John, Chairman of the General Managers' Association and himself general manager of the Rock Island line, testified

We have always gotten along comfortably well—in fact, in a very satisfactory manner—with the old orders as they exist. [167]

At the last moment, the strike was almost given a reprieve by the workers of Chicago. They supported the strikers passionately. Newsboys, for example, dropped newspapers which opposed the boycott into the sewers. [168] On June 30th, the Trades and Labor Assembly had pledged the strength of its 150,000 members in support of the strike. It sent a committee to tell the A.R.U. that, if necessary, every union member in Chicago would strike in sympathy, but Debs at that point considered the idea too extreme. Nonetheless, as the conflict deepened, pressures for a general strike continued to build. July 7th, the Building and Trades Council, representing 25,000 members, voted unanimously for a sympathetic strike and called for a nationwide general strike. Next day delegates from 100 Chicago unions met to decide on a strike. While working-class sentiments overwhelmingly supported such a move, many union officials objected because it would violate existing contracts with employers. But when the delegates heard that President Cleveland had issued a proclamation seeming to put Chicago virtually under martial law, and declaring that resistors would be considered "public enemies," all opposition to a general strike dissolved. Pullman was to be given until July 10th, however, to accept arbitration before the strike went into effect. This delay proved fatal, for by July 11th, Debs and the other A.R.U. officials had been arrested, the military was in complete control of the city, and the strike was clearly doomed to defeat. The result was that only about 25,000 non-railroad workers joined the strike in Chicago. [169]

On the demand of the Chicago unions, A.F.L. head Samuel Gompers came to Chicago, calling in as well twenty-four other national trade union officials for a conference at the Briggs House. During the first session a committee from the Cigar Makers' Union of Chicago argued that because the struggle of the A.R.U. concerned the well-being of all workers and therefore required the complete solidarity of all labor, the conference should call for a nationwide general strike to force Pullman to arbitrate. Debs likewise suggested that a general strike be called if the railroad strikers were not permitted to return to their jobs. But the A.F.L. leaders were hostile to sympathy strikes on principle, opposed to the indus-

trial unionism of the A.R.U., and allied with the railroad brotherhoods that opposed the strike. They believed that a head-on struggle between labor and capital should be avoided at all costs. Instead of appealing for a general strike, they recommended $1,000
be given for Debs' legal defense and went home. [170]

When the Chicago Building Trades Council called off its sympathetic strike in the wake of this decision, the *Chicago Tribune*
declared jubilantly:

DEBS' STRIKE DEAD
It is Dealt Two Mortal Blows by Labor
Federation Hits First
Trades Council Follows with a Crusher [171]

It is little wonder that the United States Strike Commission of 1894
declared that trade unions "have promoted conciliation, arbitration, conservatism, and responsibility in labor contentions and
agreements." [172]

How close at hand was a general strike? A number of locals in
Chicago had already struck, and the Trades and Labor Assembly
had come out for the idea. The Briggs House Conference statement
said, "While we may not have the power to order a strike of the
working people of our country, we are fully aware that a recommendation from this conference to them to lay down their tools of
labor would largely influence the members of our affiliated organizations." [173] This would seem to be borne out by Gompers' testimony that "from St. Louis and various places throughout Missouri,
Ohio, and Colorado, I was in receipt of telegrams that they had resolved to await the word that the A.F.L. conference would give as
to determining their action." [174] Instead of calling for such support, however, the Briggs House statement urged "that all connected with the A.F.L. now out on sympathetic strike should return to
work, and those who contemplate going out on sympathetic strike
are advised to remain at their usual vocations." [175] Gompers
agreed that had the executive board of the A.F.L. called a strike
even in its advisory capacity, its members would have struck, [176]
and that the strike thereupon "would have spread to a greater or
lesser extent over the whole country." [177] Many coal miners were
still on strike, and more workers joined strikes in 1894 than any
previous year. Given the stormy atmosphere of the time, Gompers'
judgment seems sound.

The workers at Pullman held out to the end. On July 6th, the
militia was sent in, replacing the strikers' guards at the works—but
the strike remained firm. Once the railroad strike was broken,
however, all hope was lost, and Pullman began to rehire his workers on his own terms, the militia standing by.

94   The real issue of the strike of course had not been simply the wages of the workers at Pullman. George Pullman defined the issue as "the principle that a man should have the right to manage his own property."[178] The secret minutes of the General Managers' Association suggested that the question was whether the railroads would "determine for themselves" what cars they would or would not handle on their lines. [179] Or, as Vice-President George Howard of the A.R.U. put it, "I always contended that the men had a right to handle or not handle anything they pleased," whereas the company announced publicly that "they would haul such cars as they chose regardless of what the delegates to the A.R.U. convention might say, or what their own employees might say." [180] The real issue was the issue of power; it was understood that this in turn would determine the other questions of wages, working conditions, and the like.

The Pullman strike showed that merely by making a non-violent strike against an industry — if the strike seriously challenged corporate power — workers would bring down upon themselves the entire organized force of society, including military force. As Debs put it,

> We have only got a number, and a limited number, of poorly paid men in our organization, and when their income ceases they are starving. We have no power of the Government behind us. We have no recognized influence in society on our side. . . . On the other side the corporations are in perfect alliance; they have all of the things that money can command, and that means a subsidized press, that they are able to control the newspapers, and means a false or vitiated public opinion. The clergy almost steadily united in thundering their denunciations; then the courts, then the State militia, then the Federal troops; everything and all things on the side of the corporations. [181]

The lesson of the strike, as one railroad worker put it, was to "demonstrate to the laboring men that they must get together; that no single organization can win . . . they have seen the united press against them; they have seen the united clergy against them; they have seen the entire judiciary against them; they have seen the entire office holders of this country against them — the United States Government against them, and all the old-time [labor] organizations . . ." [182]

The full mobilization of state power against the strikers created problems with which even the militant leadership of the American Railway Union was unable to deal. Although the A.R.U.'s structure allowed great initiative from below, local groups still looked to the national officers for leadership and direction. Consequently, when the leaders were jailed and their office broken up, the locals were unable to continue on their own. Debs gave a vivid picture of just how vulnerable the strike was to the loss of central leadership:

Our men were in a position that never would have been shaken under any circumstances if we had been permitted to remain among them. . . . but once we were taken from the scene of action and restrained from sending telegrams or issuing the orders necessary, or answering questions; when the minions of the corporations would be put to work at such a place, for instance, as Nickerson, Kansas, where they would go and say to the men that the men at Newton had gone back to work, and Nickerson would wire me to ask if that were true; no answer would come to the message because I was under arrest, and we were all under arrest. The headquarters were demoralized and abandoned, and we could not answer any messages. The men went back to work, and the ranks were broken up by the federal courts of the United States." [173]

Even had the A.R.U. officers remained at liberty, however, they would not have been able to win the strike, against a state power resolved to crush it, without a complete change of approach. The union was committed to "legal" and "orderly" tactics, even while it was being destroyed by the forces of "law and order." Initially, it made perfect sense for the workers to follow Debs' policy and "do everything in their power to maintain order, because . . . if there was perfect order there would be no pretext upon which they could call out the soldiers or appeal for the intervention of the court, and we would win without a question of a doubt." [184] Yet at the point where the courts and army intervened despite the legal and non-violent policy of the strikers, the A.R.U. was unable to change its approach. It was therefore doomed to failure, for as Debs later pointed out, even "if all the railroad men in the country were organized within one brotherhood and acted together it would be impossible for them to succeed." [185]

When the troops came in, making legal success impossible, workers throughout the country responded with mass direct action. But for the A.R.U. to adopt such a policy would have meant a challenge to the entire social order—a step from which it recoiled. Thus we are presented with the spectacle of Eugene Victor Debs, perhaps the greatest example of a courageous, radical, and uncorruptable trade union official in American history, trying to end the strike in order to prevent it from becoming an insurrection. For, as Debs testified —

We became satisfied that things were assuming too serious a phase, and that a point had been reached when, in the interest of peace and to prevent riot and trouble we must declare the strike off . . . It was in the crisis when everything was at stake, where possibly it might have eventuated in a revolution. [186]

However much of a defeat the Pullman strike may have been in terms of its immediate objectives, its real significance, as Debs saw, was the unprecedented sense of solidarity it reflected, something not embodied in any particular organization, but in what he called "the spirit of organization." As Debs testified, after the strike:

> They might as well try to stop Niagara with a feather as to crush the spirit of organization in this country. . . . It may not come up in the form of the American Railway Union, but this spirit of resistance to wrong is there, it is growing stronger constantly, and it finds its outlet in labor disturbances, in strikes of various kinds. Even if the men know in advance that they are going to meet with defeat they are so impressed with a sense of wrong under which they are suffering that they strike and take the penalty. [187]

Chapter 3: Footnotes

1. Frick to Carnegie, Oct. 31, 1892, quoted in David Brody, *Steelworkers in America, The Nonunion Era* (N.Y.: Harper & Row, Torchbooks ed., 1969), p. 53.
2. Cited in Leon Wolff, *Lockout, The Story of the Homestead Strike of 1892: A Study of Violence, Unionism, and the Carnegie Steel Empire* (N.Y.: Harper & Row, 1965), pp. 41-2.
3. Brody, p. 53.
4. U.S. House of Representatives, *Employment of Pinkerton Detectives,* 52nd Cong., 2d Sess., Report No. 2447 (Wash.: GPO, 1893), p. 23, cited in Samuel Yellin, *American Labor Struggles* (N.Y.: Harcourt, Brace and Co., 1936), p. 84.
5. Brody, p. 52.
6. *Ibid.,* p. 54.
7. Carnegie (May 1892) cited in Wolff, p. 80.
8. *Employment of Pinkerton Detectives,* p. 23, cited in Yellin, p. 80.
9. "The Fort That Frick Built," quoted in Wolff, p. 85.
10. Frick to Pinkerton (June 25, 1892), cited in Wolff, p. 86.
11. Wolff, p. 69.
12. *Ibid.,* p. 90.
13. *Ibid.,* p. 96.
14. *Ibid.,* p. 105.
15. *Ibid.,* p. 106.
16. *Ibid.,* p. 122.
17. *Ibid.,* p. 130.
18. *Ibid.,* p. 131.
19. *Ibid.,* p. 150.
20. *Ibid.,* p. 151.
21. *Ibid.,* p. 164.
22. AP dispatch, *Terre Haute Evening Gazette,* July 16, 1892, cited in Yellin, p. 93.
23. Judge Paxson, cited in Wolff, p. 213.
24. Wolff, p. 206.
25. *Ibid.,* p. 205.
26. Frick to Carnegie, cited in Wolff, p. 209.
27. *Ibid.,* Nov. 21, 1892, in Wolff, p. 225.

28. Brody, p. 58.
29. *Ibid.,* p. 28.
30. *Ibid.,* pp. 48-9.
31. *Ibid.,* p. 42.
32. *Ibid.,* pp. 45-6.
33. Foster, cited in Henry David, "Upheaval at Homestead," in *America in Crisis,* Daniel Aaron, ed. (N.Y.: Alfred A. Knopf, 1952), p. 167.
34. M.A. Hutton, *The Coeur d'Alenes, or A Tale of Modern Inquisition in Idaho,* p. 59, cited in Vernon H. Jensen, *Heritage of Conflict, Labor Relations in the Nonferrous Metals Industry up to 1930* (Ithaca, N.Y.: Cornell University Press, 1950), p. 29.
35. Jensen, p. 34.
36. Roger Wallace Shugg, "The New Orleans General Strike of 1892," in *Louisiana Historical Quarterly,* Vol. 21 (1937), p. 52.
37. *Ibid.*
38. *Ibid.,* p. 554.
39. *Ibid.,* p. 555.
40. *House Journal,* 1889, Report of special committee to investigate public prisons, pp. 306-9, 322-5; cited in A.C. Hutson, Jr., "The Coal Miners' Insurrection of 1891 in Anderson County, Tennessee," *East Tennessee Historical Society's Proceedings,* No. 7 (1935), p. 105.
41. *Birmingham Age-Herald,* Aug. 8, 1889, cited in Woodward, p. 232.
42. *Nashville Daily American,* Aug. 25, 1892, cited in Woodward, p. 233.
43. *Special Report of the Commissioner of Labor,* 1891, pp. 19-21, cited in Hutson, p. 108.
44. A. C. Hutson, Jr., "The Overthrow of the Convict Lease System," in *The East Tennessee Historical Society's Proceedings,* No. 8 (1936), p. 89.
45. Hon. Andrew Roy, *A History of the Coal Miners of the United States, from the Development of the Mines to the Close of the Anthracite Strike of 1902,* 3d Ed. (Columbus, Ohio: J.L. Trauger Printing Co., 1907), p. 302.
46. *New York Times,* April 22, 1894.
47. *New York Times,* April 13, 1894.
48. Roy, p. 303.
49. Commons, Vol. II, p. 502.
50. Roy, p. 304.
51. *New York Times,* May 1, 1894.
52. *New York Times,* May 10, 1894.
53. *New York Times,* April 24, 1894.
54. *New York Times,* May 29, 1894.
55. W.T. Stead, "Incidents of Labour War in America," in *The Contemporary Review* (July 1894), p. 67.
56. *New York Times,* May 1, 1894.
57. *New York Times,* April 30, 1894.
58. *New York Times,* May 5, 1894.
59. *New York Times,* May 10, 1894.
60. *New York Times,* June 2, 1894.
61. *New York Times,* May 26, 1894.
62. *New York Times,* May 25, 1894.
63. *Ibid.*
64. *New York Times,* May 26, 1894.
65. *New York Times,* May 25, 1894.
66. *New York Times,* May 24, 1894.
67. *Ibid.*
68. *New York Times,* May 25, 1894.

98   69. W.W. Taylor to John P. Altgeld, May 24, 1894, in *Biennial Report of the Adjustant General of Illinois to the Governor and Commander-in-Chief, 1893 and 1894* (Springfield, Ill.: Ed. F. Hartman, 1895), p. vii. (Hereafter cited as "*Report.*")

70. *Report*, p. viii.
71. *New York Times*, May 25, 1894.
72. *New York Times*, May 1, 1894.
73. *New York Times*, May 25, 1894.
74. *New York Times*, May 27, 1894.
75. *New York Times*, May 28, 1894.
76. *Ibid.*
77. *Ibid.*
78. *Ibid.*
79. *New York Times*, June 4, 1894.
80. *New York Times*, June 5, 1894.
81. *Ibid.*
82. *Ibid.*
83. *Ibid.*
84. *New York Times*, June 10, 1894.
85. *New York Times*, June 5, 1894.
86. *New York Times*, May 29, 1894.
87. *New York Times*, June 5, 1894.
88. *New York Times*, June 7, 1894.
89. *New York Times*, May 29, 1894.
90. *New York Times*, June 5, 1894.
91. *New York Times*, April 29, 1894.
92. *New York Times*, May 1, 1894.
93. *New York Times*, May 6, 1894.
94. *New York Times*, May 11, 1894.
95. *New York Times*, May 13, 1894.
96. *New York Times*, May 24, 1894.
97. *New York Times*, May 25, 1894.
98. *Ibid.*
99. *New York Times*, May 28, 1894.
100. *Ibid.*
101. *New York Times*, May 30, 1894.
102. *Ibid.*
103. *Ibid.*
104. *New York Times*, June 14, 1894.
105. Roy, p. 307.
106. *New York Times*, May 13, 1894.
107. *New York Times*, May 3, 1894.
108. *New York Times*, May 5, 1894.
109. Jensen, p. 45.
110. *Ibid.*, p. 46.
111. *Ibid.*, p. 49.
112. W.H. Carwardine, *The Pullman Strike* (Chicago: Charles H. Kerr and Co., 1894), p. 69, cited in Yellin, p. 104.
113. *Chicago Times,* June 13, 1894, p. 2, cited in Almont Lindsey, *The Pullman Strike* (Chicago: University of Chicago Press, Phoenix Books Ed., 1964). p. 127.
114. *U.S. Strike Commission Report,* Senate Exec. Doc. No. 7 53d Cong., 3d Sess. (Wash.: GPO, 1895), submitted to Pres. Cleveland on Nov. 14, 1894, p. 62.

115. Gerald G. Eggert, *Railroad Labor Disputes, The Beginnings of Federal Strike Policy* (Ann Arbor: University of Michigan Press, 1967), p. 147. 99
116. Ray Ginger, *The Vending Cross, A Biography of Eugene Victor Debs* (New Brunswick: Rutgers University Press, 1949p, p. 97.
117. *Ibid.,* pp. 97-8.
118. *Ibid.,* p. 107.
119. *Ibid.,* p. 101.
120. *Ibid.*
121. *Chicago Times,* May 13, 1894, p. 20, cited in Lindsey, p. 126.
122. Ginger, pp. 117-8.
123. *Ibid.,* p. 118.
124. *U.S. Strike Commission Report,* p. 135.
125. *Ibid.,* p. 72.
126. *Ibid.,* p. 59.
127. *Ibid.,* p. 96.
128. *Ibid.,* p. 106.
129. *Ibid.,* p. 110.
130. Ibid., p. 112.
131. *Ibid.*
132. Lindsey, pp. 134-5.
133. *New York Times,* [une 29, 1894, cited in Lindsey, p. 203.
134. *Chicago Tribune,* July 3, 1894.
135. *U.S. Strike Commission Report,* p. 140.
136. *Ibid.,* p. 28; Lindsey, p. 240.
137. Eugene Debs, in *Public Opinion,* July 5, 1894, cited in Yellin, pp. 115-6.
138. Yellin, p. 118.
139. Eugene V. Debs, *Writings and Speeches of Eugene Victor Debs,* (N.Y.: Hermitage Press, 1948), p. 45.
140. John Egan, in *Inter Ocean,* July 3, 1894, p. 3, cited in Lindsey, p. 144.
141. Lindsey, p. 142.
142. John Egan, in *Inter Ocean,* July 3, 1894, p. 3, cited in Lindsey, p. 144.
143. Olney to E. Walker, June 30, 1894, *Appendix to the . . . Report of the Attorney General . . . 1896,* p. 60, cited in Lindsey, p. 150.
144. Grover Cleveland, *The Government in the Chicago Strike of 1894* (Prince- ton' Princeton University Press, 1913), p. 232.
145. Lindsay, p. 162.
146. John Swinton, *Striking for Life* (N.Y.: Western W. Wilson, 1894), p. 92.
147. *Chicago Times,* July 3, 1894, v. 1, cited in Lindsey, p. 164.
148. Arnold to Olney, July 3, 1894, in *Chicago Strike Correspondence,* p. 66, cited in Eggert, pp. 170-1.
149. Olney, quoted in Eggert, p. 172.
150. *Strike Commission Report,* p. 39.
151. *New York Times,* July 5, 1894, cited in Lindsey, p. 175.
152. Eggert, p. 171.
153. *U.S. Strike Commission Report,* p. 214-5.
154. *New York Times,* Aug. 16, 1902, cited in Yellin, p. 122.
155. Nelson A. Miles, "The Lesson of the Recent Strikes," in *North American Review* CLIX (1894), pp. 180-8, cited in Lindsey, p. 174.
156. Waite, in *Inter Ocean*, July 7, 1894, cited in Lindsey, p. 168.
157. Lindsey, p. 250.
158. *Ibid.*
159. *Ibid.,* p. 260.
160. Eggert, p. 18.
161. Hugh D. Graham and Ted R. Gurr, *The History of Violence in America* (N.Y.:

100

        Bantam Books, 1969), p. 298.
162. *Annual Report of the Secretary of War for the Year 1894,* Vol. I (Wash.: GPO, 1894), p. 109, cited in Lindsey, p. 214.
163. *Bradstreet's,* July 28, 1894, p. 467, cited in Yellin, p. 130.
164. *Strike Commission Report,* p. xlii.
165. Ginger, p. 122.
166. *Terre Haute Evening Gadzette,* July 19, 1894, cited in Yellin, p. 123.
167. St. John, testimony in *U.S. Strike Commission Report,* p. 117.
168. Ginger, p. 143.
169. *New York Times,* July 12, 1894, cited in Lindsey, p. 225.
170. "Proceedings of Briggs Conference," p. 133, cited in Lindsey, p. 228.
171. *Chicago Tribune,* July 14, 1894, cited in Ginger, p. 150.
172. *U.S. Strike Commission Report,* p. xxviii.
173. "Proceedings of Briggs Conference," p.
174. *U.S. Strike Commission Report,* p. 190.
175. *Ibid.,* p. 192.
176. *Ibid.,* p. 194.
177. *Ibid.,* p. 199.
178. *Ibid.,* p. 556.
179. General Managers Association, *Minutes of Meetings* (Chicago, 1894), p. 94, cited in Eggert, p. 156.
180. *U.S. Strike Commission Report,* pp. 9, 11.
181. *Ibid.,* p. 169.
182. *Ibid.,* p. 76.
183. *Ibid.,* p. 146.
184. *Ibid.,* p. 50.
185. *Ibid.,* p. 161.
186. *Ibid.,* pp. 145-6.
187. *Ibid.,* p. 163.

Chapter 4
Nineteen Nineteen

"The most extraordinary phenomenon of the present time," wrote *The Nation* in October, 1919, "the most incalculable in its after effects, the most menacing in its threat of immediate consequences, and the most alluring in its possibilities of ultimate good, is the unprecedented revolt of the rank and file.

"It is a world-wide movement much accelerated by the war. In Russia it has dethroned the Czar and for two years maintained Lenin in his stead. In Korea and India and Egypt and Ireland it keeps up an unyielding resistance to political tyranny. In England it brought about the railway strike, against the judgement of the men's own executives. In Seattle and San Francisco it has resulted in the stevedores' recent refusal to handle arms or supplies destined for the overthrow of the Soviet Government. In one district of Illinois it manifested itself in a resolution of striking miners, unanimously requesting their State executive 'to go to Hell.' In Pittsburgh, according to Mr. Gompers, it compelled the reluctant American Federation officers to call the steel strike, lest the control pass into the hands of the I.W.W.'s and other 'radicals.' In New York it brought about the longshoremen's strike and kept the men out in defiance of union officials, and caused the upheaval in the printing trade, which the international officers, even though the employers worked hand in glove with them, were completely unable to control.

"The common man, forgetting the old sanctions, and losing faith in the old leadership, has experienced a new access of self-confidence, or at least a new recklessness, a readiness to take chances on his own account. In consequence, as is by this time clear to discerning men, authority cannot any longer be imposed from above; it comes automatically from below." [1]

It was this revolt which formed the underpinning for the mass strike of 1919.

In the quarter century following the Pullman strike, American capitalism had changed profoundly. Such basic industries as steel and coal grew phenomenally, rivalling the railroads in size and economic importance. These basic industries developed an organized and controlled market, dominated by one or a few firms. The United States became a world power engaged in war with Spain in 1898

102 and with the European Triple Entente in 1917, and was shaken by the world crisis of 1919.

The trade unions had succeeded in expanding around the margins of this growth, while failing to organize more than a small minority of American workers. The American Federation of Labor remained a collection of highly exclusive unions of skilled craftsmen, scornful of the unskilled and semi-skilled majority. Its avowed objective was to gain concessions for workers while preserving the harmony of employers and employees. It was safe, sane, and conservative, and as hostile to industrial unionism and the mass strike process as it had been in the days of the Pullman strike. As we shall see again and again, the A.F.L. unions were far more interested in preserving their own organizations than in responding to the needs of workers. In the vacuum left by the A.F.L. grew up the radical Industrial Workers of the World. The "Wobblies" advocated "industrial unionism" — organizing all workers in an industry into one union — in contrast to the "craft unionism" of the A.F.L. It organized the most depressed and unskilled, such as the migrant laborers of the West and the textile mill workers of the East. The I.W.W. proclaimed workers' ownership of industry its objective, and saw every strike as a preparation for revolution. It was in many ways more of a social movement than a normal union, for though it was involved in many dramatic strikes, it generally scorned negotiating a continuing relationship with the employers. The Wobblies were brutally repressed by legal and illegal means during World War I, and by 1919 had ceased to be a significant force.

During World War I, the American economy was changed overnight to a system of state-coordinated planning and management. Government boards set prices and production levels; the railroads were placed under direct government management. With immigration cut off and an overwhelming need for production, labor was suddenly placed in a uniquely powerful position. No longer could employers tolerate strikes for a few weeks or months, then easily hire strikebreakers from a steady supply of unemployed. Now strikes would halt critical war production and no unemployed workers were available as strikebreakers. As Alexander Bing, a wartime labor mediator and author of *War-time Strikes and Their Adjustment,* wrote:

> The workers could, had they seen fit to do so, have taken advantage of the scarcity of labor and the enormous need for commodities, which the war produced, and have demanded radical changes in industry, and it is very difficult to see how such demands could have been successfully resisted. [2]

In this situation, business and government developed a new

approach to trade unionism. Before World War I, employers, with some exceptions, had fought the establishment of trade unions, keeping workers under control by dealing with each one individually. Labor's new power made this strategy no longer serviceable. Consequently, employers and government turned to the unions to exercise such control. In effect, this policy took the form of a deal, in which the A.F.L. agreed to oppose strikes, in return for which it was guaranteed the right to organize, wherever the government had jurisdiction, without having its members fired. As a result, union membership increased by about two million during the war.[3] Both the A.F.L. and the war employers agreed that wages were to be set, for the duration of the war, by boards composed of business, labor, and government.

Despite this deal, two factors pushed the workers on to action. First, the war was financed in large part by an enormous inflation; the cost of living practically doubled from August, 1915, to the end of 1919. [4] Second, as Bing recalled, "the urgent need for production . . . gave the workers a realization of a strength which before they had neither realized nor possessed." [5]

Despite the appeals of patriotism and the opposition of government, business and the A.F.L., strikes mushroomed during the war. The war years 1916-1918 averaged 2.4 times as many workers on strike as 1915. [6] Big strikes practically stopped spruce lumber production and closed down the most important copper areas early in the war. In Bridgeport, Connecticut, the most important munitions center in the U.S., workers stopped production in defiance of the orders of both the National War Labor Board and their own national union leaders.

As usual, a growing spirit of solidarity developed along with increasing militance. For example, shipyard workers on the Pacific Coast tied up the yards for several months in sympathy with the lumber strikers in the Northwest, refusing to handle "ten-hour lumber." Four general strikes developed in different regions of the country. In Springfield, Illinois, a parade in support of striking streetcar workers was stopped by police; 10,000 union workers, especially miners, joined a general strike in protest. In Kansas City, Missouri, when laundry workers and drivers struck, a general strike developed in sympathy and lasted a week until the National Guard was called up to break it. At Waco, Texas, a general strike was called in support of streetcar men who had been locked out. And at Billings, Montana, icemen, city employees, gasmen, creamery workers, truck drivers, and others struck in sympathy with locked-out building trade mechanics. [7]

As World War I drew to a close, several additional factors

104   shaped the climate of industrial conflict. The enormous patriotic sentiment generated by the war was deliberately and skillfully manipulated into an hysterical fear and hatred of the growing power of labor. Employers mobilized this sentiment in their efforts to roll back the powers gained by trade unionism during the war. The workers on the other hand had been made great promises of a "new era" by the huge war propaganda, and now were eager to receive that for which they felt they had fought.

In the background of everyone's mind was the Russian revolution and the wave of revolt sweeping the whole world in the wake of the incredible suffering, destruction, and disorganization resulting from the war. Perhaps the most accurate characterization of the attitudes of American workers toward Soviet Russia was given in a study by the Interchurch World Movement, published in 1920:

> The Russian Revolution was likely a bloody business and Bolsheviks are doubtless dangerous and wild, but the Russian Government is a laboring man's government and it has not fallen down yet. Two years of newspaper reports that the Russian republic was about to fall seem to have given workingmen, even here, a sort of class pride that it hasn't fallen. [8]

The middle classes and the government, on the other hand, felt their familiar world was under attack from all quarters, and saw Bolshevism as a unified conspiracy of all that threatened them—whether Soviet Russia or the A.F.L.

Real wages had risen considerably during the war as a result of the enormous demand for labor; with the end of the great wartime industrial expansion and the return to "normalcy," it was widely felt necessary to reduce wages if profits were to be maintained. As John Maynard Keynes once pointed out, this can be done with less resistance by inflation than by direct wage cuts. So in 1919, the government simultaneously ended wartime price controls and allowed corporations to resume their traditional union-breaking policies. Between June, 1919, and June, 1920, the cost of living index (taking 1913 as 100) rose from 177 to 216. [9]

Anger, hope and militance grew as in a pressure cooker. Nowhere did this radicalization go further than in Seattle. The radical I.W.W. and the A.F.L. Metal Trades Council cooperated in sponsoring a Soldiers', Sailors', and Workingmen's Council, taking the soviets of the recent Russian revolution as their model. When a socialist and former president of the Seattle A.F.L., Hulet Wells, was convicted for opposing the draft during the war and then tortured in prison, the Seattle labor movement erupted with giant street rallies. Even the more conservative members of the Seattle labor movement supported the Bolshevik revolution and opposed the U.S. intervention against it. [10] In the fall of 1919, the Seattle longshoremen refused to load arms and munitions destined for Admiral Kolchak, leader of the counter-revolution in Siberia, and beat up the strikebreakers who tried to load them. [11] Seattle union membership increased from 15,000 in 1915 to 60,000 by the end of 1918—more than the total number of industrial workers. [12] The Seattle trade unions were formally affiliated with the A.F.L., but their ideas and action differed greatly from A.F.L. policy; as Harry Ault, editor of the union-owned *Seattle Union Record,* and a moderate in the local labor movement, put it:

I believe that 95 percent of us agree that the workers should control the industries. Nearly all of us agree on that but very strenuously disagree on the method. Some of us think we can get control through the Co-operative movement, some of us think through political action, and others think through industrial action. . . . [13]

Pamphlets on the Russian revolution circulated by the scores of thousands. A Seattle labor journalist later recalled—

For some time these little pamphlets were seen by hundreds on Seattle's streetcars and ferries, read by men of the shipyards on their way to work. Seattle's business men commented on the phenomenon sourly; it was plain to everyone that these workers were conscientiously and energetically studying how to organize their coming power.

Already, workers in Seattle talked about "workers' power" as a practical policy for the not far distant future. Boilermakers, machinists and other metal trades unions alluded to shipyards as enterprises which they might soon take over, and run better than their present owners ran them. These allusions gave life to union meetings. . . . [14]

The militant spirit and trade union growth centered among the 35,000 workers in the shipyards, an industry built with Federal funds and virtually created by the war, in which the Emergency Fleet Corporation of the United States government was the ultimate employer. Less than two weeks after the Armistice, the shipyard unions voted to authorize a strike. The unions proposed a pay scale that would raise wages for lower-paid workers and not for the skilled; the yard-owners in turn tried to split off the skilled workers by offering them alone a wage increase. The skilled workers refused the bribe and on January 21st, 1919, 35,000 shipyard workers struck. [15] Unexpectedly, Charles Piez, representing the U.S. government as head of the Emergency Fleet Corporation, telegrammed the yardowners to resist any wage increase, threatening otherwise to withdraw their contracts. "Through the 'mistake' of a messenger boy," a reporter later recalled, "one of these telegrams was delivered not to the Metal Trades Association [the employers], but to the Metal Trades Council [the workers]. The anger of the shipyard workers was thus directed against Washington." [16]

106   Faced by a government and employer determination to starve them out, the shipyard workers appealed to the Seattle Central Labor Council for a general strike. The best-known local progressive and radical leaders were in Chicago at a special conference to organize a national general strike to free Tom Mooney. (Mooney was an A.F.L. official in San Francisco who had been convicted of throwing a bomb into a 1916 preparedness parade, despite the evidence of a photograph of him standing by a clock a mile away from the scene at exactly the time the bomb was thrown.) According to one of the leaders, Anna Louise Strong, the general strike in Seattle would probably not have occurred had they been in town. "They were terrified when they heard that a general strike had been voted. . . . It might easily smash something — us, perhaps, our well-organized labor movement." [17]

At a tumultuous session of the Central Labor Council, the shipyard unions' resolution that local unions poll their members on a general strike passed with virtually no opposition. The threat of a general strike was not taken seriously except by the workers themselves; as the *Seattle Times* wrote,

A general strike directed at WHAT?
The Government of the United States? Bosh!
Not 15% of Seattle laborites would consider such a proposition. [18]

Yet within a day eight local unions endorsed the strike at their regular meetings — most of the votes nearly unanimous. Within two weeks 110 locals had voted for the strike, even some of the more conservative doing so by margins of five and ten to one.

In joining the strike, the workers knew that they were risking more than a few days' pay. First, they risked punishment from their own internationals; and second, the loss of established contracts with their employers. For example, the Longshoremen's Union imperiled (and eventually lost) a closed-shop agreement for the Seattle waterfront, and the president of the International Longshoremen's Association wired the local that he would rescind its charter if it took part in the general strike.

The Central Labor Council agreed that the strike be run by a General Strike Committee of three members from each striking local, elected by the rank and file. The 300 members of the committee — mostly not officials but rank-and-filers with little previous leadership experience — started meeting four days before the strike; they and their fifteen-man executive committee were in daily session throughout the strike, forming virtually a counter-government for the city.

A study of the strike issued later by the General Strike Committee pointed out that:

A general strike was seen, almost at once, to differ profoundly from
ny of the particular strikes with which the workers of Seattle were fa-
niliar. . . . If life was not to be made unbearable for the strikers themselves,
roblems of management, of selection and exemption, had to take the
lace of the much simpler problem of keeping everyone out of work. [19]

ipyard workers in Seattle in 1919 found themselves locked out by order of the
.S. government. Other Seattle workers felt this was the start of an attack on them
well. It was this sentiment that made them willing and eager to turn to the
ctic of a general strike.

Workers in various trades organized themselves to provide
ssential services with the approval of subcommittees of the execu-
ve committee, which granted them exemptions from the strike.
arbage wagon drivers agreed to collect wet garbage that would
reate a health hazard, but not paper and ashes. Firemen agreed to
:ay on the job. The laundry drivers and laundry workers devel-
ped a plan to keep one shop open to handle hospital laundry; be-
ɔre the strike they instructed the employers to accept no more
undry, then worked a few hours after the strike deadline to fin-
h clothes in process so they would not mildew. Vehicles author-
:ed to operate bore signs reading, "Exempted by the General
trike Committee." [20]

Employers and government officials as well as strikers came
efore the Strike Committee to request exemptions. According to

108   one correspondent,

The extent to which the city recognized the actual rather than th titular government of the community is apparent enough to anyone wh reads the carefully kept records of the strike committee, and observes wha was actually done. Before the committee, which would seem to have bee in well-nigh continuous session day and night, appeared a long successio of businessmen, city officials, and the Mayor himself, not to threaten o bully, but to discuss the situation and ask the approval of the committe for this or that step. [21]

Here are a few examples from the minutes:

"King county commissioners ask for exemption of janitors to care fo City-County building. Not granted.

"F.A. Rust asks for janitors for Labor Temple. Not granted.

"Teamsters' Union asks permission to carry oil for Swedish Hospita during strike. Referred to transportation committee. Approved.

"Port of Seattle asks to be allowed men to load a government vessel pointing out that no private profit is involved and that an emergency ex ists. Granted.

"The retail drug clerks sent in a statement of the health needs of th city. Referred to public welfare committee, which recommends that pres cription counters only be left open, and that in front of every drug stor which is thus allowed to open a sign be placed with the words, 'No good sold during general strike. Orders for prescriptions only will be fille Signed by general strike committee.'

"Communication from House of Good Shepherd. Permission grante by transportation committee to haul food and provisions only."

This is by no means all the business that came before the Committe of Fifteen in a single afternoon. An appointment of a committee of relief look after destitute homes, the creation of a publicity bureau, an ord that watchmen stay on the job until further notice. [22]

In some cases, workers improvised large-scale operations fror scratch. For instance, the milk wagon drivers initially propose to their employers that certain dairies remain open, but when th employers refused to open them except downtown, and attempte to take direction of the plan, the drivers decided to organize the own distribution system instead. They set up thirty-five neigh borhood milk stations, purchased milk from small dairymen nea the city, and distributed it throughout the city. Even more impres sive was the commissary department, which served 30,000 meals day to the strikers and community. The cooks, waiters and oth provision trade workers purchased the food, located restaura kitchens, and arranged to transport the cooked food to twenty-or eating places in halls throughout the city. This huge operation wa running smoothly by the second day of the strike.

Two days before the strike the *Union Record* asked unio

members who had served in the armed forces to come to a meeting to discuss "important strike work." [23] From this group was organized a "Labor War Veteran's Guard," designed to keep peace on the streets. Its principle was scrawled on the blackboard at one of its headquarters:

The purpose of this organization is to preserve law and order without the use of force. No volunteer will have any police power or be allowed to carry weapons of any sort, but to use persuasion only. [24]

On the eve of the general strike, an editorial in the *Union Record* tried to define the strike's significance:

On Thursday at 10 A.M.—There will be many cheering, and there will be some who fear.

Both these emotions are useful, but not too much of either.

We are undertaking the most tremendous move ever made by *LABOR* in this country, a move which will lead—*NO ONE KNOWS WHERE!*

We do not need hysteria.

We need the iron march of labor.

During the Seattle General Strike, food service workers served 30,000 meals a day in twenty-one halls throughout the city. Workers virtually ran the city, and saw this as preparation for their eventual management of society.

110 *LABOR WILL FEED THE PEOPLE.*

Twelve great kitchens have been offered, and from them food will be distributed by the provision trades at low cost to all.

LABOR WILL CARE FOR THE BABIES AND THE SICK.

The milk-wagon drives and the laundry drivers are arranging plans for supplying milk to babies, invalids and hospitals and taking care of the cleaning of linen for hospitals.

LABOR WILL PRESERVE ORDER.

The strike committee is arranging for guards and it is expected that the stopping of the cars will keep people at home.

*   *   *

A few hot-headed enthusiasts have complained that strikers only should be fed, and the general public left to endure severe discomfort. Aside from the inhumanitarian character of such suggestions, let them get this straight—

NOT THE WITHDRAWAL OF LABOR POWER, BUT THE POWER OF THE STRIKERS TO MANAGE WILL WIN THIS STRIKE.

What does Mr. Piez of the Shipping Board care about the closing down of Seattle's shipyards, or even of all the industries of the northwest? Will it not merely strengthen the yards at Hog Island, in which he is more interested?

When the shipyard owners of Seattle were on the point of agreeing with the workers, it was Mr. Piez who wired them that, if they so agreed—

HE WOULD NOT LET THEM HAVE STEEL.

Whether this is camouflage we have no means of knowing. But we do know that the great eastern combinations of capitalists *COULD AFFORD* to offer privately to Mr. Skinner, Mr. Ames and Mr. Duthie a few millions apiece in eastern shipyard stock,

RATHER THAN LET THE WORKERS WIN.

The closing down of Seattle's industries, as a *MERE SHUTDOWN,* will not affect these eastern gentlemen much. They could let the whole northwest go to pieces, as far as money alone is concerned.

BUT, the closing down of the capitalistically controlled industries of Seattle, while the *WORKERS ORGANIZE* to feed the people, to care for the babies and the sick, to preserve order — *THIS* will move them, for this looks too much like the taking over of *POWER* by the workers.

Labor will not only *SHUT DOWN* the industries, but Labor will *REOPEN,* under the management of the appropriate trades, such activities are are needed to preserve public health and public peace. If the strike continues, Labor may feel led to avoid public suffering by reopening more and more activities,

UNDER ITS OWN MANAGEMENT.

And that is why we say that we are starting on a road that leads — *NO ONE KNOWS WHERE!* [55]

Mayor Ole Hanson of Seattle described the start of the strike on February 6th, 1919: "Streetcar gongs ceased their clamor; newsboys cast their unsold papers into the street; from the doors of mill and factory, store and workshop, streamed 65,000 workingmen. School children with fear in their hearts hurried homeward. The life stream of a great city stopped." [26] The A.F.L. strikers were joined by the I.W.W., the separately organized Japanese workers, and perhaps 40,000 non-union workers who did not go to work because of sympathy, fear, closed enterprises, or lack of transportation. [27] During the strike there was not a single arrest connected with it, general police court arrests sunk to less than half of normal, and according to Major General Morrison, in charge of U.S. troops in the city, in forty years of military experience he had not seen a city so quiet and orderly. [28]

The peacefulness of the strike did not prevent middle-class Seattle from seeing it as an attempted revolution. As Mayor Hanson put it,

The so-called sympathetic Seattle strike was an attempted revolution. That there was no violence does not alter the fact. . . . The intent, openly and covertly announced, was for the overthrow of the industrial system; here first, then everywhere. . . . True, there were no flashing guns, no bombs, no killings. Revolution, I repeat, doesn't need violence. The general strike, as practiced in Seattle, is of itself the weapon of revolution, all the more dangerous because quiet. To succeed, it must suspend everything; stop the entire life stream of a community. . . . That is to say, it puts the government out of operation. And that is all there is to revolt — no matter how achieved. [29]

Local radicals thought revolution would take more; a widely circulated leaflet, often seized on as proof of the strike's revolutionary intent, read:

The Russians have shown you the way out. What are you going to do about it? You are doomed to wage slavery till you die unless you wake up, realize that you and the boss have not one thing in common, that the employing class must be overthrown, and that you, the workers, must take over the control of your jobs, and through them, the control of your lives instead of offering yourself up to the masters as a sacrifice six days a week, so that they may coin profits out of your sweat and toil. [30]

Feeling the available National Guard inadequate for the situation, the State Attorney General, acting for the Governor, telephoned Secretary of War Newton Baker for Federal troops; by Friday, February 7th, 950 sailors and marines were brought into the city and carefully placed at strategic points. The Mayor, dramatically portraying himself as the city's savior from Bolshevism, added 600 extra men to the police force and swore in 2,400 special deputies, many of them University of Washington students. By February 7th, Mayor Hanson felt he had the necessary forces to

112   issue an ultimatum:

> To the Strike Committee:
>
>   I hereby notify you that unless the sympathy strike is called off by 8 o'clock tomorrow morning, Saturday, February 8, 1919, I will take advantage of the protection offered this city by the national government and operate all the essential enterprises.
>
> Ole Hanson, Mayor [31]

    The limitations of a general strike now became apparent. The point had come where either the strikers had to try to make permanent the power they had taken over the organized life of the city—an act of revolution which would have meant an immediate military confrontation—or capitulate.

    Whether to end the strike thus became the key issue. According to Anna Louise Strong,

> . . . as soon as any worker was made a leader he wanted to end that strike. A score of times in those five days I saw it happen. Workers in the ranks felt the thrill of massed power which they trusted their leaders to carry to victory. But as soon as one of these workers was put on a responsible committee, he also wished to stop "before there is riot and blood." [32]

This situation was dramatized when the Executive Committee

In September, 1934, a textile strike swept the mills from New England through the South. Here, strikers in Patterson, New Jersey, cheer news of the strike's progress in the South.

oted thirteen to one to recommend on Saturday, February 8th, to
nd the strike that night. The 300 members of the General Strike
Committee were almost persuaded until they took a supper break
and talked with members of their own rank and file; they re-
urned to the meeting and voted overwhelmingly to continue the
strike.

The heaviest pressures to end the strike now came from the
nternational officials of the A.F.L. unions. Telegrams ordering local
unions to desert the strike poured into the Labor Temple. So did in-
ernational officers, arriving from long distances to try to force their
members back to work. These efforts began to take their toll. The
treetcar men were ordered back to work by their executive com-
nittee under pressure from an international official, but said they
would rejoin the strike if called by the General Strike Committee;
he Teamsters likewise were ordered back by an international
officer, but the rank and file called another meeting at which it
vas expected they would vote to rejoin the strike; the stereotypers
eturned "under severe pressure from their international offi-
ers" [33] and a false rumor that the strike had been called off. With
hese breaks appearing and the power of the opposition growing
ver stronger, the General Strike Committee finally voted to end
he strike Tuesday at noon. The strike was ended, as the General
Strike Committee's history stated, by

Pressure from international officers of unions, from executive committees
f unions, from the "leaders" in the labor movement, even from those very
eaders who are still called "Bolsheviki" by the undiscriminating press.
And . . . the pressure upon the workers themselves, not of the loss of their
wn jobs, but of living in a city so tightly closed. [34]

The immediate effect of the strike was inconclusive. The ship-
ard strike went on; the attack on unionism swelled in Seattle as
lsewhere; the Socialist Party headquarters, a labor printing plant,
nd the I.W.W. hall were raided and thirty-nine "Wobblies" —
.W.W. members — arrested as "ringleaders of anarchy," [35] al-
hough they played little role in the general strike.

Perhaps the greatest effect of the strike was to suddenly bring
American labor struggles into the context of the revolutionary con-
licts sweeping the world in the wake of the war. The *Union Rec-
rd,* for example, noted after the strike its similarity to the workers'
government just arising in Belfast:

They are singularly alike in nature. Quiet mass action, the tying up
f industry, the granting of exemptions, until gradually the main activ-
ies of the city are being handled by the strike committee.

Apparently in all cases there is the same singular lack of violence
vhich we noticed here. The violence comes, not with the shifting of power,

114   but when the "counter revolutionaries" try to regain the power which inevitably and almost without their knowing it passed from their grasp. Violence would have come in Seattle, if it had come, not from the workers, but from attempts by armed opponents of the strike to break down the authority of the strike committee over its own members.

    . . . Our experience, meantime, will help us understand the way in which events are occurring in other communities all over the world where a general strike, not being called off, slips gradually into the direction of more and more affairs by the strike committee, until the business group feeling their old prestige slipping, turns suddenly to violence, and there comes the test of force. [36]

                ✊

    Soon after the Armistice an eight-hour movement swept the New England textile districts. The United Textile Workers, whose members were mostly skilled, decided to ask for an eight-hour day and the employers generally agreed to it — with a corresponding reduction in pay. This was hardly satisfactory, however, to the unskilled majority of workers — mostly immigrants — who were not represented by the union and whose wages would have been reduced

Cartoon captioned "Protect the industry at all hazards!" mocks the ordering of troops against 1912 strike of textile workers in Lawrence, Massachussetts. The dozens of nationalities employed at Lawrence united for another big strike in 1919.

Historical Pictures Service

to intolerable levels by the agreement. In Lawrence, Massachusetts, they decided to strike for the shorter work week with no reduction in pay. The union refused to sanction the strike and ordered its members back to work. Nonetheless, the strike spread through New Bedford and Fall River, Pawtucket, Rhode Island, Patterson, New Jersey, and other textile centers of New England and New Jersey. In all, 120,000 workers were out.[37]

In Lawrence, the strike was directed by a general strike committee of 100 composed of striking mill workers and a few others who met every morning to receive reports and make policies. Investigator John Fitch described them:

> They are delegates from the different nationalities and as they report each morning you seem to be listening to a roll call of the nations. Russians are there and Italians, Poles, Lithuanians, Greeks, Ukranians, Syrians, Franco-Belgians, Finns and even Germans. Each nationality meets by itself in its own hall and every morning its delegates report to the strike committee.[38]

A local carpenter, "an extreme Socialist," was made chairman of the committee, and a radical minister, A.J. Muste, played an important part in leading the strike. He told the strikers "that they ought to learn everything they can about the business of making cloth so that they may have the knowledge and skill necessary when the time comes for them to operate the mills for themselves."[39]

The strikers organized their own relief operation. Fitch describes a meeting where a committee was considering the problems of milk distribution:

> Arrangements had been made with a dairyman to supply milk in quantities at central points for the children of strikers' families. Depots were being established where the people of each nationality or group of nationalities could go for their supply. It was a business arrangement requiring cooperative effort . . . some of the delegates struggling with their English . . . [40]

The strike was met with opposition from the United Textile Workers and the Lawrence Central Labor Council, fear of Bolshevism from the middle classes, and repeated brutality from the police, but after ten weeks it gained its demands. As Fitch concluded, it "is a strike for wages carried on in a revolutionary atmosphere. That is, there are serious questionings of the justice of the existing economic order. In addition to that there is a feeling on the part of the strikers that the government is against them . . . to many of them American government is personified by the Lawrence police." [41]

The strike spread to Patterson with a somewhat different pat-

116 tern. There, 30,000 silkworkers tried to cut the work week for themselves by arriving at work at eight o'clock instead of seven. When
they arrived, they found themselves locked out. They organized on
a factory-by-factory basis, with daily meetings of the delegates
from more than 100 factories. The strike spread from Patterson to
10,000 unorganized wool-workers in Passaic, New Jersey. For most
of the strikers the movement was victorious.

The strike wave reached categories of workers often considered the model of labor docility. On April 15th, for example, the
telephone operators throughout New England walked off their jobs
in a strike against the Federal government, which still retained wartime control over the telephone companies. Unionization was primarily centered in Boston, but the strike spread to dozens of unorganized cities and towns. "I do not believe," wrote one observer,
"that an industrial issue has ever before penetrated every village,
hamlet or town of New England as has this strike of telephone
girls." [42] The second day of the strike, 12,000 "inside men" of the
telephone company struck in support of the operators. The next
day the Postmaster General — in charge of the companies — capitulated and came to a settlement with the operators.[43]

In Boston the local policemen's organization, known as the
Boston Social Club, decided to affiliate with the A.F.L. When nineteen of their leaders were fired by the Police Commissioner, the
club members voted 1,134-2 to strike. The Central Labor Union ordered affiliated unions to vote on a general strike in support of
the policemen. The president of Harvard offered 1,000 students to
replace the police, and many volunteers offered their services, but
city officials preferred to let various minor disorders develop unopposed — looting of stores, stoning of trolley cars, and dice-playing
on Boston Common. The result was a huge public uproar over riot
and revolution in Boston. "Lenin and Trotsky are on their way,"
stated the *Wall Street Journal.*[44] On the second day the State
Guard occupied the city, then patrolled the streets for the next
three months. The entire police force was fired and a new one gradually recruited. Against such pressures the strike was clearly doomed, and the C.L.U. decided that "the time is not now opportune for
the ordering of a general strike." [45] The main effect of the strike
was to greatly increase fear of threats to "law and order" by showing that even the minions of law and order themselves were workers not immune to the spreading spirit of revolt.[46]

The strike wave was visible not only on a national but also on a
city-by-city basis. On February 1st, 1919, for instance, a magazine
reported:

In a small way New York City has lately been through a general labor crisis. To unemployment, daily growing more acute, have been added strikes following one another in rapid succession. The Amalgamated Clothing Workers, after several months of struggle, have won a substantial victory, the chief element of which was the achievement of a 44-hour week. The hotel workers are still on strike and 8,000 furriers have voted to go out of their demands are not granted. The harbor workers are awaiting the findings of the War Labor Board . . . comfortable . . . that at a day's notice they can tie up the whole vast traffic of New York harbor. The New York firemen . . . are backing with all their force a Socialist resolution in the Board of Aldermen requesting the establishment of a three-platoon system in the New York Fire Department. . . . Whether the firemen will strike, as they did in Cleveland, to win an eight-hour day, will probably depend upon the action of the city and the State. The most immediate and crucial sympton of the general labor unrest is the strike of some 35,000 ladies' garment workers for a 44-hour week, a 15 percent increase in wages, and 'permission to a representative of the union to visit the shops once a month in order to ascertain whether the standards established by the protocol [contract] are observed.' The deeper issue appears to be the future maintenance of the protocol. This treaty of industrial peace has in many respects proved galling to both sides. By cutting off the power of general and shop strikes it has tied the workers' hands; by depriving the employers of the right of arbitrary discharge it has inferfered in a peculiarly irritating way with the direction of business.[47]

Another magazine reported in August that "in New York City a great variety of strikes is in progress. Cigarmakers, shirtmakers, carpenters, bakers, teamsters and barbers are out in large numbers. The most depressed trades are catching the strike infection, witness the walkout last week of women workers on feathers and artificial flowers, who want a forty-four-hour week and the abolition of home work. Even the scrubwomen employed in a downtown building struck and put strikebreakers to rout with their mop handles." [48]

Another article described the "Epidemic of Strikes in Chicago." "More strikes and lockouts accompany the mid-summer heat than were ever known before at any one time . . . In rapid succession the 1,700 street sweepers, the 800 garbage collectors, drivers and workers at the reduction plant, the 900 bridge laborers, the 800 City Hall clerks and over 300 fire department engineers, with groups of workers in other departments, in all nearly 5,000 public employees, actually quit their jobs." [49] Another strike occurred at the Corn Products Refining Company in Argo, a suburb of Chicago. "The attempt to operate the works led to an uprising of the cosmopolitan population, which resulted in bloodshed and a great popular demonstration at the funeral of the men who were killed, in which many returned soldiers in uniform participated." [50] At the McCormack works of the International Harvester Company, "with-

118 out any notice whatever, without presenting any grievance or making any demands, 5,000 employees ceased work, and succeeded in
persuading 800 in the adjoining twine mill and 1,800 in the tractor
works not to continue working." [51]

Similarly, "The Crane Company, where good working conditions, including profit-sharing and an annual bonus, have been
widely considered to be satisfactory for many years, also met with a
spectacular surprise. At the noon hour one day a procession of employees started near one of the large buildings and soon numbered
thousands of workers, including those of many crafts, who marched
to an adjoining grove and did not return to work." [52] Sixteen thousand carpenters struck, closing down all construction, in violation
of a contract running to May, 1921. And "the threat of the surface
and elevated streetcar men to strike . . . has kept the public mind in
keener suspense than all the other labor troubles — and with reason,
because it would cause still more acute unrest and possibly much
more serious and prevalent disturbance."[52]

But the conflict that most held the nation's attention in 1919
was the great strike in steel.

Trade unionism in the iron and steel industry, broken in the
Homestead struggle of 1892 and faced with organized and violent
opposition by the steel trust, remained quiescent until World War
I. This did not prevent workers from striking, however, especially
as labor became scarce toward the beginning of the war. "Workmen of the most docile tendencies have been making demands . . .
insignificant little rebellions verging on strikes here and there,"
reported an investigator.[54] In early 1916 an explosion came in
Youngstown. Laborers struck for a twenty-five percent increase at
a Republic tube plant; the strike spread spontaneously to other
steel plants in the town. On January 7th, East Youngstown laborers gathered near a plant. As they pressed forward, a guard fired
on them, the strikers replied with bricks, and the guards opened
general fire. Enraged, the crowds marched through the streets and
burned property worth one million dollars. The National Guard
was rushed in to suppress the movement. Twenty strikers were
wounded, three fatally.[55]

A similar strike broke out four months later in the Pittsburgh
district, heart of the steel industry. Workers at Westinghouse in
East Pittsburgh struck in late April. They started marching from
plant to plant spreading the strike, and steelworkers at points
throughout the district began joining in. At the second march to the
Edgar Thompson Works in Braddock the company guards opened
fire, killing two. The crowd's response, as at Youngstown, was
fury. According to a local paper, they "charged plant after plant,

and many of the places were wrecked." Some mills shut down to avoid trouble, and "the whole Pittsburgh district was threatened with industrial paralysis," until troops were sent in, the Westinghouse strike leaders arrested, and the strike suppressed.[56]

Frank Morrison, Secretary of the A.F.L., visited Pittsburgh during this strike, but left in despair, considering the situation "too turbulent to be exploited by the A.F.L."[57] Nonetheless, the A.F.L. was interested in taking advantage of wartime conditions to expand its membership in the steel industry, and in August, 1918, it established the National Committee for Organizing the Iron and Steel Workers. It was composed of twenty-four trade unions which claimed jurisdiction in the steel industry and was headed by president John Fitzpatrick of the Chicago Federation of Labor, a liberal trade unionist. Secretary-treasurer in charge of detailed work was William Z. Foster, a syndicalist who at that time believed that building the A.F.L. was all-important; later he became the leading trade union figure (and eventually chairman) of the American Communist Party. The unions, in the words of the Interchurch World Movement *Report on the Steel Strike of 1919*—the basic contemporary study of the strike—"had no doubt about what they wanted—more numbers for each of their separate craft organizations . . . "[58] For Foster, as Theodore Draper wrote, "if only the trade unions—even A.F. of L. unions—could become big and strong enough, the revolution would take care of itself."[59]

Meanwhile, the mills seethed. The I.W.M. *Report* found "that three-quarters of steel employees [the unskilled] developed a frame of mind of more or less chronic rebellion, largely the physical reaction from exhaustion and deprivation. Rebellious reactions from having no 'say' in the conduct of the job was also chronic, though less so. These were fundamental facts in steelworkers' minds, of which they were constantly reminded by endless 'grievances' . . . "[60] This discontent was reflected at an individual level by high absenteeism and a phenomenal labor turnover—at Homestead, for example, 6,800 out of 11,500 workers in a year.[61] Further, a new psychology had been created during the war: steelworkers were the object of intensive propaganda stressing their essential role in the "battle for democracy." They expected after the war that their importance would be recognized with some of the fruits of democracy; instead they were met by renewed discrimination and repression. Finally, the predominantly Eastern European laborers were stirred by the overthrow of autocracy in their homelands. As the I.W.M. *Report* concluded on the basis of extensive interviews, the immigrant workers in general possessed little radical ideology, but—

120   they have a vague idea that big rich people who run things "arbitrarily," even in mills, are coming down in the world. Russia, moreover, means to them the rise of workingmen to power. They have a vague idea that poor people who have been run for a long time, on farms and in mills, are coming up in the world and are beginning to run themselves.[62]

Under these conditions an explosion was bound to come. But the steel companies through long experience had developed powerful techniques to prevent the steelworkers from organizing themselves. The first key was the division of the labor force: thirty nationalities worked in the mills, each speaking only its own language, segregated in its own community, isolated within its own traditions and customs. Nor was this a matter of chance; the divide-and-rule strategy was understood as early as 1875 by a Carnegie plant manager who wrote, "My experience has been that Germans and Irish, Swedes and what I denominate 'buckwheats' [young American country boys], judiciously mixed, make the most effective and tractable force you can find."[63] The traditional leaders within these communities were powerful, conservative, and often directly dependent on the steel companies. Finally, the companies did everything possible to instill fear in the workers—fear of firing, blacklist, labor spies, informers, arrest, and deportation made steelworkers afraid even to talk to each other, let alone organize. They knew that as soon as a man started talking union he was fired.

Labor vs. Capital—1902—Sauce for the goose but not the gander. "The steel combine: 'Drop that banner; we have a right to combine but you haven't.'"

Historical Pictures Service

But when the A.F.L. began holding mass meetings in September, 1918, around the steel district, far from having to persuade men to join all they had to do was pass out membership cards; 1,200 were signed up in one day in Joliet, 1,500 in South Chicago.[64] By the spring of 1919, nearly 100,000 workers had signed up.[65]

Conflict soon arose over the form of organization. According to the I.W.M. *Report*, "in many plants the instinct of the immigrant recruit was to associate with his shopmates of different 'crafts' rather than with his 'craft' mates from other shops. He fell more easily into a shop or plant union."[66] The local leaders, "finding that organization by shops, departments and plants was often the most natural to their inexperienced fellow-workers . . . followed that plan even though the result was industrial unionism in miniature."[67] This was heresy to the A.F.L.; "the twenty-four crafts smothered this drift,"[68] and William Z. Foster "combatted the natural tendency of sections of the rank and file toward industrial unionism."[69] The workers of each shop and plant were split up among the twenty-four unions.

The heart of the steel industry was the Pittsburgh district, including dozens of steel towns through western Pennsylvania. It was here that the decisive battles would be fought. But the mayors and burgesses of the Monongahela Valley met early in the campaign and decided to forbid all union meetings in their towns; as Mayor Crawford of Duquesne put it, "Jesus Christ himself could not speak in Duquesne for the A.F. of L.!"[70] The free speech fight in the district began in Monessen, where the Burgess had forbidden union meetings for months. To break the ban, the local organizer called a meeting for April 1st. On the date set, 10,000 miners from the surrounding coal country marched into Monessen, uniformed veterans at their head. The right to hold meetings was thereby established in fact if not by permission, and was gradually spread by similar tactics through the rest of the district.

The basic conflict between the steelworkers and the unions became more evident the stronger the movement grew. The I.W.M. *Report* characterized their positions thus:

> The raw recruits, particularly the immigrant workers, wanted to strike soon after they joined up, since they could conceive of both protection and "results" only in a universal walkout.
>
> The 24 old unions willingly put money into a campaign for new members but hesitated greatly over backing a strike in behalf of the new steel locals, which might possibly jeopardize their old membership outside the steel industry.[71]

The rank and file was particularly impatient to strike because the new union members were being fired by the hundreds up and

122   down the steel district. In order "to give the men who have waited
so long something tangible to look forward to" and to "pacify the
restless spirits," the National Committee called a conference May
25th with 583 representatives from local unions in eighty steel centers.[72] They came with specific instructions from their own members. They assumed they were empowered to call a strike and tried
to do so, but the Internationals' representatives quickly asserted
that only they had the authority to call a strike. The result was that
workers began dropping out of the unions in large numbers.

   The demand for a strike continued to mount. At the National
Committee's meeting July 11th it was reported that

in Johnstown, Youngstown, Chicago, Vandergrift, Wheeling and elsewhere great strikes are threatening. The men are letting it be known that
if we do not do something for them they will take the matter into their
own hands. Where they are not threatening to strike they are taking the
position that they will pay no more dues until they can see some results
from their efforts.[73]

   On July 20th the National Committee finally decided to authorize a strike vote, for they were faced with such ultimata as this
telegram from the Johnstown Steel Workers Council:

Unless the National Committee authorizes a national strike vote to be
taken this week we will be compelled to go on strike here alone.[74]

Believing a strike was imminent, workers flooded into the unions—
membership increased fifty percent while the strike ballot was being taken.[75] The vote was virtually unanimous for the strike.[76]

   Union organizers made a series of last-ditch efforts to head off
a strike. Fitzpatrick, who headed the nationwide organizing drive,
believed that "if only both sides could get together around a table,
it could all be straightened out,"[77] but labor's appeals to Judge
Gary, head of U.S. Steel and spokesman for the industry, were repeatedly rebuffed. Finally an appeal was sent to President Wilson,
stating that a conference with management was the only demand.
A week later union leaders wired Wilson that "it is exceedingly
difficult to withhold or restrain the men. . . . We cannot now affirm
how much longer we will be able to exert that influence." [78] Finally,
a strike date was set for September 22nd. President Wilson requested that the strike be postponed, but a flood of telegrams like
this one forced the National Committee to go ahead with the strike:

W.Z. Foster
303 Magee Bldg.
Pittsburgh, Pa.

   We cannot be expected to meet the enraged workers, who will consider us traitors if strike is postponed.

Organizers Youngstown District[79]

The extent of the strike surprised union leaders as well as management. More than 350,000 walked out, crippling most of the steel industry. Many of those who struck were not union members; as Foster had predicted, "In iron and steel, where men work together in big bunches, we can get everybody to strike even though we have only ten percent" organized.[80] The unskilled immigrants from southern and eastern Europe, who made up the great majority of the steelworkers, formed the backbone of the strike. Some of the skilled, predominantly native-born workers, long favored by the employers, joined the strike; others continued to go to work. In some places, even office workers joined the strike.

The strikers in western Pennsylvania, the heart of the industry, were met with a complete suppression of civil liberties and a reign of terror. Sheriff Haddock of Allegheny County issued a proclamation forbidding outdoor meetings anywhere in the county, and swore in 5,000 strikebreaking employees of U.S. Steel as deputies. Foster charged that the county had 50,000 deputies under arms. Indoor meetings in most steel centers were forbidden by local authorities. The isolation of the strikers, unable to meet with each other, undermined morale; investigator George Soule, comparing towns, concluded that "the absence of the right to assemble naturally had its result in the non-effectiveness of the strike . . . the effectiveness of the strike was . . . proportional to the amount of civil liberty permitted."[81]

The reign of terror was equally powerful. The I.W.M. study, based on on-the-spot investigations and hundreds of affidavits, shows the strategy of the local officials.

In Monessen, where the strikers held out solidly for a long time, with the exception of the arrest of many Russians on vague charges of "radicalism," the policy of the State Police was simply to club men off the streets and drive them into their homes. Very few were arrested. In Braddock, however, where some of the mills were partly operating, the State Police did not stop at mere beating. Ordinarily, when a striker was clubbed on the street he would be taken to jail, kept there over night, and then the Squire or the Burgess would fine him from $10.00 to $60.00. In Newcastle, the Sheriff's deputies carried the Braddock policy much further. Many of those arrested in Newcastle, who had lived in the town almost all their adult lives, were charged with being "suspicious" persons and were ordered not to be released until the strike was over. Others were released in Newcastle after they furnished bail ranging from $500 to $2,500 each. The other towns in western Pennsylvania generally followed one of the methods described above.[82]

In Newcastle, Pennsylvania, the Sheriff (also Chief of Police) admitted to arresting 100 people the first week of the strike and planning to hold at least forty of them as "suspicious persons" "un-

124   til the strike is over, even if we have to build a new jail to house them." [83] The State Police, Foster admitted, felt free to brutalize the strikers because "they realize fully that they can depend upon trade-union leaders to hold the strikers in check from adopting measures of retaliation." [84]

The U.S. government, too, played its role in breaking the strike. It no longer needed labor's support for the war effort, and felt itself threatened by the revolutionary movements sweeping the world. The Department of Justice conducted "red raids" among the steelworkers, locking up and deporting immigrants, and Attorney General Palmer warned publicly that the strike threatened Bolshevism. At Gary, Indiana, the National Guard occupied the city and forbade parades, then Federal troops were sent in when the Guard proved incapable of suppressing an "outlaw parade" of uniformed ex-soldiers and other strikers organized independently of the strike leadership. The commanding general, declaring that "the army would be neutral," had strikers arrested and picket lines broken up; soldiers were sent to arrest union officers in other trades for such offenses as threatening to call a strike on a local building operation. The army continued to occupy Gary until the strike was called off.[85] The strikers, who at the beginning had expected Wilson's public support for trade unionism to be shown in the steel industry, became bitter and disillusioned about the Federal government, convinced it was on the side of the companies.

The repression in Pennsylvania threatened all workers in the state, and pressures for a general strike grew as the strike continued. Already the coal miners were out on their own strike. On November 1st and 2nd, the Pennsylvania Federation of Labor held a special convention which resolved that "the Executive Council of the Pennsylvania Federation of Labor shall issue a call for a State-wide strike, when in its judgement it is necessary to compel respect for law and the restoration of liberty."[86] Such a general strike, of course, went against every A.F.L. principle, and according to the I.W.M., "Mr. Foster was constantly complaining of fighting the 'radicals,' meaning those who wanted to have a general strike called." [87]

One critical element in the strike was the railroad workers on lines serving the steel plants; if they had struck, production would have been stopped throughout the Pittsburgh district. The railroaders' sentiment strongly supported the strike, but their national leaders did not. As one local strike leader put it, "If the railwaymen in the steel plant yards had struck, this strike would have been won. In October the railwaymen's locals near Pittsburgh voted to strike but got no assurance of support from their Brotherhoods." [88]

In Youngstown and other places where railroadmen did join the strike their unions not only gave them no strike benefits, but did not stop other members from taking their jobs around the mills.

The leadership of the most important union in the industry, the Amalgamated Association of Iron and Steel Workers (A.A. I.S.W.) constantly undermined the campaign. In May, they tried to arrange separate negotiations with U.S. Steel, offering to help allay the "serious disturbing element in the industrial world at the present time, a great spirit of unrest that has spread over our common country." [89] Had Judge Gary not turned down this offer, it would have broken the entire strike. When the strike started, workers at mills where the A.A.I.S.W. had contracts generally joined the strike, but six weeks later the union ordered them back to work, saying the contracts would be honored "at whatever cost." Lodges that refused to break the strike had their charters revoked. According to *Iron Age,* the order "broke the strike in every plant in the [Youngstown] district with which the Amalgamated had a contract." [90] As a local strike leader described it, "When Mike Tighe [A.A.I.S.W. president] ordered back his men at that mill near Cleveland, he started an avalanche. One Amalgamated organizer got 400 men into one big union with an Amalgamated charter at a mill near Steubenville and they all struck. Mike ordered them all back and tore up that organizer's card." [91]

The employers played powerfully on the divisions among the workers. Native workers were bombarded with propaganda that it was just a "hunkie" strike; immigrants were told that the Americans had already sold them out. The following written instructions to an operative of a labor detective firm hired to fight the strike gives an indication of the company tactics:

We want you to stir up as much bad feeling as you possibly can between the Serbians and the Italians. Spread data among the Serbians that the Italians are going back to work. Call up every question you can in reference to racial hatred between these two nationalities; make them realize to the fullest extent that far better results would be accomplished if they will go back to work. Urge them to go back to work or the Italians will get their jobs. [92]

Such operatives were employed by the hundreds.

Between 30,000 and 40,000 black workers were brought into the steel districts as strikebreakers. They had few compunctions about this, since traditionally most A.F.L. unions had been white-only. The only way blacks *could* enter unionized jobs was as strikebreakers. At Youngstown, one lone black machinist striker, though he stayed on strike to the end, was still not admitted to the machinists' local.

Polish workers at a Standard Oil refinery. The American Federation of Labor often maintained that the so-called "new immigrants" from Eastern and Southern Europe were impossible to organize.

To pay strike benefits to 350,000 strikers was out of the question. To prevent workers with no resources from being starved back to work, an enormous commissary system handled food distribution for the entire strike zone. Goods were bought from the grocery co-op suppliers, packaged into half-week allotments for large or small families, and shipped to forty-five local commissaries for distribution to those in need. The total commissary cost for the entire strike averaged less than $1.40 per striker.[93]

Few workers returned to the mills under the pressure of deprivation; as long as they were convinced that the strike was succeeding they stayed out week after week, living on next to nothing. But the overwhelming power of the steel companies over communications gradually began to grind down the strikers' morale. The newspapers constantly reported that the mills had been reopened and the strike broken, for this was true in some places and therefore could be made to seem true generally. With little labor press, no public meetings, and visits to strikers' homes impossible without arrest for "intimidation," workers gradually came to believe that the strike no longer stood a chance and slowly began to filter back to work. By the end of ten weeks the number of strikers was down from 365,000 to 110,000, and on January 8th, 1920, the National Committee declared the strike at an end.

The objective of the strike from the point of view of the A.F.L. unions involved was simply to establish trade union collective bargaining. As the I.W.M. *Report* concluded,

It is possible that the workers throughout the whole steel industry might much more easily have been organized on a radical appeal. But the Strike Committee were opposed in principle to any such appeal . . . the methods of organization used in the steel strike were old fashioned and became ostentatiously so as the organizers recognized the radical possibilities of the strike. . . . By the end of the year, it was evident that the strikers were getting an old-fashioned licking.[94]

The meaning of the strike to the strikers was different, both more vague and more radical. As David Saposs described it on the basis of an intensive study of immigrant communities in the steel district,

The determination of the immigrant worker to assert himself in spite of all the opposition of dominant opinion in his own community, was the chief reason why the foreign and English press . . . considered the strike as having deeper motives than mere demands of ordinary trade unionism. Not only the mill managers, but all the governing classes in steel towns were accustomed to seeing the immigrant docile and submissive; to them any strike was indeed a revolution. . . . Thus the strike was also an outburst of the inhibited instincts for self-expression . . . The immigrant wanted not only better wages and shorter hours. He resented being treated as a chattel or a "hunkie." [95]

As the I.W.M. *Report* put it, the strike was not only for trade unionism, but was "the workers' revolt against the entire system of arbitrary control." [96] The local leaders, in contrast to the A.F.L. unions, talked freely of the workers "sharing in industrial control." As Mary Heaton Vorse said after many interviews and discussions with the strikers, "What they believed was not formulated into a dogma. It was not narrowed down to trade union bargaining." [97] Perhaps the most general sentiment was expressed by an American steelworker in Youngstown:

> If my boy could give his life fighting for free democracy in Europe, I guess I can stand it to fight this battle to the end. I am going to help my fellow workmen show Judge Gary that he can't act as if he was a king or a kaiser and tell them how long they have got to work! [98]

The steel industry agreed. "If it came to a question of wage demands alone," wrote *Iron Age*, the steel companies "might meet the union officials in a conciliatory spirit." But the real issue was whether unions "shall be allowed to dictate to the employer how he shall operate his plant." [99] Or, as *The Nation* concluded, it was

> no mere squabble over wages and hours and collective bargaining and the open shop. . . . The real question is, Who shall control our steel industry? [100]

✊

Many of the strikes of 1919 were "outlaw" or wildcat strikes, opposed as heartily by the unions as by the employers. These spread even to such citadels of trade union authority as the printing trades. But the most important of all was on the railroads.

For practical purposes, the right of railroad workers to strike did not exist after the Federal suppression of the Pullman strike. The unions generally supported this state of affairs. Thus those railroad strikes which occurred met the opposition not only of the railroads but of the unions and the government. This was all the more true during the war and post-war period because the railroads were under Federal control until March, 1920. Discontent rose with the cost of living; by April, 1920, prices had risen one hundred percent since 1914, railroad wages only fifty percent. [101] After April, 1919, the government refused all requests for wage increases. According to Commons' *History of Labor in the United States,* "in the minds of the men the pent-up resentment against this injustice became directed not only against the dilatory government officials and railway managers but also against their own union officials who apparently bore this situation with a patience unbecoming . . . " [102]

In this charged situation, a railroad worker named John Grunau, a leader of an insurgent Chicago Yardmen's Association, was demoted in the Chicago yards on April 2nd. The 700 switchmen on his line immediately walked out in protest. The strike crystallized the general discontent of the railroad workers, and within two days every railroad in the Chicago area was involved in the strike, with 9,000 switchmen out. By April 9th, the strike had spread spontaneously across the country, reaching New York, San Francisco, Los Angeles, Pittsburgh, Memphis, St. Louis, Kansas City, Omaha and Detroit. Engineers, conductors and firemen joined the striking switchmen.

In the midst of the strike the workers created several temporary organizations. For instance, 1,700 workers on nine railroads entering Cleveland voted to form a Cleveland Yardmen's Association. Similar organizations developed in Chicago, New York, Pittsburgh, St. Louis, and Kansas City; representatives from these various groups met in Washington and formed a national alliance of striking switchmen and yardmen. Sylvia Kopald describes the best-known of the outlaw organizations, the United Railway Workers of America, thus:

> Originating among the Jersey strikers, this organization, according to the statements of its accredited spokesmen, was not intended to continue after the strike. The organization had no central direction. At its head stood an Executive Committee of 15 men, including a chairman and a secretary who were chosen from the members of a General Strike committee. This latter committee in turn was composed of representatives elected from the various roads, each of which contributed 18, or three for each craft (yardmasters, engineers, firemen, conductors, road workmen and yard service men). The Executive Committee was vested with power to "conduct the strike and make such moves as seem advisable to carry it to a successful conclusion." Its actual power, however, was drastically limited by the fact that it could take no important action without the express authorization of a general meeting.[103]

The railway unions launched a bitter drive against the strike. Dozens of union officials concentrated in Chicago and other strike centers ordered the men back to work, on the grounds that the strike violated union rules and contracts—although no contracts with the employers existed, the roads having just been returned from Federal control. They red-baited the strikers as Bolsheviks and charged them with destroying the union. They threatened the strikers with expulsion if they did not return to work, and actually applied this penalty to tens of thousands of workers.

Finally, the union leaders themselves recruited hundreds of strikebreakers. For example, a Chicago officer of the Brotherhood of Railway Trainmen wired all member unions outside Chicago to send switchmen to "break the strike of Grunau's rival organiza-

130   tion." [104] An official of the Order of Railway Conductors wired members, "Strike is illegal, against our Brotherhoods and against railroads. Our existence is at stake. Our members justified under the circumstances in working in yard and road service to help us save our organization."[105] Even those who did not join the strike resented this practice, however; as a union official reported of his meetings with his rank and file:

> Many members present showed a strong sympathy for the striking switchmen and said they would not work with "scabs" or "finks." It was impossible to convince our members at this stage of the illegal strike that men who took the switchmen's places were not scabs or finks and that they were friends of bona fide organizations helping them to maintain their contracts which were made by their duly authorized representatives.[106]

At another meeting, he reported, the principal topic was "the stated fear and undesire of our men to work with what they called 'finks.'" [107]

Finally, the power of the state was turned against the strikers. Attorney General Palmer attacked the strike leaders as I.W.W.'s and Reds. On April 15th he had twenty-three strike leaders in Chicago arrested on charges of violating the Lever and Sherman Acts, and there were arrests and raids on meetings in Cleveland, New Orleans and other cities as well.

The strike succeeded in forcing President Wilson to appoint a Railroad Labor Board. The Board strengthened the hands of the official unions by agreeing to meet exclusively with them and refusing even to hear the outlaws. It granted a general wage increase in July. With the combined pressure of repression and concession, the strike gradually faded as positions were filled by strikebreakers or men returning to work.

Most protracted of all was the mass strike in the coal fields, with sporadic strikes, national strikes, and armed battles running from 1919 into 1922.

During the week of July 4th, 1919, strikes were held throughout the country to protest the imprisonment of Tom Mooney. One of the places where strikes were widespread was among the coal miners of the Belleville sub-district of Illinois. In accordance with the union contract, thousands of miners found themselves docked next payday for taking part in the wildcat protest.

When the miners in the Nigger Hollow Mine No. 2 found they had been fined for the strike, they immediately requested that the operators return the fines. At the news of the operators' refusal, the miners gathered outside the mine for a spontaneous mass meeting. A petition was drawn up asking the local union chairman to call a meeting of the local; when he ignored the request, the miners marched up a nearby hill, selected one of their own number to preside, and held their own meeting. They resolved that the collection of the Mooney Strike fines was unjustified and illegal, and voted to stop work in protest. Next the workers decided to send a committee and ask the miners of Nigger Hollow Mine No. 1, who had also been fined, to join the strike. The workers there quickly voted to do so, and proposed that a joint meeting be held that night.

At the meeting, a United Mine Workers official who urged the men to return to work was shouted down, and instead the miners decided to continue the strike and called a meeting for workers from other mines that Sunday. Meanwhile, word of the strike began to spread around the district, and the men from nearby mines independently struck and held meetings to decide what action they would advocate at the Sunday meeting.

The men from the Nigger Hollow mines decided to propose two resolutions to the Sunday meeting. One was that the miners return to work and fight through regular channels rather than continue the strike. The second was a resolution on general policy reflecting the strong socialist tradition of the Illinois miners. It read:

In view of the fact that the present-day system of Society, known as the capitalist system, has completely broken down, and is no longer able to supply the material and spiritual needs of the workers of the land, and in further view of the fact that the apologists for and the beneficiaries of that system now try to placate the suffering masses by promises of reforms such as a shorter workday and increases in wages, and in further view of the futility of such reforms in the face of the world crisis that is facing the capitalist system; therefore be it . . .

Resolved, that the next National Convention of the U.M.W.A. issue a call to the workers of all industries to elect delegates to an industrial congress, there to demand of the capitalist class that all instruments of industries be turned over to the working class to guarantee that necessities, comforts and luxuries be produced for the use of humanity instead of a parasitical class of stockholders, bondholders, and that the Congress be called upon to pass an amendment to the Constitution of the United States legalizing all such action in the aforementioned Congress.[108]

About 2,000 men arrived for the Sunday meeting. They adopted the general policy resolution by a substantial majority. The fight came over continuing the strike. A local U.M.W. official had earlier wired Illinois District President Frank Farrington:

Six mines in the Belleville District have struck this week. I have done my best to get them back to work. Three of them are still out. A mass meeting is called for Sunday at Priester's Park. The chances are a great many more miners will come out. Situation serious. If some one can come here

132 Sunday it might have some effect.[109]

To which Farrington replied,

> I have instructed Reynolds, Dobbins, Myers, Schaefer, Thomas, Walker and Mason to attend meeting to be held at Priester's Park Sunday afternoon and to use their every influence to curb the rebellious movement in the Belleville District.[110]

The issue was debated for four hours, at the end of which both the U.M.W. and the Nigger Hollow miners' resolution to end the strike was rejected, and instead it was decided to spread the strike further.

Two days later a still larger body of strikers met for what was called a "general committee meeting." They established a "policy committee" of fifty miners to handle executive work of the strike.

Meanwhile, the issues of the strike were greatly expanded. It became not just a strike against the Mooney fines, but against the contract under which all miners were then working. This contract had been established during the war by the "Washington Agreement." It established automatic fines for workers who struck—it was under this provision that the Mooney strikers were punished. It provided maximum rates of pay, which the miners now considered inadequate in the face of post-war inflation. Practically from the signing of the Washington Agreement, miners had demanded an increase in the wages it provided, and in the wake of the Armistice, mass meetings were held in mining centers throughout Illinois demanding that the union abrogate the Washington Agreement. The union not only supported the agreement, but even prevented mine operators from paying bonuses above it. The penalty clause providing fines for striking, likewise, was protested from the start by the workers. The issue became critical after the Armistice, when operators, especially in the Belleville area, began breaking down work practices the miners had long struggled to establish. When the miners retaliated by closing down the mines, they were fined under the penalty clause of the Washington Agreement. The agreement was to run "during the continuation of the war not to exceed two years from April 1st, 1918." [111] The U.S. government, the coal operators, the national and state mine union leaders all agreed that despite the Armistice the contract ran until April 1st, 1920, since no peace treaty had been signed. The rank-and-file miners throughout the country opposed continuing the old contract, and the Illinois miners' strike now became a strike to renounce the Washington Agreement and establish a new contract with a new wage scale and without the penalty clause.

Armed with this broadened program, the Belleville miners began systematically spreading their revolt across the state. They

ent bulletins and posters giving word of the strike to other mining 133
centers. Most important, they organized teams of "Crusaders,"
who traveled across the state calling mass meetings of the miners
in each area and urging them to join the strike. As the strike spread,
workers in each local elected representatives to a Policy Committee
for their own sub-district, and a State Policy Committee was
formed from representatives of each of these. The insurgent State
Policy Committee no longer merely petitioned the union for a state
convention, but decided to go ahead and call one on its own account.

Meanwhile, the union officials counter-attacked. Illinois District President Farrington issued a circular to the membership
which began:

Our union is facing a crisis. The elements of destruction are at work.
The issue is: Shall the forces of defiance and rebellion prevail and stab our
union to death, or shall reason and orderly procedure dominate the affairs
of the United Mine Workers of America? [112]

Soon the union began supplying the operators with strikebreakers
to reopen the shut-down mines. The union hired "loyal" workers to
try to intimidate or stampede the strikers back to work. "Loyal"
union men were sworn in as special deputy sheriffs, at least some
of them apparently paid directly from the union treasury. Arrests
of strikers by these deputies and other law officials were common.
The Crusaders were again and again held up on the public highways, beaten, and prevented from proceeding by these various forces. The union eventually admitted having spent $27,000 to quell
the rebellion, but refused to itemize it.

The tactics of the union in suppressing the strike roused the ire
of the miners even more. Thus a committee from Belleville was
beaten up on the highway on the way to Springfield. When they
subsequently appealed to the Springfield miners to join the strike
for a new contract, the latter were wary—but when the committee
referred to the beating they had received at the instigation of union
officials, the miners voted to strike, and remain on strike "until all
the state officers resigned their jobs." [113] By the time of the insurgent state convention perhaps half of the 90,000 miners in Illinois
had joined the outlaw strike.

Although they had opposed the convention, the union officials
understood how important it was to control it once it was called.
They headed off the attempt to spread the movement to other
states by excluding miners from Pennsylvania and other states
from participating. From then on, the union officials successfully
asserted their authority, declaring the strike called off because contract negotiations had been scheduled to begin in a month. The con-

134   tract demands of the insurgents were accepted, however, and became the basis of the rank-and-file program at the national U.M.W.
convention a month later. In addition, the convention recommended not that the mines be operated by the government — the official
U.M.W. position at that time — but that they be turned over to the
miners.

When the national U.M.W. convention met in Cleveland a
month later, a completely new situation had been created by the
Illinois insurgency, for Illinois was the heart of the union and most
reflected the mood of the rank and file. One observer described the
convention as a "fight between the men and their officials."[114] The
2,000 delegates demanded a new contract, set a strike date for November 1st if it was not gained, and instructed their officers to demand a thirty-hour week and a sixty percent wage increase. The
U.M.W. officials were forced to negotiate for a new contract.
When they failed to achieve one, the convention's strike order
went into effect and on November 1st 425,000 miners struck.

The U.S. government instantly leapt into the fray. President
Wilson declared the strike "not only unjustifiable but unlaw-
ful."[115] At the request of the U.S. Attorney General, a Federal
judge issued an injunction sequestering the union strike fund and
prohibiting the union leaders from any action furthering the strike.
Federal troops were moved into the coal fields of Utah, Washington, New Mexico, Oklahoma and Pennsylvania. On November 8th,
the Federal Court further ordered the union officials to rescind the
strike order and send the men back to work. Acting President John
L. Lewis ordered the strike call cancelled, declaring, "We are Americans, we cannot fight our Government."[116]

But the coal miners disagreed, ignored the union order, and
stayed struck, refusing to return to work for nearly a month. They
realized their power as they saw the U.S. government rationing
coal, schools closing down for lack of heat, factories shutting down,
and railroad operations drastically cut back. According to a report
in *The Survey*,

> In not a few places where temperatures were below zero, a fuel fa-
> mine existed. In the emergencies much volunteer coal mining was at-
> tempted. College and university students went into the surface mines in
> Kansas. In Montana on the other hand it was reported that Federal troops
> were used to drive miners to work. The Secretary of War announced that
> such an action was inconceivable, but there has been no public report on
> what actually occurred. In North Dakota Governor Frazier took over the
> mines under martial law and the union miners returned to work under the
> auspices of the state government.[117]

The miners reluctantly returned to work when President Wilson proposed an immediate fourteen percent wage increase and an arbitration commission to grant further demands.

The miners remained discontented with the results of the settlement, and by the summer of 1920 wildcats were common and all mining had stopped in Indiana and Illinois without declaration of a strike.

Insurgency developed even further in anthracite than in bituminous mining. In August, 1919, a U.M.W. convention formulated demands; negotiations dragged on fruitlessly until May, 1920, when the union agreed to President Wilson's proposal for arbitration. The arbitration award was totally unsatisfactory to the miners, but the union recognized that it was obliged to accept it. While the union officials were drafting the contract, 85,000 miners struck under insurgent leadership, closing down half the anthracite collieries. Union officials earnestly endeavored to end the strike, but it continued for nearly a month.[118]

Meanwhile, in response to the bituminous strike, the Governor of Kansas called a special session of the legislature to establish compulsory arbitration in major industries by means of a labor court. As soon as the proposal was passed, 400 Kansas miners walked off their jobs in a wildcat strike to show their defiance of the law, but were ordered back to work by the union the next day. Soon a test case arose when miners in Crawford County refused to work with an engineer who had helped attempts to open the mines during the national coal strike. District union officials were ordered to appear before the new labor court and were arrested for contempt when they refused. In response, the miners struck, closing down ninety percent of the mines in Kansas. They then came into Girard for a mass demonstration, where the U.M.W. district president was allowed to address them from the prison balcony. The miners returned to work only as the officials were released on bond.

Meanwhile, events in West Virginia began developing toward civil war. During and after World War I, the West Virginia coal fields had expanded enormously. The northern fields were mostly unionized, but organization was completely blocked and union organizers forbidden even to enter the southern counties of the state, whose local governments were under virtually complete control by anti-union mine operators. Miners who joined the union were fired and evicted from their homes; deputy sheriffs on company payrolls ran union organizers out of town and arrested and beat up local union sympathizers. At this point, a rumor spread around the state that women and children were being killed in Logan County. An investigator describes what happened:

On Sept. 4 hundreds of miners assembled on Lens Creek . . . 30 miles

136   from Logan County. They trudged on over the hills and by the roads. Many of them carried guns; 5,000 miners had gathered by nightfall. There were no leaders. The miners were determined, apparently, to invade Logan County... [119]

The Governor wired Frank Keeney, West Virginia U.M.W. president, who rushed to Lens Creek to try to stop the miners. "On the outskirts of the crowd he was told that his presence was useless and he might as well go back home." [120] Next both Keeney and the Governor addressed the strikers, but were only partially successful in persuading them to return home. Next day, 1,500 miners continued the march to Danville. Only when a committee they had sent to Logan County reported all there was quiet did the miners disband and go home. But this was just a prelude.

In May, 1920, a strike broke out in Mattewan over the firing of members of a new union and rapidly spread through Mingo County, West Virginia, and Pike County, Kentucky. Armed guards patrolled the Mingo County line "to prevent infiltration of union men." [121] In Mattewan, a shoot-out occurred between the local police chief, Sid Hatfield (an ex-miner and a Hatfield of the Hatfield-McCoy feud), and Baldwin-Felts detectives brought in by the operators to evict strikers. Two miners, the Mayor of Mattewan, and seven Baldwin-Felts guards were killed in a matter of minutes. In response to this and other violence, the Governor sent in state troops. On August 21st, a three-hour gun battle between strikers and guards killed six. At the Governor's request, 500 Federal troops were rushed in. District President Keeney threatened a general strike throughout the state unless the Federal troops stopped their strikebreaking activities.

The strike continued, with 1,700 people living in tent colonies. Battles flared intermittently; Federal troops were withdrawn, rushed back, and withdrawn again. Finally at a meeting of miners in the small mining camp of Marmet on August 20th, 1921, it was decided that since the union was kept out by the violence of guards, deputies and troopers, the miners would have to open the area by force of arms. Thus a second miners' march was organized, led this time by war veterans.

Patrols were flung out along the roads leading into Logan, a commissary was set up, and mess halls opened at various school houses near the front. Trains and automobiles were commandeered for the "citizens' army" and the men, armed with all sorts of weapons, were accompanied by nurses in uniform. . . . The union men wore blue overalls with red handkerchiefs around their necks. [122]

As the miners drew near to Logan County, their numbers reached 4,000. Frank Keeney, as before, tried to persuade them to disperse,

The Edgwood strike. Strikers have generally desired to avoid violence, relying instead on their ability to halt production. But where they have been met by systematic violence from the employers and government, they have repeatedly resorted to arms. This has included armed crowds, virtual guerrilla bands, and arming of picket lines, as here.

138

but when word came that armed deputies had swooped down upon a camp and killed five miners, the invasion was resumed. President Harding issued a proclamation ordering the miners to disperse but they ignored it. The miners took up position on a wide front and, advancing two miles, engaged in heavy battle at five points with deputies and volunteers defending the non-union counties. At that point, 2,100 troops of the 19th Infantry together with machine guns and airplanes were rushed into Logan County. The miners had no choice but to surrender to the Federal troops, and with company law and order restored the strike was easily defeated. Some 350 miners were indicted for treason, but never convicted.

In April, 1922, the U.M.W. called strikes in both anthracite and bituminous fields. The strikes were joined by 75,000 non-union miners in the Connellsville coke region of Pennsylvania as well. "With the zeal of new converts, the Connellsville miners became self-appointed organizers, looking to no one for orders, only anxious to spread the strike and the union gospel."[123]

After eight weeks of the strike, the Southern Illinois Coal Company began to reopen its mines in Williamson County with imported strikebreakers under heavily armed guards. When a group of miners tried to talk with the strikebreakers they were fired on by machine guns and two of them killed. Not only the miners themselves, but farmers and other workers of the area grew furious, and on June 21st, when another striker was shot dead while standing in a farmyard half a mile from the mine, men began pouring into Williamson from as far as Kansas, Indiana and Ohio. They were armed with weapons they had seized from hardware stores and American Legion halls. By dusk, 1,000 armed men advanced on the mine in skirmish waves directed by war veterans wearing trench helmets. An airplane, rented at a nearby field, flew overhead dropping dynamite bombs on the strongholds of the strikebreakers. According to a National Guard colonel, "It was a seemingly well-organized, remarkably sober, determined, resolute aggregation of men and boys."[124] As they approached they were met with continuous machine-gun fire from the mine guards. Just as they prepared to storm the mine a white flag went up and the besieged offered to surrender. Armed miners marched them away, executing the mine superintendent along the way. They then were met by a mob from town who had not taken part in the battle. The mob took over the prisoners, told them to run for it, and then began shooting at them. In this and subsequent massacres, nineteen strikebreakers were killed. Juries of local farmers refused to convict anyone for the massacre.

In July, the Federal government turned its strength against

the nationwide coal strike. President Harding officially told the operators to go home and resume operations, and wired the Governors of twenty-eight states to furnish them protection, pledging the full support of the Federal government. In response, the governors of Pennsylvania and Ohio ordered state troops to the mines, but the strike remained firm. The union finally accepted a settlement at the expense of the 75,000 non-union miners who had joined the strike; they were abandoned to their fate. A committee appointed by the Mayor of New York found their conditions "worse than the serfs of Russia or the slaves before the Civil War." [125] They continued their desperate strike for sixteen months until August, 1923, when they were finally starved out. As the 1920's wore on, the war and post-war coal boom petered out, and the industry developed a chronic coal glut. Under these conditions the United Mine Workers proved impotent, and the rest of the 1920's was a period of steady decay as the union retreated or was broken in area after area.

In 1919, we see the energy of a mass strike working both through and against trade unionism. Where — as in Seattle — the rank and file was able to control existing unions, the militance and class-consciousness of the workers gave union action radical forms; where — as in steel — unionization had been prevented, establishing trade unionism was the logical objective of strike action. In the two basic industries that had been thoroughly unionized — coal and railroads — the unions tried desperately to head off or kill off rank-and-file strike action, and the workers were forced to organize against their own unions. The unions strove to maintain their organizational security, while the workers pressed for changes which threatened that security; thus, such a conflict was inevitable.

Several important factors give mass strikes after 1900 a different character from those before. The decline in the central role of railroads dissolved the automatic process by which railroad strikes in 1877 and 1894 instantly became universal, nation-wide struggles between labor and capital. The growth of a unionism based on collective bargaining contracts tended to counteract the powerful rank-and-file solidarity and made workers tend to think of their struggle in terms of their own industry alone rather than in terms of their class as a whole; further, the contracts themselves operated as a powerful barrier to the tendency of strikes to spread to wider and wider groups. This contrasts markedly with such nineteenth-century labor organizations as the Knights of Labor and the American Railway Union, which considered the sympathetic

140 strike and the solidarity of all labor among their basic principles. The result is that twentieth-century mass strikes are far less unified than those that came before. In 1919—as later—we see the spectacle of determined groups of workers after great sacrifice going down separately to defeat.

Another important change is that by the twentieth century, workers by and large accepted the wage system and their position of subordination within it as an accomplished fact. They were far less attracted by programs designed in one way or another to recreate a nation of small independent producers, such as the producers' cooperatives of the Knights of Labor or the cooperative colonies—somewhat like contemporary rural communes—to which the American Railway Union turned after its great defeat. This had two consequences. On the one hand, it meant that workers were far more willing to accept and indeed demand stable institutions of collective bargaining and union representation that would make life under capitalism more bearable. On the other hand, it meant that when the demand for workers' power arose, it no longer took the form of demanding a return to the system of small independent producers of the past; instead workers accepted and wanted to use the new industrial technology and the large-scale, coordinated production it made possible. The idea of workers' management of industry arose in many of the struggles of 1919. It was spelled out by the workers in Seattle, in Lawrence, in Illinois, and it formed a background to the other struggles. Of course, the strikes of 1919 were not in themselves attempts to establish such a system, but they were seen by the participants—and their opponents—as part of a struggle for power which led in that direction.

Chapter 4: Footnotes

1. "The Revolt of the Rank and File," *The Nation,* Vol. 109, No. 2834 (Oct. 25, 1919), p. 540.
2. Alexander M. Bing, *War-Time Strikes and Their Adjustment* (N.Y.: E.P. Dutton & Co., 1921), p. 262.
3. *Ibid.,* pp. 168-9.
4. *Ibid.,* p. 7.
5. *Ibid.,* p. 9.
6. *Ibid.,* p. 293.
7. *Ibid.,* pp. 30, 136.
8. The Commission of Inquiry, The Interchurch World Movement, *Report on the Steel Strike of 1919* (N.Y.: Harcourt, Brace and Howe, 1920), p. 152.
9. Sylvia Kopald, *Rebellion in Labor Unions* (N.Y.: Boni and Liveright, 1924), p. 152.
10. Robert L. Friedheim, *The Seattle General Strike* (Seattle: University of Washington Press, 1964), p. 18.
11. *Ibid.*
12. William Short, *History of Activities of Seattle Labor Movement and Con-*

spiracy of Employers to Destroy It and Attempted Suppression of Labor's **141**
Daily Newspaper, the Seattle Union Record (Seattle: Union Record Publishing Co., 1919), pp. 1-2, cited in Friedheim, p. 24.

13. *Papers on Industrial Espionage* (Mss. in University of Washington Library, Seattle), report of Agent 106, June 11, 1919, cited in Friedheim, p. 29.
14. Anna Louise Strong, *I Change Worlds* (N.Y.: Henry Holt and Co., 1935), p. 68.
15. *Seattle Times,* Jan. 21, 1919, p. 1, cited in Friedheim, p. 75.
16. Strong, pp. 74-5.
17. *Ibid.,* pp. 72, 74.
18. *Seattle Times,* Jan. 28, 1919, cited in Freidheim, p. 84.
19. History Committee of the Seattle General Strike Committee, *The Seattle General Strike* (Seattle: The Seattle Union Record Publishing Co., Inc., 1920), p. 15.
20. Freidheim, p. 101.
21. William MacDonald, "The Seattle Strike and Afterwards" (written in Seattle, Feb. 28, 1919), in *The Nation,* Mar. 29, 1919, cited in Wilfrid H. Crook, *Communism and the General Strike* (Hamden, Conn.: The Shoe String Press, Inc., 1960), p. 53.
22. History Committee, pp. 21-2.
23. *Ibid.,* p. 21.
24. *Ibid.,* p. 50.
25. *Ibid.,* pp. 4-6.
26. Ole Hanson, *Americanism versus Bolshevism* (Garden City, N.Y.: Doubleday, Page, 1920), p. 84, cited in Freidheim, p. 123.
27. Freidheim, p. 124.
28. History Committee, p. 46.
29. *New York Times,* February 9, 1919, cited in Crook, p. 51.
30. For a photocopy of the original, see State's Exhibit 40, transcript of *People v. Lloyd,* p. 467; Harvey O'Connor claims authorship of "Russia Did It," in *Revolution in Seattle* (N.Y.: Monthly Review Press, 1964), p. 143, cited in Freidheim, p. 101.
31. Reprinted in *Daily Bulletin,* Feb. 8, 1919, p. 1, cited in Freidheim, p. 136.
32. Strong, pp. 81-2.
33. History Committee, p. 38.
34. *Ibid.,* p. 35.
35. *Ibid.,* p. 57.
36. *Ibid.,* p. 62.
37. Commons, Vol. IV, p. 438.
38. John A. Fitch, "Lawrence," in *The Survey,* April 15, 1919, pp. 695-6.
39. *Ibid.*
40. *Ibid.*
41. *Ibid.*
42. Commons, Vol. IV. p. 438.
43. Anne Withington, "The Telephone Strike," in *The Survey,* April 26, 1919, p. 146.
44. *Wall Street Journal,* Sept. 12, 1919, cited in Robert K. Murray, *Red Scare, A Study in National Hysteria, 1919-1920* (N.Y.: McGraw-Hill Book Co., 1964), p. 129.
45. *Boston Evening Transcript,* Sept. 12, 1919, cited in Murray, p. 129.
46. Arthur Warner, "The End of Boston's Police Strike," *The Nation,* Vol. 109, No. 2842, Dec. 20, 1919, p. 790.
47. "The Week," in *The Nation,* Vol. 108, No. 2796, Feb. 1, 1919.
48. *The Survey,* Vol. 42, Aug. 2, 1919, p. 674.

142   49. Graham Taylor, "An Epidemic of Strikes in Chicago," in *The Survey,* Vol. 42, Aug. 2, 1919, pp. 645-6.
       50. *Ibid.*
       51. *Ibid.*
       52. *Ibid.*
       53. *Ibid.*
       54. Cited in Brody, *Steelworkers in America,* p. 181.
       55. *Ibid.,* pp. 181-2.
       56. *Ibid.,* p. 183.
       57. A.F.L., *Weekly Newsletter,* Jan. 15, 1922, cited in Brody, p. 199.
       58. I.W.M. *Report,* p. 160.
       59. Theodore Draper, *The Roots of American Communism* (N.Y.: The Viking Press, Compass Books Ed., 1963), p. 320.
       60. I.W.M. *Report,* p. 147.
       61. *Ibid.,* p. 148.
       62. *Ibid.,* p. 151.
       63. Letter of manager of Edgar Thomson Works, quoted in "Inside History of Carnegie Steel Co.," by J.H. Bridge, p. 81, cited in I.W.M. *Report,* p. 127, n.l.
       64. Brody, p. 216.
       65. *Ibid.,* p. 233.
       66. I.W.M. *Report,* p. 160.
       67. *Ibid.,* p. 37.
       68. *Ibid.,* p. 160.
       69. *Ibid.,* p. 35.
       70. William Z. Foster, *The Great Steel Strike and Its Lessons* (N.Y.: B.W. Huebsch, Inc., 1920), p. 62.
       71. I.W.M. *Report,* p. 168.
       72. Brody, p. 236.
       73. I.W.M. *Report,* p. 171.
       74. Cited in Brody, p. 237.
       75. I.W.M. *Report,* p. 154.
       76. Brody, p. 238.
       77. I.W.M. *Report,* p. 165.
       78. Brody, p. 239.
       79. Cited in I.W.M. *Report,* p. 172.
       80. Cited in Brody, p. 241.
       81. Supplementary Reports of the Investigators to the Commission of Inquiry, The Interchurch World Movement, *Public Opinion and the Steel Strike* (N.Y.: Harcourt, Brace and Co., 1921), p. 173. (Cited hereafter as I.W.M. *Opinion.*)
       82. *Ibid.,* p. 178.
       83. *Ibid.,* p. 177.
       84. Foster, p. 133.
       85. Brody, pp. 140-2.
       86. Foster, p. 115.
       87. I.W.M. *Report,* p. 39.
       88. *Ibid.,* p. 181.
       89. Foster, p. 70.
       90. *Strike Investigation,* II, 632-6l, *Iron Age,* Feb. 5, 1920, p. 415, cited in Brody, p. 257.
       91. I.W.M. *Report,* p. 181.
       92. *Ibid.* p. 320.
       93. Foster, pp. 216-20.
       94. I.W.M. *Report,* pp. 39-40.
       95. I.W.M. *Opinion,* pp. 239, 241.

96. I.W.M. *Report*, p. 119.
97. Mary Heaton Vorse, *Men and Steel* (London: The Labour Publishing Co., Ltd., 1922), p. 166.
98. I.W.M. *Report*, pp. 131-2.
99. *Iron Age*, cited in Brody, pp. 242-3.
100. "The Revolution—1919," *The Nation,* Oct. 4, 1919, p. 452.
101. Kopald, *Rebellion*, p. 128.
102. Commons, Vol. IV- p. 453.
103. Kopald, *Rebellion*, p. 141.
104. *Ibid.*, p. 151.
105. *Ibid.*, p. 152.
106. Report of Jonas McBride, reprinted in Pres. Carter's "May Bulletin," cited in Kopald, p. 154.
107. *Ibid.*
108. Cited in Kopald, pp. 74-5.
109. *Ibid.*, p. 73.
110. *Ibid.*,
111. *Ibid.*, p. 62.
112. *Ibid.*, p. 84.
113. *Ibid.*, p. 87.
114. Sylvia Kopald, "Behind the Miners' Strike," *The Nation,* Vol. 109, No. 2838, Nov. 22, 1919, p. 658.
115. McAlister Coleman, *Men and Coal* (N.Y.: Farrar & Rhinehart, 1947), p. 278.
116. Cincinnati *Enquirer,* Nov. 12, 1919, p. 6, quoting Lewis; cited in Murray, p. 161.
117. *The Survey,* Vol. XLIII, No. 8, Dec. 20, 1919, p. 254.
118. Commons, Vol. IV, p. 477-9.
119. Winthrop D. Lane, *Civil War in West Virginia* (N.Y.: B.W. Huebsch, Inc., 1921), p. 106.
120. *Ibid.*
121. Commons, Vol. IV, p. 480.
122. Lane, p. 106.
123. Commons, Vol. IV, p. 483.
124. *Ibid.*, p. 483-4.
125. *Ibid.*, p. 485-6.

Chapter 5
Depression Decade
I. "Don't Starve – Fight"

The 1920's were a period of great expansion for American capitalism. For the trade unions, it was a period of decline, which they
met by trying to persuade employers to establish unionism in order to guarantee labor peace. By the late twenties, one of America's leading economists was widely seconded when he declared
that the country had entered an era of "permanent prosperity." Already, however, serious constriction had begun in such industries
as coal and textiles, and with the collapse of the stock market in
October, 1929, depression — long believed a thing of the past — set in.

With it came enormous misery — loss of jobs, homes, farms,
savings, even the means to eat. Within three years, some fifteen
million workers were unemployed. By early 1932, according to a
New York newspaperman, groups of thirty or forty men would enter chain grocery stores and ask for credit.

When the clerk tells them business is for cash only, they bid him stand
aside; they don't want to harm him, but they must have things to eat. They
load up and depart.[1]

Out of this kind of desperation the unemployed began improvising
a variety of forms of direct action to meet their needs.

Most dramatic was direct action to stop evictions. A reporter
described a typical anti-eviction "riot" in Chicago:

A woman living in a certain block in Chicago has five children; her
husband is a stockyards workman who has been out of a job a year and a
half. But on ten dollars a month sent by her brother-in-law, and borrowing
now and then from the neighbors' pantries, she has fed her family. There
is no money left for rent. So after two warnings from the landlord — a crisis.
She is to be evicted next Tuesday at five.

In the same block lives a member of the local branch of the Unemployed Council, who has been through it all before. He talks to the men
and women and together they call a meeting of all the families on the block.
Most of them have known Mrs. MacNamara for years and know that the
baby has tonsilitis. At 4:30 on Tuesday you find them in an organized
body outside the MacNamara flat. The sheriff arrives and in the face of
protest does his work. Mrs. MacNamara's bed, bureau, stove, and children
are translated to the street. Then the Council acts. With great gusto the
bed, bureau, stove, and children are put back in the house. Then the neighbors proceed to the local relief bureau, where a Council spokesman dis-
plays the children, presents the facts, and demands that the Relief Com

mission pay the rent or find another flat for the MacNamaras. The local relief worker expresses dismay but says the rent fund is exhausted. The spokesman goes through the MacNamara story again with a new emphasis, and repeats his demands. If the Commission is adamant, he leaves and reappears at general headquarters with a hundred Council members instead of fifty. Usually the Commission digs up the $6 a month rent, or the landlord throws up his hands, and Mrs. MacNamara's children have a roof over their heads.[2]

Organizations of the unemployed sprang up city by city around the country, often with initiative coming from Communist, Socialist or other leftist groups. Charles R. Walker, a labor expert, studied them in various parts of the country and described them thus:

The Unemployed Council is a democratic organ of the unemployed to secure by very practical means a control over their means of subsistence. I find it is no secret that Communists organize Unemployed Councils in most cities and usually lead them, but the councils are organized democratically and the majority rules. In one I visited at Lincoln Park, Michigan, there were three hundred members of which eleven were Communists. The Council had a right wing, a left wing, and a center. The chairman of the council, who was of the right wing, was also the local commander of the American Legion. In Chicago there are forty-five branches of the Unemployed Council, with a total membership of 22,000.

The Councils' weapon is democratic force of numbers and their functions are: to prevent evictions of the destitute, or if evicted, to bring pressure to bear on the Relief Commission to find a new home for the evicted family; if an unemployed worker has his gas or his water turned off because he can't pay for it, to investigate the case and demand their return from the proper authorities; to see that the unemployed who are shoeless and clothesless get both; to eliminate through publicity and pressure discriminations between Negroes and white persons, or against the foreign born, in matters of relief; for individuals or families and children of the unemployed who have no relief as a penalty for political views or have been denied it through neglect, lack of funds, or any other reasons whatever, to march them down to relief headquarters and demand they be fed and clothed. Finally, to provide legal defense for all unemployed arrested for joining parades, hunger marches, or attending union meetings.[3]

By direct action the unemployed were able to stop many evictions; in Chicago and other cities the public authorities were finally forced to suspend them entirely. Further, Walker reported, the amount of relief in cities he visited was directly proportional to the strength and struggle of the local unemployed council.

In many places the unemployed also made attempts to reorganize economic life on their own. In Seattle, the Unemployed Citizens' League organized self-help on a large scale. The unemployed were found fishing-boats by the fishermen's union, al-

146   lowed to pick unmarketable fruit and vegetables by nearby farmers, and permitted to cut wood on scrub timberland. Members throughout the city organized twenty-two locals, each with its own commissary at which the food and firewood thus acquired was exchanged with barbers who cut hair, seamstresses who mended clothes, carpenters who repaired houses, and doctors who treated the sick. With the end of the harvest season, however, self-help in Seattle lost its already marginal economic basis. The U.C.L. then became the machinery for distributing relief. It also became a major political power in the city; its candidate for mayor, named Dore, won with the largest plurality in the city's history, whereupon he took relief administration away from the U.C.L. and threatened to use machine guns against demonstrations of the unemployed — he quickly became known as "revolving Dore."[4] By the end of 1932 there were 330 such self-help organizations in thirty-seven states with membership over 300,000. But by early 1933 most of them, including the Seattle U.C.L., were in collapse, discovering the limitations of a self-help movement living off the scraps of an already collapsed economy.

    The most dramatic — and illegal — form of self-help was the bootleg coal industry in Pennsylvania. Small teams of unemployed coal miners simply dug small mines on company property and mined out the coal, while others took it by truck to nearby cities and sold it below the commercial rate. A miner named William Keating composed a ballad in 1932 which typifies the attitudes of the "coal-leggers":

> While the woes of unemployment were increasing,
> While the price of foodstuff swelled the grocer's till,
> For to fix 'gainst next winter's chill breeze,
> Lest our poor families do freeze,
> We dug a wee coal hole on God's hill.
>
> But our terrible toil was wasted; we worked in vain,
> Two Cossack-mannered coal and iron cops came.
> On next winter's cold nights,
> We'll have no anthracite,
> 'Cause the cops caved in our wee coal hole.
>
> My mule-driving record proves at Oak Hill mine,
> I'm unfairly unemployed for four years' time.
> To no soup house I'll be led,
> Because I'll dig my family's bread,
> Or by cops be killed, in my wee coal hole.
>
> Right demands I keep my family fed and warm,

God put coal 'neath these hills; here I was born.
So call it bootleg or what,
I'll have coal in my cot,
While there's coal in Good God's coal vein.[5]

By 1934, coal bootlegging was an important industry, producing some five million tons of coal worth $45 million and employing 20,000 men and 4,000 vehicles. The coal companies fumed, but community opinion solidly backed the bootleggers — local officials would not prosecute the miners, juries would not convict, and jailers would not imprison. When company police tried to stop the bootlegging the miners defended themselves by force. In Shamokin, when the company started stripping operations on the "Edgewood Bootleggers' Tract," where 17,000 illegal miners dug coal, the men promptly dynamited the steam shovel and told the company men to "beat it"; nobody was arrested. At Tremont, a thousand bootleggers prepared to battle fifty police until the latter withdrew. The private police of another company blew up more than 4,000 holes in 1934, but in that time at least 4,000 new ones were dug on their property. An investigator reported several bootleggers telling him, "If they close our holes, we'll gang up on their collieries and close *them*." [6]

In coal bootlegging the miners took over use of private property and began producing for themselves. But as long as the rest of the economic system remained unchanged, bootleg mining had severe limitations. Miners had little equipment save shovels, ropes and buckets; the primitive technology required much more labor for a given amount of coal. With bootleg coal priced below commercial coal, the bootleggers ended with a wage of about $14 a week. Had the bootleg competition cut seriously into regular producers' profits, the latter would have had to cut their wages, thus worsening conditions of employed miners and turning them against the bootleggers. And with no money for safety devices, the bootleggers faced an accident rate far worse even than that of ordinary miners.

Desperate revolt was by no means limited to the unemployed. As wages were cut again and again, strikes broke out and spread spontaneously. In High Point, North Carolina, for example, a few hundred stocking boarders walked out at six hosiery mills one July morning in 1932 when the second wage cut of the year was posted at their mills. Other hosiery workers joined and by the end of the day 1,600 had walked out. The next day bands of strikers and unemployed workers marched through High Point and nearby Kernersville, Jamestown, Lexington and Thomasville, closing 100 factories of all kinds employing 15,000 workers. Next day twenty-five unemployed workers forced their way into a High Point moviehouse and demanded admission, saying that they were out of work and entitled to entertainment. When the police drove them out, they wrecked a motor and turned off the town's electricity, "to teach the big fellows that we hain't going to stand for no more bad treatment." [7] The hosiery strike was finally settled through the intervention of the Governor, with a rescinding of the wage cut. Out of the conflict developed the Industrial Association of High Point, a union open to all industrial workers in the city, with 4,000 members and committees in each of the mills.

Although trade union strikes were rare and ineffectual during the early years of the depression, such spontaneous revolts developed in all parts of the country. As Charles R. Walker foresaw, there were

increasing outbursts of employed and unemployed alike—a kind of spontaneous democracy expressing itself in organized demonstrations by large masses of people. I use the word organized and I use the word democracy advisedly. They will not be mobs—though the police will often break them up—but will march and meet in order, elect their own spokesmen and committees, and work out in detail their demands for work or relief. They will present their formulated needs to factory superintendents, relief commissions, and city councils, and to the government at Washington . . . Another social tendency . . . is to suppress by any means at hand this rough-and-ready democracy. Meetings, marches, unions, and councils will be greeted in many cases—as they were in Detroit—with bullets and not relief. . . . As long as the American crisis lasts these two political tendencies —"spontaneous but organized" protest, and suppression by violence—will fight it out. [8]

Leftist organizations received little support in the early years of the Depression, but it was widely felt that such spontaneous mass action would become a revolutionary movement if conditions continued to worsen. As one unemployed organizer wrote of the coal bootleggers,

All that is really necessary for the workers to do in order to end their miseries is to perform such simple things as to take from where there is, without regard to established property principles or social philosophies, and to start to produce for themselves. Done on a broad social scale it will lead to lasting results; on a local, isolated plane it will be either defeated, or remain an unsuccessful attempt unable to serve the needs of the working class. When the large masses face a similar general situation as the Pennsylvania miners faced in their specific case, we have every reason to assume that they will react in the same way. The bootleg miners have shown in a rather clear and impressive way, that the so much bewailed absence of a socialist ideology on the part of the workers, really does not prevent workers from acting quite anti-capitalistically, quite in accordance with their own needs. Breaking through the confines of private property in order to live up to their own necessities, the miners' action is, at the same time a manifestation of the most important part of class consciousness—namely, that the problems of the workers can be solved only by themselves.[9]

At this point Franklin Roosevelt, the New Deal, and the National Recovery Administration offered workers the hope that they would not have to solve their problems by themselves. From the day of his first inaugural address, Roosevelt captured the imagination and confidence of the nation with the promise of government action to meet the social crisis. He acted quickly to end the financial panic that had closed the nation's banks by putting the credit of the U.S. government behind them. He created a national relief system which effectively prevented mass starvation in the face of the virtual breakdown of local welfare resources, and established public works programs to provide employment, going far to pacify the unemployed. Many workers developed an almost religious faith in the new President. From the Carolinas, Martha Gellhorn wrote,

Every house I visited—mill worker or unemployed—had a picture of the President. These ranged from newspaper clippings (in destitute homes) to large colored prints, framed in gilt cardboard. The portrait holds the place of honour over the mantel; I can only compare this to the Italian peasant's Madonna.[10]

One central feature of the early New Deal was the National Recovery Administration. The NRA was largely modelled on the War Industries Board of World War I, of which its head, General Hugh S. Johnson, had been an official. The National Recovery Act was in essence a suspension of the anti-trust laws which allowed trade associations for each industry to fix prices and establish production quotas for each company. A "Code of Fair Competition" was established for each industry, with a Code Authority to enforce the agreements and set minimum wages and maximum hours. Following the precedent of World War I, (and with the tacit support of the U.S. Chamber of Commerce), labor support for the program was won by including as Section 7A of the National Recovery Act the provision that

employees shall have the right to organize and bargain collectively through representatives of their own choosing, and shall be free from the interference, restraint or coercion of employers. . . . [11]

Until the formation of the NRA, the American trade union movement had become practically defunct. The A.F.L. had failed to combat the layoffs and wage cuts that accompanied the Great Depression, and membership, far from increasing with popular discontent, went down with the slump. Workers had largely lost interest in trade unions and had turned on a considerable scale to

150 various forms of direct action. But with Section 7A guaranteeing the right to organize and appearing to make trade unionism part of the President's plan for economic recovery, workers throughout the country rushed to join unions, with high hopes that Roosevelt and the A.F.L. would cure their ills. In the Appalachian hills they sang

> When you all work for the NRA
> You work shorter hours and get the same pay
> Sweet thing, baby mine.[12]

The great mass of unorganized industrial workers flooded into such industrial unions as the United Mine Workers, and where none existed, they joined the newly formed "federal locals" directly under the A.F.L. In 1933, the United Mine Workers signed up tens of thousands of members simply on the slogan, "The President wants you to join the union"—admitting only if challenged that they meant the president of the union, not of the United States.

2. Nineteen Thirty-Four

With the passage of Section 7A, longshoremen in San Francisco, like workers elsewhere, began pouring into the available unions. During July and August, 1933, nearly ninety-five percent of the San Francisco longshoremen joined the International Longshoremen's Association.[13] Their greatest grievance was the shape-up, a system of hiring which the longshoremen referred to as "the slave market." Every morning at 6 a.m., everyone seeking a day's work longshoring would crowd along the Embarcadero, where the foremen would pick out those they wanted for the day. The effect was that longshoremen could never count on steady work, had to suck up to or even bribe the foremen, and had to work to exhaustion or not be hired again, Yet the I.L.A. into which they flooded made no attempt to challenge the shape-up.

Consequently the more militant workers began forming a rank-and-file movement within the union. (Its most prominent figure was an Australian, Harry Bridges, and it included many members of the Communist Party.) The rank-and-file movement forced the calling of a West Coast convention in February, 1934, from which paid officers of the union were excluded as delegates, and forced union officials to accept a program they had no desire to fight for: abolition of the shape-up and its replacement by a union hiring hall, with a strike if this was not accepted within two weeks.

Faced with a strike, the Waterfront Employers Association made a somewhat vague offer to recognize the I.L.A. and set up a

dispatching hall whose control was not specified. The I.L.A. leaders accepted the proposal, whereupon the membership repudiated
it and suspended the local president for being "too conservative."
On May 9th, longshoremen in Bellingham, Seattle, Tacoma, Aber-
deen, Portland, Astoria, San Francisco, Oakland, Stockton, San Pe-
dro and San Diego struck, cutting off nearly 2,000 miles of coast-
land.

The lines of the conflict rapidly began to spread. The employers imported large numbers of strikebreakers—eventually 1,700,
many of them recruited from the University of California—to un-
load the ships. The strikebreakers were housed in floating board-
ing houses (which were rapidly boycotted by union employees) and
thus protected from pickets; those who sneaked ashore, however,
were systematically brutalized by the strikers. Strikebreaking
would have seriously threatened the strike, but within four days
mass meetings of Teamsters in San Francisco, Los Angeles, Oakland and Seattle decided overwhelmingly not to haul goods to and
from the docks, thus making the strikebreakers' efforts fruitless;
many of the Teamsters joined the picket lines as well. In San Francisco, as much as seventy percent of the Teamsters' work was on
the waterfront. The feelings stirred by seeing the struggle of the
longshoremen, combined with their own fear that if the longshoremen were broken the Teamsters would be attacked next, gave them
strong motivation for sympathetic action. Before long the strike began to idle unrelated industries; lumber mills shut down in Oregon,
for example, because they were unable to ship their products.

At the same time, the strike spread to other maritime workers.
As ships came to port, entire crews walked off and joined the longshoremen. By May 21st, 4,500 sailors, marine firemen, water ten-
ders, cooks, stewards and licensed officers had struck. They established a Joint Marine Strike Committee with five representatives
from each of the ten unions involved. Breaking a tradition of scab-
bing on each other, each agreed not to return to work until the others had settled.

Meanwhile, the longshoremen resisted numerous efforts by
government and union officials to get them to work without the union hiring hall. At the outset the strike had been postponed at the
request of President Roosevelt, who appointed a Federal Mediation Board; the proposal this Board worked out with the employers
and West Coast leaders of the I.L.A. was repudiated by the rank
and file, who went ahead and struck anyway. Next Assistant
Secretary of Labor Ed McGrady, Roosevelt's top mediator, flew to
San Francisco and asked the longshoremen to empower their
negotiating committee to enter a final settlement; but the San

152   Francisco local voted unanimously to refuse and to require any
agreement to be ratified by the strikers themselves. Then Joseph
Ryan, president of the I.L.A., flew to San Francisco and announced
absurdly that "the only vital point at issue" was "recognition of the
I.L.A." When he negotiated a settlement similar to past proposals,
he was met with catcalls and voted down almost unanimously by
the I.L.A. locals in Portland and San Francisco. [14] Two weeks later
Ryan signed a new agreement to send the longshoremen back to
work; Michael Casey and Dave Beck, San Francisco and Seattle
Teamster bosses, guaranteed the agreement by promising to resume working on the docks; but Ryan was again booed down by his
own membership, which rejected the agreement by acclamation at
a mass meeting in San Francisco, Finally, President Roosevelt appointed a National Longshoremen's Board to mediate the conflict.

Pacification efforts notwithstanding, the conflict itself grew
steadily more violent. On the first day of the strike, police broke up
a 500-man picket line. On May 28th, pickets armed with brickbats
fought police, who ended the battle by firing with sawed-off shotguns directly into the pickets after failing to quell them with billy
clubs and tear gas. As the *Clarion*, organ of the conservative Central Labor Council, put it,

> To parade strike-breakers through the streets on the way to the docks un-
> der police guard and to use public property and city employees in convey-
> ing these outcasts to their nefarious work was an invitation to vio-
> lence. . . . [15]

After forty-five days, San Francisco's economy was reeling,
and the business community decided the time had come to break
the strike. At a meeting on June 23rd, representatives of the Industrial Association, Chamber of Commerce, Police Commissioners,
Chief of Police, and Harbor Commissioners agreed to open the port,
with the assurance of the Chief of Police that "every available police officer in San Francisco will be detailed to the waterfront to
give the necessary protection." [16] On July 3rd a cordon of freight
cars was set up and 700 policemen armed with tear gas and riot
guns. A police captain brandishing a revolver declared, "The port
is open," and five trucks manned by strikebreakers rolled from the
pier toward the warehouses. Thousands of strikers and sympathizers
on the picket line attacked the police lines. As the *New York Times*
described it,

> Mounted and foot police swung their clubs and hurled tear-gas bombs,
> strikers hurled bricks and rocks, battered heads with clubs and railroad
> spikes and smashed windows. . . . Mounted and foot police relentlessly
> drove the pickets behind these freightcar barriers. The safety line remain-
> ed intact but on its fringes pandemonium raged. [17]

Twenty-five people were hospitalized as a result of the battle, about half pickets, half police.

After the Independence Day holiday, battle resumed July 5th. In the morning police charged 2,000 pickets who had gathered to stop trucks coming off the pier, and dispersed them after an hour and a half of street and barricade fighting. By the afternoon a crowd of 5,000 gathered, and when the police could no longer control them with gas, they switched to guns on a large scale. The crowd grew increasingly furious in the face of police shootings, and when the word spread that evening that the National Guard would take over the waterfront that evening, they made a last concerted effort to seize the belt-line railway on the waterfront before the troops arrived. Unarmed demonstrators were no match for the police, however, and were driven back in a bloody battle. One reporter wrote, "It was as close to actual war as anything but war itself could be." [18] Two strikers and a bystander were killed, 115 people were hospitalized.

That night the Governor of California ordered in 1,700 National Guardsmen, who enclosed the Embarcadero with barbed wire and machine gun nests, patrolled the area with armored cars, and were given orders to shoot to kill. Under this protection, freight moved steadily from the docks to the warehouses. The balance of forces had shifted decisively against the strikers; as Harry Bridges said, "We cannot stand up against police, machine guns, and National Guard bayonets." [19]

But the conflict had generated a whole new body of allies for the strikers. In the early weeks of June, the feeling had begun to spread among San Francisco workers that a general strike might be necessary to back up the longshoremen. The strikebreaking activities of the police daily roused their ire. A general strike was felt as a way of expressing their power against all employers. Even relatively conservative workers felt the need to protect themselves against the employer offensive; The *Clarion* wrote:

Workers in other groups have been impelled to stand behind the marine and waterfront workers under the general belief that they represented the 'shock troops' in a general defense of the Trade Union position against the assault upon the union shop and for the installation of the "open shop," even in industries which had recognized union contracts for generations. [20]

In mid-June, the Painters Local circulated a letter among A.F.L. unions requesting support for a general strike if necessary. On June 20th the Machinists Local voted to join such a strike when called. The longshoremen began sending first small committees and then mass delegations of fifty to four hundred men to other

154 unions asking for support by a vote for a general strike.

The movement for a general strike did not become irresistable, however, until after the violent opening of the port. The street fighting itself had roused a spirit of combat, and the killing of unarmed strikers by police roused the resentment of virtually all the city's workers. The sending in of the National Guard to break the strike aggravated them still further. And with every other tactic defeated, a general strike was evidently the only means by which the longshoremen could be saved from defeat.

The day after the entry of the National Guard, the Joint Marine Strike Committee appealed for a general strike. Next day fourteen unions in San Francisco voted to strike in sympathy with the longshoremen, and similar sentiment developed in Portland and Seattle. At the crucial meeting of the Teamsters, Local President Casey warned the drivers that their contract restricted and their union constitution forbade sympathetic strikes, but they voted 1,220 to 271 to strike Thursday, July 12th, if the maritime strike had not been settled. "Nothing on earth," Casey said, "could have prevented that vote. In all my thirty years of leading these men I have never seen them so worked up." [21]

On July 9th, a mass funeral procession for the strikers killed in the opening of the port rallied tens of thousands. As Paul Eliel, director of industrial relations for the Employers' Industrial Association, later wrote, "the funeral was one of the strangest and most dramatic that had ever moved along Market Street." It created a "tremendous wave of sympathy for the workers," and with it "a general strike . . . became for the first time a practical and realizable objective." [22] By July 12th, twenty-one unions had voted to strike, most of them unanimously. At a second mass meeting the Teamsters sang, "We'll hang Michael Casey from a sour apple tree," and shouted him down when he argued passionately against a strike. [23]

By Thursday, a partial general strike was under way; 4,000 Bay Area Teamsters walked out and picketed the roads entering the city, stopping all trucks except those carrying such exempted goods as milk, bread and laundry. In the city, Teamsters established a system of strike exemptions — as in Seattle in 1919:

San Francisco's food and gasoline problems . . . were taken to the Teamster's Union. . . . Emissaries of corporations and hospitals made their way through the crowd of striking truck drivers up the dingy stairs and waited their turn at the door behind which union officials sat. . . . Anyone not a representative in some way of a charitable institution or hospital was turned away with curt words before he reached that door, usually to the accompaniment of jeering laughter. . . . Union truck placards were granted without ado to the hospitals. [24]

Restaurants began to shut down. Next day 2,500 taxi drivers were scheduled to walk out. Cleaners and dryers struck for their own demands. Boilermarkers in sixty shops left their jobs.

The Central Labor Council was now faced with a general strike of which it wanted no part. Three weeks before it had passed a resolution condemning the "Communist" leadership of the maritime strikers, and resolutions calling for a general strike had been ruled out of order at its meetings week after week. After the forcible opening of the port, when the Joint Maritime Strike Committee had appealed for a general strike, the Central Labor Council did not even take up the question. Instead, it appointed a "Strike Strategy Committee" of seven conservative union officials, none of them from the striking unions. "The action of the conservative element in the labor council in naming the strike strategy committee . . . successfully sidetracked the plan of more radical groups to incite and promote a general walkout immediately," the *New York Times* reported.[25] The Committee was appointed to kill the strike, not to organize it.

The momentum of general strike sentiment was too great, however, for the city's A.F.L. leadership to head off. When a convention called by the Strike Strategy Committee met Friday, July 13th, the general strike, though not yet complete, was already a fact. The convention, with five members from each union, voted 315-15 for a general strike. By Monday, the strike deadline, virtually all San Francisco unions except the Bakery Wagon and Milk Wagon Drivers — who were instructed to stay at work — had voted to join the strike. The Oakland Central Labor Council similarly voted for a general strike. The movement spread up the Pacific Coast; in Portland the Central Labor Council voted for a general strike, but left the date to a Strategy Committee.

Unable to stop the strike, the leadership of the San Francisco Central Labor Council decided to assume direction in order to bring it to an end as quickly as possible. They established a General Strike Committee of Twenty-five, all conservatives. The head was Vandeleur, who as chairman of the Labor Council had consistently opposed the strike, and the vice-chairman was C.W. Deal. Deal was head of the Ferryboatmen's union, one of the few in the city not to join the strike. Vandeleur was head of the Municipal Streetcar Workers' Union; when his members walked out on Monday he ordered them back to work on the grounds that they were breaking civil service contracts; he thus created the first breach of the strike the very first day. The General Strike Committee made no provision for meeting the needs of the strikers and the city's population, but instead issued an ever-increasing number of

156 strike exemptions, which created the impression that the strike was dissolving. They also organized their own strike police to keep pickets from interfering with those they had sent back to work.

According to the press, Harry Bridges planned to recommend—

the immediate establishment of food distribution depots in every section of the city, with sub-committees of strikers to prevent profiteering, to regulate distribution of vegetables and fruit, and to prevent hardship.[26]

But this system never developed. Bridges concluded, "The general strike was broken by the return of the carmen and the lifting of restrictions upon food and gasoline." And as an article in *Editor and Publisher* pointed out, the bitterly anti-strike newspapers fully realized and abetted the objective of the labor leaders: "Newspaper editorials built up the strength and influence of the conservative leaders and aided in splitting the conservative membership away from the radicals..."[27]

Nevertheless, the strike effectively crippled the life of the city. Some 130,000 workers were out. With taxis, trolleys, and street railway workers out and gasoline for private cars embargoed by the strikers, transportation in the Bay Area virtually stopped. Many small shops closed down in sympathy with the strike or because delivery of goods had stopped. Food trucks were given permits to enter the city and markets remained open; a limited number of restaurants were permitted to run; gasoline was supplied for doctors; electric power workers and newspaper printers continued to work. The violence which had raged for weeks came to a halt with the general strike.

The strike was met with a powerful counter-attack. Five hundred special police were sworn in and the National Guard contingent was raised to 4,500, complete with infantry, machine gun, tank and artillery units; state officials were poised on the edge of declaring martial law. The leading California publishers set up a headquarters at the Palace Hotel and undertook a coordinated attack on the strike, combining a desire to weaken trade unions with an effort to embarrass President Roosevelt and a real fear that the general strike was the beginning of a revolt that might sweep the country. Typical was an editorial in the *Los Angeles Times:*

The situation in San Francisco is not correctly described by the phrase "general strike." What is actually in progress there is an insurrection, a Communist-inspired and led revolt against organized government. There is but one thing to be done—put down the revolt with any force necessary.[28]

The NRA chief, General Johnson, arrived in town and after meeting with the publishers declared the general strike a "menace to the government" and "civil war." The Governor declared that

the general strike "challenges the authority of government to maintain itself," and Senator Hiram Johnson, California's elder states-
man, declared, "Here is revolution not only in the making but with
the initial actualities." [29] President Roosevelt followed the strike
closely, but felt it had been provoked by the employers and saw no
need to intervene for, as Secretary of Labor Perkins informed him,
the General Strike Committee of Twenty-five was "in charge of
the whole strike . . . and represents conservative leadership." [30]

On July 17th, Charles Wheeler, vice-president of the McCor-
mick Steamship Lines, said that raids on radical centers would
start soon, with government consent. That day a series of vigilante
raids began up and down the coast on the Marine Workers Industrial Union, the Ex-Service Men's League, the Western Worker,
and many other radical organizations and gathering places. According to the *New York Times,* the vigilantes "were connected
with the Committee of 500 organized by prominent citizens at the
behest of Mayor Rossi." [31] The raids followed a regular pattern:
men in leather jackets drove up, broke in, smashed windows, furniture and typewriters, and beat up those within; the police invariably arrived just after the attackers departed and arrested those they
had beaten. U.S. Army and immigration officials interrogated
many of those arrested and held some of them for possible deportation. Radicals faced a virtual reign of terror.

The general strike succeeded in preventing the crushing of the
longshoremen for the moment, but the Labor Council leadership began maneuvering to bring it to an end almost before it began. On
July 18th, President Green of the A.F.L. disowned the strike. The
second day of the strike the General Strike Committee called for
arbitration of all issues, thus giving up the basic demand which the
strike was all about, the union hiring hall. The third day it reopened all union restaurants and butcher shops and ended embar-
goes on gasoline and fuel oil. This generated irresistable pressures
on those still striking for, as the strike strategy committee in the
East Bay declared, "it would be unfair to the unions to continue the
strike in view of the return of some San Francisco organizations to
work." By the fourth day, the General Strike Committee voted 191
to 174 to end the general strike.[32]

With the end of the general strike, the longshoremen were
forced to accept arbitration of all issues by the Longshoremen's
Board. The Board established jointly operated hiring halls with union dispatchers but employer choice among available workers.
Each employer won the right "to introduce labor-saving devices
and to institute such methods of discharging and loading cargo as
he considers best suited to the conduct of his business." [33]

158   This far from ended the struggle on the waterfront, however, for the longshoremen now moved to direct action on the job to fight the speed-up authorized in the 1934 settlement. A journalist described the conflicts which followed:

> . . . every dock gang elected from among themselves a so-called gang or dock steward . . . There were endless disputes, some resulting in "job action" on the part of workers or quick strikes ("quickies") localized to one dock. Suddenly, in the midst of unloading a ship, the longshore gang would walk off, causing the stubborn employer sailing delay, considerable additional expense, and general irritation . . .
>
> . . . the employer called the union hiring-hall for another gang, which came promptly enough, but as likely as not pulled another "quicky" an hour later; and so on, till the employer yielded to, say, a demand that the slingload be made two or three thousand instead of four thousand pounds.[34]

Between January 1st, 1937, and August 1st, 1938, more than 350 such work stoppages occurred in the maritime industry on the Pacific Coast.[35]

Another bloody struggle broke out at the auto parts plant in Toledo, Ohio. The local A.F.L. union struck, went back, and on April 12th, 1934, struck again. Fewer than half the workers joined the strike, and the employers hired strikebreakers and kept the plants running. Under such conditions the strike seemed doomed to failure, until a large number of unemployed began joining the picket lines. As a newspaperman wrote privately,

> The point about Toledo was this: that it is nothing new to see organized unemployed appear in the streets, fight police, and raise hell in general. But usually they do this for their own ends, to protest against unemployment or relief conditions. At Toledo they appeared on the picket lines to help striking employees win a strike, though you would expect their interest would lie the other way—that is, in going down and getting the jobs the other men had laid down.[36]

The Lucas County Unemployed League was affiliated with the American Workers Party, a small radical organization led by A.J. Muste, which emphasized mutual support of employed and unemployed workers, and A.W.P. leaders played an important part in the conflict.

When the strikers and unemployed blocked the plant gates with mass picketing, the employers got an injunction limiting them to twenty-five pickets at each gate. The Unemployed League, determined to "smash the injunction," continued picketing, and when leaders were arrested for contempt of court, hundreds of unem-

Police and deputies chase strikers near the Auto-Lite plant in Toledo, Ohio, May 23rd, 1934. The unemployed of Toledo joined with Auto-Lite workers to "smash the injunction" against mass picketing.

One of those shot by National Guardsmen in the Auto-Lite strike. Two were killed and fifteen wounded in a single battle. More soldiers were called up than ever before in Ohio in peacetime.

ployed packed the courtroom and cheered and sang as the trial progressed. On May 21st, 1,000 gathered for a noon mass meeting at the gates of the Toledo Auto-Lite plant; next day 4,000 came to the noon rally, and the third day 6,000.

At this point, Sheriff David Krieger decided, as he later testified in court, that the time had come to take the offensive. Unwilling to rely on the local police, who were disaffected themselves and sympathetic to the strikers, he deputized special police, paid for by

National Guardsmen attacked the picket lines and evacuated strikebreakers from Auto-Lite plants, but were driven back by the crowds. Guardsmen advanced again with bayonets; they were ordered to fire.

Auto-Lite. He then began arresting pickets, and a deputy began beating an old man in front of a crowd of 10,000 which had gathered. This was too much for the crowd, which proceeded to surround the Auto-Lite plant, holding 1,500 strikebreakers inside. The special deputies dropped tear gas on the crowd from the plant and attacked them with fire hoses, iron bars and some gunfire. The crowd systematically collected bricks and stones, deposited them in piles around the streets, and heaved them through the factory windows. Three times the strikers broke into the factory and were driven out in hand-to-hand fighting. The battle raged for seven hours.

At dawn next morning 900 National Guardsmen, complete

with machine-gun units, were rushed into Toledo from elsewhere in the state — Sheriff Krieger being unwilling to call up the local Guard. The Guardsmen evacuated the strikebreakers from the plant, but failed to intimidate the crowds, who stoned them and drove them against the factory walls. The Guardsmen advanced with bayonets. The crowd drove them back again, and were in turn pushed back with bayonets. As the crowd advanced the third time the troops were ordered to fire; they let go, killing two and wounding fifteen. Even this did not disperse the crowd, which attacked again that night and was again fired on by the Guard. Only the sending of four more militia companies to the plant — more troops than ever seen in Ohio before in peacetime — and the agreement of the companies to close down finally pacified the situation. Meanwhile, eighty-five local unions pledged themselves to support a general strike in sympathy with another dispute, growing from the demands of workers at the electric power company. The strike was headed off when the company offered a twenty-two percent wage increase and union recognition.

Leaders of the unemployed were arrested and one was seized by the Guard and held incommunicado. With their plants closed, the auto parts makers finally agreed to recognize the union, grant a wage increase, and rehire the strikers. Rehiring proceeded slowly as the plants reopened until a crowd began gathering at the Auto-Lite gates and the company, fearing a renewal of direct action, re-hired all the strikers at once.

Meanwhile, in Minneapolis there developed a conflict which clearly demonstrated the process of polarization of social classes occurring throughout the country. Early in 1934, Teamsters who worked in Minneapolis coalyards struck, caught the employers by surprise, and closed down sixty-five of the town's sixty-seven coal yards; the employers capitulated in three days and granted recognition for Teamsters Local 574. The local held a catch-all charter making it virtually industrial in character, and truckdrivers and helpers in all trades began pouring in. Unofficial leadership for the unions was given by the Dunne brothers and Karl Skogeland, who were American followers of Leon Trotsky. When the truckers refused to sign any agreement with the union, the Teamsters voted at a mass meeting May 12th to strike. Most businesses were hit by the strike — general and department stores, groceries, bakeries, cleaners and laundries, meat and provision houses, all building materials; all wholesale houses, all factories; gas and oil companies, stations and attendants; breweries, truck transfer and warehouses; all

162   common carriers. As the Sheriff later put it, "They had the town
tied up tight. Not a truck could move in Minneapolis." The only exceptions were the unionized milk, ice and coal companies, which
were given strike exemptions.[37]

The key tactic of the strike was the "flying squadron," a system of mobile pickets operating out of the strike headquarters, an
old garage rented for the strike. There were never less than 500
strikers at the headquarters, day or night. In the dispatchers' room
four telephones took in messages from picket captains throughout
the city with instructions to call in every ten minutes.

> Truck attempting to move load of produce from Berman Fruit, under
> police convoy. Have only ten pickets, send help.

> Successfully turned back five trucks entering city. . . . Am returning
> Cars 42 and 46 to headquarters.[38]

On the basis of such information, the dispatchers sent cars from the
garage wherever they were needed. A motorcycle squad cruised
the city reporting trouble. The strikers listened to police radio instructions on a special short-wave radio, and conducted phone calls
in code when their phones were tapped. Pickets guarded fifty
roads into the city, turning back non-union trucks. A crew of 120
prepared food day and night; at the peak of the strike, 10,000 people ate at the headquarters in a single day. A hospital was established with two doctors and three nurses in constant attendance.
And a machine shop with fifteen auto mechanics kept the 100
trucks and cars of the flying squadrons in repair. Guards policed
the headquarters and watchmen with tommy guns stood guard on
the roof. Constant PA announcements and nightly mass meetings
attended by thousands of strikers and supporters kept strikers in
touch.[39] A rank-and-file committee of 100 truckdrivers formed the
official strike authority.

Support for the strike among other Minneapolis workers
was passionate. Thirty-five thousand building trades workers
walked out in sympathy, as did all the taxi drivers in the city. The
Farm Holiday Association, a militant farmers' organization, made
substantial contributions of food, and other unions contributed to
the strike fund. Hundreds of non-Teamster workers showed up at
strike headquarters daily saying, "Use us, this is our strike."[40]

The city polarized as the business forces, too, began to organize. Leading them was the Citizens' Alliance, one of the most powerful employers' associations in the country, with its own corps of
undercover informers. It was dedicated to keeping unionism out of
Minneapolis and for a generation it had been almost completely
successful. Business leaders developed their own strike headquarters with barracks, hospital and commissary. As the conflict deep-

ened they called for a "mass movement of citizens" to break the strike and began organizing a "citizen's army," [41] many of whose members were deputized as special police.[42] With an unusual clarity, two organized social classes stood face to face, poised for battle.

The battle was seriously joined on Monday, May 21st. A group of men and women pickets had been severely beaten when they were sent into a police trap by a stool pigeon who had infiltrated the strike headquarters. One striker described the effect thus:

Nobody had carried any weapon or club in the first days of the strike. We went unarmed but we'd learned our lesson. All over headquarters you'd see guys making saps or sawing off lead pipe . . .[43]

As the citizens' army began to occupy the market and move trucks, the strikers hit with military precision. A strike leader described it:

We built up our reserves in this way. At short time intervals during an entire day we sent fifteen or twenty pickets pulled in from all over the city into the Central Labor Union headquarters on Eighth Street. So that although nobody knew it, we had a detachment of six hundred men there, each armed with clubs, by Monday morning. Another nine hundred or so we held in reserve at strike headquarters. In the market itself, pickets without union buttons were placed in key positions. There remained scattered through the city, at their regular posts, only a skeleton picket line. The men in the market were in constant communication through motorcycles and telephone with headquarters. The special deputies [citizens' army] were gradually pushed by our pickets to one side and isolated from the cops. When that was accomplished the signal was given and the six hundred men poured out of Central Labor Union headquarters. They marched in military formation, four abreast, each with their clubs, to the market. They kept on coming. When the socialites, the Alfred Lindleys and the rest who had expected a little picnic with a mad rabble, saw this bunch, they began to get some idea what the score was. Then we called on the pickets from strike headquarters who marched into the center of the market and encircled the police. They [the police] were put right in the center with no way out. At intervals we made sallies on them to separate a few. This kept up for a couple of hours, till finally they drew their guns. We had anticipated this would happen, and that then the pickets would be unable to fight them. You can't lick a gun with a club. The correlation of forces becomes a little unbalanced. So we picked out a striker, a big man and utterly fearless, and sent him in a truck with twenty-five pickets. He was instructed to drive right into the formation of cops and stop for nothing. We knew he'd do it. Down the street he came like a bat out of hell, with his horn honking and into the market arena. The cops held up their hands for him to stop, but he kept on; they gave way and he was in the middle of them. The pickets jumped out on the cops. We figured by intermixing with the cops in hand-to-hand fighting, they would not use their guns because they would have to shoot cops as well as strikers. Cops don't like to do that.

164   Casualties for the day included for the strikers a broken collar bone, the cut-open skull of a picket who swung on a cop and hit a striker by mistake as the cop dodged, and a couple of broken ribs. On the other side, roughly thirty cops were taken to the hospital.[44]

The Monday battle was not decisive, however, and the reserves on both sides mobilized in the market again the next day. An extra 500 special police were sworn in, and according to Charles R. Walker's study of the strike, *An American City,* "Nearly every worker who could afford to be away from his job that day, and some who couldn't, planned to be on hand in the market."[45] Twenty to thirty thousand people showed up. No battle was planned; the melee began when a merchant started to move crates of tomatoes and a picket threw them through his store window. The pickets, armed with lead pipes and clubs, fought viciously with the police, driving them out of the market within an hour, then continuing to battle them all over the city. By nightfall there were no police to be seen in Minneapolis. Strikers were directing downtown traffic.

After the "Battle of Deputies Run," a settlement of sorts was patched together by the Governor and Federal mediators, leaving the real issues unsettled, and events moved toward a second strike.

Strikers applied military tactics in battle with police and "Citizen's Army" during 1934 Minneapolis teamsters strike. Workers marched in military formation between the two forces, then sallied in among police to break them up.

The Chief of Police requested a virtual doubling of his budget to add 400 men to the force, to maintain a training school, and to buy machine guns, rifles and bayonets, steel helmets, riot clubs and motorcycles. The employers sponsored an enormous press and radio campaign against the union, stressing an attack by the head of the International Brotherhood of Teamsters calling the local leadership Communistic. The workers laid in food for a forty-day seige.

On July 5th the largest mass meeting in the history of Minneapolis, preceded by a march of farmer and labor groups with two airplanes flying overhead, mobilized support for the Teamsters and displayed the forces that would support them in the event of another showdown. When the Teamsters struck again on July 16th, they re-established in still more perfected form the strike organization, published a hugely popular strike daily paper (circulation went from nothing to 10,000 in two days), and kept farmer support by allowing all members of farmers' organizations to drive their trucks into town and establish their own market.

The first few days of the strike were peaceful, then the police tried to break it by terror. On July 20th, a truck accompanied by fifty police armed with shotguns started moving in the market. A second truck with ten pickets arrived and cut across the convoy's path. The police opened fire, and within ten minutes sixty-seven persons, including thirteen bystanders, were wounded, two fatally. A commission appointed by the Governor to investigate the "riot" later concluded:

> Police took direct aim at the pickets and fired to kill.
> Physical safety of police was at no time endangered. . . .
> At no time did pickets attack the police. . . .
> The truck movement in question was not a serious attempt to move merchandise, but a "plant" arranged by the police.
> The police department did not act as an impartial police force to enforce law and order, but rather became an agency to break the strike.
> Police actions have been to discredit the strike and the Truck Drivers' Union so that public sentiment would be against the strikers.[46]

These actions were hardly accidental. As the secretary of the Citizens Alliance, whose leaders met with the Police Chief just before the attack, stated later,

> Nobody likes to see bloodshed, but I tell you after the police had used their guns on July 20 we felt that the strike was breaking. . . . There are very few men who will stand up in a strike when there is a question of they themselves getting killed.[47]

That night an enormous protest meeting ended in a march on City Hall to lynch the Mayor and Police Chief. The march was headed off by National Guard troops. This, together with a huge mass funeral for one of the killed pickets—attended by an esti-mated 50,000 to 100,000—revealed that whatever its intentions, the massacre had strengthened rather than undermined the workers' determination and solidarity.

In this situation Farmer-Labor Governor Floyd B. Olson—who had personally contributed $500 to the strike fund and declared, "I am not a liberal . . . I am a radical"—declared martial law. The Governor's official policy was that neither pickets nor trucks (ex-cept those delivering food) would operate; but by the second day of martial law, military authorities announced that "more than half the trucks in Hennepin County were operating."[48] Faced with the imminent breaking of the strike, the workers decided at a mass meeting attended by 25,000 to resume picketing in defiance of the Governor and the National Guard. The Governor replied by sur-rounding the strike headquarters at 4 a.m., August 1st, occupying it, arresting most of the top strike leaders, and instructing the rank and file to elect new leaders. The strikers replied with intensified picketing. As the press reported:

> Marauding bands of pickets roamed the streets of Minneapolis today in automobiles and trucks, striking at commercial truck movement in widespread sections of the city. . . . National Guardsmen in squad cars made frantic efforts to clamp down. The continued picketing was regarded as a protest over the military arrest of Brown and the Dunnes, strike leaders, together with 68 others during and after Guardsmen raided strike headquarters and the Central Labor Union.[49]

Charles Walker wrote, "The strike's conduct had been such that a thousand lesser leaders had come out of the ranks and the pickets themselves by this time had learned their own jobs. The ar-rest of the leaders, instead of beheading the movement, infused it, at least temporarily, with demoniac fury." [50] As one worker said, "We established 'curb headquarters' all over the city. We had twen-ty of them." [51]

In the face of this situation, the Governor was forced to back down. He released the captured leaders, turned back the strike headquarters, and raided the Citizens Alliance to save face with his labor constituents. The strike continued and with the city reel-ing after a month of conflict the employers succumbed to the enor-mous pressures for a settlement and capitulated. The strike sup-porters celebrated with a twelve-hour binge.

The most extensive conflict of the NRA period was the nation-al textile strike of 1934. The Depression hit the textile industry long before the rest of society and by early 1929 the mill towns, especial-

In second battle, Minneapolis strikers totally routed police, and ended the day patrolling the streets and directing traffic themselves. Workers first began making saps and clubs a few days before when pickets had been lured into a trap and severely beaten.

168 ly in the South, were seething with discontent. The great grievance was the "stretch-out"; at one mill at Monroe, North Carolina, for example, spinners were required to work twelve rather than eight spindles, four doffers did the work of five, and crews of four carders were cut to three. The result, as Herbert J. Lahne wrote in *The Cotton Mill Worker,* was that, "a powder train of strikes flashed through an astonished South," many of them "without unionism at all and . . . under purely local leadership whose main concern was . . . the stretch-out." [52] We have described above one such explosion at High Point, North Carolina.

With the coming of NRA, textile workers flooded into the United Textile Workers union; its paper membership went from 27,500 in 1932 to 270,000 in 1934. The NRA Cotton Textile Industry Committee was headed by George Sloan, who happened to be the chief industry spokesman as well. The code set a minimum wage of twelve dollars per week in the South and thirteen dollars in the North. It utterly failed to prevent more stretch-out, or to stop employers from firing workers who joined the union.[53] Further, in order to restrict over-production, the NRA ordered a cut-back to thirty hours a week per shift, cutting wages by twenty-five percent. The U.T.W. threatened to strike the industry, but withdrew the threat in exchange for a seat on the Cotton Textile Industrial Relations Board and a government "study" of the industry.

Textile workers were furious at the union's backdown. For the Southern cotton mill workers, as Irving Bernstein put it, "NRA had become a gigantic fraud." [54] In Alabama, forty of forty-two U.T.W. locals voted to strike, and 20,000 workers walked out on July 16th, 1934. The president of the U.T.W. advised workers in other states not to join the strike, adding to resentment at the cancellation of the previous strike; "He killed the other strike," a worker in Birmingham remarked, "we're not going to let him kill this one." [55] The strike held solidly, revealing an unexpected commitment and solidarity, and a month later a U.T.W. national convention, with the militant Southern rank and file in control, voted without opposition for a general strike in the industry, and required the officers to call it within two weeks. The workers condemned NRA bitterly and were only kept from boycotting it by a special appeal from union officers and prominent outsiders.

The strike began in North Carolina on Labor Day, September 3rd, 1934, when 65,000 workers walked out. That day National Guardsmen were ordered to guard three mills in South Carolina where the strike was expected next day. The workers not only quit work, but immediately formed "flying squadrons," which moved through the area, closing non-striking mills. A reporter described a typical example:

> Workers in the Shelby, N.C., mills, thoroughly organized, refused to permit the opening of their plants early today, formed a motorcade which swept into King's Mountain, a dozen miles away, and succeeded in closing eleven plants. They met with no resistance and persuaded 2,800 non-union workers to quit their posts.[56]

The strikers' tactics showed great creativity in other ways; for example, at Macon, Georgia (and later at various other points), a group of pickets, many of them women, sat down on a plant railroad track and prevented the movement of trains carrying finished goods. Before and at the start of the strike, mass demonstrations were held throughout the South, such as a meeting of 1,000 at Charlotte, North Carolina, and a parade of 5,000 in Gastonia, North Carolina, designed to show the workers' strength.

The strike spread rapidly throughout the eastern seaboard; newspaper surveys reported 200,000 out on September 4th and 325,000 out the next day.[57] The flying squadrons were largely responsible for the spread:

> Moving with the speed and force of a mechanized army, thousands of pickets in trucks and automobiles scurried about the countryside in the Carolinas, visiting mill towns and villages and compelling the closing of the plants . . . strikers in groups ranging from 200 to 1,000 assembled about mills and demanded that they be closed. . . .

> The speed of the pickets in their motor cavalcades and their surprise descent on point after point makes it difficult to follow their movements and makes impossible any adequate preparation by mill owners or local authorities to meet them.[58]

What happened when the flying squadrons arrived depended on conditions of the moment, the mood of the crowd, the degree of resistance and similar factors. Sometimes they simply picketed peacefully, at others they battled guards, and at times they entered mills, unbelted machinery, broke threads, and fought non-strikers.

Although the flying squadrons created a sensation throughout the country, they were a natural form of action in isolated mill towns. They were at first tolerated and perhaps encouraged by union officials, but as the squadrons led to confrontations, union officials tried to bring them to a halt. Francis Gorman, chairman of the U.T.W. strike committee, repudiated their use and denied that they were ever sanctioned by the national leadership.[59]

Practically from the beginning of the strike, confrontations and small-scale violence developed in numerous places. In Fall River a crowd of 10,000 imprisoned 300 strikebreakers in a mill, and in

Deputies attack a crowd of pickets at the Tube Company Plant near Pittsburgh in 1933. Strikes in the early Depression were often desperate and bloody.

Library of Congress

172   North Carolina pickets stormed a mill in which strikebreakers were working. The flying squadrons and other mass actions developed a momentum of their own, and as early as September 5th the *New York Times* warned on page one that "The grave danger of the situation is that it will get completely out of the hands of the leaders. Indications of that were in evidence today." Women were reported "taking an increasingly active part in the picketing, egging on the men," with "the pickets apparently prepared to stop at nothing to obtain their objectives."[60] The *Times* added ominously,

> The growing mass character of the picketing operations is rapidly assuming the appearance of military efficiency and precision and is something entirely new in the history of American labor struggles.
>
> Observers . . . declared that if the mass drive continued to gain momentum at the speed at which it was moving today it will be well nigh impossible to stop it without a similarly organized opposition with all the implications such an attempt would entail.[61]

The opposition was not long in starting. On September 5th, the Governor of North Carolina called out the National Guard to aid local authorities, declaring, "The power of the State has been definitely challenged," and "local authorities have proven unequal to the test." More Guardsmen were ordered out in South Carolina, and on September 9th partial martial law was established in that state.[62] The Governor declared that a "state of insurrection" existed.[63] Mills in the Carolinas were reported "feverishly preparing to resist . . . by mobilizing special guards equipped with shotguns and teargas bombs and by arming workers who remained at the looms."[64] But as a reporter wrote from the storm-center in North Carolina, "Despite efforts of strike leaders to prevail upon the strike pickets 'to put on the brakes,' . . . picketing activity showed no abatement . . . "[65]

More than fifty strike squadrons were in action in the Carolinas, in detachments of 200 to 650. They moved south on a 110-mile front between Gastonia, North Carolina, and Greenville, South Carolina, garrisoning the towns along the line of battle to ensure that the mills would stay closed. As they approached Greenville they were met by National Guardsmen who informed them they had orders to "shoot to kill," but "the strikers, apparently undeterred by the presence of the troops, were determined to capture Greenville . . . "[66] where the strike had not yet spread.

The conflict naturally became more violent, for "the situation was rapidly assuming the character of industrial civil war . . . "[67] On September 5th, a striker and a special deputy were killed in a two-hour battle at a mill in Trion, Georgia (pop. 2,000); a policeman shot three pickets, one fatally, in Augusta; 2,500 textile work-

ers rioted in Lowell, Massachusetts; at Danielson, Connecticut,
Macon, Georgia, and other points, mill officials' cars were attacked.[68] On September 6th at Honea Path, South Carolina, sheriff's deputies and armed strikebreakers fired on pickets:

> Without warning came the first shots, followed by many others, and for a few minutes there was bedlam. Striker after striker fell to the ground, with the cries of wounded men sounding over the field and men and women running shrieking from the scene. [69]

Seven pickets were killed and a score wounded in the attack. The killings were seen as marking "the beginning of the second bloody phase of the strike," as "one town after another reported completion of preparations to resist the flying squads and the picketing activity of the strikers." [70]

Commissaries were set up in various textile centers, and hundreds of strikers canvassed for contributions of food and money. At Hazleton, Pennsylvania, 25,000 workers shut down the town in a one-day general strike on September 11th in support of the textile workers. George Googe, chief A.F.L. representative in the South, urged other workers to give support "without joining the strike," emphasizing that his appeal was not to be interpreted as "a move toward extending the strike to other industries . . . " [71] Workers from other industries joined in many of the confrontations that occurred at mills throughout the country, turning them into community struggles.

Meanwhile, violent conflict spread through New England. The first strike shooting there occurred in Saylesville, Rhode Island, on September 10th. A crowd of 600 pickets attempting to close a mill (particularly hated for having broken previous strikes) was driven back by state troopers with machine guns. A smaller group of pickets then tried to outflank the troopers and attack the rear of the plant; deputy sheriffs opened fire on them with buckshot. Next afternoon a much larger crowd, estimated at 3,000 to 4,000, imprisoned strikebreaking employees in the mill. As the shift was due to end, the crowd surged forward, captured the mill gate, ripped up a fire hydrant, overturned a gate house, and appeared about to take possession of the plant. In reply, deputy sheriffs began firing buckshot with automatic weapons into the crowd, hitting five. Some 280 National Guardsmen then rode into the scene on caissons. They were pelted with paving stones torn up by the pickets as they clubbed their way to the mill. The crowd tried unsuccessfully to capture the pumping station and set fire to the mill.

That night the pickets deployed themselves behind the tombstones of a nearby cemetery, and shouting "Let's get the militia!" 2,000 of them broke through police lines and battled the troops.[72]

174   By the next afternoon, the crowd had grown to 5,000. Hurling pieces of gravestones from the cemetery, they charged the troops and drove them back behind the barbed wire enclosure surrounding the plant. The Guardsmen fired into the crowd, critically wounding three. That night another crowd stoned the Guard, which again fired on them. In the face of such serious disorder, the Sayles plant finally decided to shut down, giving the signal for many other plants in the area to do the same.

   By September 12th, National Guardsmen were on duty in every New England state except Vermont and New Hampshire. At Danielson, Connecticut, 1,500 pickets battled state troopers. A flying squadron of 200 from Fall River, Massachusetts, was turned back from a factory in Dighton, Massachusetts, when they found every approach barricaded with sandbags manned by police and seventy-five special deputies armed with shotguns. Other confrontations occurred at Lawrence and Lowell, Massachusetts, and Lewiston, Maine, but the New England violence reached its peak at Woonsocket, Rhode Island.

   The mill which was the original scene of rioting there had been organized six months before, whereupon the union members were fired, leaving much bitterness behind. The evening of September 12th, Governor Green of Rhode Island read a proclamation over the radio urging rioters to return to their homes. Instead, ever-increasing masses began to pour down on the Woonsocket Rayon Plant in a "sullen and rebellious mood." At midnight a crowd of about 500 let fly a barrage of bricks at the police guards at the plant, then attacked. The police replied with tear gas grenades, many of which were caught and thrown back "with telling effect" by the crowd. Word of the conflict spread, and the crowd grew quickly to 2,000. At this point, National Guardsmen took a hand, firing 30 shots into the front ranks of the crowd, hitting four, one fatally. At the shooting, a correspondent reported, "The crowd went completely wild with rage."

News of the shooting, carried back into the heart of the city, brought recruits to the strikers' forces. . . . Men and women and boys too, pounded up and down the business district, and where they ran the crash of broken plate glass and tearing splintering wood was heard.[73]

The crowd grew to 8,000 and was only quelled by the arrival of two more companies of National Guardsmen, who put the city under military rule. The Woonsocket Rayon Mill, source of the conflict, was closed.

   Declaring that "there is a Communist uprising and not a textile strike in Rhode Island," Democratic Governor Green called the legislature into special session to declare a state of insurrection and

ton, detachments of regular Army troops began mobilizing at strategic points, prepared to leave for Rhode Island "at a moment's notice." [74] The union leadership agreed with the Governor's assessment of the riots:

. . . Communists . . . were solely responsible for the serious uprisings that
took place in both Saylesville and Woonsocket.

. . . the [Rhode Island] strike committee has instructed each union to
place trustworthy men and women of their unions at strategic points in
strike areas for the sole purpose of cooperating with police and all other
law enforcement agencies in driving Communists not only from strike areas but from the state." [75]

The strike — like the industry — was centered in New England
and the South, but it spread through the rest of the eastern seaboard as well. In Pennsylvania, for example, 47,000 struck, eleven
cars filled with special guards were attacked and some of them
overturned, and in Lancaster, police charged that women strikers
were using "old-fashioned hat pins" to attack non-strikers.

Meanwhile, the struggle in the South reflected "a grim determination on both sides to hold on at any cost." [76] A road approaching the Cherryville mill in Gaston County, North Carolina, was dynamited September 10th, as was a mill generator at Fayetteville,
North Carolina, a few days later. Five pickets in a crowd of 400
wearing "peaceful picket" badges were bayoneted by soldiers as
they yelled "scab" at strikebreakers entering a mill at Burlington,
North Carolina. Non-striking workers in Aragon, Georgia, armed
by their employer and led by a deputy sheriff, dispersed a flying
squadron by threat of force.

By September 17th, the Southern employers were ready for
their big counter-offensive. They met in advance in Greenville,
North Carolina, and planned "a gigantic effort . . . to break through
the strike lines and start the movement back to the mills." [77] An army of 10,000 National Guardsmen was mobilized in Georgia,
South Carolina, North Carolina, Alabama and Mississippi, supple-
mented by 15,000 armed deputies. Numerous Southern mills tried
to reopen under heavy armed guard. The *New York Times*
described as typical the response of 1,000 pickets at the Hatch
Hosiery Company in North Carolina:

Refusing to budge even when a wedge of troops with bayonets tried
to cross the road to break their lines, the pickets shouted "Boy Scouts!"
and "Tin Soldiers!" . . . A committee of four pickets was assured that the
mill would not resume operations during the day and the picket line dispersed until tomorrow.[78]

Such confrontations continued all week throughout the South. The

176   employers' effort to stampede the strikers back to work failed overwhelmingly: on September 18th, the AP reported 421,000 on strike,
20,000 more than the week before.

In Georgia, Governor Talmadge declared martial law. National Guardsmen started mass arrests of flying squadrons and incar-
cerated them without charges in what was described as a concentration camp near the spot where Germans had been interned during World War I. Thirty-four key strike leaders in whose names
strike funds were held were arrested and held incommunicado,
thus crippling the strike relief system in the state. Organizers were
beaten and arrested throughout the South. By September 19th, the
death toll in the South reached thirteen. Union officials stated September 20th that "force and hunger" were sending strikers back to
the mills, but only 20,000 of 170,000 on strike in the South had returned to work in the previous six days, many of them to mills still
too understaffed to operate, and they were offset by many thousands of additional workers who had joined the strike.[79]

On September 20th, the Board of Inquiry for the Cotton Textile Industry, which President Roosevelt had appointed toward the
start of the strike, issued its report. A new Textile Labor Relations
Board of "neutral" members should be established; it would set up
a subcommittee to "study" workloads; the Federal Trade Commission should study the capacity of the industry to raise hours and
employment; the Department of Labor should survey wages to see
whether differentials had been maintained. As Irving Bernstein
noted, "There was little of tangible benefit to either the textile
workers or U.T.W. . . . In fact, the only recommendation that was
immediate and tangible in effect was imposed on the union: to terminate the strike."[80] Nonetheless, the U.T.W. strike committee
hailed the Board's recommendation as "an overwhelming victory"
and on September 22nd ordered the strikers back to work.[81] Thus
ended what Robert R.R. Brooks described as "unquestionably the
greatest single industrial conflict in the history of American organized labor."[82]

President Roosevelt urged textile firms to rehire strikers without discrimination, but by October 23rd, the U.T.W. reported, 339
mills had refused to do so, leaving thousands of workers unemployed. Martha Gellhorn wrote from North Carolina that textile
workers "live in terror of being penalized for joining unions; and
the employers live in a state of mingled rage and fear . . . "[83]

The textile workers felt an extreme disillusionment with both
the government and the union. As Robert R.R. Brooks concluded,

The thousands of militiamen, sheriffs, and armed strikebreakers
which were thrown into strike territories and the numerous deaths at the

hands of drunken deputies and nervous guardsmen linked the forces of law and order so clearly with the interests of the textile employers that northern newspaper reporters repeatedly referred to the situation as "the employers' offensive." The significance of this was not lost upon the strikers. In the space of a few weeks thousands of workers received a practical education in the philosophy of class relations which was clearly reflected in conversation, tactics, and general attitude.[84]

Mill workers were likewise extremely bitter at the union and its officials for claiming a victory, calling off the strike, and putting their faith in government boards, when the employers had conceded nothing. Herbert Lahne reported he found that "in many interviews . . . with Southern cotton mill workers in 1938 this resentment was clearly expressed." [85]

3. Sitdown

The bloody conflicts of 1934 certified the failure of the NRA's Section 7A. By the end of the year, workers who had previously looked to the NRA for a solution to their problems were referring to it as the National Run-Around. Local radicals played important parts in the strikes of 1934 — Communists in San Francisco, Musteites in Toledo, Trotskyists in Minneapolis; significantly, in each case it was not their particular party line and party organization that was responsible for this, but the fact that their own militance coincided with that of the workers.

U.M.W. head John L. Lewis, according to his biographer Saul Alinsky, "read the revolutionary handwriting on the walls of American industry," [86] and moved to establish the Committee on Industrial Organization within the A.F.L. to utilize the newly revealed militance to establish unionism in the basic mass-production industries. New Dealers in Congress began pushing for a National Labor Relations Act to enforce the system of orderly collective bargaining in industry which the NRA had promised but had manifestly failed to establish. Meanwhile, the workers themselves, largely fed up with both the unions and the NRA, began to develop their own methods of struggle. The key weapon they created was the sitdown; the crucible in which it was forged was Akron, Ohio.

By the time of the Depression, Akron was the rubber center of America, home of the great Goodyear, Firestone, and Goodrich plants and more than twenty factories of lesser companies. At peak production the Akron rubber industry employed nearly 40,000 workers, but by 1933 one-third to one-half of Akron's workers were unemployed, Firestone and half a dozen smaller companies were closed down, and Goodyear was on a two-day week.[87]

178   With the passage of the NRA in 1933, Akron's rubberworkers
poured into unions set up by local trade unionists. As Ruth McKenney wrote in her over-dramatized but valuable study of the Akron
labor movement, *Industrial Valley,* "the first weeks of the new rubber union were something like a cross between a big picnic and a
religious revival . . . "[99] Forty to fifty thousand rubberworkers,
mostly in Akron, took out union cards in 1933. They expected the
union, backed by the government, to save them.

> Always the cry was "join up." But nobody said what came after you joined.
> The rubberworkers believed blindly, passionately, fiercely, that the union
> would cure all their troubles, end the speedup, make them rich with wages.
> They had no clear idea, and nobody told them, just how the union would
> accomplish these aims. Vaguely, they thought President Roosevelt might
> just order the rubber bosses to raise wages and quit the speedup.[89]

The next two years would see their disillusionment with that belief
and their discovery of how to act on their own.

The A.F.L. assigned an organizer, Coleman Claherty, to Akron. His first step was to try to separate the rubberworkers, who
had established locals representing all the workers in each plant,
into various crafts. The workers joined the unions to which they
were assigned but proceeded to ignore the divisions, coming to the
meetings of their plant local anyway. Claherty's slogan was "Rome
wasn't built in a day," and he did everything possible to "pack ice
on the hot-heads" who were pushing in every union meeting for action. Ruth McKenney describes a Goodyear local meeting one Sunday which Claherty was addressing on the NRA:

> "We want action," a big tirebuilder bawled, bored with the NRA.
> "Sure you do," Claherty shot back, "and you're going to get it." . . .
> Claherty never liked the curious atmosphere of Akron union meet-
> ings. He tried to prevent the back talk. He deplored the universal notion
> of rubberworkers that a man had a right to get up and have his say, when-
> ever he felt like it, at his own union meeting.
> But the rubberworkers had carried over the technique of Baptist
> prayer sessions, where anybody was free to "testify" as the spirit moved
> him, to their union meetings. Tirebuilders rose in the Federal locals to
> "testify" about "why ain't this union gittin' anywheres," whenever the
> thought struck them...
> "We shall demand that the rubber industry recognize our unions,"
> Claherty thundered this Sunday.
> "How you goin' to git 'em to dew that?" somebody yelled. . . .
> "He asks a question like that," Claherty shot back, "when everybody
> in this room knows that President Roosevelt is for the unions."
> It was a good answer. A lot of the men clapped and the mill-room
> man in the back of the hall seemed satisfied. . . .
> "It won't be long now," some of the men said . . . "Roosevelt will fix

"Every labor gain," he [Claherty] told his assistant . . . "is a gradual one. You can't expect to get everything the first five years. The fellows expect the moon on a platter all in a month." [90]

On June 19th, 1934, tirebuilders at the General Tire and Rubber Co. walked out when a foreman announced some wage rate changes — the first step in introducing the "Bedeaux plan" to speed up production. The tirebuilders began cussing out the foreman. One of them yelled, "I ain't going to stand for it. Let's quit, boys," and the entire shift walked out. Outside the plant the men decided to have a meeting the next day and take a strike vote. At the meeting the local union's executive committee recommended that the workers accept a wage increase the company had offered in response to the strike and go back to work — they were booed off the platform and physically attacked by the strikers. A local officer was hissed off the platform for saying the strike wasn't legal because the United Rubber Council executive board had to give permission to strike. "Who said they had to OK what we do? We ain't never heard anything about that before," a man yelled from the floor. The rubberworkers voted to strike and established their own strike organization, selecting their own picket captains and organizing food committees. After a month, the company granted a number of the strikers' demands and they went back to work.[91]

By the end of 1934, the labor relations board of the NRA denounced the companies for refusing to bargain collectively and ordered representation elections in the Goodyear and Firestone plants. The government had ballots printed and polling places set up. The rubberworkers fully expected the government to force the companies to recognize them. Then two days before the election the companies asked for and got an injunction against the election from a Federal court, thus tying up the issue in the courts indefinitely. The rubberworkers were shocked and bitterly disappointed; their belief that the government would solve their problems was killed at a blow. As Ruth McKenney put it, "Rubberworkers spent three passionate weeks hoping that the government would cure the speed-up and low wages in Akron — and then the NRA and its NLRB went blooey as far as the man on the tire machine was concerned." [92]

The final disillusionment with the union came in the spring of 1935. Workers were flooding out of the unions, and Claherty recognized that he had to give at least the appearance of doing something. On March 27th he announced a strike vote. By April 8th, A.F.L. president William Green was announcing to the press, "There is no hope of averting the strike." [93] The rubberworkers were set to strike on the 15th, and began feverish preparations. Then Claherty and the local presidents went to Washington and, at the last minute, signed a government-mediated agreement not to strike and to await court action on a representative election. As Goodyear announced, the agreement made "no change in employee relations since the provisions are in complete accord with the policies under which Goodyear has always operated." [94]

The rubberworkers considered it a complete sell-out. They stood on street corners tearing up their union cards, thinking it futile even to vote against the settlement. As one put it, "You can't do nothin' about that. They run the union, and they run it for the bosses, not for us. I'm through. I'd see myself in hell before I ever belong to another dirty stinking union." [95] Union membership in Summit County — mostly rubberworkers — dropped from 40,000 to 5,000, with most of those remaining paper members.

In the face of this collapse of confidence in trade unionism and the government, work conditions remained intolerable. As a rubberworker in Akron wrote to the local paper,

Only our machines are alive. We must treat them with respect or they turn against us. Last week one of the boys who had been back only a month grew a little careless, or maybe the long layoff had made him dull or maybe he had grown so accustomed to the change from sleeping at night to working at night — and his mill swallowed his hand and part of his arm. . . .

The mills stopped only long enough for us to pull him out, and then they resumed their steady turn. Two of the boys carried him to the hospital and the foreman called for a Squad man to take his place.

Unbelievably it is 3 A.M., and we hastily gulp tasteless sandwiches, working and eating at once. The soapstone which is flying around everywhere clogs our throats and tongues and nostrils so that they seem dry. If we drink much water, we become fat and bloated, so we chew great handfuls of licorice-flavored tobacco.

Someone has grown drowsy. "Ha, ha," we laugh. "Old Bill has forgotten to weigh his batch. That's a good one, ha, ha." Bill doesn't laugh. He knows that to do this once more will cost him his job. The foreman has warned him. . . .

We used to work eight hours and feel fine when the quitting whistle blew. Now we work six hours and are dead-tired.

We can't be cheerful, remembering the hard days of the past three years, and knowing that the work may not last much longer. We've nothing to look forward to. We're factory hands. [96]

Disillusioned with trade unionism and tormented by the speedup, workers in Akron developed a new tactic — the sitdown — which they themselves could directly control without need for any outside leaders. When Louis Adamic later visited Akron to find out how the sitdowns had begun, he was told that the first had occurred not in a rubber factory but at a baseball game. Players from two factories refused to play a scheduled game because the umpire, whom they disliked, was not a union man. They simply sat down on the diamond, while the crowd for a lark cheered the NRA and yelled for an umpire who was a union man, until the non-union umpire was replaced.[97]

Not long after, a dispute developed between a dozen workers and a supervisor in a rubber factory. The workers were on the verge of giving in when the supervisor insulted them and one of them said, "Aw, to hell with 'im, let's sit down." The dozen workers turned off their machines and sat down. Within a few minutes the carefully organized flow of production through the plant began to jam up as department after department ground to a halt. Thousands of workers sat down, some because they wanted to, more because everything was stopping anyway. What had happened, workers wanted to know? "There was a sitdown at such-and-such a department. A sitdown? Yeah, a sitdown; don't you know what a sitdown is, you dope? Like what happened at the ball game the other Sunday." [98]

Adamic describes the response:

Sitting by their machines, cauldrons, boilers, and work benches, they talked. Some realized *for the first time how important they were in the process of rubber production.* Twelve men had practically stopped the works! Almost any dozen or score of them could do it! In some departments six could do it! The active rank-and-filers, scattered through the various sections of the plant, took the initiative in saying, "We've got to stick with 'em!" And they stuck with them, union and non-union men alike. Most of them were non-union. Some probably were vaguely afraid not to stick. Some were bewildered. Others amused. There was much laughter through the works. Oh boy, oh boy! Just like at the ball game, no kiddin'. There the crowd had stuck with the players and they got an umpire who was a member of a labor union. Here everybody stuck with the twelve guys who first sat down, and the factory management was beside itself. Superintendents, foremen, and straw bosses were dashing about. . . . This sudden suspension of production was costing the company many hundreds of dollars every minute. . . . In less than an hour the dispute was settled—full victory for the men! [99]

Between 1933 and 1936 this tactic gradually became a tradition in Akron, with scores of sitdowns—the majority probably not instigated even by rank-and-file union organizers, and almost invariably backed by the workers in other departments. It became an understood principle that when one group of workers stopped work everyone else along the line sat down too. To explain this, Adamic listed the advantages of the sitdown strike "from the point of view not so much of the rank-and-file organizer or radical agitator as of the average workingman in a mass-production industry like rubber."

To begin with, the sitdown is the opposite of sabotage, to which many workers were opposed.

It destroys nothing. Before shutting down a department in a rubber plant, for instance, the men take the compounded rubber from the mills, or they finish building or curing the tires then being built or cured, so that nothing is needlessly ruined. Taking the same precautions during the sitdown as they do during production, the men do not smoke in departments where benzine is used. There is no drinking. This discipline . . . is instinctive.[100]

Sitdowns are effective, short, and free from violence.

There are no strikebreakers in the majority of instances; the factory management does not dare to get tough and try to drive the sitting men out and replace them with other workers, for such violence would turn the public against the employers and the police, and might result in damage to costly machinery. In a sitdown there are no picket lines outside the factories, where police and company guards have great advantage when a fight starts. The sitdown action occurs wholly inside the plant, where the workers, who know every detail of the interior, have obvious advantages. The sitters-down organize their own "police squads," arming them — in rubber — with crowbars normally used to pry open molds in which tires are cured. These worker cops patrol the belt, watch for possible scabs and stand guard near the doors. In a few instances where city police and company cops entered a factory, they were bewildered, frightened, and driven out by the "sitting" workers with no difficulty whatever.[101]

The initiative, conduct, and control of the sitdown came directly from the men involved.

Most workers distrust — if not consciously, then unconsciously — union officials and strike leaders and committees, even when they themselves have elected them. The beauty of the sitdown or the stay-ins is that there are no leaders or officials to distrust. There can be no sell-out. Such standard procedure as strike sanction is hopelessly obsolete when workers drop their tools, stop their machines, and sit down beside them.

Finally, the sitdown counters the boredom, degradation and isolation of the factory.

Work in most of the departments of a rubber factory or any other kind of mass-production factory is drudgery of the worst sort — mechanical and uncreative, insistent and requiring no imagination; and any interruption is welcomed by workers, even if only subconsciously. The conscious part of their mind may worry about the loss of pay; their subconscious, however, does not care a whit about that. The situation is dramatic, thrilling.

. . . the average worker in a mass-production plant is full of grievances and complaints, some of them hardly realized, and any vent of them is welcomed.

The sitdown is a social affair. Sitting workers talk. They get acquainted. And they like that. In a regular strike it is impossible to bring together under one roof more than one or two thousand people, and these only for a meeting, where they do not talk with one another but listen to speakers. A sitdown holds under the same roof up to ten or twelve thousand idle men, free to talk among themselves, man to man. "Why, my God, man" one Goodyear gum-miner told me in November, 1936, "during the sitdowns last spring I found out that the guy who works next to me is the same as I am, even if I was born in West Virginia and he is from Poland. His grievances are the same. Why shouldn't we stick?" [102]

Late in 1935, Goodyear announced that it was shifting from the six- to the eight-hour day, admitting that 1,200 men would be laid off and that other companies would follow suit. The announcement created shock in Akron — unemployment was still high and six hours under speed-up conditions were already so exhausting that rubberworkers complained, "When I get home I'm so tired I can't even sleep with my wife." [103] As the companies began "adjusting" piece rates in preparation for introducing the eight-hour day, a wave of spontaneous work stoppages by non-union employees forced a slowing of production.

On January 29th, 1936, the truck tirebuilders at Firestone sat down against a reduction in rates and the firing of a union committeeman. The men had secretly planned the strike for 2 a.m. When the hour struck,

the tirebuilder at the end of the line walked three steps to the master safety switch and, drawing a deep breath, he pulled up the heavy wooden handle. With this signal, in perfect synchronization, with the rhythm they had learned in a great mass-production industry, the tirebuilders stepped back from their machines.

Instantly, the noise stopped. The whole room lay in perfect silence. The tirebuilders stood in long lines, touching each other, perfectly motionless, deafened by the silence. A moment ago there had been the weaving hands, the revolving wheels, the clanking belt, the moving hooks, the flashing tire tools. Now there was absolute stillness, no motion anywhere, no sound. . . .

"We done it! We stopped the belt! By God, we done it!" And men began to cheer hysterically, to shout and howl in the fresh silence. Men wrapped long sinewy arms around their neighbors' shoulders, screaming, "We done it! We done it!" [104]

The workers in the truck tire department sent one committee around the plant to call out other departments, another to talk with the boss, and a third to police the shop. Within a day the entire Plant No. 1 was struck, and after fifty-three hours the workers at Plant No. 2 announced they had voted to sit down in sympathy. Management capitulated completely. Two days later, pitmen at Goodyear sat down over a pay cut, were persuaded to return to work by the company union, sat down again and were cajoled back

184 to work, sat down a third time and returned to work under threat of immediate replacement. On February 8th, the tire department at Goodrich sat down over a rate reduction. The strike spread through the rest of the plant, stopping it completely within six hours, and management rapidly capitulated to the sitdowners. The sitdown had shaken each of the rubber big three within a ten-day period.

The crisis finally came February 14th. A few days before, Goodyear had laid off 700 tirebuilders and the workers assumed that this was the signal for introducing the eight-hour day. At 3:10 a.m., 137 tirebuilders in Department 251-A of Goodyear's Plant No. 2 — few if any of them members of the union — shut off the power and sat down. The great Goodyear strike was on.

Meanwhile, the Rubberworkers Union had been regaining support. It had refused to accept Claherty as president, installed former rubberworkers in office, and allied itself with the new C.I.O. With each sitdown, the union signed up the participants, and now workers flooded back into the union halls. The initiative for the sit-downs, however, did not come from the union; indeed, as Irving Bernstein has noted, "The U.R.W. . . . disliked the sitdown." [105] Thus, U.R.W. officials now persuaded the Goodyear sitdowners to leave and marched them out of the plant. Goodyear offered to take the laid-off men back, but by now the rubberworkers of the entire city were up in arms, determined to make a stand against the eight-hour day. Fifteen hundred Goodyear workers met and voted unanimously to strike, but four days later the president of the local was still saying the strike was not a U.R.W. affair.

The workers made it their affair. They began mass picketing at each of the forty-five gates around Goodyear's eleven-mile perimeter, putting up 300 tarpaper shanties to keep warm. They elected picket captains who met regularly, coordinated strike action, and set the strike's demands. Inside Plant No. 1, hundreds of men and women staged a sitdown — until a union delegate marched them out. At the union hall, "committees sprang up almost by themselves" to take care of problems as they arose. A soup kitchen developed out of the sandwich- and coffee-making crew, staffed by volunteers from the Cooks and Waitresses Union. On the sixth day of the strike the C.I.O. sent in half-a-dozen of its top leaders, and the U.R.W. executive board finally sanctioned the strike.

The company now tried to break the strike by force. They secured an injunction against mass picketing, which the workers simply ignored. The Sheriff put together a force of 150 deputies to open the plants, but 10,000 workers of all trades from all over the city gathered with lead pipe and baseball bats and the charge was called off at the last possible second. Next a Law and Order League,

which claimed 5,200 organized vigilantes, was organized by a for-   185
mer mayor with money from Goodyear. Word spread that an attack
was planned for March 18th. The union went on radio all that night
while workers gathered in homes throughout the city ready to rush
any place an attack was made. The Summit County Central Labor
Council declared it would call a general strike in the event of a
violent attack on the picket lines. In the face of such preparations,
the vigilante movement was paralyzed.

President Roosevelt's ace mediator, Ed McGrady, proposed
that the workers return to work and submit the issues to arbitration.
To this and other proposed settlements the workers at their mass
meetings chanted, "No, no, a thousand times no, I'd rather die than
say yes." [106] After more than a month Goodyear capitulated on
most of the demands, although without agreeing to formal recognition of the union. The rubberworkers returned to work largely victorious and proceeded to implement their position with the sitdown.
In the three months after the strike there were nineteen recorded
sitdowns at Goodyear alone, with many "quickies" unrecorded.
Louis Adamic described the situation he found in Akron in 1936:

> A week seldom passed without one or more sitdowns. . . . A typical
> one took place on November 17, when I was in Akron, in the huge Good-
> year No. 1 plant. After an inconclusive argument with the management
> over an adjustment in wage rates, ninety-eight workers in one of the de-
> partments sat down, stopping the work of seven thousand men for a day
> and a half, at the end of which period the company promised speedy ac-
> tion on the adjustment.
>
> Officials of rubber companies, with whom I talked, were frantic in
> their attempts to stop the sitdowns. They blamed them on "trouble-
> makers" and the union movement in general. They tried to terrorize un-
> ion sympathizers. The Goodyear management, for instance, assigned two
> non-union inspectors to a department with instructions to disqualify tires
> produced by known union men. After pelting them with milk bottles for a
> while, the men sat down and refused to work till the inspectors were re-
> moved. The company rushed in forty factory guards with clubs, but a 65-
> year-old union gum-miner met the army at the entrance and told them to
> "beat it." They went — and the non-union inspectors were replaced.
>
> Akron sitdowns were provoked by various other causes. In the early
> autumn of 1936, S.H. Dalrymple, president of the U.R.W.A., was beaten
> by thugs employed by a rubber factory, whereupon the factory workers
> sat down in protest, forcing the company to close for a day. When work
> was resumed, the next night, a K.K.K. fiery cross blazed up within view of
> the plant. This caused the men to sit down again — and to despatch a squad
> of "huskies" to extinguish the cross. [107]

Such use of the sitdown gave rubberworkers virtually a dual
power over the production process in Akron.

186   Machine Operator No. 8004 worked in the camshaft department of the Chevrolet factory in Flint, Michigan. The men he worked with produced 118 shafts per shift, naturally producing a few
more in the first half, when they were fresh, than in the second.
One day in 1935, the management suddenly announced that they
would have to increase production in the second half to the level of
the first, turning out 124 instead of 118 a shift. The men accepted
the increase, but then organized informally to prevent any further
speed-up. As one of them put it, "Any man who runs over 124 every night is only cutting his own throat." [108] They also carefully
planned not to produce more in the first half, lest management
again use the differential against them. If they ran past sixty-two
shafts, they would hide the extras in the racks under the machines,
covering them with rough stock. The pickup man checked every
hour to see how many shafts were completed and passed the information along, allowing the workers to keep a steady and equalized
pace. If a worker turned out seventy shafts, he picked up only sixty-
two of them.

          Machine Operator No. 8004 fought the movement, telling his
fellow workers to "knock the production out and forget about trying to set an amount for each man to run;" [109] he was almost beat-
en up for his pains. This case of workers controlling the speed of
production is documented — unlike thousands of others that have remained unrecorded — because Machine Operator 8004 was a labor
spy whose periodic reports were published by the Senate Civil Liberties Investigating Committee, popularly known as the La Follette
Committee.

          As a study of the auto industry in 1934 by the NRA Division of
Research and Planning revealed prophetically, the grievance

mentioned most frequently . . . and uppermost in the minds of those who
testified is the stretch-out. Everywhere workers indicated that they were
being forced to work harder and harder, to put out more and more products in the same amount of time and with less workers doing the job. . . .
If there is any one cause for conflagration in the Automobile Industry, it is
this one. [110]

According to Sidney Fine, whose *Sitdown* is the basic scholarly
study of the great General Motors strike of 1936-1937, the speed-
up was resented not only because of the absolute rate of production, but also because the mass-production worker "was not free,
as perhaps he had been on some previous job, to set the pace of his
work and to determine the manner in which it was to be performed." [111] A Buick worker complained, "You have to run to the
toilet and run back. If you had to . . . take a crap, if there wasn't
anybody there to relieve you, you had to run away and tie the line

up, and if you tied the line up you got hell for it." [112] The wife of a
General Motors worker complained,

"You should see him come home at night, him and the rest of the men in the busses. So tired like they was dead, and irritable. My John's not like that. He's a good, kind man. But the children don't dare go near him, he's so nervous and his temper's bad. And then at night in bed he shakes, his whole body, he shakes."

"Yes," replied another, "they're not men any more if you know what I mean. They're not men. My husband is only 30, but to look at him you'd think he was 50 and all played out." [113]

"Where you used to be a man . . . now you are less than their cheapest tool," one worker complained, and another summed up, "I just don't like to be drove." [114]

The development of unionism in the auto industry followed closely that in rubber. Herbert Harris estimated that with the coming of the NRA, 210,000 auto workers joined the A.F.L. auto locals, though the figure may be excessive. [115] Since the employers refused to give any significant concessions, important auto locals voted to strike and a strike throughout the industry seemed inevitable. Workers flooded into the unions to take part in the strike — 20,000 in Flint alone. [116] The A.F.L. leadership, however, wanted no part in a strike, and managed to postpone it again and again.

Finally, William Collins, top A.F.L. official in the auto industry, asked President Roosevelt to intervene. Roosevelt immediately demanded that the strike be postponed. Collins told union leaders, "You have a wonderful man down there in Washington and he is trying hard to raise wages and working conditions." [117] According to Henry Kraus, editor of the union paper in Flint, "The attitudes of the auto workers toward the President those days bordered on the mystical"; [118] the local representatives agreed to cancel the strike. Thereupon Roosevelt announced a settlement conceding nothing to the workers but an Automobile Labor Board to hear discrimination cases, legitimizing company unions, and virtually exempting the auto industry from Section 7A. [119]

"We all feel tremendously happy over the outcome in Washington," a General Motors vice-president reported. [120] In the words of Sidney Fine, "The President made the victory of the automobile manufacturers complete on the issue of representation and collective bargaining." [121] Leonard Woodcock (today president of the United Auto Workers) recalls that when the workers in Flint heard of the settlement they felt "a deep sense of betrayal," and began to tear up union cards. By October, 1934, paid-up membership in Flint had plummeted to 528. In several subsequent local strikes, the A.F.L. played a strikebreaking role, even marching its members

188   with a police escort into a motor products plant struck by another union. Those few, mostly young and militant, who remained in the auto union bitterly fought A.F.L. control, and eventually took control of the union and aligned it with the newly emerging C.I.O. (The C.I.O., the alliance of unions aiming to unionize the unorganized basic industries, was soon to be expelled from the A.F.L. and establish itself as a new union federation, the Congress of Industrial Organizations.)

Like the rubberworkers, the auto workers turned to the sitdown and other forms of job action against the speed-up; we have given one example in a camshaft department above. Quickies occurred sporadically, especially in auto body plants in Cleveland and Detroit, from 1933 through 1935. By late 1936, the highly visible sitdowns in Akron were being imitated by auto workers all over, especially since it was the "grooving-in" period during which new models are introduced. Management as usual tried to increase speed and cut piece rates on new jobs, raising resentment to a peak. In Flint, heart of the General Motors empire, there were seven work stoppages in the Fisher Body No. 1 plant in one week. One day the trim shop knocked off an hour early as a protest. Workers in another shop struck for an extra man and got the line slowed

Pickets outside the Ford Motor Company plant in St. Louis, Missouri, November, 1937. The impact of the General Motors sitdowns of early 1937 spread through the rest of the auto industry, but Ford held out against the U.A.W. until 1941.

from fifty to forty-five units. Another action won restoration of a twenty percent wage cut. Henry Kraus describes this as "largely a spontaneous movement onto which the union had not yet securely attached itself."[122] He tells of Bud Simons, a union leader in the Fisher plant, coming to Bob Travis, the U.A.W. organizer in Flint, and saying, "Honest to God, Bob, you've got to let me pull a strike before one pops somewhere that we won't be able to control!"[123]

The union tried to win the confidence of the workers by supporting the sitdowns and making itself the agency through which they could be spread. On November 12th, for example, supervision reduced by one the number of "bow-men" who welded the angle irons across car roofs. The other bow-men were two brothers named Perkins and an Italian named Joe Urban; none of them was in the union, but they had been reading about a sitdown at Bendix. Adopting the idea, they simply stopped working. The foreman and superintendent rushed over and tried to talk them into going back to work, but the men just sat there arguing until twenty unfinished jobs had passed on the production line. The whole department followed the argument with intense excitement. Finally the bow-men agreed to go back to work till they could talk with the day-shift about it, but everyone left that night talking about the sitdown. Next day when the Perkins came to work they were sent to the employment office and told that they were fired. They showed their firing slips to Bud Simons and he and the other union committeemen ran through the "body-in-white" department where the main welding and soldering work was done, crying, "The Perkins boys were fired! Nobody starts working!"

The whistle blew. Every man in the department stood at his station, a deep, significant tenseness in him. The foreman pushed the button and the skeleton bodies, already partly assembled when they got to this point, began to rumble forward. But no one lifted a hand. All eyes were turned to Simons who stood out in the aisle by himself.

The bosses ran about like mad.

"Whatsamatter? Whatsamatter? Get to work!" they shouted.

But the men acted as though they never heard them. One or two of them couldn't stand the tension. Habit was deep in them and it was like physical agony for them to see the bodies pass untouched. They grabbed their tools and chased after them. "Rat! Rat!" the men growled without moving and the others came to their senses.

The superintendent stopped by the "bow-men."

"You're to blame for this!" he snarled.

"So what if we are?" little Joe Urban, the Italian cried, overflowing with pride. "You ain't running your line, are you?"

That was altogether too much. The superintendent grabbed Joe and started for the office with him. The two went down along the entire line, while the men stood rigid as though awaiting the word of command. It was like that because they were organized but their organization only went that far and no further. What now?

Simons, a torch-solderer, was almost at the end of the line. He too was momentarily held in vise by the superintendent's overt act of authority. The latter had dragged Joe Urban past him when he finally found presence of mind to call out:

"Hey, Teefee, where you going?"

It was spoken in just an ordinary conversational tone and the other was taken so aback he answered the really impertinent question.

"I'm taking him to the office to have a little talk with him." Then suddenly he realized and got mad. "Say, I think I'll take you along too!"

That was his mistake.

"No you won't!" Simons said calmly.

"Oh yes I will!" and he took hold of his shirt.

Simons yanked himself loose.

And suddenly at this simple act of insurgence Teefee realized his danger. He seemed to become acutely conscious of the long line of silent men and felt the threat of their potential strength. They had been transformed into something he had never known before and over which he no longer had any command. He let loose of Simons and started off again with Joe Urban, hastening his pace. Simons yelled:
"Come on, fellows, don't let them fire little Joe!"

About a dozen boys shot out of line and started after Teefee. The superintendent dropped Joe like a hot poker and deer-footed it for the door. The men returned to their places and all stood waiting. Now what? The next move was the company's. The moment tingled with expectancy.

Teefee returned shortly, accompanied by Bill Lynch, the assistant plant manager. Lynch was a friendly sort of person and was liked by the men. He went straight to Simons.

"I hear we've got trouble here," he said in a chatty way. "What are we going to do about it?"

"I think we'll get a committee together and go in and see Parker," Simons replied.

Lynch agreed. So Simons began picking the solid men out as had been prearranged. The foreman tried to smuggle in a couple of company-minded individuals, so Simons chose a group of no less than eighteen to make sure that the scrappers would outnumber the others. Walt Moore went with him, but Joe Devitt remained behind to see that the bosses didn't try any monkeyshines. The others headed for the office where Evan Parker, the plant manager, greeted them as smooth as silk.

"You can smoke if you want to, boys," he said as he bid them to take the available chairs. "Well, what seems to be the trouble here? We ought to be able to settle this thing."

"Mr. Parker, it's the speed-up the boys are complaining about," Simons said, taking the lead. "It's absolutely beyond human endurance. And now we've organized ourselves into a union. It's the union you're talking to right now, Mr. Parker."

"Why that's perfectly all right, boys," Parker said affably. "Whatever a man does outside the plant is his own business."

The men were almost bowled over by this manner. They had never known Parker as anything but a tough cold tomato with an army sergeant's style. He was clearly trying to play to the weaker boys on the committee and began asking them leading questions. Simons or Walt Moore would try to break in and answer for them.

"Now I didn't ask you," Parker would say, "you can talk when it's your turn!" In this way he sought to split the committee up into so many individuals. Simons realized he had to put an end to that quickly.

"We might as well quit talking right now, Mr. Parker," he said, putting on a tough act. "Those men have got to go back and that's all there is to it!"

"That's what you say," Parker snapped back.

"No, that's what the men say. You can go out and see for yourself. Nobody is going to work until that happens."

Parker knew that was true. Joe Devitt and several other good men who had been left behind were seeing to that. The plant manager seemed to soften again. All right, he said, he'd agree to take the two men back if he found their attitude was okay.

"Who's to judge that?" Simons asked.

"I will, of course!"

"Uh-uh!" Simons smiled and shook his head.

The thing bogged down again. Finally Parker said the Perkins brothers could return unconditionally on Monday. This was Friday night and they'd already gone home so there was no point holding up thousands of men until they could be found and brought back. To make this arrangement final he agreed that the workers in the department would get paid for the time lost in the stoppage. But Simons held fast to the original demand. Who knew what might happen till Monday? The Perkins fellows would have to be back on the line that night or the entire incident might turn out a flop.

"They go back tonight," he insisted.

Parker was fit to be tied. What was this? Never before in his life had he seen anything like it!

"Those boys have left!" he shouted. "It might take hours to get them back. Are you going to keep the lines tied up all that time?"

"We'll see what the men say," Simons replied, realizing that a little rank and file backing would not be out of the way. The committee rose and started back for the shop.

As they entered a zealous foreman preceded them, hollering: "Everybody back to work!" The men dashed for their places.

Simons jumped onto a bench.

"Wait a minute!" he shouted. The men crowded around him. He waited till they were all there and then told them in full detail of the discussion in the office. Courage visibly mounted into the men's faces as they heard on the unwavering manner in which their committee had acted in the dread presence itself.

192   "What are we going to do, fellows," Simons asked, "take the company's word and go back to work or wait till the Perkins boys are right here at their jobs?"

"Bring them back first!" Walt Moore and Joe Devitt began yelling and the whole crowd took up the cry.

Simons seized the psychological moment to make it official.

"As many's in favor of bringing the Perkins boys back before we go to work, say Aye!" There was a roar in answer. "Opposed, Nay!" Only a few timid voices sounded — those of the company men and the foremen who had been circulating among the workers trying to influence them to go back to work. Simons turned to them.

"There you are," he said.

One of the foremen had taken out pencil and paper and after the vote he went around recording names. "You want to go to work?" he asked each of the men. Finally he came to one chap who stuck his chin out and said loudly, "Emphatically not!" which made the rest of the boys laugh and settled the issue.

Mr. Parker got the news and decided to terminate the matter as swiftly as possible. He contacted the police and asked them to bring the Perkins boys in. One was at home but the other had gone out with his girl. The police short-waved his license number to all scout cars. The local radio station cut into its program several times to announce that the brothers were wanted back at the plant. Such fame would probably never again come to these humble workers. By chance the second boy caught the announcement over the radio in his car and came to the plant all bewildered. When told what had happened the unappreciative chap refused to go to work until he had driven his girl home and changed his clothes! And a thousand men waited another half hour while the meticulous fellow was getting out of his Sunday duds.

When the two brothers came back into the shop at last, accompanied by the committee, the workers let out a deafening cheer that could be heard in the most distant reaches of the quarter-mile-long plant. There had never been anything quite like this happen in Flint before. The workers didn't have to be told to know the immense significance of their victory. Simons called the Perkins boys up on the impromptu platform. They were too shy to even stammer their thanks.

"You glad to get back?" Simons coached them.

"You bet!"

"Who did it for you?"

"You boys did."

Simons then gave a little talk though carefully refraining from mentioning the union.

"Fellows," he said amid a sudden silence, "you've seen what you can get by sticking together. All I want you to do is remember that."[124]

Largely in response to this victory, United Auto Workers' membership in Flint increased from 150 to 1,500 within two weeks. The union's objective was to win recognition as the bargaining representative for the auto workers. Discontent was seething in the auto plants and breaking out in strikes all over. Since the auto companies were not willing to recognize the union voluntarily, the obvious approach for the union was to "attach itself" to this strike movement, lead it on a company-wide basis, and use it to negotiate for recognition by the company. As one U.A.W. National Council member had put it some time before, "the only means we have now is to strike . . . we must prove to the automobile workers we can help them." [125]

Indeed, such "organizational strikes" became the basic tactic of the C.I.O. unions in winning union recognition. Yet the union leadership was ambivalent about a strike. According to J. Raymond Walsh, later research and education director for the C.I.O., "The C.I.O. high command, preoccupied with the drive in steel, tried in vain to prevent the strike . . . "[126] Leadership of the U.A.W. believed a strike was necessary, but wanted to postpone it until they were better organized — membership from April to December, 1936, averaged only 27,000 for the entire industry — and resisted attempts to spread various strikes that broke out in November and December.

This attitude was based on the fact that General Motors would be little hurt by strikes in peripheral plants, whereas if the Fisher Body plants in Cleveland and Flint could be closed, perhaps three-quarters of General Motors' production could be crippled. On the other hand, local leaders often reflected the turbulence of the workers in the shops. Thus Adolph Germer, C.I.O. representative for the auto industry, complained,

> There is . . . a strong undercurrent of revolt against the authority of the laws and rules of the organization. . . . It is not that the boys are defiant of the organization; I attribute it rather to their youth and dynamic natures. They want things done right now, and they are too impatient to wait for the orderly procedure involved in collective bargaining.[127]

The union finally requested a collective bargaining conference with General Motors, the key company in the industry. It also announced the goals with which it hoped to gain leadership of the workers: an annual wage adequate to provide "health, decency, and comfort," elimination of speed-up, seniority, an eight-hour day, overtime pay, spreading work through shorter hours, safety measures, and "true collective bargaining."[128] It expected events to move toward a head sometime in January. Events, however, did not wait. The workers all over began striking on their own; as Germer complained, "It seems to be a custom for anybody or any group to call a strike at will. . . ."[129]

In Atlanta, on November 18th, the local called a sitdown over piece rate reductions, to the consternation of national officials of

194　the U.A.W. A week later, the U.A.W. local at the Bendix Corporation in South Bend won a contract after a nine-day sitdown, and a sitdown at Midland Steel Frame Company in Detroit won a wage increase, seniority, and time and a half for overtime. In early December a sitdown at Kelsey-Hayes Wheel Company in Detroit forced union recognition. In Kansas City on December 16th, workers sat down over the firing of a union man for jumping over the conveyor to go to the toilet. Detroit experienced a virtual sitdown wave in December, 1936, with workers at the Gordon Baking Company, Alcoa, National Automotive Fibers, and Bohn Aluminum and Brass Co. all sitting down.

Those union leaders who wanted a strike against General Motors were most worried about whether the Fisher plant in Cleveland would come out—many union workers there had lost their jobs in the wake of previous strikes, and no more than ten percent of the workers were in the union. But resentment was running high over grooving-in speed-up, and when on December 28th management postponed a long-awaited meeting to discuss grievances, workers in the quarter panel department said, "to hell with this stalling," and pulled the power switch. Workers in the steel stock, metal assembly and trim departments quit work and soon 7,000 workers were sitting down.[130] The local leadership was "taken completely by surprise."[131]

Meanwhile, events in Flint moved toward the decisive conflict. Two days after the Cleveland strike began, fifty workers sat down spontaneously at the Fisher Body No. 2 plant in Flint to protest the transfer of three inspectors who had been ordered to quit the union and refused. Later that night workers in Fisher plant No. 1 discovered that the company was loading dies—critical for the making of car bodies—onto railroad cars for shipment to plants elsewhere. General Motors followed a policy described by Knudson as "diversification of plants where local union strength is dangerous"; half the machinery in the Toledo Chevrolet plant, for example, had been removed after a strike in 1935, leaving hundreds out of work. The workers were furious, and streamed over to the union hall across from the plant where a meeting had been announced for lunchtime. Kraus, who was present, reports that "everybody's mind seemed made up before even a word was spoken."[132] When an organizer asked what they wanted to do, they shouted, "Shut her down! Shut the goddam plant!"[133] They raced back into the plant, and a few minutes later one of them opened a third story window and shouted, "Hurray, Bob! She's ours!"[134]

The occupiers rapidly faced the problem of organizing themselves for life inside the plant. (The following description is largely

drawn from Fisher No. 1, but the pattern was similar in the small-
er sitdowns elsewhere.) The basic decision-making body was a daily meeting of all the strikers in the plant. "The entire life of the sitdown came into review here and most of its ideas and decisions originated on the spot," Henry Kraus reported.[135] The chief administrative body was a committee of seventeen that reported to the strikers; available records indicate that virtually all its decisions were cleared with the general meeting of strikers. The strikers inside the plant, according to Sidney Fine, "displayed a fierce independence in their relationship with the U.A.W. leadership on the outside." For example, Flint U.A.W. organizer Bob Travis, though personally respected by the strikers, had to ask their permission to send one of his men into the plant to gather material for the press, and he was only allowed in on condition his notes were cleared by the strike executive. A sitdowner told a reporter that he and his companions would not leave the plant even under orders from the union president or John L. Lewis, "unless we get what we want."[136]

Social groups of fifteen, usually men who worked together in the shop, set up house and lived together family-style in their own corner of the plant, usually with close camaraderie. Each group had its own steward, and the stewards met together from time to time. The actual work of the strike was done by committees on food, recreation, information, education, postal services, sanitation, grievances, tracking down rumors, coordination with the outside, and the like. Each worker served on at least one committee, and was responsible for six hours of strike duty a day. The sitdowners sent out their own representatives to recruit union members, coordinate relief, and create an "outside defense squad."

Special attention was paid to the question of defense. A "special patrol" made hourly inspections of the entire plant day and night, looking for signs of company attack. Security groups were assigned to doorways and stairwells. Strikers set up "a regular production line"[137] to make blackjacks out of rubber hoses, braided leather and lead, and covered the windows with metal sheets with holes for fire hoses. The men conducted regular drills with the hoses, and collected piles of bolts, nuts, and door hinges for ammunition.

Sanitation likewise was stressed. At 3 p.m., a crane whistle would blow and all the men would line up at one end of the plant. The first wave would pick up refuse, behind them the second would put things in order, and the third would sweep the floor. The commissary floor was cleaned once an hour. The men showered daily. These measures were aimed at preserving both morale and

196 health. Likewise the workers protected the machinery, in some cases even oiling it, organized fire protection and inspected for fire hazards. Food was prepared on the outside by hundreds of volunteers and brought to the sitdowners by striking trolley coach employees.

Workers established courts to punish infractions of rules. The most serious "crimes" were failures to perform assigned duties by not showing up, sleeping on the job, or deserting the post. Others included failing to bus dirty dishes, littering, not participating in daily clean-up, smoking outside the plant cafeteria, failure to search everyone entering and leaving buildings, bringing in liquor, or making noise in sleeping areas or the "Quiet Zone" where absolute silence was available twenty-four hours a day. Punishments were designed to fit the crime; for example, men who failed to take a daily shower were "sentenced" to scrub the bathhouse. The ultimate punishment, applied only after repeated infractions, was expulsion from the plant. The courts were generally conducted with a good deal of humor and treated as a source of entertainment. For example, a striker who entered a plant without proper credentials was sentenced to make a speech to the court as his punishment; reporter Edwin Levinson observed that "there is more substantial

Workers at the Cleveland Fisher Body plant triggered the great General Motors strike when 2,000 said "to hell with this stalling" and sat down on the job. Local union leaders were taken completely by surprise.

than in a season of Broadway musical comedies." [138]

This kind of informal gaiety and creativity seemed to burgeon in the strike community. A favorite pastime was for the men to gather in a circle and call out the name of a member, who would then have to sing, whistle, dance, or tell a story. Each plant had its own band, composed of mandolins, guitars, banjos and harmonicas. The strikers made up verse after verse about the strike to dozens of popular and country tunes. General meetings, by the strikers' decision, opened and closed with singing; the favorite was "Solidarity Forever." A sitdowner wrote home, "We are all one happy family now. We all feel fine and have plenty to eat. We have several good banjo players and singers. We sing and cheer the Fisher boys and they return it." [139] Another wrote, "I am having a great time, something new, something different, lots of grub and music." [140] A psychologist declared that, "the atmosphere of cooperativeness" created "a veritable revolution of personality," indicated, for example, by workers more frequently saying "we" and "I." [141] As a reporter in Paul Gallico's novelette on the sitdown sensed, "They had made a palace out of what had been their prison." [142]

Outside the factories, a network of committees supported the

Wide World Photos

This sitdown, in March, 1937, at a St. Louis Chevrolet plant, was one of hundreds that month. Workers organized elaborate defenses, food supply, and entertainment as part of the sitdowns.

198 strike, organizing defense, food, sound cars, picketing, transportation, strike relief, publicity, entertainment, and the like. Women were particularly important in the outside organization. (The union leadership had decided that only men would occupy the plants, to the anger of some women workers.) Wives' support was essential to strike morale, a fact recognized by the company, which sent representatives calling on them to pressure their husbands back to work. But strikers' wives and women workers poured into the commissary and worked on the various committees. Following a street dance New Year's Eve about fifty women decided to form a Women's Auxiliary, and set up their own speakers' bureau, day care center for mothers on strike duty, first-aid station, welfare committee and the like. After battles began with the police, women established a Women's Emergency Brigade of 350, organized on military lines, ready to battle police. "We will form a line around the men, and if the police want to fire then they'll just have to fire into us," announced a leader.[143] "A new type of woman was born in the strike," one of the women said. "Women who only yesterday were horrified at unionism, who felt inferior to the task of organizing, speaking, leading, have, as if overnight, become the spearhead in the battle of unionism."[144] Another recalled, "I found a common understanding and unselfishness I'd never known in my life. I'm living for the first time with a definite goal. . . . Just being a woman isn't enough anymore. I want to be a human being with the right to think for myself." [145]

The union coordinated the strike and put forward union recognition as its central demand. What recognition meant was never clarified, but workers assumed it meant a powerful say for them in industrial decisions and they supported it enthusiastically. The strike spread rapidly from Flint and other initial centers throughout the General Motors system. Auto workers sat down at Guide Lamp in Anderson, Indiana, at Chevrolet and Fisher Body in Janesville, Wisconsin, and Cadillac in Detroit; regular strikes developed at Norwood and Toledo, Ohio, and Ternstedt, Michigan. General Motors was forced to halt production at Pontiac, Oldsmobile, Delco-Remy, and numerous other plants.[146] G.M.'s projected production for January of 224,000 cars and trucks was cut to 60,000, and in the first ten days of February, it produced only 151 cars in the entire country.

General Motors refused to bargain until the plants were evacuated and started a counter-attack on three levels: legal action, organization of an anti-strike movement, and direct violence against the strikers. The third day of the strike, G.M. lawyers requested and received an injunction from Judge Edward Black ordering

strikers to evacuate the plants, cease picketing, and allow those
wanting to work to enter. The Sheriff read the injunction to the sitdowners, who jeered him menacingly until he fled. Then a quick-
witted union lawyer checked and discovered that Judge Black
owned 3,365 shares of General Motors stock valued at $219,900.
This revealed the judge as a party in interest and made the injunction worthless, as well as showing dramatically the corporation's
power over government.

The company's next move was to organize the Flint Alliance
"for the Security of Our Jobs, Our Homes, and Our Community."
It was headed by George Boysen, a past and future General Motors official, and as a state police investigator reported, it was "a
product of General Motors brains." The Alliance worked in close
cooperation with Flint City Manager Barringer.[147] It began anti-
strike publicity and started recruiting anti-union workers, businessmen, farmers, housewives, schoolchildren and anyone else who
would sign a card; a large enrollment was desired, according to
Boysen, for "its moral effect toward smothering the strike movement."[148]

For almost two weeks there was little violence in Flint. But on
January 11th, supporters carrying dinner to the sitdowners in Fisher No. 2 were stopped at the gate by plant guards, whom the strikers had allowed to hold the ground floor of the factory. The pickets
started taking food up a twenty-four-foot ladder, but the guards
formed a flying wedge and seized the ladder. Suddenly police
closed off all traffic approaches to the plant. An attempt was clearly
underway either to starve out the sitdowners or evict them by
force, and unless the workers took the gates it would succeed.
Twenty sitdowners, armed with blackjacks, marched downstairs
and demanded the key to the gate. "My orders are to give it to nobody," the company policeman in charge replied.[149] The sitdowners gave them to the count of ten, then charged the gate. The
guards fled and locked themselves in the ladies room. The sitdowners put their shoulders to the wooden gates and splintered them, to
the cheers of the pickets who had quickly gathered outside.

Then suddenly patrol cars drew up and city policemen began
pouring out, throwing gas grenades at the pickets and into the
plant. At this point the earlier defensive preparations came in han-
dy; the sitdowners dragged firehoses to the windows and showered the police with two-pound door hinges. Within five minutes
the police, drenched and battered, retreated from the vicinity. The
police attacked again, but the outside pickets regrouped and drove
them off. In retreat the police began firing their guns, wounding
thirteen.

200   The conflict was quickly dubbed the Battle of the Running Bulls. It was considered a great victory for the strikers and a demonstration that they could hold out against police attack; in its wake, hitherto hostile workers flooded into the union. It also caused Governor Frank Murphy to order the National Guard into Flint.

Murphy was a New Deal Governor *par excellence.* In Detroit he had been one of the most liberal mayors in the country, providing exceptional public assistance to the unemployed and preventing the police from suppressing radicals. He was elected Governor with overwhelming labor support, and had insisted on making welfare relief available to strikers. He was also on close terms with such auto magnates as Walter Chrysler and Lawrence Fisher of Fisher Body, whose plants were the chief target in Flint. Although it was not known at the time, Murphy was also the owner of 1,650 shares of General Motors stock worth $104,875.[150]

Murphy did not intend to use the Guard to drive the sitdowners out by force. In this decision he was fully supported by General Motors, whose officials told Murphy privately that they did not want the strikers "evicted by force." [151] Knudson stated publicly that G.M. wanted the strike settled by negotiation rather than violence. Murphy, who believed the sitdown illegal but feared bloodshed in evicting the strikers, used the Guard to prevent vigilante attacks while holding the threat of a starve-out over the workers' heads. Murphy even succeeded in arranging a truce in which the union would evacuate the plants in exchange for a company pledge not to remove machinery or open the plants for fifteen days. This would have given away the strikers' strongest point, their possession of the plants, but it was scotched when the union labelled G.M.'s plans to negotiate with the Flint Alliance a double-cross and called off the truce.

Failing to evacuate the plants by negotiation, G.M. applied for a new injunction from a different judge. Meanwhile pressure built up as strikers were attacked by police in Detroit, vigilantes in Saginaw, and both in Anderson, Indiana. At this point the local leaders in Flint devised a bold initiative to shift the balance of forces by seizing the giant Chevrolet No. 4 plant. The problem was that union strength at Chevrolet No. 4 was limited and the plant was heavily protected by company guards. At a meeting of carefully selected Chevrolet workers which deliberately included company spies, Bob Travis announced a sitdown at Chevrolet No. 9 at 3:20 the next day, February 1st. Key leaders at No. 9 were told that they need only hold the plant for half an hour, as the real target was No. 6. As expected, company guards next day had been pped off and shifted from the No. 4 to the No. 9 area. At 3:20 orkers sat down at No. 9, company guards rushed in, and the di- ersionary battle began. Meanwhile, a handful of workers in Chev- olet No. 4 who knew the plan marched around the factory shout- ig, "Shut 'er down!" [152] but were too few even to be heard. Those on the plan in plant No. 6, meanwhile, led a small group over to o. 4. They were still too few to close down the huge plant, how- ver, and it seemed as if the plan had failed. But when they re- urned to No. 6, they found the whole plant on strike, and the work- rs marched en masse back to No. 4 and shut it down. About half le No. 4 workers joined the sitdown, the rest dropping their lun- hes in gondolas for the sitdowners as they left.

The capture of Chevrolet No. 4 changed the balance of forces. : demonstrated that the workers, far from being exhausted, were :ill able to expand their grip on the industry. As a result, General 1otors agreed to negotiate without evacuation of the plants. The w and order forces tried one more offensive, however. January nd, Judge Gadola issued a new injunction ordering evacuation of he plants and an end to picketing within twenty-four hours; when he workers ignored it he issued a writ of attachment and claimed uthority to have the National Guard enforce it without approval f the Governor. In the final crisis, thousands of workers poured nto Flint from hundreds of miles around — auto plants in Detroit nd Toledo were shut down by the exodus of workers to Flint. To void the appearance of provocation, the mobilization was de- lared Women's Day and women's brigades came in from Lan- ing, Pontiac, Toledo and Detroit. The crowd of perhaps 10,000 irtually occupied Flint, parading through the heart of the city, hen surrounding the threatened Fisher No. 1 plant, armed with hirty-inch wooden braces provided from the factory.

Learning that the Guard would not evict the sitdowners, City 1anager Barringer ordered all city police on duty and decided to rganize a 500-man "army of our own." "We are going down there hooting," he announced. "The strikers have taken over this town nd we are going to take it back." [153]

The tenor of events is suggested by a plan worked out without nion knowledge by the Union War Vets, who had taken respon- ibility for guarding strike leaders outside the plants. Had leaders een arrested under the Gadola writ, the veterans "would muster n armed force among their own number and in defense of the J.S. Constitution, of 'real Patriotism,' and the union, would take ver the city hall, the courthouse and police headquarters, capture nd imprison all officials and release the union men." [154]

The rug was pulled from under City Manager Barringer's

"army" when a G.M. official asked him to demobilize, saying "The last thing we want is rioting in the streets," [155] a result the workers' mass mobilization would have made inevitable.

General Motors agreed to recognize and bargain with the union in the struck plants and promised not to deal with any other organization in them for six months. As Sidney Fine wrote,

> What the U.A.W., like other unions at the time, understood by the term "recognition" has always been rather nebulous, but the union believed, and it had reason to, that it had been accorded a status of legitimacy in G.M. plants that it had never before enjoyed. It was confident that it would be able to consolidate its position in the 17 plants during the six-month period because it had no rivals to contend with. [156]

But if the agreement established the *union* firmly enough, it did little for the concrete grievances of the workers. When Bud Simons, head of the strike committee in Fisher No. l, was awakened and told the terms of the settlement, he remarked, "That won't do for the men to hear. That ain't what we're striking for." [157] When the union presented the settlement to the sitdowners, they asked, "How about the speed of the line? How about the bosses—would they be as tough as ever?" Did the settlement mean everything stood where it did when they started? [158]

The workers' forebodings were borne out by the negotiations which followed the evacuation of the plants. In the words of Irving Bernstein, "The corporation's policy was to contain the union, to yield no more than economic power compelled and, above all, to preserve managerial discretion in the productive process, particularly over the speed of the line." [159] The fundamental demand of the strike from the point of view of the workers had been "mutual determination" of the speed of production, but under the collective bargaining agreement signed March 12th, local management was to have "full authority" in determining these matters—if a worker objected, "the job was to be restudied and an adjustment was to be made if the timing was found to be unfair." [160] Further, instead of having a shop steward for every twenty-five workers, directly representing those they worked with, the union agreed to dealing with management through plant committees of no more than nine members per plant. Finally, the union agreed to become the agency for repressing workers' direct action against speed-up and other grievances, pledging that

> There shall be no suspensions or stoppages of work until every effort has been exhausted to adjust them through the regular grievance procedure, and in no case without the approval of the international officers of the union. [161]

Such agreements were not enough to control workers who had

just discovered their own power. Workers assumed victory in the
strike "would produce some radical change in the structure of status and power in G.M. plants," and they "were reluctant to accept the customary discipline exercised by management"; they "ran wild in many plants for months." [162] As one worker later recalled, "every time a dispute came up the fellows would have a tendency to sit down and just stop working." [163] According to Knudson, there were 170 sitdowns in G.M. plants between March and June, 1937.[164]

For example, on March 18th, 200 women sat down in a sewing room in the Flint Fisher Body No. 1 plant in a dispute over methods of payment. An hour later 280 sat down in sympathy with them in another sewing room. Next, sixty men sat down in the shipping department. Soon the entire plant was forced to shut down. "Since the strike was clearly in violation of the agreement . . . in which the union promised to protect the company against sitdowns during the life of the agreement, union officials hurried to Flint to settle the matter." [165]

Two weeks later 935 men struck in the final Chevrolet assembly plant. Then the parts and service plant struck in sympathy, closing Fisher Body Plant No. 2. Finally, workers in all departments of the Chevrolet complex walked out in sympathy. Meanwhile, the Fisher Body Plant and the Yellow Truck and Coach Plant in Pontiac were closed by workers protesting discharge of fellow workers. In all, 30,000 workers were involved in the wildcats at this time. This indicated that the workers had developed the ability to coordinate action between plants and even between cities without the union. Union officials told Governor Murphy that they were "mystified" by the sitdowns and that "their representatives in the plants told them they had been 'pushed into' the new sitdowns without union authorization."[166] Equally important, the workers won control over the rate of production, despite the union contract that conceded this authority to management. The *New York Times* reported April 2nd,

> Production in the Chevrolet Motor plants has been slowed down to nearly 50 per cent of former output during the last several weeks by concerted action of the union workers, with key men on the mother line stopping work at intervals to slow down production.[167]

Despite the failure of the union to win control over the production rates, a Fisher No. 1 worker who had opposed the big strike wrote,

> The inhuman high speed is *no more*. We now have a voice, and have slowed up the speed of the line. And [we] are now treated as human beings, and not as part of the machinery. The high pressure is taken off. . . . It proves clearly that united we stand, divided or alone we fall.[168]

204   The top leadership of the union considered these wildcat work stoppages a serious threat to union authority. A *New York Times* article entitled "Unauthorized Sit-Downs Fought by C.I.O. Unions" described the steps they took against them:

> (1) As soon as an unauthorized strike occurs or impends, international officers or representatives of the U.A.W. are rushed to the scene to end or prevent it, get the men back to work and bring about an orderly adjustment of the grievances.
>
> (2) Strict orders have been issued to all organizers and representatives that they will be dismissed if they authorize any stoppages of work without the consent of the international officers, and that local unions will not receive any money or financial support from the international union for any unauthorized stoppage of, or interference with, production.
>
> (3) The shop stewards are being "educated" in the procedure for settling grievances set up in the General Motors contract, and a system is being worked out which the union believes will convince the rank and file that strikes are unnecessary.
>
> (4) In certain instances there has been a "purge" of officers, organizers and representatives who have appeared to be "hot-heads" or "trouble-makers" by dismissing, transferring or demoting them.[169]

John L. Lewis and U.A.W. leaders blamed wildcats that idled tens of thousands in early April on Communist agitation, and the *New York Times* reported Lewis might soon "send some 'flying squadrons' of 'strong-arm men' from his own United Mine Workers to Flint . . . to keep the trouble-makers in line."[170] But William Weinstone, Michigan secretary of the Communist Party, hotly denied the charges that Communists were responsible; he himself denounced "helter-skelter use of the sit-down." [171] He added, "I have personally visited Flint today . . . and have not found a single Communist party member who countenanced or supported in the slightest the recent sit-down . . ." [172]

The Communists' general attitude toward the sitdown closely followed that of the C.I.O.; at a party strategy meeting an Akron Communist leader put it thus:

> The sitdown is an extremely effective organizational weapon. But credit must go to Comrade Williamson for warning us against the danger of these surprise actions. The sitdowns came because the companies refused to bargain collectively with the union. Now we must work for regular relations between the union and the employers—and strict observance of union procedure on the part of the workers.[173]

The lengths to which union opposition to wildcats went is illustrated by an incident in November, 1937. Four workers were fired from a Fisher Body plant and several hundred of their fellow workers struck and occupied the plant in protest. U.A.W. leaders denounced the strike, but were unable to persuade the workers to leave, and therefore resorted to strategem. They persuaded the workers to divide into two shifts and take turns occupying the plant, concentrated their supporters in one of these shifts, and marched the workers out of the plant, turning possession back to the company guards. When the other shift of strikers arrived to take their turn, they found themselves locked out.

It is not surprising that a *New York Times* reporter found the continuing sitdowns due in part to "dissatisfaction on the part of the workers with the union itself," and that "they are as willing in some cases to defy their own leaders as their bosses."[174] They had not reckoned on having the union become the agency for enforcing work discipline in the shops. Yet this had always been the essential policy of the C.I.O. unions, however much they might utilize sitdowns as an organizing tactic. C.I.O. Director John Brophy made this clear in a carefully worded statement issued before the General Motors strike:

> In the formative and promotional stages of unionism in a certain type of industry, the sitdown strike has real value. After the workers are organized and labor relations are regularized through collective bargaining, then we do urge that the means provided within the wage contract for adjusting grievances be used by the workers.[175]

Len De Caux, editor of the C.I.O. Union News Service, elaborated:

> . . . the first experience of the C.I.O. with sitdowns was in discouraging them. This was in the Akron rubber industry, after the Goodyear strike. C.I.O. representatives cautioned . . . the new unionists against sitdowns on the grounds that they should use such channels for negotiating grievances as the agreement provided . . .
>
> . . . when collective bargaining is fully accepted, union recognition accorded and an agreement reached, C.I.O. unionists accept full responsibility for carrying out their side of it in a disciplined fashion, and oppose sitdowns or any other strike action while it is in force.[176]

John L. Lewis was even more blunt: "A C.I.O. contract is adequate protection against sit-downs, lie-downs, or any other kind of strike."[177] Held up as a model was the C.I.O.'s largest union, the United Mine Workers, whose "agreement with coal companies now includes guarantees that there shall be no cessation of work during the term of the contract, and its constitution includes definite penalties, including fines, discharges and even a blacklist for anyone calling or participating in an unauthorized strike."[178] "The new unions, it is held in C.I.O. quarters, must educate and discipline their members or invite a situation of chaos and anarchy which could very well be utilized by either Leftists or Rightists in seizing political power," the *Times* concluded ominously.[179] Des-

pite the efforts of the union and management, however, the wildcats in the auto industry continued — and continue to this day.

✊

In the wake of the General Motors strike, people throughout
the country began sitting down. Even excluding the innumerable
quickies of less than a day, the Bureau of Labor Statistics recorded
sitdowns involving nearly 400,000 workers in 1937.[180] It would be
impossible of course even to summarize them all here, but we can
learn something of their range and pattern by examining a number
of those that occurred in the peak of the wave during and just after
the General Motors sitdown.

The most immediate impact was in the auto industry. The union began negotiations with Chrysler, and the company offered to
accept the General Motors agreement. According to the *New York
Times*, at the start of negotiations

> . . . the union committee started the discussion on the issue of senior-
> ity, but said that the rank-and-file demanded that sole bargaining be put
> first on the agenda.
> Then the various union locals held meetings and passed resolutions
> ordering the union committee to present an ultimatum demanding a yes-
> or-no answer from the company on sole bargaining by the following Mon-
> day.
> When the company replied in the negative, according to the union,
> the men themselves sat down without being ordered out by their lead-
> ers.[181]

The company secured an injunction ordering the 6,000 sitdowners
to leave, but as the hour it ordered evacuation came near, huge
crowds of pickets gathered — 10,000 at the main Dodge plant in
Hamtramck, 10,000 at the Chrysler Jefferson plant, smaller numbers at other Chrysler, Dodge, Plymouth and DeSoto plants—
30,000 to 50,000 in all, demonstrating the consequences of an attempted eviction. "It is generally feared," the *Times* reported,
that an attempt to evict the strikers with special deputies would
lead to an "inevitable large amount of bloodshed and the state of
armed insurrection . . ." [182]

Governor Murphy warned that the State might have to use
force to restore respect for the courts and other public authority,
to protect personal and property rights, and to uphold the structure of organized society, emphasizing that the State must prevent
"needless interruption to industry, commerce and transportation." [183] He established a law and order committee, but when top
U.A.W. officials refused to serve on it, "strikers inside the plant
could be seen waving their home-made blackjacks in jubilation. In-

side the gate about 150 women who had been serving meals in the company cafeteria engaged in a snake-dance, beating knives and forks against metal serving trays." [184]

Shop committees in the occupied plants voted not to leave the plants until they had won sole bargaining rights. Nonetheless on March 24th, John L. Lewis, representing the C.I.O., agreed to evacuate the plants on the basis of the General Motors settlement, which Chrysler had accepted even before the strike began. Many strikers considered the settlement a surrender, but they reluctantly left the place.

The Chrysler strike was merely the largest of dozens of simultaneous sitdowns in the Detroit area. About 20,000 additional auto workers were out as a result of a sitdown at the Hudson Motor Company. [185] Wildcat sitdowns in General Motors plants, as we have seen, occurred by the score during this period, many of them involving tens of thousands of workers at a time; by April 1st there were more than 120,000 auto workers on strike in Michigan. Workers occupied the Newton Packing Co. in late February and, after eleven days, turned off refrigeration of $170,000 worth of meat, stating they were "through fooling." [186] In early March, clerks sat down in the Crowley-Milner and Frank & Sedar department

Police break up a picket line at the West Philadelphia plant of the General Electric Company in February, 1946, after a court order banning mass demonstrations in front of plant gates.

stores. Thirty-five women workers seized the Durable Laundry, as the proprietor fired a gun over organizers' heads "to scare them away."[187] The same day, Detroit's four leading hotels were all closed by sitdowns and lockouts, the auto workers providing a mass picket line in one case. Women barricaded themselves in three tobacco plants for several weeks; in one case residents of the neighborhood battled their police guard with rock-filled snowballs. Eight lumberyards were occupied by their workers. Other sitdown strikes occurred at the Yale & Towne lock company and the Square D electrical manufacturers.

Unable to challenge the giant Chrysler strike, police moved forcefully against the lesser sitdowns. Early in the afternoon of March 20th, police evicted strikers from the Newton Packing Company. Three hours later 150 police attacked sitdowners at a tobacco plant.

> Hysterical cries echoed through the building as, by ones and twos, the 86 women strikers, ranging from defiant girls to bewildered workers with gray hair, were herded into patrol wagons and sped away, while shattering glass and the yells of the street throng added to the din.[188]

Such action could clearly be an entering wedge against the auto workers, and the U.A.W. responded by calling a mass protest rally in Cadillac Square and threatening to call a strike of 180,000 auto workers in the Detroit area (excluding those at G.M. for whom they had just signed a contract) and hinting that it would ask for a city-wide general strike unless forcible evictions of sitdowners in small stores and plants was halted. In the judgment of Russell B. Porter of the *New York Times*,

> ... it is wholly possible that the automobile workers' union might get the support of the city's entire labor movement, now boiling over with fever for union organization ... for a city-wide general strike.[189]

Telegrams went out to U.A.W. locals in Detroit to stand by in preparation to strike, but the city quickly halted its drive against the more than twenty remaining sitdowns.

In the two weeks March 7th-21st, Chicago experienced nearly sixty sitdowns. Motormen on the sixty-mile freight subway under Chicago shut off controls and sat down when the employer decided to ship a greater proportion of goods above ground and laid off thirty-five tunnel workers. The motormen were joined by 400 freight handlers and other employees who barricaded their warehouses. On March 12th, sitdowns hit the Loop, with more than 9,000 men and women striking—including waitresses, candy makers, cab drivers, clerks, peanut baggers, stenographers, tailors, truckers and factory hands. Eighteen hundred workers, including

three hundred office workers, sat down at the Chicago Mail Order
Co. and won a ten percent pay increase; 450 employees at three de
Met's tea rooms sat down as "the girls laughed and talked at the
tables they had served" until they went home that night with a
twenty-five percent pay increase [190]; next day sitdowns hit nine
more Chicago firms.

The range of industries and locations hit by sitdowns was virtually unlimited. Electrical workers and furniture workers sat down
in St. Louis. Workers at a shirt company sat down in Pulaski, Tennessee. In Philadelphia, workers sat down at the Venus Silk Hosiery Co. and the National Container Co. Leather workers in Garard,
Ohio, sat down, as did broom manufacturing workers in Pueblo,
Colorado. Workers sat down at a fishing tackle company in Akron,
Ohio. Oil workers sat down in eight gasoline plants in Seminole,
Oklahoma. The list could go on and on.

Sitdowns were particularly widespread among store employees, so easily replaced in ordinary strikes. Women sat down in two
Woolworth stores in New York. Pickets outside one store broke
through private guards, opened windows from a ledge fifteen feet
above ground, and passed through cots, blankets, oranges and
food packets to the strikers, who ate with china and silver from the
lunch counter. Similar sitdowns occurred in five F. & W. Grand
stores; in one, strikers staged an impromptu St. Patrick's Day cele-
bration and a mock marriage to pass the time. Having no chairs to
sit down on, 150 salesgirls and 25 stock boys in Pittsburgh staged a
"folded-arms strike" in four C.G. Murphy five-and-ten stores for
shorter hours and a raise; they also complained that "we have to
pay for our uniforms and washing them and have to sweep the
floor." [191] Twelve stores in Providence, Rhode Island, locked out
their employees to prevent an impending sitdown, whereupon the
unions called a general strike of retail trades.

Nor was the sitdown restricted to private employees. In Am-
sterdam, New York, municipal ash and garbage men sat down on
their trucks in the city Department of Public Works garage when
their demands for a wage increase were refused; when the Mayor
hired a private trucking firm, the strikers persuaded the men not
to work as strikebreakers. A similar strike occurred in Bridgeport,
Connecticut, when sixty trash collectors sat down demanding immediate reinstatement of a fellow-employee and the firing of the
foreman who had fired him. In New York, seventy maintenance
workers, half white, half black, barricaded themselves in the kitch-
en and laundry of the Hospital for Joint Diseases; services were
continued for patients, but not for doctors, nurses and visitors. A
series of similar sitdowns occurred in the Brooklyn Jewish Hospi-

210 tal. Forty grave-diggers and helpers prevented burials in a North Arlington, New Jersey, cemetery by sitting down in the toolhouse to secure a raise for the helpers. Seventeen blind workers sat down to demand a minimum wage at a workshop run by the New York Guild for the Jewish Blind, and were supported by a sympathy sit-down of eighty-three blind workers at a workshop of the New York Association for the Blind. Draftsmen and engineers in Brooklyn sat down against a wage cut in the office of the Park Department. W.P.A. workers in California sat down in the employment office as flying squadrons spread a strike through the Bay Area.

An important aspect of the sitdown was the extent to which it was used to challenge management decisions. We have already seen various examples of this, such as the Chicago freight subway workers' challenge to the decision to move more freight on the surface. On March 11th, workers at the Champion Shoe Company sat down when they found the company had secretly transferred fifty machines to a new plant elsewhere. Two hundred and fifty workers, more than half of them women, occupied a Philadelphia hosiery mill which management intended to close and prepared to block efforts to move the machinery.

A hundred and fifteen workers at the Yahr Lange Drug Company in Milwaukee, who had resisted efforts to unionize them, sat down in protest against a company policy of firing workers as soon as their age and length of service justified a raise. Their sole demand was removal of Fred Yahr as general manager of the company. "The girls sat around and played bridge and smoked, and the men gathered in knots awaiting the results. The telephone was not answered, and customers were not served. Salesmen on the road were notified of the strike by wire and responded that they were sitting down in their cars until it was settled." After a long conference with the workers, management announced that Mr. Yahr had resigned. The strikers, in effect, had "fired the boss."[192]

Far from being limited to employer-employee relationships, sitdowns were used to combat a wide range of social grievances. In Detroit, for example, thirty-five women barricaded themselves in a welfare office demanding that the supervisor be removed and that a committee meet with the new supervisor to determine qualifications of families for relief. Thirteen young men sat down in an employment agency where they had paid a fee for jobs that had then not materialized. In New York, representatives of fifteen families who lost their homes and belongings in a tenement fire sat down at the Emergency Relief Bureau demanding complete medical care for those injured in the fire and sufficient money for rehabilitation, instead of token sums the Bureau had offered. A few days later forty-five people sat in at another relief office, demanding aid for two families and a general forty percent increase for all families on home relief. In Columbus, Ohio, thirty unemployed men and women sat down in the Governor's office demanding $50 million for poor relief. And in St. Paul, Minnesota, 200 people demanding action on a $17 million relief plan staged a sitdown in the Senate chamber. In the Bronx, two dozen women sat down in an effort to prevent the eviction of two neighbors by twenty-five policemen.

Prisoners in the state prison in Joliet, Illinois, sat down to protest working in the prison yard on Saturday afternoon, usually a time of rest, as did prisoners in Philadelphia against a cut in prison wages. Children sat down in a Pittsburgh movie theater when the manager told them to leave before the feature film, as did children in Mexia, Texas, when a theater's program was cut. At Mineville, New York, 150 high school students struck because the contracts of the principal and two teachers had not been renewed. Women students at the Asheville Normal and Teachers College in North Carolina sat down to protest parietal rules. In Bloomington, Illinois, wives went on a sitdown strike, refusing to prepare meals, wash dishes, or answer door bells until they received more compensation from their husbands. In Michigan, thirty members of a National Guard company which had served in Flint during the G.M. sitdown staged a sitdown of their own in March because they had not been paid.

The sitdown idea spread so rapidly because it dramatized a simple, powerful fact: that no social institution can run without the cooperation of those whose activity makes it up. Once the example of the sitdowns was before people's eyes, they could apply it to their own situation. On the shop-floor it could be used to gain power over the actual running of production. In large industries it could be used for massive power struggles like the G.M. strike. In small shops it could force quick concessions. Those affected by public institutions — schools, jails, welfare departments and the like — could use similar tactics to disrupt their functioning and force concessions; these conflicts showed that ordinary people's lack of power over their daily lives led them to revolt not only in the workshops but in the rest of society as well. The power and spread of the sitdowns electrified the country: in March, 1937, alone there were 170 industrial sitdowns reported with 167,210 participants — no doubt a great many more went unrecorded.[193]

The sitdowns provided ordinary workers an enormous power

which depended on nobody but their fellow workers. As Louis Adamic wrote of the non-union sitdowns in Akron,

> The fact that the sitdown gives the worker in mass-production industries a vital sense of importance cannot be overemphasized. Two sitdowns which completely tied up plants employing close to ten thousand men were started by half a dozen men each. Imagine the feeling of power those men experienced! And the thousands of workers who sat down in their support shared that feeling in varying degrees, depending on their individual power of imagination. One husky gum-miner said to me, "Now we don't feel like taking the sass off any snot-nose college-boy foreman." Another man said, "Now we know our labor is more important than the money of the stockholders, than the gambling in Wall Street, than the doings of the managers and foremen." One man's grievance, if the majority of his fellow-workers in his department agreed that it was a just grievance, could tie up the whole plant. He became a strike leader; the other members of the working force in his department became members of the strike committee. *They* assumed full responsibility in the matter; formed their own patrols, they kept the machines from being pointlessly destroyed, and they met with management and dictated their terms. *They* turned their individual self-control and restraint into group self-discipline. . . . *They* settled the dispute, not some outsider.[194]

In the face of the sitdown wave, a great many employers decided to deal with unions voluntarily, and by World War II unions were established in practically all large industrial companies. Most significant was the largest corporation of them all, U.S. Steel, which reversed its bitter tradition of anti-unionism to recognize the C.I.O.'s Steel Workers Organizing Committee (S.W.O.C.). As Irving Bernstein wrote, it made sense for the corporation to engage in collective bargaining "on a consolidated basis with experienced and responsible union officials like Lewis and Murray rather than with disparate local groups led by men with no background in bargaining." U.S. Steel head Myron Taylor "had good reason to trust Lewis and Murray," whom he had been bargaining with already in the coal industry.[195]

The new contract cost U.S. Steel little—a wage increase they recouped twice over in a price increase, limitation on hours which was required anyway if they wanted to bid on government contracts, and some deference to seniority in laying off workers. In return, the contract provided that

> differences . . . should be taken up without cessation of work, with the final decision, if an agreement was not reached, to rest with an impartial umpire named by the company and union.[196]

S.W.O.C. was in a strong position to enforce this strike ban: its officials were appointed by the C.I.O., not elected by the steelworkers; all initiation fees and dues went through the central office, and locals were forbidden to sign an agreement or call a strike without its approval. As Myron Taylor wrote a year after the contract went into effect, "The union has scrupulously followed the terms of its agreement." [197]

In early 1937 Louis Adamic had an interesting interview with the head of a small steel company that had voluntarily recognized the C.I.O. soon after U.S. Steel, suggesting how union recognition looked to an employer faced with rising labor militancy. The employer described how he had been visited by a C.I.O. organizer who "began to sell me on the idea of letting the C.I.O. start a union in our plant." The organizer started to tell him "all about the petty troubles and pains-in-the-neck we'd had in the mill the past few weeks, which . . . amounted to a lot of trouble and expense" which "were bound to increase as the years went by . . ."

Why? Because, he said, in shops where the union was fought and men belonged to it secretly all sorts of damned things happened all the time, which led to fear, nervousness, and jitters among the men, to secret sabotage and loafing on the job. . . . he proceeded to tell me, too, that if we let the union come in, it would form a grievance committee consisting of workers in the mill; all the union men in the shop would be required, and others allowed, to take their grievances to the committee, which would assemble all the kicks and complaints and what-nots, then take them up with us — the management . . . say once a week; and many, perhaps most, of the grievances would be smoothed out by the committee itself without bothering us with them. . . . We signed an agreement for a year, the union was formed, about half the men joined, a grievance committee was organized and sure enough, the thing began to work out. . . . It seemed to act as a sort of collective vent. . . .

The men bring their grievances to committee members, then argue about them, then the first thing they know, in many instances, the grievances disappear.[198]

His only complaint was that grievance committee members "are new, green, inexperienced fellows, apt to get excited about nothing at all. As yet they can't quite handle authority and responsibility. They get 'tough' with us over little matters."

Workers had used the sitdown to establish a direct counter-power to management — freedom to set the pace of work, to tell the foreman where to get off, to share the work equitably, to determine their share of the product, and the like. They saw trade unionism as a way to guarantee this power. The new C.I.O. unions — like any political organizations trying to win a following — presented themselves as the fulfillment of the workers' desires. The objective of the C.I.O. organizing campaigns was that magical phrase "union recognition" — magical because it could mean all things to all people.

U.S. Steel Corporation willingly accepted collective bargaining, but the "little steel" companies decided to resist. Here police "hammer strike demonstrators into submission" near Chicago in May, 1937. Attacks on strikers were deliberate policy.

Unable to move against the giant Chrysler sitdown, Detroit police began breaking up various smaller sitdowns. Here they remove a striker from the Yale and Towne Co. Auto workers threatened to retaliate against the evictions with a general strike.

Brutality reached a peak in the "little steel" strike on Memorial Day, 1937, when police attacked unarmed pickets at the gates of the Republic Steel Company, fatally wounding ten demonstrators—shooting seven in the back and three in the side.

The "little steel" strike was marked by violence throughout. Here strikers and strikebreakers engage in a battle at a Republic Steel plant in Cleveland during which sixty were injured.

216   To the workers the C.I.O. proclaimed that union recognition meant an end to speed-up, shorter hours, higher wages, better working conditions, vacations with pay, seniority, job security, and —in the words of John L. Lewis—"industrial democracy." Furthermore—and here it won over the great number made cynical about unionism by their experience with the A.F.L.—the C.I.O. proclaimed that the union meant all the workers would be organized together and fighting the employers. It was this image that allowed the C.I.O. to appear as the champion of the great sitdown wave, even as it was systematically opposing and crushing sitdown movements.

Meanwhile, to management, it was able to declare itself with equal honesty as a system for disciplining the work force, managing workers' discontent, and protecting "against sit-downs, lie-downs, or any other kind of strike"—a claim whose validity it was able to demonstrate in practice. Thus with the cooperation of the government, which created a rigid institutional structure for collective bargaining through the Wagner Act and its National Labor Relations Board, the C.I.O. was able to channel the sitdown movement back into forms of organization which, far from challenging the power of the corporate rulers, actually reinforced their power over the workers themselves.

Chapter 5: Footnotes

1. Louis Adamic, *My America 1928-1938* (N.Y.: Harper & Brothers, Publishers, 1938), p. 309.
2. Charles Walker, "Relief and Revolution" in *The Forum*, September 1932, p. 156.
3. *Ibid.*, pp. 155-6.
4. Irving Bernstein, *The Lean Years, A History of the American Worker 1920-1933* (Baltimore, Md.: Penguin Books, 1960), p. 417.
5. *Ibid.*, pp. 423-4.
6. Adamic, p. 323.
7. Bernstein, *Lean Years*, p. 421.
8. Walker, p. 158.
9. Paul Mattick Sr., "What Can the Unemployed Do," in *Living Marxism*, No. 3, May 1938, p. 87. Author's italics.
10. Irving Bernstein, *Turbulent Years, A History of the American Worker 1933-1941* (Boston: Houghton Mifflin Co., 1970), p. 171.
11. Cited *Ibid.*, p. 34.
12. "Songs from the Depression," New Lost City Ramblers.For a vivid picture of popular feelings during the Depression, especially in Appalachia, this record is well worth attention.

13. Samuel Yellin, *American Labor Struggles* (N.Y.: Harcourt, Brace and Co., 1936), p. 328.
14. Bernstein, *Turbulent Years,* p. 266.
15. *Clarion,* May 18, 1934, cited in Wilfred H. Crook, *Communism and the General Strike* (Hamden, Conn.: The Shoe String Press, 1960), p. 112.
16. Bernstein, *Turbulent Years,* p. 271.
17. *New York Times,* July 4, 1934, cited in Crook, p. 116.
18. *San Francisco Examiner,* July 5, 1934, cited in Crook, p. 117.
19. *Ibid.*
20. Cited in Crook, p. 112.
21. Bernstein, *Turbulent Years,* p. 280.
22. *Ibid.,* p. 282.
23. *Ibid.,* p. 283.
24. *San Francisco Examiner,* July 13, 1934, cited in Crook, p. 120.
25. *New York Times,* July 8, 1934, cited in Yellin, p. 344.
26. *New York Times,* July 16, 1934, cited in Crook, p. 138.
27. E. Burke, "Dailies Helped Break General Strike," *Editor and Publisher,* July 28, 1934, cited in Yellin, p. 348.
28. *Los Angeles Times,* cited in Yellin, p. 347.
29. Bernstein, *Turbulent Years,* p. 287.
30. *Ibid.,* p. 288.
31. *New York Times,* July 18, 1934, cited in Yellin, p. 350.
32. Bernstein, *Turbulent Years,* p. 293.
33. *Ibid.,* p. 295.
34. Adamic, p. 370.
35. George O. Bahrs, *The San Francisco Employers' Council* (Phila.: Wharton School of Finance and Commerce, 1948), p. 7.
36. Roy W. Howard of Scripps-Howard newspapers to Louis Howe in the White House, cited in Bernstein, *Turbulent Years,* p. 221.
37. Charles R. Walker, *American City, A Rank-and-File History* (N.Y.: Farrar & Rinehart, 1937), pp. 97-8.
38. *Ibid.,* pp. 99-100.
39. *Ibid.,* pp. 102-3.
40. *Ibid.,* pp. 110-1.
41. *Ibid.,* p. 109.
42. *Ibid.,* p. 110.
43. *Ibid.,* p. 111.
44. *Ibid.,* pp. 113-4.
45. *Ibid.,* p. 120.
46. Cited *Ibid.,* pp. 168-9.
47. Cited *Ibid.,* pp. 171-2.
48. *Ibid.,* p. 181.
49. *Ibid.,* pp. 208-9.
50. *Ibid.,* p. 211.
51. *Ibid.,* p. 208.
52. Herbert J. Lahne, *The Cotton Mill Worker* (N.Y.: Farrar & Rinehart, 1944), p. 216.
53. Bernstein, *Turbulent Years,* pp. 302-4.
54. *Ibid.,* p. 306.
55. Alexander Kendrick, "Alabama Goes on Strike," in *The Nation,* Aug. 29, 1934, p. 233.
56. *New York Times,* Sept. 4, 1934.
57. *New York Times,* Sept. 5 & 6, 1934.
58. *New York Times,* Sept. 5, 1934.

218

59. *New York Times,* Sept. 16, 1934.
60. *New York Times,* Sept. 5, 1934.
61. *Ibid.*
62. Robert R.R. Brooks, "The United Textile Workers of America" (unpublished Ph.D. dissertation, Yale University, 1935), p. 376.
63. *New York Times,* Sept. 10, 1934.
64. *New York Times,* Sept. 6, 1934.
65. *Ibid.*
66. *Ibid.*
67. *Ibid.*
68. *Ibid.*
69. *New York Times,* Sept. 7, 1934.
70. *Ibid.*
71. *New York Times,* Sept. 10, 1934.
72. *New York Times,* Sept. 12, 1934.
73. *New York Times,* Sept. 13, 1934.
74. *New York Times,* Spet. 14, 1934.
75. *Ibid.*
76. *New York Times,* Sept. 12, 1934.
77. *New York Times,* Sept. 16, 1934.
78. *New York Times,* Sept. 18, 1934.
79. Brooks, p. 378; *New York Times,* Sept. 19, 1934.
80. Bernstein, *Turbulent Years,* p. 314.
81. *Ibid.*
82. Brooks, p. 379.
83. Cited in Bernstein, *Turbulent Years,* p. 315.
84. Brooks, pp. 384-5.
85. Lahne, p. 231.
86. Saul Alinsky, *John L. Lewis, an unauthorized biography* (N.Y.: G.P. Putnam's Sons, 1949), p. 72.
87. Bernstein, *Turbulent Years,* p. 99.
88. Ruth McKenney, cited in Bernstein, *Turbulent Years,* p. 98.
89. Ruth McKenney, *Industrial Valley* (N.Y.: Harcourt, Brace and Company, 1939), p. 101.
90. *Ibid.,* pp. 134-5.
91. *Ibid.,* pp. 166-9, 178.
92. *Ibid.,* p. 188.
93. *Ibid.,* pp. 194-5.
94. Bernstein, *Turbulent Years,* p. 591.
95. McKenney, pp. 198-9.
96. Cited in McKenney, pp. 133-4.
97. Adamic, p. 405.
98. *Ibid.,* pp. 405-6.
99. *Ibid.,* p. 406.
100. *Ibid.,* p. 407.
101. *Ibid.,* p. 408.
102. *Ibid.,* pp. 408-9.
103. McKenney, cited in Bernstein, *Turbulent Years,* p. 99.
104. McKenney, pp. 261-2.
105. Bernstein, *Turbulent Years,* p. 593.
106. *Ibid.,* p. 595.
107. Adamic, p. 411.
108. Henry Kraus, *The Many and the Few* (Los Angeles: Plantin, 1947), p. 8.
109. *Ibid.,* p. 9.

110. Herbert Harris, *American Labor* (New Haven: Yale University Press, 1939), p. 272.
111. Sidney Fine, *Sit-Down, the General Motors Strike of 1936-1937* (Ann Arbor: University of Michigan Press, 1969), p. 55.
112. *Ibid.,* p. 56.
113. Harris, p. 271.
114. Fine, pp. 59, 57.
115. Harris, p. 281.
116. Kraus, p. 10.
117. Bernstein, *Turbulent Years,* pp. 182-3.
118. Kraus, p. 12.
119. Bernstein, *Turbulent Years,* pp. 184-5.
120. Cited in Fine, p. 31.
121. *Ibid.*
122. Kraus, p. 42.
123. *Ibid.*
124. *Ibid.,* pp. 48-54.
125. Fine, p. 75.
126. J. Raymond Walsh, *C.I.O. — Industrial Unionism in Action*
127. Cited in Bernstein, *Turbulent Years,* p. 501.
128. Fine, p. 97.
129. Germer to Brophy, Nov. 30, 1936, cited in Fine, p. 136.
130. Bernstein, *Turbulent Years,* p. 524.
131. *Ibid.*
132. Kraus, p. 87.
133. *Ibid.,* p. 88.
134. *Ibid.,* p. 89.
135. *Ibid.,* p. 93.
136. *New York Times,* Feb. 1 & 9, 1937, cited in Fine, p. 172.
137. Fine, p. 165.
138. Edward Levinson, "Labor on the March," in *Harper's Magazine* CLXXIV (May 1937), cited in Fine, p. 160.
139. Cited in Fine, pp. 173-4.
140. Cited in Fine, p. 171.
141. Solomon Diamond, "The Psychology of the Sit-Down," in *New Masses,* *XXIII* (May 4, 1937), p. 16. *cited in Fine, p. 157.*
142. Paul Gallico, "Sit-Down Strike," p. 159, cited in Fine, p. 171.
143. Genora Johnson, cited in Fine, p. 201.
144. Cited in Fine, p. 201.
145. *Ibid.*
146. Bernstein, *Turbulent Years,* p. 525.
147. Fine, p. 189.
148. *Ibid.,* p. 188.
149. Kraus, p. 128.
150. Fine, p. 155.
151. *Ibid.,* p. 236.
152. Kraus, p. 211.
153. Fine, p. 281.
154. Kraus, p. 248.
155. Fine, p. 282.
156. *Ibid.,* pp. 306-7.
157. *Ibid.,* p. 307.
158. Kraus, p. 287.
159. Bernstein, p. 551.

220
160. Fine, p. 325.
161. *New York Times,* April 11, 1937.
162. Fine, p. 321.
163. *Ibid.*
164. Bernstein, *Turbulent Years,* p. 559.
165. *New York Times,* Mar. 19, 1937.
166. *New York Times,* Apr. 2, 1937.
167. *Ibid.*
168. Alfred H. Lockhart to Gernsley F. Gorton, Mar. 7, 1937, William H. Phelps Papers, Michigan Historical Collection, cited in Fine, p. 328.
169. *New York Times,* Apr. 11, 1937.
170. *New York Times,* Apr. 4, 1937.
171. *New York Times,* Apr. 7, 1937.
172. *Ibid.*
173. McKenney, p. 340.
174. *New York Times,* Apr. 11, 1937.
175. Adamic, p. 415.
176. Harris, pp. 290-1.
177. *Ibid.,* p. 291.
178. *New York Times,* Apr. 11, 1937.
179. *Ibid.*
180. Bernstein, *Turbulent Years,* p. 500.
181. *New York Times,* Mar. 27, 1937.
182. *New York Times,* Mar. 19, 1937.
183. *New York Times,* Mar. 18, 1937.
184. *Ibid.*
185. *New York Times,* Mar. 21, 1937.
186. *New York Times,* Mar. 9, 1937.
187. *New York Times,* Mar. 18, 1937.
188. *New York Times,* Mar. 21, 1937.
189. *Ibid.*
190. *New York Times,* Mar. 31, 1937.
191. *New York Times,* Mar. 21, 1937.
192. *New York Times,* Apr. 15, 1937.
193. Fine, p. 331.
194. Adamic, p. 408.
195. Bernstein, *Turbulent Years,* p. 468.
196. *New York Times,* Mar. 18, 1937.
197. Bernstein, *Turbulent Years,* p. 468.
198. Adamic, pp. 431-3.

Chapter 6
Postscript: The War
and Post-War Strike Wave

The pattern of mass strikes was significantly transformed by the institutional structures developed in the 1930's. To see the effects of the new relations established among workers, unions, employers, and government, let us turn to World War II and its aftermath, a period which shared some but by no means all of the characteristics of the other mass strikes we have studied.

With the coming of World War II, the separation of the trade unions and the workers' own action became complete. When the United States entered the war, both A.F.L. and C.I.O. leaders pledged that for the duration of the war there should be no strikes or walkouts. Thus, at a time when profits were "high by any standard" and a great demand for labor meant "higher wages could be secured . . . and a short stoppage could secure immediate results," the unions renounced the one method by which workers could have gained from the situation. Instead, they took on the function of administering government decisions affecting the workplace, disciplining the workforce, and keeping up production. " . . . To cease production is to strike at the very heart of the nation," proclaimed the A.F.L.; the C.I.O. announced it would "redouble its energies to promote and plan for ever-increasing production." [2] Over the radio, Philip Murray of the C.I.O. urged labor to "Work! Work! Work! Produce! Produce! Produce!" [3]

Interestingly, the unions with Communist leadership carried this policy furthest. As *Business Week* noted,

A more conciliatory attitude toward business is apparent in unions which once pursued intransigent policies. On the whole, the organizations involved are those which have been identified as Communist-dominated.

. . . Since Russia's involvement in the war, the leadership in these unions has moved from the extreme left-wing to the extreme right-wing position in the American labor movement.

Today they have perhaps the best no-strike record of any section of organized labor; they are the most vigorous proponents of labor-management cooperation; they are the only serious labor advocates of incentive wages. . . . In general, employers with whom they deal now have the most peaceful labor relations in industry.

Complaints to the union's national officers usually will bring all the organization's disciplinary apparatus to focus on the heads of the unruly local leaders.[4]

222   As in World War I, the government established a tripartite National War Labor Board, empowered to impose final settlements on all labor disputes. On request of the President, Congress passed an Economic Stabilization Act, essentially freezing wages at the level of September 15th, 1942; the Board retained power to make exceptions in cases of maladjustment and substandard wages. Thus the widespread modern practice, in which the government participates in setting wages, even in ordinary wage disputes, in the interest of "economic stability," was established.

"We're going to have to call on the leaders of labor to put this [wage stabilization] over," the chairman of the War Labor Board declared in an interview. "That is another reason for upholding the hands of leaders of organized labor."[5] In exchange for enforcing the no-strike pledge, unions had their hands upheld by being granted rights that greatly aided their growth, while making them less vulnerable to pressure from their own rank and file. The unions' problem, as Joel Seidman put it in his study *American Labor from Defense to Reconversion,* was this:

Since the right to strike was suspended, how could they produce the rapid improvements in wages and working conditions and the prompt and satisfactory settlement of grievances that would sell unionism to nonmembers and keep old members paying their dues? How could they co-operate with management to boost production as required by war needs, if their time and energy had to go, month after month, into the routine but exhausting tasks of signing up new members and keeping old ones satisfied, so that union strength would be preserved and the treasury maintained? How could they build the responsible type of unionism demanded by the nation at war without the power afforded by a security clause to discipline those who violated the contract or broke union rules? How could they afford to be discriminating on grievances, refusing to waste valuable time on those of little or no merit, if the workers thus offended were free to quit the union and persuade their friends to do likewise? If union leaders were to meet their responsibilities under wartime conditions, they argued, they had to be assured that their membership would remain high and their treasuries full.[6]

In most cases, the Board met this need for "union security" by setting up maintenance-of-membership provisions, under which no union member could quit for the duration of the contract. Thus the union was "safe-guarded against a shrinkage of membership and relieved of the necessity of reselling itself to the membership every month."[7] Maintenance of membership "protected the union from those new employees who did not wish to join or those old employees who became dissatisfied."[8] And by making the unions dependent on the government instead of on their members, it kept them "responsible." As the Board decision on maintenance-of-membership put it,

By and large, the maintenance of a stable union membership makes for the maintenance of responsible union leadership and responsible union discipline, makes for keeping faithfully the terms of the contract, and provides a stable basis for union-management cooperation for more efficient production. If union leadership is responsible and cooperative, then irresponsible and uncooperative members cannot escape discipline by getting out of the union and thus disrupt relations and hamper production.[9]

The Board also declared:

Too often members of unions do not maintain their membership because they resent the discipline of a responsible leadership. A rival but less responsible leadership feels the pull of temptation to obtain and maintain leadership by relaxing discipline, by refusing to cooperate with the company, and sometimes with unfair and demagogic attacks on the company. It is in the interests of management, these companies have found, to cooperate with the unions for the maintenance of a more stable, responsible leadership.[10]

Further, the Board could hold the threat of refusing maintenance-of-membership as a club over any unions that did not cooperate. "Even a stoppage of a few hours, when engaged in deliberately by a union, was enough evidence of irresponsibility for the Board to deny it the protection of the membership maintenance clause." [11] For example, on September 19th, 1942, the Board denied a union security clause for an A.F.L. union at the General Electric Company in Buffalo because it had gone on strike for a few hours in June.

The unions thrived under these conditions; the greatest growth of union membership in American history may well have come in this period of collaboration with management and government. By 1946, sixty-nine percent of production workers in manufacturing were covered by collective bargaining agreements, including almost all of the largest corporations.[12]

At first, the power of the government and the unions, combined with general support for the war, virtually put an end to strikes. The chairman of the War Labor Board called labor's no-strike policy an "outstanding success." [13] Five months after Pearl Harbor he reported that there had not been a single authorized strike and that every time a wildcat walkout had occurred union officials had done all they could to end it. With the exception of a series of successful strikes by the United Mine Workers in 1943, the unions continued to hold to this role until the end of the war.

Faced with this united front of government, employers, and their own unions, workers developed the technique of quick unofficial strikes independent of and even against the union structure on a far larger scale than ever before. The number of such strikes began to rise in the summer of 1942, and by 1944—the last full year of

224   the war—there were more strikes than in any previous year in American history,[14] averaging 5.6 days apiece.[15] Jerome Scott and George Homans, two Harvard sociologists studying wildcats reported that "the responsible leaders of the unions were as weak as management in dealing with 'quickies,' and the government, for all its new machinery, almost as weak."[16] They described a detailed study of 118 work stoppages in Detroit auto plants in December, 1944, and January, 1945:

> ... only four strikes ... might be attributed to wages and more specifically attributable to union organization. Most of the strikes were protests against discipline, protests against certain company policies, or protests against the discharge of one or more employees.[17]

Many involved all three. For example, one strike record read,

> 7 employees stopped work in protest of discharge of employee for refusing to perform his operation; 5 of this 7 were discharged when they refused to return to work; 320 employees then stopped work and left plant.[18]

"If one added to this, that the international union was unsuccessful, and that the War Labor Board succeeded only after a time, in getting the men to go back to work, one would have the picture of a characteristic quickie," they concluded.[19]

The sense of solidarity was strong enough so that wildcats often reached large proportions. In February, 1944, 6,500 Pennsylvania anthracite miners struck to protest the discharge of a fellow worker. Ten thousand workers at the Briggs Manufacturing Company in Detroit struck for one day over a cutback in work schedules. Ten thousand workers at the Timken Roller Bearing Co. in Canton, Ohio, struck twice in June, 1944, over the general refusal of the employer to settle grievances. In September, 1944, 20,000 workers struck for two days at the Ford Willow Run Bomber plant against the transfer of workers in violation of seniority rules.[20]

This form of resistance became an industrial tradition, into which new workers were initiated. For instance, one company set a high output standard in an operation in which many young and inexperienced workers were employed. The newcomers strove to meet the standard until an old-timer came and told them they ought to stick together and turn out a good deal less. The company fired the old-timer and several of the new workers, and the other workers in the plant responded with a wildcat.[21] Those who worked together functioned as an informal organization. As Scott and Homans found, "In almost all instances a wildcat strike presupposes communication and a degree of informal group organization. The strike had some kind of leadership, usually from within the group, and the leaders do some kind of planning, if only but a few hours or minutes ahead."[22] Many official labor leaders, in con-

trast, "were dealing more with War Labor Board decisions and policies relating to the union as a whole than with the feeling of the
men in the lines . . . no company president could have been more bewildered and irritated than a representative of the central office of
the union, called in to stop a wildcat strike.[23]

In many cases the strikes were directed against decisions of
the War Labor Board. For example, in October, 1943, the union representing workers at the National Malleable and Steel Castings
Company in Cleveland requested a wage increase from the Board.
After nine months the Board granted an increase of only two and
one-half cents an hour; in late July, 1,100 workers struck against
the award. Similarly, maintenance men in twenty Detroit-area auto
plants struck in October, 1944, idling 50,000 men when their request for an eleven-cent increase in hourly wages had sat before
the Board for nine months without action.[24]

The unions and the employers worked hand-in-hand to suppress the wildcats. For example, at the Bell Aircraft Corporation
plant in Marietta, Georgia, employees in the electrical department,
most of them women, left their jobs after the transfer of a supervisor. Union officials ordered them back to work, but the workers
held out for six hours. Next they were called to a meeting in the
plant labor relations office; union officials told them they had for-
feited union protection when they broke the no-strike pledge, then
company officials handed out discharge slips to the seventy workers.[25] In the Akron rubber industry, "some plants had work stoppages almost daily over minor grievances, dissatisfaction with
wage rates." In a typical response, United Rubber Workers President Sherman H. Dalrymple one week expelled seventy-two combat tire band builders who participated in a wildcat at General
Tire and Rubber Co., and two mill-room workers blamed for leading a strike at Goodyear. This amounted to firing, for

management was obliged to conform to the maintenance of membership
clause in the rubber contracts and dismiss the expelled workers because
they are no longer union members in good standing. . . . General and Goodyear are expected to notify the appropriate local draft boards of the dis-
missals, and the change in occupational status of the strikers may subject
them to reclassification,

Business Week reported.[26] Dalrymple's home local, Goodrich Local 5, then retaliated by voting to expel him for violating the union
constitution, whereupon the union's General Executive Board
backed down and reinstated all but seven of the wildcatters.

Detroit, the center of defense production, was likewise the center of the strike movement. Detroit papers had carried reports on a
dozen strikes a week on the average for the first three months of

226 1944. At Ford, two or three a week were common. Occasionally they became violent. For example, a crowd of workers overpowered a plant protection man and demolished the office and records of a labor relations officer for whom they were searching. The president of the Ford local promised to take "whatever measures are necessary to wipe out rowdyism in Local 600." Twenty-six "ringleaders" were fired and ninety-five more were disciplined with the tacit approval of the U.A.W. officials. "Implementation of this policy in the Ford case was hailed by management people, who feel that only a few examples of this kind are necessary to bring labor relations back to a level keel," *Business Week* reported.[27] When members of Local 600 moved a strike vote against the penalties, the officers quickly adjourned the meeting.

During the forty-four months from Pearl Harbor to V-J Day, there were 14,471 strikes involving 6,774,000 strikers—more than during any period of comparable length in United States history.[28] In 1944 alone there were 369,000 steel and iron workers, 389,000 auto workers, 363,000 other transportation equipment workers, and 278,000 miners involved in strikes.[29] In many cases, the "quickie" tactics were extremely effective in improving working conditions and easing the burden of company discipline. Workers virtually made extra holidays for themselves around Christmas and New Year's, holding illicit plant parties and cutting production to a trickle. Workers often created free time for themselves on the job by other means. On one occasion workers in an aircraft plant staged a necktie-cutting party in the middle of working hours, roaming through the plant snipping off ties of fellow workers, supervisors, and management men. The wildcat tradition and organization gave workers a direct counter-power over such management decisions as the speed of work, numbers of workers per task, what foremen were acceptable, and how the work was organized. While the effects are impossible to measure, it is worth noting that industry spokesmen claimed a decrease of "labor efficiency" of twenty to fifty percent during the war period.[30]

No doubt the unions would have liked a continuation of wartime conditions—protection by government and cooperation with management—into the post-war period. Presidents Murray and Green of the C.I.O. and A.F.L. signed a "Charter of Industrial Peace" with Eric Johnston, president of the U.S. Chamber of Commerce, in March, 1945—"It's Industrial Peace for the Post-war Period!" read the front-page headline of the *C.I.O. News*.[31] But this was mostly wishful thinking. As early as July, 1944, the *New*

York Times was observing "labor-management antagonisms which forecast a post-war period of great turmoil in labor relations . . . " [32] The real question was not whether there would be strikes, but whether they would be union-controlled or wildcat. *Business Week* found many who expected

> large numbers of quickie strikes. . . . these analysts admit that the end results of such stoppages may prove as substantial as those of the premeditated, big-league strikes. [33]

"Business was resolved to 'restore efficiency' and raise productivity — in many cases below pre-war standards — by breaking the de facto control of production won by the workers during the war. To this end employers demanded from the unions "company security" against wildcats and a recognition of management's "right to manage." The unions' program after the war was, as Clark Kerr put it, "a continuation substantially of the *status quo* . . . " [34] They set as their main bargaining objective the maintenance of wartime incomes. Through loss of overtime and downgrading of workers, the weekly wages of non-war workers decreased ten percent between the spring of 1945 and the winter of 1946; war workers lost thirty-one percent, [35] and were making eleven percent less spendable income than in 1941. [36] A government study released in May, 1946, found that "in most cases, wages during the first phase of reconversion were inadequate for the maintenance of living standards permitted by earnings in the year preceding the Pearl Harbor attack." [37] To compensate for these losses and to re-establish rank-and-file support, the unions bargained for substantial increases in hourly wages.

With the end of the war, the expected strike wave began. In September, 1945, the first full month after V-J Day, the number of man-days lost to strikes doubled, and doubled again in October. [38] Forty-three thousand oil workers struck in twenty states on September 16th. Two hundred thousand coal miners struck on September 21st to support the supervisory employees' demand for collective bargaining. Forty-four thousand Northwest lumber workers struck, seventy thousand Midwest truck drivers, forty thousand machinists in San Francisco and Oakland. East Coast longshoremen struck for nineteen days, flat glass workers for 102 days, and New England textile workers for 133 days. [40] And these were but a prelude to the great strikes of 1945-1946.

Three days after V-J Day, the United Auto Workers requested a thirty percent increase in wage rates without a price increase at General Motors to maintain incomes; the company offered a ten percent cost-of-living increase and told the union its prices were none of the union's business. U.A.W. President R.J. Thomas

228   stated he hoped that a settlement could be reached "without a work stoppage," but by early September some ninety auto and auto-part plants around Detroit were already on strike, and the union decided to order a strike vote.[41] When G.M. failed to respond to a union offer to have all issues settled by arbitration if the company would open its books for public examination, 225,000 workers walked out November 21st.

The auto strikers were soon joined by workers throughout industry. On January 15th, 1946, 174,000 electrical workers struck. Next day 93,000 meatpackers walked out. On January 21st, 750,000 steelworkers struck, the largest strike in United States history. At the height of these and 250 lesser disputes, 1,600,000 workers were on strike.[42] On April 1st, 340,000 soft-coal miners struck, causing a nation-wide brown-out; and a nation-wide railroad strike by engineers and trainmen over work-rule changes on May 23rd brought "an almost complete shutdown of the nation's commerce."[43] The first six months of 1946 marked what the U.S. Bureau of Labor Statistics called "the most concentrated period of labor-management strife in the country's history," with 2,970,000 workers involved in strikes starting in this period.[44] Nor was the strike wave limited to industrial workers. Strikes were unusually widespread among teachers, municipal and utility workers, and there were more strikes in transportation, communication, and public utilities than in any previous year.[45] By the end of the year, 4.6 million workers had been involved in strikes; their average length was four times that of the war period.[46]

The government moved in quickly to contain the strike movement; as President Truman wrote, "it was clear to me that the time had come for action on the part of the government."[47] In the auto dispute, he appointed a "fact-finding board" and appealed to the strikers to return to work pending its decision; similar boards followed for numerous other industries. The findings of the General Motors strike board, generally followed by the other boards as well, recommended a 19.5 percent wage increase, six cents above the corporation's last offer and a little more than half of what the union demanded as necessary to retain wartime incomes. General Motors refused to accept the recommendation.

Where fact-finding boards were not sufficient to set limits to the strike wave, the government turned to direct seizures, still authorized under wartime powers. On October 4th, 1945, the President directed the Navy to seize half the refining capacity of the United States, thus breaking the oil workers' strike.[48] On January 24th, 1946, the packinghouses were seized on the grounds that the strike was impeding the war effort — months after V-J Day — and the strike was thus broken. The nation's railroads were seized May 17th to head off a nation-wide strike. Workers struck anyway on May 23rd and only the President's threat to draft the strikers and call up the Army to run the railroads forced them back to work. On May 21st, the government seized the bituminous coal mines; the miners continued to strike, however, forcing the government to grant demands unacceptable to the operators and continue its control of the mines for many months. On November 20th, the miners struck again, this time directly against the government. The government secured an injunction against the U.M.W., and when the miners struck anyway the union was fined $3.5 million for contempt. As President Truman wrote, "We used the weapons that we had at hand in order to fight a rebellion against the government . . . "[49]

The unions made little effort to combat the government's attack, despite their demonstrated power virtually to stop the entire economy. Except for the miners, they returned to work when the government seized their industries, and in most cases they accepted the recommendations of the fact-finding boards, even though these admittedly meant a decline in workers' incomes below wartime levels. Indeed, by May, 1947 — a year after the big strikes — the average worker had less purchasing power than he had had in January, 1941[50]; in March, 1947, auto and basic steelworkers were making almost twenty-five percent less than two years before.[54]

Nor did the unions generally attempt to combine their strength, even within the A.F.L. or C.I.O.; each union made settlements without consideration of others still on strike. Thus the division of the working class that had been the source of so much criticism of craft unionism was reproduced on a larger scale by industrial unionism. This contrasts with the high level of rank-and-file solidarity, indicated not only by the nation-wide strikes of 1946 but also by general strikes in Lancaster, Pennsylvania, Stamford, Connecticut, Rochester, New York, and Oakland, California.

Indeed, the union leaderships would have preferred to avoid the strikes of 1946 altogether; they led them only because the rank and file were determined to strike anyway and only by leading the strikes could the unions retain control of them. In a widely-cited *Collier's* article, Peter F. Drucker pointed out that in the major strikes of 1945-1946,

it was on the whole not the leadership which forced the workers into a strike but worker pressure that forced a strike upon the reluctant leadership; most of the leaders knew very well that they could have gained as much by negotiations as they finally gained by striking. And again and again the rank and file of the union membership refused to go back to work . . .[52]

230   The attitude of the unions was not accidental; we have seen it develop throughout the course of this book. It was embodied in the preamble to the 1947 U.S. Steel contract, in which company officials pronounced that they were not anti-union, and union officials stated they were not anti-company, but were "sincerely concerned with the best interests and well-being of the business . . . " [53]

Far from trying to break the unions, management in the large corporations had learned how to use them to control the workers; G.M.'s number one demand in 1946 auto negotiations was "union responsibility for uninterrupted production." [54] The unions were more than willing to continue their role in disciplining the labor force; ninety-two percent of contracts in 1945 provided automatic arbitration of grievances,[55] and by 1947 ninety percent of contracts pledged no strikes during the course of the agreement.[56] Wildcat action on the part of workers was the natural result of this union-management cooperation; in U.S. Steel alone there were sixty-three unauthorized strikes in 1946.[57]

The war integrated the American economy more than ever before. The conditions affecting workers in 1946 cut across industry lines, leading to the closest thing to a national general strike of industry in the twentieth century. The potential capacity of the workers to paralyze not just one company or industry but the entire country was demonstrated. At the same time, even simple wage settlements affected the entire economy, so that the government took over the function of regulating wages for the whole of industry. In this situation, the trade unions played an essential role in forestalling what might otherwise have been a general confrontation between the workers of a great many industries and the government, supporting the employers. The unions were unable to prevent the post-war strike wave, but by leading it they managed to keep it under control. Nonetheless, they were unable to prevent wildcat strikes and other direct challenges by workers to management control.

Chapter 6: Footnotes

1. John T. Dunlop, "The Decontrol of Wages and Prices," in *Labor in Postwar America,* Colston E. Warne, Ed. (Brooklyn, N.Y.: Remsen Press, 1949), pp. 4-5.
2. Joel Seidman, *American Labor from Defense to Reconversion* (Chicago: University of Chicago Press, 1953), pp. 78, 79.
3. Philip Murray, cited in Art Preis, *Labor's Giant Step, Twenty Years of the CIO* (N.Y.: Pioneer Publishers, 1964), p. 198.
4. "Bridges' Setback," in *Business Week,* Mar. 18, 1944, pp. 83-4.
5. Davis, cited in Preis, p. 155.
6. Seidman, pp. 91-2.
7. *Ibid.,* p. 62.
8. *Ibid.,* p. 94.

9. Republic Steel Corporation, etc., *I. War Labor Report* 325 (July 16, 1942), pp. 340-1, cited in Seidman, p. 101.
10. Cited in Preis, p. 155.
11. Seidman, p. 105.
12. Bureau of Labor Statistics, *Bulletin 909* (1947), p. 1.
13. Davis, cited in Seidman, p. 134.
14. Bureau of Labor Statistics, *Bulletin 878* (1946), p. 3.
15. *Ibid.*
16. Jerome F. Scott and George C. Homans, "Reflections on Wildcat Strikes," *American Sociology Review* (June 1947), p. 278.
17. *Ibid.,* p. 280.
18. *Ibid.*
19. *Ibid.*
20. *Monthly Labor Review,* Apr. 1944, p. 783; Aug. 1944, p. 357; Nov. 1944, p. 1018.
21. Scott & Homans, p. 281.
22. *Ibid.,* p. 283.
23. *Ibid.,* p. 282.
24. *Wall Street Journal,* Aug. 22, 1944; *Monthly Labor Review,* Apr. 1944, p. 1218.
25. *Business Week,* Nov. 25, 1944, p. 110.
26. *Business Week,* Jan. 15, 1944, p. 88.
27. *Business Week,* Mar. 18, 1944, pp. 88-89.
28. Preis, p. 236.
29. *Handbook of Labor Statistics,* Bureau of Labor Statistics, Bulletin 916, 1947, p. 137.
30. Bruce R. Morris, "Industrial Relations in the Automobile Industry," in Warne, p. 416.
31. *C.I.O. News,* Apr. 2, 1945, cited in Preis, p. 257.
32. *New York Times,* July 30, 1944.
33. *Business Week,* Dec. 16, 1944, p. 82.
34. Clark Kerr, "Employer Policies in Industrial Relations, 1945 to 1947," in Warne, p. 45.
35. Bureau of Labor Statistics, *Bulletin 876,* (1946), p. 8.
36. *Ibid.,* p. 17.
37. *Ibid.,* p. 1.
38. Seidman, p. 221.
39. Preis, pp. 262-3.
40. *Ibid.*
41. *Ibid.,* p. 262.
42. Bureau of Labor Statistics, *Bulletin 918,* (1947), p. 8.
43. Seidman, p. 235.
44. *Ibid.*
45. *Ibid.,* pp. 12-3.
46. *Ibid.,* p. 1.
47. Harry S. Truman, p. 498.
48. Richard B. Johnson, *Government Seizure in Labor Disputes* (Phila., University of Pennsylvania, 1948), p. 106.
49. Truman, p. 504.
50. Morris, p. 416.
51. H.M. Douty, "Review of Basic American Labor Conditions," in Warne, p. 130.
52. Peter F. Drucker, "What to Do About Strikes," in *Collier's,* Jan. 18, 1947, p. 12.
53. Frank T. De Vyver, "Collective Bargaining in Steel," in Warne, p. 390.
54. Morris, p. 409.
55. Fred H. Joiner, "Developments in Union Agreement," in Warne, pp. 40-1.
56. *Ibid.,* p. 35.
57. De Vyver, p. 390.

Part 2
The Significance of
American Strikes

Chapter 7
The Significance
of Mass Strikes
I. The Mass Strike Process

If, as Rosa Luxemburg wrote, mass strikes form "a perpetually moving and changing sea of phenomena," how is it possible to make sense of them? What ties together the disparate local, national, and general strikes, occupations, street fights, armed confrontations, and other actions we have seen arise during these peak periods of social conflict?

Let us start by isolating three related processes: the challenge to existing authorities, the tendency of workers to begin taking over direction of their own activities, and their development of solidarity with each other.

These processes begin in the cell-unit of industrial production, the group of those who work together. As Elton Mayo discovered in his study of factories,

> In every department that continues to operate, the workers have— whether aware of it or not—formed themselves into a group with appropriate customs, duties, routines, even rituals; and management succeeds (or fails) in proportion as it is accepted without reservation by the group as authority and leader.[1]

The development of these work groups was studied in 1946 by the Committee on Human Relations in Industry at the University of Chicago. In a number of factories in the Chicago area, they found that most work groups established a "quota" beyond which the group expects that no individual worker will produce. The new employee was systematically "indoctrinated" by the work group. The work group "expects him to conform to its system of social ethics."[2] This system was backed by the workers' knowledge that management would use higher production by one of them to speed up everyone else. As one worker expressed it, "They begin by asking you to cut the other guy's throat, but what happens is that everybody's throat is cut, including your own."[3] The workers worked intensively for a short time to meet the quota, then used the remaining free time as their own.

Much of the time accumulated in this fashion was used "shooting the breeze" or reading newspapers in the toilet. The observers, however, believe . . . that the greater part was spent in "government work." Such work included making the "illegal" devices and fixtures which served as short-cuts in production, repairing parts damaged by men in other departments so that repair tickets might be avoided, and making equipment for their automobiles and homes. Most workers did not like to be idle for too great a time, but all of them preferred "government work" to production work.[4]

The workers saw the cooperation and sociable relaxation created by such action as valuable in themselves. As one put it, "Sure, I think most of us would admit that we could double our take-home if we wanted to shoot the works, but where's the percentage? A guy has to get something out of life. Now my little lady would rather have me in a good humor than have the extra money. The way it works out none of us are going to be Van-Asterbilts so why not get a little pleasure out of living together and working together."[5]

The work groups also created their own ways of getting the work done, contradicting those of management. The scheduling of work was often reorganized so that machine operators could eliminate extra time setting up the work. Each work group had special cutting tools, jigs, and fixtures, usually made on "government time," through which operations could be performed in a fraction of the time allowed for them. As the study concluded,

Such restrictive (and, from management's point of view, illegal) devices make necessary a system of social controls imposing, upon the individual, responsibility to the group. Essentially what results is an informal secret organization . . . workers employ a social ethic which requires that each individual realize his own goals (social and pecuniary) through cooperation with the work group.[6]

It is in these groups that the invisible, underlying process of the mass strike develops. They are communities within which workers come into opposition to the boss, begin acting on their own, and discover their need to support each other and the collective power they develop in doing so. The end product of this process is precisely the rejection of management as "authority and leader," and the transformation of the work group into what one industrial sociologist described as a guerrilla band at war with management.[7]

Although the unofficial actions of these groups generally go unnoticed and unrecorded, we have been able to catch glimpses of them from the cooperative action of the railroad workers in each town in 1877 to the wildcat strikes and informal control of production by factory workers during World War II.

The large-scale struggles of periods of mass strike develop out of the daily invisible and unrecorded skirmishes of industrial life in normal times. Clayton Fountain, later a U.A.W. official, but at the time an auto worker so untouched by unionism he was still willing to cross picket lines, describes such a conflict at a Briggs auto plant in 1929, one of the quietest years for industrial conflict in American history:

According to the theory of incentive pay, the harder and faster you worked, and the more cushions you turned out, the more pay you received. The employer, however, reserved the right to change the rules. We would start out with a new rate, arbitrarily set by the company time-study man, and work like hell for a couple of weeks, boosting our pay a little each day. Then, bingo, the timekeeper would come along one morning and tell us that we had another new rate, a penny or two per cushion less than it had been the day before.

One day when this happened we got sore and rebelled. After lunch the whistle blew and the line started up, but not a single worker on our conveyor lifted a hand. We all sat around on cushions waiting to see what would happen.

In a few minutes the place was crawling with big-shots. They stormed and raved and threatened, but our gang stood pat. We just sat on the cushions and let them rant and blow. When they got too abusive, we talked back and told them to go to hell. We told them that the Briggs plant was run by a bunch of rats who did nothing but scheme how to sweat more production out of workers and that we didn't care a damn how many of us they fired; we just weren't going to make any more cushions or backs at the new low rate.

We didn't belong to a union and we had no conception of organization. There were no leaders chosen by us to deal with the angry bosses; we all pitched into the verbal free-for-all with no epithets barred. Some of the workers threatened to take the bosses outside and beat the hell out of them — in fact, they had a damn good notion to do it right then and there inside the plant.

Finally, after about forty-five minutes of confusion, the bosses relented. They agreed to reinstate the previous piecework rate. With this assurance, we went back to work. Looking back, I can see that, in a small and disorganized fashion, we tasted the power of the sitdown strike on that far-away day in the Briggs plant in 1929.[8]

This miniature revolt and innumerable ones like it, unknown to all but those directly involved, form the submerged bulk of the iceberg of industrial conflict, of which the headline-making events of mass strikes are the visible tip. Because workers do not direct production, they find it is directed to their disadvantage — in a way that tries to hold down their income, extract more labor, and increase the power of the employers over them. Against this, as in the example above, workers are forced to fight back, thus discovering their own power.

Out of the day-to-day conflict in the workplace, the sense of exploitation revealed in inadequate wages, and the general resentment against subordination, develops the sentiment for a strike. As the Interchurch World Movement's *Report* on the 1919 steel strike

236   put it,

> It cannot be too strongly emphasized that a strike does not consist of
> a plan and a call for a walkout. There has been many a call with no resul-
> tant walkout; there has been many a strike with no preceding plan or call
> at all. Strike conditions are conditions of mind.[9]

Whether triggered by a relatively trivial incident or by a strike call,
at some point in the accumulation of resentment workers quit work.
Already this is a kind of revolt, as Alvin Gouldner put it, "a *refusal
to obey* those socially prescribed as authorities in that situation,
that is, management." [10]

Workers are immediately faced with the problem of making
the strike effective by preventing production. This means in effect
denying the owner free use of his own property. The result is a natural tendency toward de facto seizure of the productive apparatus
by sitdown strikes, crowd action, and mass picketing. We find this
as early as 1877, when railroad workers and supporting crowds virtually took possession of the railroad system of the country; it was
dramatically illustrated by the sitdowns and mass picketing of the
1930's.

When strikes seriously disrupt production for long, they generally call forth state intervention. For one thing, as the official
History of Violence in America by the President's Commission on
Violence wrote, "Today, as always, employers have the legal right
to move goods and people freely across a picket line and the duty
and practice of police has tended to safeguard this right." [11] Further, the government has generally been held to have the right and
responsibility to end strikes which create an "emergency" by dis-
rupting the ordinary life of society. Finally, the government has
frequently defined strikes as insurrections to be suppressed by
military action. According to the official *History of Violence in
America* there have been no fewer than "160 occasions on which
State and Federal troops have intervened in labor disputes."[12]
Leon Wolff hardly exaggerated in his study of the Homestead
strike when he concluded:

> The decisive effect of militiamen cannot be overemphasized; one
> searches United States labor history in vain for a single case where the
> introduction of troops operated to the strikers' advantage. In virtually all
> conflicts before and after 1892 the state guard acted, in effect, as a strike-
> breaking agency . . . [13]

Use of guards, deputies, police, militia and army in turn have generated frequent large-scale battles between crowds and occasionally armed bands of strike supporters and the forces of "law and order." Thus by a natural progression we have observed dozens of
times, strikes move toward miniature civil wars between workers
and the state.

In the course of strike actions, the ordinary life of workers, in which they act under the constant direction of their boss, ceases, and they have to think, act, and coordinate their actions for themselves. Even in shop conflicts over speed and organization of production they begin to coordinate their own action and to take over part of the management function. Once a strike begins, it involves a tremendous amount of activity, including picketing, countering employer and governmental violence, providing food, health care and other vital needs of the strikers, coordinating activity, and setting strike strategy. If the strike seriously affects the population, the strikers often find it necessary to continue part of their usual work to show their social responsibility and keep public sympathy; for example, railroad strikers have generally run passenger and mail trains. This tendency of strikers to conduct social activities under their own management perhaps reached its height in the Seattle general strike of 1919, when the various trades provided the necessary services for an entire city.

Though the cell-units of mass strikes may be the individual work groups, industrial conflicts by no means remain limited to them, but rather tend to spread in wider and wider circles. Indeed, in many cases we have seen solidarity spread across even the deepest divisions within the working class. The range of this process can be seen by selecting a few examples from the many we have described above. Practically the whole body of railroad workers in America joined in the sympathetic strike with the Pullman workers, who were not even railroadmen, as did workers of a great variety of trades in Chicago and elsewhere. Scores of traditionally hostile nationality groups separated by religion, language, history, and the deliberate policy of the employers joined together with close cooperation and mutual trust in the steel strike and the Lawrence textile strike of 1919. Black and white workers in such Southern cities as St. Louis in 1877 and New Orleans in 1892 joined together in general strikes supporting each others' demands.

Numerous general strikes throughout the periods covered in this book reveal the willingness of workers in completely unrelated trades and industries to support each other. The railroad strike of 1877 and the Toledo Auto-Lite strike of 1934 illustrate the unemployed and impoverished joining together in the streets with those on strike. The Homestead strike showed mutual support between skilled and unskilled workers. The General Motors sitdown of 1936-1937 showed employed women taking a full part and non-employed wives, whose social participation had previously been limited to home and family, emerging to play an active role in the struggle. The tendency of mass strikes — never fully realized — is toward joint action of all working people.

If the mass strike is a process marked by workers' challenge to existing authority, direction of their own activity, and spreading solidarity, what is its source? If workers possessed society's means of production and managed them themselves, there would be no basis for strikes against management. But since they do not, they have to work for those who do. The result is that all workers share a subordination to the control of managers, who have the power to make decisions which shape their daily lives.

While the particular issues which trigger workers' resistance to this domination may vary, their underlying source—control of production and the product by others—is thus always the same. This is why the most intense battles may be fought over the most trivial issues, such as a fraction of a cent in wages; in such struggles "the issue is not the issue." The real issue is an attempt of workers to wrest at least a part of the power over their lives away from the industrial managers and exercise it themselves. This is frequently recognized explicitly by management; as an employer in Milwaukee said during the 1886 May Day strikes for the eight-hour day, it was a question of "my right to run my works and your right to sell me your time and labor." [14] Or as President Sloan of General Motors wrote at the height of the 1936-1937 G.M. sitdown, the "real issue" was, "Will a labor organization run the plants of General Motors . . . or will the Management continue to do so?" [15] Because it challenges the real power-holders of our society—the industrial managers—and because carried to its logical conclusion it would have to replace them, the mass strike can be considered in essence a revolutionary process.

This revolutionary process is not merely a struggle for power between two groups, however. For out of the very necessities of that struggle develop the two other aspects of mass strikes we have emphasized above: the tendencies toward self-management and toward solidarity—qualities which if extended could form the basis of a society different from any now existing. Most people in their work life and community life are passive—submitting to control from above. They are also atomized—separated from each other. What we see in mass strikes is the beginning of a transformation of people and their relationships from passivity and isolation to collective action.

The tendency toward self-management is rooted in the simple fact that unless people direct their own activities, somebody else will direct them in a way which does not let them pursue their own ends. Self-management is the only alternative to management by somebody else. At one level it arises out of the immediate needs of the struggle—keeping the plant closed, feeding the strikers and the like. At a more profound level, all the actions of a mass strike are responses to the fact that when a small minority manage society, they will generally do so in a way that conflicts with the needs of the majority; mass strikes are thus implicitly an attack on the elite organization of management.

Of course, self-management is not the only tendency within mass strikes; it is always possible that the authority wrested from the old managers will be taken up by some new power. We can see this, for example, in the establishment of industrial unionism in the 1930's when the unions subsequently took over much of management's responsibility as the instrument of labor discipline. Where this occurs, however, conflict next arises between the agency attempting to assert the new authority and the subjects of that authority.

Solidarity likewise is a response both to the immediate needs of the struggle and the fundamental problems of society. In the course of social struggles it arises directly out of the realization that the struggles will be lost without it. But fundamentally it is a response to the obsolescence of individual solutions to people's problems. As the powerlessness of ordinary individuals makes their position look less and less tenable, the psychology of "looking out for number one" becomes futile, the need to support others who in turn will support you becomes obvious, and a spirit of all-for-one and one-for-all spreads in a bond which is at once intellectual recognition of reality and emotional feeling of union. The reason this sense of solidarity crystallizes so suddenly is that "I will only make sacrifices for you when I can sense that you will grasp the need to make sacrifices for me." This mutual trust develops in a thousand miniature experiments taking place in the background of a mass strike. As an Akron rubberworker quoted above put it,

during the sitdowns last spring I found out that the guy who works next to me is the same as I am, even if I was born in West Virginia and he is from Poland. His grievances are the same. Why shouldn't we stick?[19]

The end product of this process is the sense of being part of a class, in some ways comparable to the sense of being part of a nation which can be seen developing, for example, in the American Revolution, the Confederacy during the Civil War, or more recently the Algerian revolution or the Quebec nationalist movement. But its source and result are different from those of nationalism. The common situation of workers is that individually they are powerless, but together they embody the entire productive force of society; their solidarity is the discovery of this. It reflects the fact of modern society that individuals can only gain control of the social

240 forces that determine their lives by working together. Thus, "individualism" keeps the individual weak, while solidarity increases his control over his life; once the consciousness of this develops, it becomes impossible to say whether the motive for an act such as joining a sympathetic strike is altruistic or selfish, for the interest of the individual and the collective interest are no longer in conflict: they have come to be the same.

This unity of individual and collective interest and the feelings of unity it generates are the necessary basis of a society based on cooperation rather than competition. From one perspective, therefore, the mass strike can be seen as a process in which workers are transformed from competitors to cooperators. Combined with a replacement of managers by self-management, this would result in a society of free human beings working together to meet their own needs by meeting each others' needs. Thus we may consider the mass strike as a revolutionary process whose outer expression lies in contesting the power of the existing authorities, and whose inner expression is the transformation of those who do society's work from passive and isolated individuals to a collective of self-directing cooperators. (Of course, not all the organized manifestations of mass strikes have these characteristics; see "containment of mass strikes" below.) The last chapter of this book will try to project that process beyond the stages it has reached so far.

There are a number of evident objections to this concept of the mass strike. The most obvious is that those who have taken part in the actions described in this book simply have not aimed for any such revolution, but rather at much smaller and more specific changes in wages, hours, and working conditions. While it is true that strikes do in fact have such specific goals, this does not prove they have no other implications; similarly, the fact that the Boston Tea Party protested the English stamp tea tax did not thereby rob it of meaning in the struggle for national independence. As sociologist Robert E. Park put it,

> While a strike may be regarded as a single collective act in which minor clashes and individual cases of violence are incidents, every individual strike may be regarded as a single episode in a larger revolutionary movement, a movement of which the participants are perhaps only dimly conscious.[17]

Or as *Business Week* once put it, such industrial disputes are not "a series of isolated battles for isolated gains. Rather, they are part of a long-term, irrepressible struggle for power."[18] In fact, revolutionary movements rarely begin with a revolutionary intention; this only develops in the course of the struggle itself. To take a classic example, the Third Estate in the French Revolution did not initially intend to replace the monarchy; at first it demanded only specific reforms. Then the Constituent Assembly aimed to exercise a counter-power to the King. Since such a dual power is inherently unstable and can hardly last forever, the new class is sooner or later forced either to replace the old or to fall back into subordination. Thus even if replacing the old power — revolution — is not the deliberate aim, it may be necessary to achieve or hold other aims; therefore, the struggles of a subordinate class for greater power can still be understood as part of a revolutionary process, even when its members do not consciously assert such a goal.

A second objection is based on a neat distinction between political and economic struggles. The former are seen as challenges to the state and therefore potentially revolutionary. The latter, on the other hand, are merely attempts to win better conditions within the existing framework of society. The lack of working-class political action in America, combined with the extraordinary struggles of American workers at the point of production, is therefore interpreted as satisfaction with the existing system combined with an effort to make maximum gains within it.

But in a period of mass strike, the political/economic distinction breaks down. Strikes aim not just to win concessions but to increase the power of workers within industry — a quintessentially political objective. For industry itself is a system of political power — indeed, in our society the central one. The challenge to it is revolutionary. Indeed, forms of action which changed the state but left the organization of power in industry and other production intact would be no revolution at all from the standpoint of the ordinary worker. The relative disinterest of American workers in traditional forms of political action largely reflects the irrelevance of traditional politics to their daily problems; their militance at the workplace *is* their mode of political action. But the economic/political distinction breaks down for another reason as well. Even purely "economic" strikes, as we have seen, arouse the direct political and military opposition of the state — making the conflict political even in the most narrow sense. In the final analysis, state authority and industrial authority function as parts of a unified system.

Of course, not all strikes challenge the organization of industrial power. The classic trade union bargaining strike takes the power organization as given, and plays only on the marginal disadvantage a strike causes the employer in the market place. It is precisely to the extent strike actions go beyond this to the altering of power relations that their implications are revolutionary.

Another, related criticism is the assertion that strikers aim to increase their power only in the narrow sense of their bargaining

242   power in the market. This is the usual view of economists and of many labor leaders, who see workers essentially as people selling a commodity—their labor—in the market. If the price is too low, they withdraw their labor from the market. Since this is ineffective if done by individual labor-sellers, they join together in trade unions and withdraw their labor together—strike—until their commodity's price is raised. The emphasis placed by unions on the timing of strikes, bargaining strategy, organization of the labor market, and the like flows from this perspective. Above all, their conception of "what is possible" flows from their conception of what is possible in the existing market, a view which is applicable enough to collective bargaining strikes in ordinary times, but which renders incomprehensible the kind of social struggles reviewed in this book. For in them the workers think, speak and act not as vendors in a market, but as oppressed and exploited human beings in revolt. Their criterion is what they need, not "what the market will bear." Their strikes are not timed to the balance of supply and demand, but to the felt intolerability of their present condition. Their relation to employers and to each other is not expressed in terms of buyers and sellers, but in terms of anger at their oppressors and human solidarity with each other.

In the late 1960's, the nation's campuses were rocked by massive confrontations between students and administrators backed by police. Student discontent grew largely from resentment at being processed to be merely cogs in the corporate machine. It was fed by anger at the war in Vietnam and poverty and racism at home. Students turned naturally to the mass action techniques of strikes, demonstrations, and occupations to gain their objectives.

2. The Course of Mass Strikes

If the inner dynamic of mass strikes is generally the same, the particular forms they take are always different. To discover why a period of mass strike developed in the particular way it did requires looking at its particular circumstances — the approach we have followed in the bulk of this book. But we can identify a number of factors affecting their general course, and make a number of comparisons among them.

The course of each mass strike is naturally set by the existing structure of industrial society. Before the widespread development of industry and employees, there could be no mass strikes. In the nineteenth century, by far the most important aspect of capitalism was the railroads, and so the core of the 1877 and 1894 mass strikes were railroad strikes. Because railroads were so dominant and reached every industrial center, railroad strikes tended to spread rapidly to national proportions and to workers in all industries.

In the twentieth century, no single industry played this role. In 1919, the basic industries of steel and coal, along with other mass

Management personnel attempting to cross a picket line of striking electrical workers at General Electric's plant in Schenectady, N.Y., in October, 1969. 150,000 workers participated nationwide in the long and bitter strike.

244 employers of the unskilled, formed the mass strike storm center.
By the 1930's, the automobile was the new heart of the economy,
and Teamsters, auto and auto-parts workers, and rubberworkers
were the most prominent in the strikes of 1934-1937. Generally
speaking, the units of production have become larger and larger
through the years, so that the size of individual strikes has tended
to grow.

The cyclical development of capitalist economy affects the occurrence of mass strikes. Periods of depression generate widespread social misery and bitterness among workers; not only are
millions unemployed, but wages are cut and managers try to cut
labor costs through speed-up. The large number of unemployed at
such times as 1877 and 1934 add a potential mass urban crowd of
extreme bitterness ready to join street battles in support of strikers.
Strikes during depressions are often extremely bitter, but they are
difficult to win because employers have little margin of profit from
which to grant wage increases or improvements in working conditions, and little to lose by closing down. During periods of business
recovery, on the other hand, workers take advantage of their improved bargaining position to conduct a great many strikes. These
tend, however, to be primarily aimed toward making up ground
lost during the previous downturn. Finally, periods of rapid inflation, such as after World Wars I and II, cause real wages to drop
for virtually all workers at a time of relatively full employment,
thus generating discontent at a time when strikes can generally be
won.

The conventional wisdom that high labor conflict is exclusively a product of depression, or of the business upswing, or of any other particular part of the business cycle, does not hold up on examination. Yet at another level, there can be no question that mass
strikes are part of the periodic crises — whether economic, political,
or military — which have marked industrial capitalist society from
the time of its establishment. The mass strikes of 1877, 1886, and
1894 were each phenomena of world-wide depression, as were
those of the 1930's. Those of 1919 and 1946 were part of the reorganization that followed industrial capitalism's greatest crises,
World Wars I and II.

Such crises potentiate industrial action even when (as in
World Wars I and II) they raise workers' wages. This is in large
part because they undermine the rhythms of daily life, the pattern
of adaptation to which people have become accustomed, and to
which they tend to cling even when it is impoverished. After all,
people will try to adapt to even the most unpleasant situation if it
seems stable and they feel unable to change it — that is why they are

not in a state of revolt continuously. Only when something disrupts the normal life pattern and makes it impossible to go on living in the old way or provides a new sense of potential power will large numbers of people cease to act in accustomed ways.[19] Once objective forces have broken these familiar patterns, people begin acting in new ways. The fact that mass strikes are a response to crises in the system of industrial capitalism gives them a further significance. For it means that mass strikes are essentially mass responses to the failures and irrationalities of that system.

At a time of growing discontent, in which invisible, low-level conflicts at the shop level are everywhere generating the potential basis for solidarity, the action of one group of workers often serves as the triggering example to large numbers of others. The strike and defeat of the militia in Martinsburg, West Virginia, started a chain reaction in the Great Upheaval of 1877; victory over the nation's most notorious industrial magnate in the first Gould strike was a major factor in precipitating the struggles of 1886; similarly, the Great Northern strike laid the basis for the Pullman strike and the mass strikes of 1894; and it was the successful sitdowns of the rubberworkers that triggered the sitdown wave of 1936-1937. Each exemplary action demonstrated the power workers held because they could stop production, often backed by their willingness and capacity to withstand violence by company or state forces, thus infusing other workers with self-confidence and an appreciation of their own power.

It is not only workers' victories that lay the basis for mass strikes, however. In many cases it is defeat or impending defeat that drives home the need for a wider solidarity and stronger tactics. The dramatic defeat of the Homestead strike of 1892 at the hands of the Carnegie Steel Company and the state militia had a great impact on workers throughout the country, laying the groundwork for the sense of class war that accompanied the 1894 Pullman strike and the intense solidarity revealed in that struggle. Similarly, the San Francisco general strike of 1934 resulted from the impending defeat of the longshoremen by the National Guard. And the solidarity that marked the General Motors strike of 1936-1937 grew largely from the experience of defeats in the preceding years in isolated plants in Toledo, Cleveland, and elsewhere. Thus within mass strikes we can see an evolution based on lessons learned from the successes and failures of the recent past.

The visible events that compose mass strikes are in large part community or national polarizations. As the impact of a strike on daily life grows greater, it tends to dissolve the infinite variety of subcommunities into two opposed camps: those who identify with

246   the strikers and those who identify with the employers. This polarization can be seen most dramatically in general strikes, such as
those in Seattle in 1919 and San Francisco in 1934. Here the entire
population divides into two organized blocs with the social fabric
that usually holds them together virtually dissolved. Violence or
armed state intervention often plays a critical role in precipitating
this polarization—an important reason why those in positions of
authority generally prefer to avoid them. Once blood is drawn or
troops intervene, social struggles are dramatized as fundamental
struggles over power, to which members of each side respond by
coming to the aid of their fellows. It is through such events that the
hidden development of class solidarity becomes manifest.

   The same process of polarization occurs nationally, although it
is often less visible due to the vastness and diversity of the country,
and less tangible because it takes place largely in the realm of public opinion rather than direct action. It can be seen most vividly in
the Pullman strike of 1894; but in all the periods we have studied,
national sentiment became polarized on class lines as a result of
dramatic strikes and confrontations. The development of public
opinion on the employers' side is easy to trace; it is revealed in
newspapers, statements by public figures, and the action of government officials, stressing law, order, authority, and property rights.
The change in workers' attitudes, on the other hand, is extremely

Alan Copeland/Photon West

When all the usual pressures are no longer sufficient to keep people in line, any
ruling group may be expected to turn to physical force to maintain its position.
Here the San Francisco Tactical Squad clears City Hall steps in 1970.

hard to investigate, except as it is revealed in mass actions. However, a few observations can be made on the development of workers' consciousness during periods of mass strike.

In normal times, American workers do not have a strong sense of being part of a class that is separate from the rest of society. As Charles R. Walker put it, "In everyday life . . . [the working class] tends with slenderer means to approximate the social fashions and cultural content handed to it"[20]; their style of living is as close as they can bring it to the classes above them. This is in contrast, for example, to England, where the awareness of being part of a separate class is expressed in a wide range of cultural forms — pubs, co-ops, and benefit societies, entertainment, folklore, neighborhood, family, and the like — regardless of the current level of industrial conflict. In the United States, such separate subcultures tend to divide much more on ethnic and generational lines. This does not mean that workers have not felt exploited and kicked around; they have felt consistently that the managers are powerful and that they are powerless, and others are rich while they are barely able to get by. But class consciousness involves more than an individual sense of oppression. It requires the sense that one's oppression is a function of one's being part of an oppressed group, whose position can only be dealt with by the action of the entire group. It is this consciousness that arises in the course of mass strikes, revealed in workers' attitudes as well as in concrete acts of solidarity. For, as Walker continued, members of the working class

are united by a common insecurity and despite variations a common way of making a living — by wages and not profits. They are united as well by the union against them — in time of crisis — of all other forces in society. At such times, the working class for brief periods develops ideas of its *own* interest apart from the middle class, and the faint beginnings of an original culture. It produces leaders, thinks up fresh forms of organization and strategy, and above all scans skeptically its own relation to the rest of society.[21]

This transformation can at times be seen in individual lives. In normal times American workers generally look to individual advancement for themselves or their children as the means to escape working-class status; in periods of mass strike millions of them risk their jobs, their meagre savings, and whatever security they have built up through respectability, trade unionism, or relations with their employer, to engage in collective action.

But the most important change in consciousness in periods of mass strike is the heart of revolutionary consciousness — "people's understanding that they can initiate and control action and themselves make the decisions about their lives."[22] This awareness is of course only partial, but we can see it in every mass strike action, superceding the feeling of impotence that marks life in ordinary times.

Occasionally, this consciousness has reached a realization that workers need and are able to take over the direction of production and society. The participants in the Seattle general strike explicitly saw their own activities in management during the strike as a preparation for the time that workers would run society. As the *Seattle Union Record* wrote,

If by revolution is meant that a Great Change is coming over the face of the world, which will transform our method of carrying on industry, and will go deep into the very sources of our lives, to bring joy and freedom in place of heaviness and fear—then we do believe in such a Great Change and that our General Strike was one very definite step towards it.

We look about us today and see a world of industrial unrest, of owners set over against workers, of strikes and lock-outs, of mutual suspicions. We see a world of strife and insecurity, of unemployment, and hungry children. It is not a pleasant world to look upon. Surely no one desires that it shall continue in this most painful unrest. . . .

We see but one way out. In place of two classes, competing for the fruits of industry, there must be, eventually ONLY ONE CLASS sharing fairly the good things of the world. And this can only be done by THE WORKERS LEARNING TO MANAGE. . . .

When we saw, in our General Strike:

The Milk Wagon Drivers consulting late into the night over the task of supplying milk for the city's babies;

The Provision Trades working twenty-four hours out of the twenty-four on the question of feeding 30,000 workers;

The Barbers planning a chain of co-operative barber shops;

The Steamfitters opening a profitless grocery store;

The Labor Guards facing, under severe provocation, the task of maintaining order by a new and kinder method;

When we saw union after union submitting its cherished desires to the will of the General Strike Committee:

THEN WE REJOICED.

For we knew that it was worth the four or five day's pay apiece to get this education in the problems of management. Whatever strength we found in ourselves, and whatever weakness, we knew we were learning the thing which it is NECESSARY for us to know. . . .

Some day, when the workers have learned to manage, they will BEGIN MANAGING. . . .

And we, the workers of Seattle, have seen, in the midst of our General Strike, vaguely and across the storm, a glimpse of what the fellowship of that new day shall be.[23]

The outlaw coal strikers of 1919 similarly saw their actions as a first step toward taking over "the mines for the miners," and attempted to spread the aim of a workers' take-over of production to other groups. More typically, however, workers have aimed for some kind of counter-power over management, neither realizing the inherent problems of such a state nor feeling their own power to direct society.

Of course, the mass consciousness at any moment is always full of contradictions. Workers often feel that big business controls everything in America including the government, but simultaneously believe that America and its government represent the ordinary people and should be supported by them. Indeed, they resist believing that the government is their enemy. It is painful and unpatriotic to believe that the government systematically uses armed force against its own people to protect the interests of the wealthy, for that belief means giving up hope that anything can be gained without revolutionary change.

This conservatism of thought is quite natural. The Declaration of Independence puts it: "all experience hath shewn that mankind are more disposed to suffer, while evils are sufferable, than to right themselves by abolishing the forms to which they are accustomed." Here lies the explanation of the Homestead strikers, one day indicted for treason for levying war against the State of Pennsylvania, and the next voting for Cleveland, the very man who was to suppress the Pullman strike. Seemingly conservative ideas can be deceptive, however; for instance, at the height of the General Motors sitdown, union war veterans planned to take over the city hall and jail—a completely insurrectionary act—yet planned to take over authority in the name of the Constitution as well as the union. It is a cliche that people walk into the future facing backward; a radical intention is often clothed in the language of the past. For, as Leon Trotsky wrote, there is a "chronic lag of ideas and relations behind new objective conditions," so that the process of revolution "consists in the gradual comprehension by a class of the problems arising from the social crisis—the active orientation of the masses by a method of successive approximations." [24] Only the first stages of this process can be seen in U.S. history.

One other change in consciousness—indeed in life—develops in mass strikes. This is the break they create within the day-to-day boredom, monotony, subservience, and limitation of individual possibilities of which most people's daily lives are made up. This is revealed in the frequent statements to the effect that "suddenly I felt like a human being, not a machine." It comes out in the gaiety, the festival atmosphere that marks so many of the mass actions we have described, even when they were colored by anger and bitterness as well. And it can be observed in the explosion of spontaneous creativity in tactics, in songs, in organization, that we have

250 seen. It is this which most of all foreshadows a real change in ordinary life, in which human activity flows from individual and group creativity, rather than from a minority who direct the social activity of others in their own interest. No mere increase in "leisure time" provided by the present system can provide this sense of liberation from the limits imposed on all of us by those who now determine social life.

3. The Containment of Mass Strikes

Although in this book we have focused on the actions of the workers, this is of course only half the story—the other half is the action of those who oppose them. It is a truism that ruling groups try to control challenges from those subordinate to them by a combination of repression and concessions. The detailed history of employer and government labor policy during mass strikes can in most cases be reduced to various combinations of these two tactics. For, as Peter Drucker wrote,

> A strike is essentially a revolt. . . . Historically, revolts have been ended in one of two ways: by force of arms or by giving the rebels what they wanted and thus taking the steam out of the revolution.[25]

Ruling groups call on force and violence only reluctantly, for it is a great liability to do so. It shatters their image of benevolence and fairness to all parties, revealing them instead as oppressors ready to kill to retain their privileges. It reveals that their authority is breaking down, that they no longer receive automatic obedience by consent but must obtain it by force. In turn, violence pushes its victims into more extreme forms of opposition. Nonetheless, the industrial managers and the state have again and again had to resort to force to maintain their position. An entire history could be written of the apparatus constructed for this purpose, from the armories built in American cities in the wake of the Great Upheaval of 1877, to the Pennsylvania Coal and Iron police, to the industrial munitions uncovered by the La Follette Committee, to the military surveillance of potential sources of civil disturbances—demonstrations, strikes, and riots—revealed by Senate investigations in 1971.

A general pattern marks the mobilization of the forces of repression in the periods we have studied. Generally speaking, the industrial managers wield enormous power over the local politicians in strike areas, and with their assistance can put together a force of company guards, sheriff's deputies (often paid for by the employer), local police, vigilantes, and the like. They try to break up the picket lines and generally harass and intimidate the strikers. If this is insufficient to break the strike, the next step is the calling in of the National Guard. Often the tensions generated by the conflict have already led to confrontations which can be used to justify this step; if not, the employers can easily provoke or fabricate them. Once the National Guard enters the scene and allows free entrance to the plants, the strike can generally be broken unless the workers respond with mass action on a large scale. Oftentimes, a conservative Governor will himself want to send in the Guard in order to assert the power of "law and order" and assist his political allies.

But, as we have observed, liberal Governors elected by labor votes may also end up calling out the Guard against strikers. A vivid example is Governor Floyd B. Olson of Minnesota, elected by a Farmer-Labor Party representing the unions and radical farmers' organizations, who personally contributed $500 to the Teamsters strike fund and stated, "I am not a liberal . . . I am a radical" — yet who sent in the National Guard to arrest the Minneapolis Teamsters strike leaders and capture strike headquarters in 1934. The reason for this seeming anomaly is that the government, its supposed neutrality in labor matters notwithstanding, is bound to protect private property rights and the orderly processes of society, and any politician who fails to do so will stand condemned for failing to fulfill his job and creating anarchy.[26]

The formal division between State and Federal government allows the Federal government in most cases to avoid the onus of repression, thus maintaining its appearance of neutrality between labor and capital. Of course, this appearance is illusory, for the various National Guards are trained, equipped, and supported by the U.S. Army. And when the National Guard is unable to do the job, the U.S. Army is always there to help out. We have seen Federal troops directly suppressing strikes in the Great Upheaval of 1877, and in the Pullman Strike of 1894 (without the request and over the objections of the Governor); we have seen them poised to intervene in the textile strike of 1934 and the railroad strike of 1946, as well as in various plant seizures during and after World War II. Such events are an index of the extent to which the normal authority of the rulers has broken down and they are driven to resort to naked force.

But force is only one face of their policy; the granting of concessions is equally important. No doubt the greatest number of strikes are ended simply by wage increases and related concessions, giving the appearance of a victory for the workers while leaving the

252 power of their employers intact. Very often the government steps in at a point of deadlock, bringing conciliators, mediation, arbitration, fact-finding boards, and the like to propose or impose a settlement of this kind. Unlike armed intervention, this presents the state as neutral or even pro-labor, since it generally recommends concessions from the employers. In fact, of course, it throws the authority of the government behind a return to work on terms that do not threaten the powers or prosperity of the industrial managers.

More significant than the granting of particular concessions, however, has been the recognition of trade unions and the acceptance of collective bargaining. Industrial management has been far more reluctant to grant these than wage increases, for it has seen in them a threat to its own powers. The government, on the other hand, has frequently supported collective bargaining, recognizing (as the much-cited report of the English Royal Commission on Labor argued as early as 1894) that —

the evidence . . . points to the conclusion that on the whole and notwithstanding occasional conflicts on a very large scale, the increased strength of [labor] organization may tend toward the maintenance of harmonious relations between employers and employees.[27]

Collective bargaining was endorsed by all twentieth-century Presidents [28] and finally required by the Wagner Act. Union representation left the subordinate position of workers intact, but provided a mechanism for eliminating those grievances which could be rectified without undermining the profit-making of the employer.

Management and government often started by supporting various schemes for collective bargaining through company unions, works councils, and other "house unions." But unions that are formally opponents of the employers are superior to company unions in disciplining the workforce for a very simple reason — workers will not obey leaders they think represent the boss. Thus a high police official in San Francisco in 1934 reported that the trouble which culminated in the general strike began when regular A.F.L. leaders lost control because "the rank-and-file workers became convinced that their leaders were too much hand-in-glove with the industrial interests of the city." [29]

Trade unions often started when the industrial work-groups we described above simply formed into permanent organizations. As they grew their character changed, however, and they became quite separate from the workplace, controlled from above by professional officials kept in office by their own political machines. This division between the union organization and the workers who may be its members can be seen in normal times in the "discipline" imposed by union officials on workers defying company or union authority, as in wildcat strikes; in times of mass strike, the conflict between the trade union organization and the so-called rank and file becomes one of the dominant realities, as we have seen repeatedly. The formal democratic structure of many trade unions does not contradict, but merely ratifies the division between ordinary workers and the trade union leadership. As E.A. Ross wrote in a study of collective bargaining,

> There are few institutions in the economic or social life of the nation with so many channels of communication between the rank and file and the leadership.

It does not follow, however, that trade union wage policy is actually made up of rank-and-file decisions, in any real sense. And in point of fact, the rank and file is extremely dependent on the leadership for guidance on what is equitable, what is possible, and what is acceptable. The most important business of meetings and conventions is to permit the officers to communicate with the members. The essential function of the strike vote and the referendum is to demonstrate the solidarity of the union in support of its leaders.[30]

Furthermore, as Ross argues, this centralization of union power in the leadership grows out of the very function of the trade union, bargaining for the workers:

> The wage policy of a union, like the foreign policy of a nation, is a matter poorly suited to the methods of primitive democracy . . .

> To expect a rank-and-file determination of bargaining strategy is about as plausible as to expect the government of the United States to conduct its foreign policy through a monthly plebescite of registered voters. . . . At some point or other, it is wise to conclude negotiations (or terminate hostilities) and sign a treaty for another year. This is another strategic decision which the rank and file is not equipped to make.

> Thus, trade union wage policy is inevitably a leadership function. The reason is not that the leadership has wrested dictatorial power from the rank and file but that it alone is in possession of the necessary knowledge, experience and skill to perform the function adequately.[31]

It is not for combat that the union leadership is needed, but for diplomacy. Even democratic procedures on the part of the leadership do not belie this, according to Ross.

It is interesting to observe how the procedures for rank-and-file participation in the wage bargain have increasingly become tools for the use of leadership. Originally intended to implement the final authority of the rank and file, they have gradually undergone a subtle metamorphosis, until they have become a means of conditioning the membership, communicating indirectly with the employer, and guarding the flank against rival leadership . . . the procedures originally designed to guarantee control *by* the rank and file have become devices for control *of* the rank and file.[32]

Militant gestures on the part of the union leadership play a similar role.

254   From time to time, prudence may also require the vigorous prosecution of lost causes. A group of workers may feel strongly about some fancied grievance, or a grass-roots wage demand. . . . Notwithstanding the virtual certainty of defeat, the issue may be militantly pressed in collective bargaining. Employers frequently understand that union officials are required to support improbable demands, and develop a spirit of tolerance toward the practice if it is not carried too far. If it is politically impossible for the officials to accept a refusal, the issue may be carried to arbitration, again without expectation of success. All of these procedures are part of the equipment of successful trade union leaders.[33]

Ross concludes that trade unions must be considered as organizations with aims quite separate from their own members. "The formal rationale of the union is to augment the economic welfare of its members; but a more vital institutional objective—survival and growth of the organization—will take precedence whenever it comes into conflict with the formal purpose."[34]

The key to understanding the role of trade unions in periods of mass strike is the labor contract. For the past half-century, this has essentially been an exchange of certain concessions from management for a union pledge to prevent strikes during the term of the contract. (Such contracts have been the objective of all modern American unions, though many unions in the nineteenth century and the I.W.W. in the twentieth did not sign contracts running fixed times. Labor organizations which do not make such contracts can hardly be considered trade unions in the modern sense, and they are not necessarily subject to the dynamics we discuss here.) As long as such a contract does not exist, a union will support and encourage the most militant action on the part of workers, including spontaneous strikes, violence, and occupations. Once employers accept a contract, however, the existence of the union and the jobs of its officials will depend on its enforcing the contract—that is, preventing strikes. The union's central office

detaches itself from the masses it regiments, removing itself from the fickle eddy of moods and currents that are typical of the great tumultuous masses. The union thus acquires the ability to sign agreements and take on responsibilities, obliging the entrepreneur to accept a certain legality in his relations with the workers. This legality is conditional on the trust the entrepreneur has in . . . [the union's] ability to ensure that the working masses respect their contractual obligations.[35]

Thus we have seen unions lead determined struggles with illegal means and full encouragement of mass initiative, only to turn around after winning recognition and apply the full panoply of employers' strikebreaking tactics—including red-baiting, physical attack, importation of strikebreakers, loss of employment and blacklisting—to put down workers' strikes. This is not necessarily the result of personal corruption. Indeed, it flows from the very function of unionism—setting the terms on which workers will submit to the managers' authority. This function can only be carried out if the workers do in fact submit.

This development in the role of unions helps clarify their contribution to the two elements of labor struggles which foreshadow a different society: self-directed action and solidarity. In the pre-recognition period, unions generally offer themselves as the vehicle of workers' self-initiative; where there is serious discontent but they fail to do so, as with the A.F.L. in the 1930's, new leaders or unions offer themselves for this role. The union attempts to build support by championing the workers' acts of defiance against the employer, and does not oppose spontaneous strikes except on the basis of bad timing. Once a contract is signed, however, the statements of the union leaders—including radical leaders—suddenly ring with the need for discipline and order. The responsibility of the workers is no longer to act, but to obey union orders. When a conflict arises in the workplace, the union leaders immediately tell the workers not to take impulsive action, but to let the union authorities take care of it through the grievance machinery. (Of course occasional shop-floor militants do not take this attitude, but, reflecting their own position not as officials but as workers, encourage their co-workers to use their power directly; this is one of the reasons that the lowest level of union officials are frequently involved in wildcat strikes not authorized by the union.) Above all, the workers are not to strike—that is a violation of the contract which jeopardizes the union's whole relation to the employer and thereby its existence.

J. Raymond Walsh, professor of economics at Harvard and one-time director of research and education for the C.I.O., explained the methods by which unions try to forestall strike movements:

> . . . the records demonstrate that most unions make every effort to settle disputes without recourse to the strike. Many unions guard against hasty strike judgements by taking from their locals all authority in such matters, and concentrating it in the hands of national officers. Frequently the national officials, removed from the heat of the dispute [and the miseries that engender it, we might add], are much more likely to be reasonable and willing to mediate than are local officials, or an irritated rank-and-file.
>
> . . . National officers . . . are much easier to deal with than union committees from the shop. Far from fomenting trouble, they spend most of their time settling disputes before the strike stage is reached.[36]

256   Of course to retain support of the workers, a union must appear to fight the employer. It does this by means of the collective bargaining strike when the contract expires. In these strikes, however, the union generally tries to limit workers' initiative by keeping them under strict discipline, although pent-up feelings sometimes break out in mass action initiated by the workers themselves, and the workers often refuse to accept the limited objectives proposed by the unions, or refuse their terms of settlement.

The same development applies to solidarity. In the pre-recognition period, unions try to show that workers' problems can be solved only through collective action. They try to build up the sense of solidarity first among those who work together directly, then throughout the whole industry. When a strike breaks out, unless they consider it poorly timed, they try to spread it, at least to all of those who would be covered by the same contract. Once a contract is achieved, however, the process is reversed. If a strike breaks out, everything possible is done to isolate it and prevent its spread. Any direct coordination by the workers outside union channels is either taken over or fought by all means necessary. Solidarity with workers in other trades, industries and unions is undermined most of all. This occurs continuously through the context created by unions in which only those in a particular union advance together. The unions' divisive role becomes most clear in the bitterness with which union leaders oppose sympathetic strikes and general strikes, on the grounds that they violate the sanctity of the contract.

Finally, trade unions play an important role in circumscribing the aspects of life with which workers are supposed to concern themselves. First, the union contract explicitly recognizes the right of management to make the basic decisions affecting the company. This perpetuates the unpleasant and demeaning character of work by preventing workers from attempting to organize the work more to suit their own convenience. It also prevents them from taking any responsibility for what is produced, how well it is made, whether the production process poisons the environment, and similar questions. Thus workers are prevented from trying to make their work serve each others' needs rather than those of their employer. Second, the union framework limits workers to questions which affect their particular sector, rather than the more general questions of social organization and policy that affect all workers in common. The first blocks development toward workers' management of production, the second toward their management of society.

Of course, these characteristics of trade unionism have not always been clear either to the workers who supported it or to the employers who fought it. Generally speaking, both parties saw in trade unionism a steadily encroaching control by the workers, leading to a power at least equal to that of the employers. As Judge Gary of U.S. Steel, long champion of the open shop, put it,

the contemplated progress of trade unions, if successful, would be to secure the control of the shops, then of the general management of business, then of capital, and finally of government.[37]

But in fact trade unions turned out to be a means for taking unformed aspirations toward such control and channeling them into demands which were "realistic"—in the sense that employers could meet them without giving up their power or going out of business. With rare exceptions, trade unions have opposed as irresponsible and unrealistic workers' demands which went beyond this.

Since 1877, the trade union leadership as a whole has recognized the mass strike process and consciously opposed it, even when trying to use certain of its manifestations. This is vividly revealed in Terence Powderly's attempt to break up the 1886 general strike out of fear of another 1877; in Samuel Gompers' and the A.F.L.'s killing off of the Pullman strike; and in the C.I.O.'s attempt to break up the sitdown movement in 1937-1938.

What about the radical parties and organizations whose self-proclaimed goal is not just marginal improvements but a different kind of society? We have run across them from time to time in the course of this book—Communists, Socialists, Trotskyists, Musteites, Socialist Labor and other parties, as well as their members in the A.F.L., C.I.O., and dualist trade unions. Yet they have had little significant role in instigating the mass struggles we have described. They have generally been preoccupied with building their own organization, whether party or union, and have seen the significance of mass movements in their possible addition to the membership or support for such organizations. They have done little to clarify the possible revolutionary significance of mass actions or to develop their more radical potentialities. For example, the Communist and Socialist union leaders involved in the Flint sitdowns of 1936-1937 made a point of emphasizing that the sitdowners did not even discuss the idea of reopening the plants—then or eventually—under their own management. When radical leaders have succeeded in gaining organizational control over unions, the unions have operated within the framework of orderly collective bargaining like any others. In those cases where their members have played a radical role in mass movements, they have generally done so in response to the conditions they shared with other participants, not as a result of their organizational connections. The most radical upheavals have generally been as much a surprise to the radicals as to everyone else.

If mass strikes constitute a revolutionary process, they have never yet in America made a revolution. On the whole, workers have believed—or at least hoped—that their needs could be met within the framework of the existing society. Further, they have believed in the inevitability of that society, and have believed themselves powerless to change it fundamentally. Only rarely has it occurred to them that they could run society themselves.

Even when workers discovered their own power, they retained the gravest doubts about its legitimacy. For it contradicted all the long-inculcated values of law, order, authority and property. They understood instinctively that such action undermined the "republican" form of government by substituting direct action for state action. The belief in existing political forms has thus served as a constant brake on more radical forms of action.

The failure of American mass strikes to pass over into revolution requires two levels of explanation. First, we must look at factors largely beyond control of the workers. American capitalism started out without a feudal class, and therefore escaped constraints and struggles against them which have generated revolutionary tendencies in many other countries. Similarly, it has experienced unique opportunities for continental and then world expansion, and consequently has been able so far to grant considerable concessions to its own workers without undermining its profit-making capacity. And it has so far gained enormously from the cataclysmic wars of the twentieth century while escaping relatively unscathed from the devastation that generated revolutions elsewhere.

In the last chapter of this book, we will examine three foreign cases in which workers during periods of mass strike tried to take over the means of production and run them themselves. In each case, the repressive power of the state was seriously shaken, while at the same time the old owners were unable to make further concessions without giving up their control of production or going bankrupt, and therefore had taken the offensive against the workers through lockouts or civil war. While the conditions under which a mass strike develops revolutionary goals are not completely clear, the weakening of the apparatus of repression and the lack of a margin for making concessions seem to be most important. The failure of American mass strikes to attempt revolution is in large part the result of the fact that so far the state, its army and police forces, have remained solvent and intact, and that the industrial corporations have been able to make concessions on wages and trade union issues while retaining their profitability.

But if the power and wealth of the existing system has been the main factor in containing American mass strikes, it is important

to look at the limitations of the working class' own response. Perhaps the most important of these was workers' lack of appreciation
of their own potential power. Even when they discovered, for instance, that they could shut down their department, plant, or industry, this was rarely seen as revealing their ability to stop—and
therefore to change—the entire society. And even when they exercised a counter-power over production or organized the complexi-
ties of social life under strike conditions, they did not draw the conclusion that therefore they could manage society and production.

For this reason, workers have always assumed that at the end
of any strike, no matter how large or powerful, they would end up
going back to work for somebody else. And this assumption automatically limited their objectives, even in periods of mass strike, to
improvements within the system rather than an end to the rule of
the boss. Trade unionism was felt to offer a counter-power, in
which workers would be presented with management plans and
could challenge them—backing up the challenge with a strike if
necessary. No organizational alternative to trade unionism—based
on a refusal to accept the established rights and powers of the industrial managers—developed, even though the workers were repeatedly contesting those prerogatives, even in opposition to the
unions. Workers continued to accept trade unionism in general,
even when actually opposing trade unions in their own actions, because trade unionism represented the concessions the employers
were willing and able to grant, and workers could not envision getting rid of this limitation by getting rid of the employers.

A sense of powerlessness is natural in a society where the real
power is held by a small minority. Workers—indeed, everyone but
the managers—have little experience in controlling anything outside their private lives. They are kept in ignorance of how society is
managed. Their education from kindergarten upward is designed
to impress upon them their limitations, and to unfit them for the
exercise of power. As adults they are limited to highly specialized
and often stultifying jobs. Under these conditions, they naturally
doubt their ability to direct their own workplace, let alone society.
This feeling of powerlessness is accentuated by the ever-
increasing concentration of decision-making in the hands of the
managers. In short, the division of labor between those who decide
and those whom they order to carry out their decisions leaves the
latter feeling incompetent to do anything but obey.

The sense of powerlessness is of course enormously increased
by the actual power workers find facing them in this society. The
importance of direct economic dependence on the employers cannot be underestimated; the result of disobedience on the job is sim-

260   ply getting fired. While a main purpose of unions was to modify this power through seniority, union hiring halls, and other forms of job security, they have become another instrument of this control by themselves authorizing or even demanding the firing of workers who engage in wildcats and other acts of rebellion. Once workers do rebel they find not only the employer, the local police and state militia, and eventually the U.S. Army ranged against them, but also their own union. In the fact of such power, resistance seems hopeless and a fatalistic adaptation the wiser course.

Further, the ideology of the existing society exercises a powerful hold on workers' minds. The longing to escape from subordination to the boss is most often expressed in the dream of going into business for yourself, even when you realize that the odds against success are overwhelming. The civics book cliche that the American government represents the ordinary people and is therefore legitimate survives even in those who find the government directly opposing their own needs in the interests of their bosses. The desire to own a house, a car, or perhaps an independent business maintains a belief in private property which makes an expropriation of the great corporations seem a personal threat. The idea that everybody is really out for himself, that it can be no other way, and that therefore the solution to one's problems must come from beating

When the U.S. invaded Cambodia in May, 1970, campuses erupted in a nationwide student strike calling for a total withdrawal from Southeast Asia, an end to campus complicity with the war, and freeing Bobby Seale and all political prisoners.

the others rather than cooperating with them is inculcated over and over by the very structure of life in a competitive society.

The divisions within the working class keep workers from realizing the power they have together by turning them against each other instead of against their common rulers. This has often been fostered by the employers, who deliberately imported mutually hostile nationalities, used women, blacks and students as strikebreakers, and played skilled and unskilled, blue- and white-collar workers against each other. But these divisions have also been deliberately perpetuated by the workers themselves. In part this has been the result of traditional prejudice, suspicion, ignorance and racism. But to a great extent it has resulted from a deliberate policy of maintaining a favored position at the expense of other workers. This is seen most vividly in the craft unions, which operate as closed guilds — often controlled by particular ethnic groups, and almost invariably by white men — to exclude outsiders from the trade. But it is true of all unions insofar as they use their bargaining power primarily to improve their position vis-a-vis other workers. And it is true of all who hold privileged positions within the working class: skilled, male, white, native-born, and white-collar workers. The more these groups have turned their power against other workers, the weaker has been the working class as a whole. As S.M. Lipset and Reinhard Bendix wrote in *Social Mobility in Industrial Society* (1959):

> A real social and economic cleavage is created by widespread discrimination against . . . minority groups and this diminishes the chance for the development of solidarity along class lines. . . . This continued splintering of the working class is a major element in the preservation of the stability of the American social structure.[38]

The process of mass strike which we have described in this chapter is the process of overcoming these weaknesses. In the mass strike, workers learn that they are powerless only insofar as they are divided; that together they represent the entire productive force of society. So far, however, mass strikes in America have failed to develop far enough to replace the existing organization of society. Whether they may do so in the future depends upon the rapidly changing social context in which they occur.

But even in terms of the workers' position within capitalism, mass strikes have not been a failure. As a railroad engineer put it after the suppression of the Pullman strike, "If there had never been a strike or a labor organization I am satisfied that every railway employee in the country would be working for one-half what he has been working for of late. Strikes are not generally successful, but they entail a heavy loss on the company and it is to avoid

262 that loss that the company ever meets us at all." [39] The same is true of the various "reforms" like the Wagner Act, grievance procedures, seniority system, and the like: they are the result of the threat of disruption and revolution contained in the mass strike. In our society, even reform has occurred only under threat of revolt.

✊

Chapter 7: Footnotes

1. Elton Mayo, *The Human Problems of an Industrial Civilization* (Harvard, 1946), cited in Paul Romanto and Ria Stone, *American Worker* (Detroit: Facing Reality Publishing Co., 1947), p. 53.

2. Orvis Collins, Melville Dalton and Donald Roy, "Restriction of Output and Social Cleavage in Industry" in *Applied Anthropology* (Summer 1946), p. 4.

3. *Ibid.*

4. *Ibid.,* p. 8.

5. *Ibid.,* p. 7.

6. *Ibid.,* p. 9.

7. Donald Roy, "Making Out: A Counter-System of Workers Control of Work Situations and Relations," in *Industrial Man,* Tom Burns, ed. (Baltimore: Penguin Books, 1969).

8. Clayton W. Fountain, *Union Guy* (N.Y.: Viking Press, 1949), pp. 28-9.

9. The Commission of Inquiry, Interchurch World Movement, *Report on the Steel Strike of 1919* (N.Y.: Harcourt Brace and Howe, 1920), p. 147.

10. Alvin W. Gouldner, *Wildcat Strike, A Study in Worker-Management Relationships* (N.Y.: Harper & Row, Torchbooks ed., 1965), p. 66.

11. Hugh D. Graham and Ted R. Gurr, *The History of Violence in America, A Report to the National Commission on the Causes and Prevention of Violence* (N.Y.: Bantam Books, 1969), p. 380.

12. *Ibid.*

13. Leon Wolff, *Lockout, The Story of the Homestead Strike of 1892: A Study of Violence, Unionism and the Carnegie Steel Empire* (N.Y.: Harper & Row, 1965), p. 228.

14. *Milwaukee Daily Journal,* May 5, 1886, cited in Roger Simon, "The Bay View Incident and the People's Party in Milwaukee," unpublished paper, 1967, p. 9.

15. Sloan, cited in Sidney Fine, *Sit-Down, The General Motors Strike of 1936-1937* (Ann Arbor, Mich.: University of Michigan Press, 1969), p. 182.

16. Louis Adamic, *My America 1928-1938* (N.Y.: Harper & Brothers, Publishers, 1938), p. 409.

17. Robert E. Park, in introduction to E.T. Hiller, *The Strike* (Chicago: University of Chicago Press, 1928), p. x.

18. *Business Week,* Mar. 8, 1941, p. 52, cited in Joel Seidman, *American Labor from Defense to Reconstruction* (University of Chicago Press, 1953), p. 46.

19. See "Keep on Trucking," by Mac Brockway, in *Root and Branch* No. 3 for a discussion of this phenomenon.

·20. Charles R. Walker, *American City, a Rank-and-File History* (N.Y.: Farrar & Rinehart, 1937), p. 239.

21. *Ibid.*

22. Paul Mattick Jr., in introduction to Anton Pannekoek, *Workers Councils* (Root & Branch Pamphlet 1) 1970, p. ii.

23. History Committee of the Seattle General Strike Committee, *The Seattle General Strike* (Seattle: The Seattle Union Record Publishing Co., Inc., 1920), pp. 7-8.

24. Leon Trotsky, *The Russian Revolution,* Selected and edited by F.W. Dupee (Garden City, N.Y.: Doubleday Anchor Books, 1959), introduction, pp. x-xi.
25. Peter Drucker, "What to Do About Strikes," in *Collier's,* Jan. 18, 1947, p. 12.
26. See for example C.R. Walker, pp. 73-6, 203.
27. "Final Report of the Royal Commission on Labor," *Parliament Papers,* 1894, V. xxxv.
28. Graham & Gurr, p. 387.
29. *New York Post,* July 19, 1934, cited in Wilfrid H. Crook, *Communism and the General Strike* (Hamden, Conn.: Shoe String Press, 1960), pp. 142-3.
30. E.A. Ross, "The Trade Union as a Wage-Fixing Institution," in the *American Economic Review,* Sept. 1947, p. 582.
31. *Ibid.*
32. *Ibid.,* pp. 582-6.
33. *Ibid.,* p. 587.
34. *Ibid.*
35. Antonio Gramsci, "Unions and Councils — II," *L'Ordine Nuovo,* June 12, 1920, in *New Left Review,* No. 51, p. 39.
36. J. Raymond Walsh, *C.I.O.,* pp. 173-4.
37. Judge Gary, *Steel Institute Yearbook* (1920), p. 19, cited in David Brody, *Steelworkers in America, the Nonunion Era* (N.Y.: Harper Torchbooks, 1969), p. 275.
38. S.M. Lipset and Reinhard Bendix, *Social Mobility in Industrial Society* (Berkeley and L.A.: University of California Press, 1963), p. 106.
39. U.S. Strike Commission, p. 121.

Chapter 8
The Current Scene

Shortly before his death in 1970, United Auto Workers President Walter Reuther reported, "There is a new breed of workers in the plant who is less willing to accept corporate decisions that pre-empt his own decisions. . . . There is a different kind of worker than we had twenty-five or thirty years ago." [1] A recent *New York Times* article detailed the change:

The younger generation, which has already shaken the campuses, is showing signs of restlessness in the plants of industrial America.

Many young workers are calling for immediate changes in working conditions and are rejecting the disciplines of factory work that older workers have accepted as routine.

Not only are they talking back to their foremen, but they also are raising their voices in the union halls complaining that their union leaders are not moving fast enough.

Leaders and young workers . . . said in recent interviews that they saw increasing dissatisfaction and militancy.

The new, younger workers, they say:

Are better educated and want treatment as equals from the bosses on a plant floor. They are not as afraid of losing their jobs as the older men and often challenge the foreman's orders.

Do not want work they think hurts their health or safety, even though old-timers have done the same work for years.

Want fast changes and sometimes bypass their own union leaders and start wildcat strikes.

And at the heart of the new mood, the union men said, there is a challenge to management's authority to run its plants, an issue that has result-ed in some of the hardest-fought battles between industry and labor in the past.

"The worker wants the same rights he has on the street after he walks in the plant door," said Jim Babbs, a 24-year-old worker who is a U.A.W. officer at Wixom. "This is a general feeling of this generation whether it's a guy in a plant or a student on a campus, not wanting to be an I.B.M. number," he said.

. . . the president of U.A.W. Local 36 . . . pointed to a paragraph in a 1967 contract and said:

"If there isn't a change in this section soon there's going to be a re-volt against the union here."

The section says that the company retains the sole right to maintain order and efficiency in its plants and operations; to hire, lay off, assign, transfer and promote employees, and to determine the starting and quit-ting time and the hours worked.

"To the young guy this means the company has all the rights and he's

The young fight back, he said, by challenging the orders of foremen in the sprawling assembly plant that turns out luxury Lincoln and Thunderbird cars. . . .

When they challenge a foreman, he added, they may be disciplined, and that raises another cry of injustice.

The foreman can immediately discipline a worker by barring him from the plant but a worker who feels he has been punished unjustly must follow a grievance procedure that sometimes lasts up to a year.

"They're willing to strike to win that one. . . . They want to change the idea that you're guilty until proven innocent. And just like the students they want it changed now."

A steelworkers union official said,

"Most of the older workers in my area are immigrants. They're somewhat afraid of authority. When a foreman pushes them around they take it. The young generation coming in now won't take that. They want to be asked to do something, not to be told to do it."

He recalled that young workers had sparked several wildcat strikes over the way an employee had been treated by a foreman. Last month, he said, young workers led a three-day wildcat strike in a brick manufacturing plant after a foreman disciplined a worker for carelessness in operating a lift truck.

"The older generation would have filed a grievance," he said. "The young people have no faith in that. They want it settled right away. There's a big explosion coming in the industrial unions and the young people are going to come out on top." [2]

Alan Copeland/ Photon West

Hundreds of campuses joined the 1970 student strike in response to the invasion of Cambodia. Mass demonstrations, attacks on R.O.T.C. buildings, and battles with police and in some cases National Guardsmen were widespread.

The argument that workers should be satisfied with the gains won by the unions cuts little ice with younger workers.

I.W. Abel, the president of the steel workers union, said that one cause of the unrest was that "young workers don't appreciate what the union has built."

"They didn't go through the rough times," he said.[3]

Young workers are far less willing to go along with the position of subordination, of accepting the employers' power, on which trade unionism is based. As U.A.W. education director Brendan Sexton complained,

The style of the young is very different from that of the old-timers. . . . They understand a lot less about power, the potential and the limits."

The young are impatient for change and more militant, said Mr. Sexton, while compromise is part of the union movement. "Even in the toughest unions there comes a time to settle," he said.[4]

The result has been the development of widespread action by workers—especially younger workers—independent of and even against the unions. It can be seen at many levels—resistance to management and union authority on the job, work stoppages, wildcat strikes, strikes over "local issues," and opposition to union-negotiated contracts. While these actions by no means yet constitute the kind of movement we have called a mass strike, nor even indicate such a period is necessarily on the way, they certainly reflect the same underlying processes we have seen in such periods in the past.

The *Wall Street Journal* reported in the summer of 1970 that workers were piling up so many grievances that "observers of the labor-management scene . . . almost unanimously assert that the present situation is the worst within memory." An official of a large U.A.W. local in Detroit complained, "I've had more grievances dumped on my desk in the past two months than I had all last year." A large proportion of these grievances resulted from company efforts to cut labor costs in the face of the recession, through laying off and downgrading workers and through speed-up. As a Chicago shop steward put it, "A foreman with a fast monkeywrench can speed up a line quite a bit. It's a constant battle you have to fight, and it's gotten much worse lately."[5]

Significantly, workers did not respond to the recession by driving themselves harder in their work. According to the *Journal*, corporate officials have been surprised to learn that "morale in many operations is sagging badly, intentional work slowdowns are cropping up more frequently and absenteeism is soaring."[6]

Production workers in some facilities, long accustomed to fat paychecks due to overtime, began to stretch out their work to keep the overtime coming, and to forestall any layoff.

. . . men such as Mr. Burke at Otis [Elevator Co.] contend the problem [of declining worker productivity] is so widespread it's their major headache at the moment.

Another factor that contributes to lower productivity, according to Prof. Cummins at Case Western Reserve, is the pickup in "group therapy sessions," when employees gather around watercoolers and elsewhere to moan about layoffs, past or pending. An office worker at the Otis unit in Cleveland says he noticed that such sessions were well attended "almost every time I went to the men's room." . . .

A metallurgist at an Ohio steel plant that downgraded some workers says many felt the company was unfair to them and slowed down "to get even with the company." [7]

We can see here at work the very processes at the cell level of production — the work-group — that we have found underlying mass strikes. Although these processes have been accelerated by the recession, they were visible even before it. In 1968, a young man named Bill Watson went to work in an auto factory in the Detroit area. In the year he spent there he discovered what he considered a "new form of organization," informal, separate from the union, whose purpose was not negotiation with management, but "taking control of various aspects of production," introducing a virtual "counter-planning" by the workers opposing the plans of management.

One dramatic example concerned a six-cylinder model hastily planned by the company without any interest in the life or precision of the motor. It ran roughly, workers in the motor-test area complained, and workers submitted dozens of suggestions for improving the motor and modifying its design. Workers throughout the plant became interested, and were convinced that certain changes would solve the problems, but all suggestions were ignored.

. . . the contradictions of planning and producing poor quality, beginning as the stuff of jokes, eventually became a source of anger. In several localities of the plant organized acts of sabotage began. They began as acts of misassembling or even omitting parts on a larger-than-normal scale so that many motors would not pass inspection. Organization involved various deals between inspection and several assembly areas with mixed feelings and motives among those involved — some determined, some revengeful, some just participating for the fun of it. With an air of excitement, the thing pushed on.

Temporary deals unfolded between inspection and assembly and between assembly and trim, each with planned sabotage. Such things were done as neglecting to weld unmachined spots on motor heads; leaving out gaskets to create a loss of compression; putting in bad or wrong-sized spark plugs; leaving bolts loose in the motor assembly; or, for example, assembling the plug wires in the wrong firing order so that the motor appeared to be off balance during inspection. Rejected motors accumulated.

268   In inspection, the systematic cracking of oil-filter pins, rocker-arm covers, or distributor caps with a blow from a timing wrench allowed the rejection of motors in cases in which no defect had been built in earlier along the line. In some cases motors were simply rejected for their rough running.

There was a general atmosphere of hassling and arguing for several weeks as foremen and workers haggled over particular motors. The situation was tense, with no admission of sabotage by workers and a cautious fear of escalating it among management personnel.

In the end, the entire six-cylinder assembly and inspection operation was moved to an area at the end of the plant where new workers were brought in to man it. "In the most dramatic way, the necessity of taking the product out of the hands of laborers who insisted on planning the product became overwhelming." [8]

Just before the time for model changeover, the company attempted to build the last V-8's with parts rejected during the year. The motor-test area protested, but management sent down representatives to insist that inspectors pass the motors.

It was after this that a series of contacts, initiated by the motor-test men, took place between areas during breaks and lunch periods. Planning at these innumerable meetings ultimately led to plant-wide sabotage of the V-8's. As with the 6-cylinder-motor sabotage, the V-8's were defectively assembled or damaged en route so that they would be rejected. In addition to that, the inspectors agreed to reject something like three out of every four or five motors.

The result was stacks upon stacks of motors awaiting repair, piled up and down the aisles of the plant. This continued at an accelerating pace up to a night when the plant was forced to shut down, losing more than 10 hours of production time. At that point there were so many defective motors piled around the plant that it was almost impossible to move from one area to another.

These actions aimed at partial control of what was produced. Others were designed to get control of working time.

A plant-wide rotating sabotage program was planned in the summer to gain free time. At one meeting workers counted off numbers from 1 to 50 or more. Reportedly similar meetings took place in other areas. Each man took a period of about 20 minutes during the next two weeks, and when his period arrived he did something to sabotage the production process in his area, hopefully shutting down the entire line. No sooner would the management wheel in a crew to repair or correct the problem area than it would go off in another key area. Thus the entire plant usually sat out anywhere from 5 to 20 minutes of each hour for a number of weeks due to either a stopped line or a line passing by with no units on it. [9]

In other cases, large-scale contests and games, such as water fights with fire hoses on hot days were organized "to turn the working day into an enjoyable event." [10]

Likewise, workers imposed counter-plans of how to get the work done. For example, workers established

a complete alternative break system . . . whereby they create large chunks of free time for each other on a regular basis. This plan involves a voluntary rotation of alternately working long stretches and taking off long stretches. Jobs are illegally traded off, and men relieve each other for long periods to accomplish this. The smuggling of men through different areas of the plant to work with friends is yet another regular activity requiring no small amount of organization.[11]

On one occasion, management scheduled an inventory which was to last six weeks.

They held at work more than 50 men who otherwise would have been laid off with 90 per cent of their pay. The immediate reaction to this was the self-organization of workers, who attempted to take the upper hand and finish the inventory in three or four days so they could have the remaining time off. Several men were trained in the elementary use of the counting scales while the hi-lo truck drivers set up an informal school to teach other men to use their vehicles. Others worked directly with experienced stock chasers and were soon running down part numbers and taking inventory of the counted stock. In several other ways the established plan of ranking and job classification was circumvented in order to slice through the required working time.[12]

Management forced this process to a halt, even though it would have saved money, claiming that legitimate channels of authority, training and communication had been violated.

Watson notes that a majority of the workers were either black or newly arrived Southern whites. "Despite the prevalence of racist attitudes . . . these two groups functioned together better than any other groups in the plant . . . women were no less active than men . . . workers from eighteen to thirty-five were the most militantly anti-union and the most willing to go beyond the established channels in their work actions." [13]

What stands out in all this is the level of cooperative organization of workers in and between areas. While this organization is a reaction to the need for common action in getting the work done, relationships like these also function to carry out sabotage, to make collections, or even to organize games and contests which serve to turn the working day into an enjoyable event. . . . There is planning and counter-planning in the plant because there is clearly a situation of dual power.[14]

"Within these new independent forms of workers' organization," Watson concludes, "lies a foundation of social relations at the point of production which can potentially come forward to seize power in a crisis situation and give new direction to the society." [15]

It would be difficult to tell just how typical these actions are of other workplaces. No doubt, many have not reached such a high level of organization, but there can be no question that activities of this general type are today widespread.

Workers' desire for more control over workplace conditions has led to a steadily rising number of strikes over so-called "local issues." In 1970, General Motors, for example, received more than 39,000 "local demands." [16] According to G.M., demands included

shift schedules, vacations, work assignments, entertainment or recreation for employees, providing legal advice, additional wash-up facilities, nursery care for (children) of working parents in the plant, employees' cars to be serviced and maintained at company expense, and health and safety.

Other demands dealt with assignment of overtime, speed of production lines, the amount of relief time, choices of work turns, the use of new technology and grievance procedures.[17]

These issues dealt with every aspect of life in the factory.[18]

In 1955, what was hailed as a great union victory over G.M. was unexpectedly followed by a coast-to-coast wildcat over "local issues" which crippled production; in response, union and management agreed to incorporate local issues into the national collective bargaining agreement and thus control such strikes. Nonetheless, as the *Wall Street Journal* wrote, "To the auto companies and the U.A.W.'s top leaders, these disputes have become a nightmare." [19] Indeed, while headlines during strikes focus on wage issues, "local issues" have increasingly become the heart of labor disputes, in the auto industry above all. One measure of this is the fact that between 1955 and 1967, General Motors estimates that it lost 14.9 million man-hours of work in strikes over national issues, but 101.4 million man-hours in "local disputes." [20]

The right to strike over local disputes even during the life of the contract has become a major issue in the steel industry. Typical was the complaint of the president of Local 2698 in Monessen, Pennsylvania, who said that management had refused to use a better grade of coal in its coke ovens to cut down pollution. When workers refused to work in the polluted area, the company used supervisors to replace them. In order to get more influence over company policy and regain control of such wildcat actions, the local union leadership demanded the right to strike. Steelworker President I.W. Abel persuaded a conference of 600 local presidents in March, 1971, not to vote on a motion to allow such strikes, although Abel conceded that a majority would have voted for it.[21]

The strikes over "local issues," like the informal control of production described above, represents a reaching out for control over the production process itself. So far this movement has not been explicitly formulated by those who take part in it as a struggle for control in the workplace, let alone in society. It is impossible to foretell whether this movement — starting off like the black and student movements protesting particular results of powerlessness — will, like them, discover in the process that its problem lies in the fundamental division of social power, and resolve to challenge it.

Nor has the independent action of workers been limited to single workplaces; we have seen a series of national strikes independent of the official labor movement. Perhaps the most dramatic of these — and the recent event most resembling the pattern of past mass strikes examined in this book — was the postal wildcat of March, 1970, the first major strike in the history of the Post Office, indeed of the Federal government.

A government study in 1968 had reported "widespread disquiet" among postal workers as a result of "antiquated personnel practices . . . appalling working conditions . . . and limited career opportunities . . ." [22] The explosion finally came in New York City, where high living costs forced many mailmen onto welfare to supplement incomes eroded by the inflation of the late 1960's, and where several small wildcats had already been pulled, such as a "sick-out" the year before by seventy-two or more employees at the Kingsbridge Station in the Bronx. [23] Letter carriers voted March 17th, 1970, to strike, and set up picket lines around the city's post offices which were honored by 25,000 drivers and clerks, bringing postal operations to a standstill. The strike began to spread almost instantly, with workers throughout New York State, New Jersey, and Connecticut joining within a day or two. The strikers organized themselves through informal channels; by March 19th, the New York local said it had received unsolicited telephone calls from letter carriers in fifty-eight communities in a number of states saying they would join the strike. [24]

Government and union officials moved quickly against the strike. The walkout was of course illegal from the start, since it is a felony for government employees to strike, and the courts quickly issued an injunction against the New York strikers. James Rademacher, head of the letter carriers union, announced he would send a telegram to Gus Johnson, president of the New York local which launched the strike, warning that the union's executive council was considering expelling the local because of its strike action, which was contrary to union policy. Johnson in turn urged members to go back to work.

Postmaster General Blount stated that national leaders of the postal unions had assured the Post Office of their cooperation. [25] The government also promised concessions if the wildcatters returned to work. On March 20th, "The Administration won an agreement from postal union leaders . . . to urge their striking workers

272 back to work in return for prompt consideration of their demands." [26] That night, however, 6,000 mailmen in Chicago — the postal system's central distribution point — ignored Rademacher's urgings and voted to join the strike, and the next day New York postal workers "voted almost unanimously to defy their leaders and the back-to-work agreement":

Branding their national union leaders "rats" and "creeps" for urging a return to work, the rank and file . . . roared their refusal to accept the proposed settlement.

Signs behind the rostrum in a Manhattan armory where the employees met read "Hang Rat-emacher" and "We won't take rat poison." An effigy of the union president hung nearby. [27]

Rademacher nonetheless predicted that "reason will prevail over emotion . . . and ninety percent of the mail will be moving on Monday." [28] But the action of the New York letter carriers had crystallized discontent throughout the country; by March 21st, the strike had spread to more than 200 cities and towns from coast to coast, including Chicago, Detroit, Philadelphia, Cleveland, Pittsburgh, San Francisco, Minneapolis, Denver and Boston. "We're very close to paralysis," said a Post Office official. "What is still functioning is hardly worthy of calling a postal system." [29] At the Post Office's emergency command center, "increasingly thick clusters" of flashing red lights indicating struck areas blinked in twelve states. "No blue lights — indicating struck areas where employees were returning to work — flashed on the big map." [30]

Even more alarming, the strike seemed on the verge of spreading to other government employees. John Griner, head of the American Federation of Government Employees, reported that he had to intervene personally to prevent several strikes by his locals. Nathan Wolkomer, head of the National Federation of Federal Employees, said that N.F.F.E. locals throughout the country had indicated that they wanted to strike in support of the postal workers. [31] "There's no doubt that our members are in complete sympathy with the postal workers. The strike definitely could spread throughout the Federal service." [32] Alan Whitney, vice-president of the National Association of Government Employees, reported that "tremendous pressure" was being put on the union to authorize strikes, especially in "one of our biggest locals whose primary duty is to supply our war effort in Southeast Asia." Whitney added,

We have been receiving phone calls from our various local presidents in various agencies throughout the government and throughout the country. They have watched events of the past days and have seen postal workers striking with a degree of impunity, and their question to us is, if they can do it, why can't we? [33]

The union leadership was able to head off any spread of the

strike beyond the postal workers, but the groundwork was nonetheless laid for future strikes of government employees. As one government strike advocate was quoted in the *Washington Star,* "We've learned from the postal workers that if practically everybody strikes, then nobody is going to be hurt . . . After all, they can't fire everybody."

The postal strike itself, meanwhile, continued to hold. In most cities, other postal workers refused to cross letter carriers' picket lines, ignoring another plea from the Administration and from the seven major postal unions that they return to work.[34] In all, over 200,000 postal workers in fifteen states joined the wildcat. They ignored injunctions throughout the country.

And so the President, turning to his last resort, declared a national emergency and ordered the U.S. Army and National Guard into New York to break the strike at its most militant point. In a nation-wide television address, he echoed Grover Cleveland's declaration in sending Federal troops to break the 1894 Pullman strike that "the mails must go through," and stressed that the postal workers were striking "not only . . . against the best interests and the best traditions of their service, but against the recommendations of their national union leaders."[35] Soon some 25,000 state and Federal troops arrived and began to sort the most pressing commercial mail, whose stoppage had threatened to close business and even the stock exchange. Though the Administration maintained its stance of refusing to negotiate until the postmen re-

Wide World Photos

Wildcat postal strikers defy national leaders to picket Post Office in New York City, March 1st, 1970. U.S. soldiers called in to sort mail fraternized with strikers and deliberately created chaos inside to support them.

turned to work, Congressional spokesmen emphasized that they would act immediately on pay increases as soon as the strike was over.

In the midst of this squeeze play, Rademacher called 500 local union officials to Washington. These officials recognized that the strike was being forced to a close, but ordered Rademacher to call a new nation-wide strike unless their demands were quickly met. A week after they had struck, the mailmen returned to work and negotiations began, with the New York local constantly threatening to trigger another strike, even calling a rump meeting of local leaders throughout the country to discuss plans for a slowdown.[36]

In strictly financial terms, the strike was a modest success, forcing Congress to grant an immediate six percent pay increase to all government workers and an additional eight percent for postal workers on passage of the postal reorganization plan. It also represented a new stage in the current action of American workers. It was the first nation-wide strike of government employees, and the first nation-wide strike in recent times to be carried on not only independently of, but in opposition to, the national union establishment.

The strikers did not play by the rules of the game. The risks they took were considerable. Striking against the government is a felony, punishable by a year and a day in jail and a $1,000 fine.[37] For the unions, opposition to the strike was a matter of institutional survival. Rademacher warned that continuation of the strike would put the union "practically out of business," since government unions whose members strike lose their right to the dues checkoff by which members' union dues are automatically collected by the employer. Fortunately, for the union officials, the government was fully aware of union efforts to break the strike, and therefore tried to strengthen its hand. Indeed, in the new postal reorganization, the government has gone out of its way to build the authority of the major unions that supported it against the postal strikers in 1970.

This development of rank-and-file independence from the trade union leadership and from orderly collective bargaining was likewise illustrated in the 1970 Teamsters wildcat. After what was described as the "most orderly series" of negotiations in Teamsters' history — credit for which management officials gave to acting Teamsters President Fitzsimmons [38] — union and management agreed to a new contract granting $1.10 in wage increases over thirty-nine months. But drivers in sixteen cities, including such central distribution centers as San Francisco, Los Angeles, St. Louis, Cleveland, Atlanta, Chicago, Detroit, Harrisburg, Akron, Columbus, Toledo,

Buffalo, Kansas City and Milwaukee quickly wildcatted against
the agreement in what the *New York Times* described as "a revolt
against the national union leadership and a $1.10-an-hour raise
that has been accepted in a national contract." [39] The strikers
quickly established mobile pickets to enforce the strike. The head
of Lee Way Motor Freight, Inc., complained, "We've been unable
to operate into the East because of the Teamsters union in St. Louis,
whose roving pickets have stopped all our drivers at various Mississippi River crossings." He said the company had tried to route
its truckers across the Mississippi at Cairo, Illinois, but they had
been stopped there, too.[40] From Cleveland the *New York Times*
reported,

> Strikers here have set up a roving patrol system that they say can
> muster 300 men within an hour to stop any truck moving goods in the
> area. The strikers are allowing trucks carrying food, drugs and beer to
> continue, but they have become outraged when they have found food
> trucks carrying other cargo.
> There has been rock throwing, windshields have been smashed,
> tires slashed and air hoses cut.[41]

Mayor Stokes of Cleveland stated that violence had been associated with the strike in two-thirds of the counties in Ohio. [42] The
United Press estimated that a half-million people were out of work
as a result of the strike.[43]

As the wildcat spread, acting Teamster President Fitzsimmons
sent telegrams to 300 locals, urging members to return to work.[44]
Fitzsimmons had pledged, "We will never tie up the over-the-road
freight operation of this country." [45]) A spokesman for the employers vowed, "We'll stay out till the snow falls" rather than accept
the rank-and-file wage demands, and stated that the Teamsters
union was "standing by" the agreement it had negotiated.[46] Local
and national Teamsters officials unanimously endorsed the agreement, and the director of the Federal Mediation Service issued a
statement urging all striking truck drivers to return to work pending a vote to ratify the contract—all to no avail.

Since none of the walkouts were legally sanctioned, trucking
companies secured numerous injunctions against the strikers. In
California, workers who were enjoined from striking simply called
in sick.[47] Teamsters in St. Louis ignored an injunction against them
for a month, then were cited for contempt until they returned to
work.[48] In Los Angeles, where strikers ignored a court back-to-
work order, the conflict developed a special bitterness. Teamsters
initially struck over the "local issue" of lack of sick pay. The companies responded by sending 10,000 strikers telegrams telling them
they were fired, presumably so they could rehire them without

276   seniority. The workers responded by demanding not only ten days' sick leave with pay but a full amnesty.[49]

Meanwhile, the Governor of Ohio ordered 4,100 National Guardsmen to duty to combat the strike and put the rest of the 13,000-man force on standby alert to combat what he called "open warfare" on the highways of Ohio.[50]

Helmeted troops, armed with M-1 rifles, were stationed in pairs on some overpasses, while other Guardsmen rumbled along on patrol in quarter-ton trucks.

Guard officers said their men were also guarding truck terminals and, in response to requests from truck companies and the state police, had escorted about four convoys of from 5 to 20 trucks.

. . . 200 rock-throwing strikers drove back about 50 policemen and guardsmen and the three-truck convoy they were attempting to escort out of the Yellow Freight Line terminal.[51]

The 145th Infantry — which had intervened in four or five ghetto riots in the previous two years and was soon to be rushed to Kent State University — patrolled west of Akron, where a number of truck terminals were operating in defiance of the strike.

They sought out and neutralized the strong points, identifying two bars where striking teamsters hung about and from which they poured out to heave everything from invective to rocks whenever trucks moved out of nearby terminals. The National Guard simply set up squads to meet the Teamsters as they rushed out.

One Guardsman reported, "They'd pull up short, stare at us for a while, and then go back into the bar for another drink."[52]

Despite the combined opposition of union, employers, courts and military, the strike held firm. After twelve weeks, employers in Chicago capitulated, undermining the entire national contract, forcing a wage increase two-thirds higher than union and management had originally agreed to.[53] This victory in turn strengthened the resistance of workers throughout the society to the policy of solving current economic problems by holding down wages.

Wildcat actions have become endemic in a number of other areas. A notable example is the coal industry, where, as a recent *Fortune* article pointed out, "the aims, interests, and policies of the union and the companies became inextricably intertwined . . . and the threat of a strike in the coalfields disappeared from the land," during the 1950's and '60's. According to Monsignor Charles Owen Rice, "The union that once protected the men from the bosses has become the union that protects the bosses from the men." As union president Boyle described union policy, "The U.M.W.A. will not abridge the rights of mine operators in running the mines. We follow the judgement of the coal operators, right or wrong."[54] In response, the miners' traditional solidarity has become divorced from the union and has emerged in wildcat actions; as *Fortune* put it, "Pensions, health, and safety are issues so close to a miner's heart that he will strike for them at the sight of a single picket sign, whoever carries it." [55] Management is therefore faced with "the problem of dealing with a work force that is no longer under union discipline . . ." [56]

Perhaps the most dramatic example was the Black Lung wildcat in West Virginia. One cold morning in February, 1969, a miner at Winding Gulf District Mine in Raleigh County, West Virginia, fed up with the lack of progress on health and safety conditions, spilled his water out on the ground. This act of rebellion was the traditional appeal to other miners to join in the strike. His fellow-workers quit working, and within five days the wildcat spread to 42,000 of West Virginia's 44,000 coal miners. They continued to strike for twenty-three days until the state legislature finally passed a bill to compensate victims of pneumonoconiosis — Black Lung — the miners' most dreaded disease. [57]

Sporadic wildcats have continued on other issues. Three thousand miners in southern Illinois struck and ignored union back-to-work orders in a dispute over filling a repairman's job.[58] On June 22nd, 1970, 19,000 miners in Pennsylvania, Ohio, and West Virginia struck to protest non-enforcement of the Federal mine safety act. The *Wall Street Journal* reported that "the nation's coalfields are seething with anger and disappointment over the new law."[59] "Rebel miners and others charge that the Bureau [of Mines] is acting in concert with the Boyle leadership and coal operators" to undermine implementation of the law. [60] A court order drove many of the miners back to work. Similarly, a series of three wildcats in Virginia, West Virginia and Kentucky, eventually involving 15,000 workers at ninety mines, was met by union opposition and court restraining orders. The strike's primary aim was union hospital benefits for disabled miners and widows.[61] A simultaneous wildcat in Pennsylvania was ended when a court ordered the miners to go to work "or go to jail." [62] All these cases followed the miners' traditional pattern of walking out of the mines when roving pickets appear.

In other industries, discontent has simmered without yet boiling over into large-scale wildcats. In March, 1970, for example, railroad shopcraft workers were so fed up with repeated delays in settling work-rule issues that William P. Winpisinger, chief union negotiator, reported them "right on the rigid edge of being out of control," and warned of a "carbon copy of the current Post Office strike," in which, as the *Wall Street Journal* added, "the rank-and-file workers defy efforts of union leaders and the government to

278   keep them on the job." Labor Secretary Shultz agreed that "though wildcat strikes have been contained, thanks to the action of responsible union leaders, I fear another delay might fuel the fires of impatience." [63] Similar situations exist in a wide range of industries.

To date, all of the wildcat movements have eventually been brought back under control. But the cost has often been great. The government's economic "game plan," based on restoring profits by reducing wages through unemployment, was essentially defeated by the wildcat Teamsters strike, which broke the previous pattern of wage settlements based on the General Electric contract of early 1970 — of which Walter Reuther said the gains weren't enough even to offset what workers had lost in purchasing power because of inflation in recent years.[64] In the year following the Teamsters wildcat, real after-tax wages for the average worker increased by 1.8 percent despite inflation and unemployment, "because of the large wage increases that have taken place." [65] This reversed the decline in real wages of the previous four years.

The government has had repeatedly to pit its power against workers through injunctions, wage policies, National Guard and Army, undermining their previous deep commitment to the state. This shift was symbolized by the construction workers who had beaten up students in support of Nixon's Vietnam policies in 1970, but were picketing against him a year later, side by side with students, to protest his wage policies for the construction industry.

War protestors burn draft cards before police at Oakland, California, Induction Center, October, 1969. While increasing numbers refused induction at home, soldiers in Vietnam began systematically resisting orders and "fragging" superiors.

Employers' plans to extricate themselves from the narrowest profit squeeze since 1938 by de facto wage cuts have been defeated in many cases, at least hampered in others. Finally, the unions have been largely discredited with their own members, especially the young.

If the economy is able to provide workers a constantly rising standard of living without forcing a further deterioration of working conditions, the unions will be able to contine to "win gains" and retain some support. If the economy fails to do so, the unions will be forced to accept and enforce wage cuts and speed-up in a way which will present them as the direct enemy of the workers.

In the course of recent strikes, union and management officials at the bargaining table have often appeared as partners trying to devise a formula and a strategy which will get the workers back to work and keep them there. As the *New York Times* wrote of the July, 1971, telephone strike, "Union and management . . . were manifestly less concerned about any real differences between them than about how to fashion an agreement that would satisfy the inflated expectations of a restless union rank and file." [66]

The strike itself is sometimes actually part of the strategy to control the workers—albeit a costly one. A fascinating series of articles in the *Wall Street Journal* described "union-management cooperation" to get the workers back to work and build up the authority of the union in the course of the 1970 General Motors strike. According to the series, after U.A.W. President Reuther died suddenly, "G.M. had to consider the crisis at Solidarity House, the U.A.W.'s headquarters, and the problems of a new union president—problems that could influence U.A.W. control over the men in G.M. plants." [67] G.M.'s "goal was union help to bolster productivity." [68] From the union-management viewpoint, a strike was necessary for three reasons. First, a long strike would

help to wear down the expectations of members, expectations that in the current situation have been whetted by memories of recent good times and by the bite of inflation. This trimming of hopes eases the difficult task of getting members to ratify settlements leaders have negotiated. (More than one of every 10 agreements hammered out by union officials is rejected by union members.) [69]

As one U.A.W. official put it privately, "The guys go out on strike expecting the moon. But after a few weeks of mounting bills and the wife raising hell about his hanging around the house all day watching TV while she works, the average worker tends to soften his demands." [70]

Second, a long strike would "create an escape valve for the frustrations of workers bitter about what they consider intolerable

280   working conditions imposed by companies' single-minded drive for greater production and profits." [71]

Third, a long strike would foster union loyalty and pull together various rank-and-file factions by uniting them against a common enemy, and strengthen the position of union leaders, who must stand for re-election regularly by a membership that is constantly turning over and that is wary of leaders in general, union leaders included. [72] The strike "permits union leaders to assert their manhood — at least in the eyes of their followers. It is the best way they have to demonstrate that they are 'tough' and thus to refute the assertion, common among workers, that the union's leaders are really in bed with management." [73]

But, the *Journal* points out, it is not only union leaders who recognize these functions of official strikes.

Surprisingly, among those who do understand the need for strikes to ease intra-union pressures are many company bargainers. . . . They are aware that union leaders may need such strikes to get contracts ratified and to get re-elected. In fact, some company bargainers figure strikes actually help stabilize fragmented unions and, by allowing workers to vent their "strike need," actually buy peace in future years. [74]

Unfortunately, from the union-management point of view, this approach nearly backfired in the General Motors strike. In order to generate pressure for settlement of "local issues," "top negotiators for both sides . . . indicated they won't return to serious bargaining on national issues until the bulk of the union's 155 local bargaining units reach agreement with G.M.," [75] even though "company and union officials say they can reach a national agreement after settling local issues in about ten days . . . " [76] Cooperation was so close that General Motors lent the U.A.W. $30 million to pay the medical insurance bills of the striking workers. [77] "Both sides want G.M. to be able to resume operations quickly after a national agreement is reached." [78] But workers simply refused to agree to local settlements, raising the spectre of a long strike going out of union control and defeating its original purpose.

Both sides agree that if the strike had dragged on past Thanksgiving, it would have paved the way for an epic dispute continuing into the new year. Such a possibility could have tipped the scales within the U.A.W. from a "heroic struggles" strengthening of Mr. Woodcock to a messy strike beyond the control of the top leaders. [79]

To forestall this threat, top G.M. and U.A.W. negotiators went into secret talks to settle the national contract despite the unresolved local disputes. The contract did not fulfill G.M.'s dream of cutting labor costs by strengthening work discipline, but, wrote the

the knowledge that peace is probably assured when it next bargains with the U.A.W., in 1973, and perhaps for many years thereafter (at least over national contract issues); the prospect that the U.A.W. . . . emerged stronger and thus may be able to speak more confidently for its members who are younger, less loyal and increasingly distrustful of employer and union alike." [80]

Though we can see in these developments the beginnings of the mass strike process, there is no guarantee that the result will be a renewed sense of solidarity in revolt among all kinds of workers which has marked mass strikes in the past.

It is often suggested that today's renewed labor militance differs from that of the past in that today's strikers are "only out for themselves," rather than seeing their actions as part of a broader struggle. This is often expressed in the phrase that today's strikers are not "socially conscious." There is considerable truth in this view, and it reflects one of the main weaknesses of the present movement, since it means that the gains of one section of workers are easily taken out of the rest, and workers are not able to draw on each others' strength. But as we have seen, solidarity is not a static attitude; it is something that develops with the process of struggle itself. During the relative labor peace in the post-World War II period, workers' revolt was sporadic and isolated. The tendency was strong to identify with the present system and its rulers, rather than with other workers. The present renewed militance of particular groups of workers is the first step toward a broader solidarity, for only when workers are actually struggling can the fact that they need each other for that struggle become apparent.

Workers are also very much divided today — black and white, young and old, male and female, skilled and unskilled — and these groups are easily played off against each other. Whether the need for solidarity will overcome these divisions, as it has to some extent in past periods of mass strike, remains to be seen.

It is likewise argued that the affluence of today's workers makes a repetition of the bitter conflicts of the past unlikely. There has indeed been a substantial increase in the incomes of industrial workers. For example, the real spendable earnings of the average private production worker with three dependents increased from $60 per week in 1949 to $78 per week in 1969.[81] Yet the image of the affluent, satisfied worker is exaggerated to say the least — in part because of the high wage rates of a few skilled crafts. The average production worker in 1969 made $5,980 [82] before taxes. This is substantially below the level the government describes as "mod-

282   est but adequate" for an average family of four. One index of what such income levels mean is the statement of George Romney, head of the Department of Housing and Urban Development, that fifty percent of the people in this country can't afford a decent home.[83]

However, the continuing stability of even this level of incomes has now become questionable. Real wages of industrial workers declined steadily from 1965 to 1970, a period which included both boom and recession. Further, the widely held view that depressions are now a thing of the past has been badly shaken. In 1970, for example, not only did unemployment top six percent and the stock market plunge, but corporate profit margins hit their lowest rate since 1938.[84]

The dominant position of American goods on the international market since World War II has been seriously undermined, a leading cause of recurring international financial crises. The resultant drive to make American goods more competitive is already generating substantial pressure to reduce wage rates which are high in relation to other countries. The conditions shaping the long postwar expansion—which has allowed workers to expect wages to be a little higher each year—seem to have been reversed. The introduction of wage and price controls in August, 1971, may well follow the pattern we have observed during World War II, in which wages were effectively frozen, while prices continued to rise. As the *Times* wrote, November 7th, 1971, "the essential purpose of the whole complicated system of boards, commissions, and councils created to manage the drive against inflation" was to "tighten the knot on future wage settlements and increase pressure on unions to acquiesce in the arrangement."

The image of the affluent worker has largely been based on that of unionized, white, male workers who entered the labor force in the 1930's and 1940's, and who, as a recent study points out, "have reaped a greater increase in standard of living . . . than any other group of workers in the history of American capitalism."[85] They have indeed supported the status quo, at least until recently. But they are only a minority of the working class—roughly sixty-six percent of the labor force is composed of blacks, women, and men under thirty-five who entered the labor force after 1950.[86] All these groups face depression-level unemployment. Blacks and women receive little more than half the wages of white men. And young workers' real incomes have been falling since 1957[87]

Another common argument is that automation is making the working class an ever smaller and less important part of society. There has indeed been a transformation of the American class structure. But its effect has not been to make workers less numerous or significant, at least if workers are defined as those who do not possess society's means of production and therefore must work for others who do. In fact, the most important change in American class structure has been the steady erosion over the past 100 years of the self-employed middle class from a majority of society to a small minority, transforming this traditional middle class into workers as we have defined them. The working class now represents at least eighty percent of the occupied labor force.

Of course, the composition of the working class has changed. White-collar workers have become more numerous than blue-collar. Service workers have increased relative to those producing goods. Government employment has expanded far faster than private employment. But such changes are nothing new; as we have seen, each stage of capitalist development has brought new categories of workers to the fore and reduced others, and the decline in the proportion of production-line workers in the mid-twentieth century no more heralds the end of the working class than did the decline of industrial craftsmen at the end of the nineteenth. The growing sector of white-collar workers, indeed, is undergoing a transition similar to that which struck blue-collar workers with the rise of modern industry. A recent article in *Fortune* detailed changes which are levelling the status of white- and blue-collar workers:

The strong mutual loyalty that has traditionally bound white-collar workers and management is rapidly eroding. . . . Now there are platoons of them instead of a privileged few, and instead of talking to the boss they generally communicate with a machine.
. . . The younger white collars are swept by some of the same restlessness and cynicism that afflict their classmates who opted for manual labor. . . . All too often, the keypunch operator spends the workday feeling more like an automaton than a human being. . . .
Now that they are needed by the millions, white-collar workers are also expendable. The lifetime sinecure is rapidly disappearing as management experts figure out another way to streamline the job, get in another machine, and cut down overhead. . . . When an unprofitable division is closed or a big contract slips away to a competitor, layoffs are measured in thousands, and the workers usually hit the streets with no more severance pay benefits than management feels willing and able to provide.
Production workers made an average of $130 a week last year and clerical workers only $105. . . . A 29-year-old secretary in a government agency in Washington says, "We're lower people. Down at our level we're peons, that's what they think of you."

Since 1965, a survey found,

Worker satisfaction with job security has dropped by 17% and with pay by 45%. There has been a 30% decline in the belief that companies deal fairly without playing favorites, and a 39% decline in the belief that the company will do something about individual problems and complaints.

As *Fortune* concludes,

> There is a terrible, striking contrast between the fun-filled, mobile existence of the young opulents of America as shown on television, and the narrow, constricting, un-fun existence that is the lot of most white-collar workers at the lower job levels. You can't buy much of what television is selling on the salaries these young workers earn; about all you can do is stay at home watching those good things go by on the screen. The result is frustration, sometimes bitterness, even anger. Workers in this stratum cannot but notice that the federally defined poverty standard is climbing toward their level from below, while above them the salary needed to enjoy the glittery aspects of American life soars ever higher, further and further out of reach.[88]

In short, far from the workers becoming middle class, what was once the middle class has largely been transformed into workers. This is reflected in the forty-six percent increase in white-collar unionism from 1958 to 1968 [89], and the fact that teachers, hospital workers, government employees, and other white-collar groups have been the focus of the most significant unionization drives of recent years. It is also revealed by the turning of large numbers of non-industrial workers to the workers' traditional weapon, the strike. In the public sector, where most white-collar growth is concentrated, there were some fifteen strikes in 1958, two hundred and fifty-four in 1969.[90]

In evaluating claims that labor insurgency has become a thing of the past, it is important to keep in mind that such beliefs have been a commonplace of the periods of relative labor peace between mass strikes. In 1888 — two years after the May Day general strike and six years before the Pullman strike — the great analyst of American society James Bryce observed:

> There are no struggles between privileged and unprivileged orders, not even that perpetual strife of rich and poor. . . . Not one of the questions which now agitate the nation is a question between rich and poor. Instead of suspicion, jealousy, and arrogance embittering the relations of classes, good feeling and kindliness reign. . . . The poorer have had little to fight for, no grounds for disliking the well-to-do, few complaints to make against them.[91]

Much the same has been said of today's workers.

But the labor insurgency of today is not simply a rerun of that of the past. For a number of new attitudes — albeit with precursors in the past — mark the action of today's younger workers. These changes in attitude are subtle, hard to pin down and harder to measure; any description can only be impressionistic. But they undermine some of the fundamental constraints that in the past contained mass strikes within the limits of the existing social structure.

Workers in the 1930's, for example, even when they engaged in such direct action as the sitdown strikes, saw the solution to their problems in building up the power of union and government officials, welfare bureaucracies, and the like, who would win for them more favorable conditions. Increasingly, people today experience the institutions that have been set up to "help" them — the unions, the schools, the welfare agencies, and the like — as alien and even hostile forces. They no longer look to such agencies to solve their problems, for the past failures of these agencies have become a dominant fact of everyday experience. So, instead, people are forced to begin solving their problems themselves; the kind of informal organization we have described in the auto plant is a striking example of this process. What is crucial, Bill Watson pointed out, is that "while sabotage and other forms of independent workers' activity had existed before . . . that which exists today is unique in that it follows mass unionism and is a definite response to the obsolescence of that social form." [92]

In the past, even when workers have engaged in direct action to gain counter-power over management, they have envisioned this power as embodied in a formal institutional structure — the trade union, which, in the words of Professor Jack Barbash, created "a system of bilateral, constitutional government through collective bargaining." [93] But now it is just that structure which is called into question. So instead of trying again to create such a structure, younger workers today use direct action to force immediate solutions to their own problems. This still requires solidarity and therefore organization, but unlike trade unionism it does not require representation by a specialized leadership skilled in determining just what compromise can be made between worker and boss.

This is turn involves a basic change of attitude concerning the question of leadership. In the 1930's such figures as Franklin Roosevelt and John L. Lewis were viewed almost with reverence. Workers, out of their own weakness, felt the need for strong leaders; what they demanded was that their leaders be given a part in decision-making by business and government. This in part they won, only to find themselves still powerless over their own lives. It is the union official who breaks up their wildcat strikes and the "pro-labor" politicians who fight for wage controls. Today there is an enormous cynicism about leaders and organizations of all sorts, whatever their rhetoric; even when workers vote for a politician or a union official, they often consider him a crook or a sell-out like his opponents. This cynicism often looks like apathy, especially to aspiring leadership groups like union insurgents and leftist parties trying to "activate the workers." But it also means that if and when large numbers of workers again move into action, they will be better innoculated against the appeals of "leaders" and may try to keep control of the struggle in their own hands.

If this happens, new movements will create something different from the bureaucracies that emerged from past struggles. What that will be they themselves will have to determine; some of the possibilities are sketched in the last chapter of this book. We can get some idea of their starting point by analyzing the Akron sitdowns of the 1930's. Here the workers shop-by-shop became groups working together to control production on the basis of their own ability to stop it. This control started with the speed of production and spread to control of the number of workers employed in the industry as a whole by controlling the hours of work. Finally, it developed a counter-power to the Akron city government. These powers were held by the ordinary production workers, without any intermediaries, simply through their ability to halt production. We have already described the beginning of such developments today, such as the "new form of organization" described by Bill Watson. But the difference is that today workers are far less inclined to hand these powers back over to outside leaders of any kind.

This change is related to a pervasive change in current thinking about society. In the past, the alternative to the irrationalities of the status quo has usually been seen as increasing the realm of state authority and public bureaucracy. Liberals and social democrats proposed to do this by augmenting the present state, various revolutionary groups by creating a new state based on their own organization. Today the spontaneous tendency of social criticism and opposition is to transfer decision-making from the present authorities to those the decisions affect. Current demands for community control, participatory democracy, black power, and women's liberation, their ambiguities notwithstanding, all reflect this tendency.

There is another shift in attitude, difficult to pin down but significant, especially among younger workers today. This is a breakdown of psychological identification with their job and their role as a worker. Their job, no matter how dull and deforming, was previously experienced by most American workers as the source of meaning in their lives, the proof of stature as a mature adult. This was revealed in the total collapse of personality that frequently followed unemployment in the early 1930's and the general feeling that being able to get and keep a job is the definition of a valid life. The idea of a worker's "right to his job," so prominent in the 1930's, reflects this feeling perfectly. Today the sense of pride in the social role of the worker is much less important; concomitantly, the sense of shame at not working, living on public support, is far weaker than formerly. Work is just something unpleasant you have to do to earn a living; your identity is centered in living the rest of your life. This attitude has several implications. It constitutes a revolt against the idea that man should serve the machine, that life should serve production, rather than vice versa. As such, it suggests that future working-class movements will differ from those in the past in aiming not to stabilize the position of workers through quasi-judicial protection in the shop and state intervention in the economy to guarantee full employment, but instead will seek to challenge the whole position of the worker as a servant of the production process. Lack of identification with the job also makes the worker less afraid of losing his job and therefore more willing to risk fighting back. On the other hand, this attitude leads workers to consider work life as relatively unimportant, something to be gotten through rather than something to change. This attitude leads away from the struggle to control the point at which social misery is produced.

These changes are part of the overall change in social values of which the "hippie" movement of the 1960's was the most visible, middle-class expression. At the most fundamental level, it is a response to the fact that modern technology has made the subordination of life to the needs of production obsolete and irrational. The expansion of wealth and industrial production for its own sake is less and less seen as the great objective of society. Our society's imperative to accumulate wealth is now seen as the source of many of its greatest problems — its environmental pollution, its stressful and atomized way of life, its constant international conflicts. Industrial expansion, in the past considered a virtually unmixed blessing, is today perceived as a threat to health and life. Direction of production to meet needs, rather than continued expansion per se, is widely seen as the proper goal of society.

One other change undermines an important bastion of social conservatism. Traditionally, American workers have been motivated in part by a deep craving for respectability within the framework of middle-class society. Socially they were outcasts who wanted in. (This feeling was heightened among those suffering inferior status as immigrants.) Anger at the shame of social exclusion was a powerful force motivating workers' action. But it also made them reluctant to act in ways considered unrespectable by middle-class society. Even more important, it meant that they would welcome "concessions" of status — being addressed as "Mr." or "Mrs." at work, flattered by politicians, receiving an income that allowed the

288   appearance though not the reality of a middle-class standard of life, and receiving a "recognition" for the union and its leaders, even though that recognition left the workers powerless as ever.

Such concessions cost the rulers little and left the workers in the same essential position as before. This sentiment is still visible as a driving force in the struggles that most resemble those of the 1930's—for example, the Hospital Workers' Local 1199, whose members are genuinely proud of their newly-won respectability. But in most current labor struggles, respectability is no longer a major theme, especially among younger workers. A revealing case in point was the New York police wildcat of January, 1971, which the older strikers described as a demand for more respect for policemen, while the younger ones were unconcerned with that and primarily wanted the salary increases they felt they had been promised by the city. For them, as for younger workers in general today, respectability seems no longer to be the issue.

The challenge to existing institutions is not, of course, limited to the workplace but extends to every aspect of contemporary society. It can be seen in the series of bitter university struggles that started with the Berkeley strike of 1964 and became a virtual nation-wide student uprising at the start of the U.S. invasion of Cambodia in 1970. It is perhaps even more significant, if less visible, in high schools, where forty-five percent of teachers polled by the National Education Association in 1970 reported student unrest [94], and where a recent study found that—

the great majority of students are angry, frustrated, increasingly alienated by school. They do *not* believe they receive individual justice or enjoy rights of dissent or share in critical decision-making affecting their lives within the school. Our schools are now educating millions of students who are *not* forming an allegience to the democratic political system simply because they do not experience such a democratic system in their daily lives in school. [95]

The challenge to established authority has been seen in dramatic form in the great black riots that began with Watts and became a unified nation-wide movement in the 1967 upheaval following the death of Martin Luther King, Jr. Similarly, a number of American cities have seen street battles over control of turf—highlighted by the struggle to establish People's Park in Berkeley, which was suppressed only with helicopters and rifle fire. Rent strikes and squatters' movements reflect the same trend in housing. Direct action has developed over welfare issues in dozens of cities. The Women's Liberation Movement has made a direct assault on the institutions of male dominance, without waiting for legislation to "guarantee" equality—just as the black movement earlier moved from the courts to the streets. Prisons have become the scene of repeated revolts, often bloodily suppressed.

Ohio National Guard fired on student demonstrators at Kent State University, killing four and wounding eleven, during nationwide student strike of May, 1969. Guard units had just come from breaking a wildcat Teamsters strike.

In 1969, citizens of Berkeley, California, occupied a vacant lot owned by the University of California to turn it into a People's Park. They were driven off by repeated police attacks, backed by helicopter.

Even the idea of unconditional subordination to the foreign interests of the State has been seriously undermined in recent years. From 1969 to 1971, workers, like the rest of the population, developed an overwhelming opposition to the Vietnam war. For the first time, the costs of American expansion abroad have come to mean a deterioration of conditions for American workers. Of special significance was the development of widespread resistance to authority and mini-mutinies among American soldiers in Vietnam—mostly working-class young men. In 1969 and 1970, soldiers gradually began to refuse to go on dangerous patrols and do other tasks they disliked. The normal punishment for refusing to obey an order under combat conditions is death. To prevent this, soldiers developed the technique of "fragging." The *New York Times* reported:

A growing number of incidents in which enlisted men have attacked their leaders because of hostilities caused by racial problems, attitudes toward the Vietnam war and what seems to be an increasing antagonism toward unpopular officers and sergeants. . . .

Some young soldiers resist orders to risk their lives and resent the attitude of the "lifers"—career officers and noncommissioned officers—who are impatient with a lack of discipline.

The incidents are called "fraggings," a term derived from the fragmentation grenade—the weapon most often used in such attempts on the lives of Army leaders because it destroys all evidence with its explosion.

. . . in the 101st Airborne Division near Hue, there were 42 "serious incidents" against officers and sergeants that resulted in at least 9 deaths last year.[96]

Senator Mike Mansfield reported that the Pentagon told him that in Vietnam of 1970 there were 209 incidents of American servicemen using fragmentation grenades to kill other Americans, usually officers or non-commissioned officers.[97]

In sum, we see a breakdown of the institutions which adapt people to the status quo, a rise of resistance to their authority, and organized efforts by ordinary people to impose their own, rather than the official, solutions to their problems.

The forces of repression have not been slow in responding to these developments. Police, National Guard, and Army civil disturbance programs have been greatly expanded, coordinated, and given the latest of technical gadgetry—often modelled on that developed for counter-insurgency in Vietnam. A secret directive issued by the Army in February, 1968, and uncovered by a Senate committee, reveals that senior officers at that time feared the development of "a true insurgency"; another from May, 1968, ordered surveillance of "strikes and labor and civil disturbances of sufficient magnitude to indicate a probable employment of Federal troops to preserve or restore order." The order was based on what the Army called a long-standing tradition of rendering assistance to state or local authorities in peacetime.[98] A command center was established—

to procure, evaluate, interpret, and disseminate . . . intelligence relating to any actual, potential or planned demonstrations or other activities related to civil disturbances within the continental U.S. which threaten civil order or military security.[99]

Testimony of Assistant Secretary of Defense Robert Froehike revealed that the program was initiated and supervised by the very highest civilian officials, including Attorney General Ramsey Clark, Secretaries of Defense Robert McNamara and Clark Clifford and special assistant to the President Stephen Pollak.[100] In the twenty-nine months from January, 1968, through May, 1970, the National Guard was used on 324 occasions to suppress civil disorders.[101] By 1970, 680,000 men of the active Armed Forces and Reserve components of the U.S. had been trained for civil disturbance duty.[102]

The actors for future dramas are prepared. But they will have to write their own lines.

Chapter 8: Footnotes

1. *Wall Street Journal,* Apr. 20, 1970.
2. *New York Times,* June 1, 1970.
3. *Ibid.*
4. *Ibid.*
5. *New York Times,* June 15, 1970.
6. *Wall Street Journal,* June 26, 1970.
7. *Wall Street Journal,* Aug. 6, 1970.
8. Bill Watson, "Counter-Planning on the Shop Floor," in *Radical America,* Vol. 5 (May-June 1971), p. 78.
9. *Ibid.,* pp. 79, 80.
10. *Ibid.*
11. *Ibid.,* p. 82.
12. *Ibid.,* p. 84.
13. *Ibid.,* p. 85.
14. *Ibid.,* pp. 80-1, 82.
15. *Ibid.,* p. 85.
16. *Wall Street Journal,* Nov. 24, 1970.
17. *Ibid.*
18. Martin Glaberman, "Marxism, The Working Class and The Trade Unions," in *Studies on the Left,* Vol. 4, No. 3 (Summer 1964), p. 68.
19. *Wall Street Journal,* Nov. 24, 1970.
20. *Ibid.*
21. *New York Times,* Mar. 31, 1971.
22. President's Commission on Postal Organization, headed by Frederich R. Kappel, quoted in *Wall Street Journal,* Mar. 19, 1970.
23. *Ibid.*
24. *Ibid.*
25. *Ibid.*

Strike / The Current Scene

292
26. *Washington Post,* Mar. 22, 1970.
27. *Ibid.*
28. *Ibid.*
29. *Ibid.*
30. *Ibid.*
31. *Root and Branch,* No. 1 (June 1970), p.3.
32. John Griner, quoted in *Washington Star,* in *Root and Branch,* p. 3.
33. Alan Whitney, radio interview, quoted *Ibid.*
34. *Wall Street Journal,* Mar. 23, 1970.
35. *Wall Street Journal,* Mar. 24, 1970.
36. *Wall Street Journal,* May 1, 1970.
37. *Wall Street Journal,* Mar. 23, 1970.
38. *Wall Street Journal,* Mar. 23, 1970.
39. *New York Times,* May 1, 1970.
40. *Wall Street Journal,* April 8, 1970.
41. *New York Times,* May 1, 1970.
42. *Ibid.*
43. *Washington Star,* May 6, 1970.
44. *Wall Street Journal,* April 8, 1970.
45. *Wall Street Journal,* Jan. 27, 1970.
46. *Wall Street Journal,* April 10, 1970.
47. *Wall Street Journql,* April 8, 1970.
48. *Wall Street Journal,* Apr. 10, 1970.
49. *Wall Street Journal,* Apr. 13, 1970.
50. *New York Times,* Apr. 30, 1970.
51. *New York Times,* May 1, 1970.
52. *New York Times Magazine,* June 21, 1970, p. 64.
53. *Wall Street Journal,* July 7, 1970.
54. Thomas O'Hanlon, "Anarchy Threatens the Kingdom of Coal," in *Fortune,* Jan. 1971, pp. 78, 82.
55. *Ibid.,* p. 78.
56. *Ibid.*
57. Paul Nyden, "In Memory of Joseph Yablonski, Coal Miners, 'Their' Union and Capital," unpublished paper, Jan. 22, 1970, pp. 26-7.
58. *Wall Street Journal,* Mar. 13, 1970.
59. *Wall Street Journal,* June 25, 1970.
60. *Wall Street Journal,* June 23, 1970.
61. *Wall Street Journal,* July 23, 1970.
62. *New York Times,* June 26, 1970.
63. *Wall Street Journal,* Mar. 24, 1970.
64. *Wall Street Journal,* Mar. 13, 1970.
65. *New York Times,* July 24, 1971.
66. Editorial, *New York Times,* July 21, 1971.
67. *Wall Street Journal,* Nov. 20, 1970.
68. *Ibid.*
69. *Wall Street Journal,* Oct. 29, 1970.
70. *Ibid.*
71. *Ibid.*
72. *Ibid.*
73. *Ibid.*
74. *Ibid.*
75. *Wall Street Journal,* Oct. 5, 1970.
76. *Ibid.*
77. *New York Times,* July 18, 1971.

78. *Wall Street Journal,* Nov. 20, 1970.
79. *Wall Street Journal,* Oct. 5, 1970.
80. *Ibid.* See also "Notes on the Official Strike in 1970," unpublished paper by Joel Stein.
81. Bureau of Labor Statistics, *Handbook of Labor Statistics,* 1969, Table 103, p. 209.
82. *Ibid.*
83. George Romney, quoted in *Newsweek,* June 22, 1970, p. 69.
84. *New York Times,* Economic Review, Jan. 10, 1971.
85. Joe Eyer, "Living Conditions in the United States," in *Root and Branch,* No. 2, 1971, p. 23.
86. 1969 *Handbook of Labor Statistics,* Table 4, p. 32.
87. Eyer, p. 24.
88. Judson Gooding, "Who's Down There?—III. The Fraying White Collar," in *Fortune,* Dec. 1970, pp. 78, 79, 109.
89. *Ibid.,* p. 79.
90. "The U.S. Can't Afford What Labor Wants," in *Business Week,* Apr. 11, 1970, p. 106.
91. James Bryce, 1888, quoted in Henry David, *The History of the Haymarket Affair* (N.Y.: Collier Books, 1963), p. 39.
92. Bill Watson, p. 77.
93. Jack Barbash, "The American Labor Movement," in *Oberlin Alumni Magazine,* Dec. 1962, p. 6.
94. National Education Association Press Release, Aug. 18, 1970.
95. Teachers College, Columbia University, Press Release, Sept. 1, 1970, p. 4.
96. *New York Times,* Jan. 11, 1971.
97. *New York Times,* Apr. 21, 1970.
98. *New York Times,* Mar. 1, 1970.
99. *New York Times,* June 22, 1971.
100. *New York Times,* Mar. 3, 1971.
101. Testimony of Major General Wilston P. Wilson, Chief, National Guard Bureau, before the President's Commission on Campus Unrest, 116 Cong. Rec. E 7302 (daily ed., Aug. 4, 1970), in "The National Guard and the Constitution," American Civil Liberties Union Legal Study, mimeographed, 1971, p. 1.
102. S/AS/91/1, 1970 I p. 293.

Chapter 9
From Mass Strike
to New Society

We have seen how mass strikes might lay the basis for a new society. We have noted occasions when, as in the Seattle general
strike, workers themselves envisioned "reopening more and more
activities under . . . [their] own management," and situations such
as the bootleg coal industry where they have actually done so. We
have observed the development of "new independent forms of
workers' organization" within which lie "a foundation of social relations at the point of production which can potentially come forward to seize power in a crisis situation and give new direction to
society." But how can such a new society come about? In this chapter we shall try to project the mass strike process beyond the limits
it has so far reached in the U.S.

   To start with, let us look briefly at three occasions when workers in other countries — Russia, Italy, and Spain — have tried to take
over the means of production and run them for themselves. They
are presented not as models to be followed — all took place under
circumstances that practically guaranteed failure — but as experiments showing how in certain conditions mass strikes can turn into revolutions, and revealing some of the problems they then face
and the solutions that come to hand.

   In February, 1917, a spontaneous general strike followed by
street fighting shook Russia, especially the capital, and led to the
collapse of the Czar's government. Revolutionary discontent
spread through the peasantry and the peasant-based army. Meanwhile, workers' committees sprang up in the factories of every major industrial center of European Russia.[1] As historian E.H. Carr
wrote,

> The first demands were for the 8-hour day and for increased wages.
> But these demands soon culminated in more or less organized attempts by
> the workers, sporadic at first, but becoming gradually more frequent, to
> interfere with managements and themselves take possession of factories.
> This . . . was the inevitable reaction of the workers in a revolutionary situa-
> tion to refusals of their demands . . .[2]

Widespread strikes and lockouts developed over these attempts:

> There was a common feature to these struggles: the employers were
> prepared to make concessions through increased wages but categorically

refused to recognize any rights to the Factory Committees. The workers in struggle . . . were prepared to fight to the bitter end not so much on the question of wage increases as on the question of the recognition of their factory organizations.[3]

Starting in May, the Factory Committees in the capital area began holding conferences to coordinate their action. The second conference passed such rules as these:

"All decrees of the Factory Committee" were declared compulsory "for the factory administration as well as for the workers and employees", unless revoked "by the Central Soviet [council] of Factory Committees.

Committees would meet, with pay, during working hours.

Factory Committees were to have "control over the composition of the administration and the right to dismiss all those who could not guarantee normal relations with the workers or who were incompetent for other reasons." "All administrative factory personnel can only enter into service with the consent of the Factory Committee, which must declare its hirings at a General Meeting of all the factory or through departmental or workshop committees."

Factory Committees were to have their own press and "to inform the workers and employees of the enterprise concerning their resolutions by posting an announcement in a conspicuous place."

The "internal organization" of the factory — working time, wages, holidays, and the like — was to be determined by the Factory Committee.[4]

On the eve of the October Revolution, an All-Russia Conference of Factory Committees met in Petersburg. It called for the creation of a central organ "for the regulation of the national economy," to be elected by the all-Russia organization of Factory Committees, and to function within the trade union structure.[5]

By October, a great revolutionary wave was sweeping Russia, and largely with the support of the Factory Committees the Bolshevik Party seized state power in the name of the workers, peasants, and soldiers. As a contemporary commentator wrote, "workers' control" stood side by side with "land" and "peace" as the "most popular and widely current slogans of the October Revolution" among the workers.[6] In many situations where the management deserted their enterprises, the Factory Committees simply took over in the name of the workers. Where they were strong enough, the committees "boldly ousted the management and assumed direct control in their respective plants."[7]

As a Bolshevik historian wrote, "During its struggle for a 'factory constitution,' the working class had become aware of the need itself to manage production."[8] The means to do so were laid out in December, 1917, in a *Practical Manual for the Implementation of Workers' Control in Industry,* published by the Central Council of the Petrograd Factory Committees. Each Factory Committee was

296   to establish a "production commission." It would establish the necessary links between the different sections of the factory, supervise the state of the machinery and its depreciation, deal with deficiencies in the arrangement of the plant, determine the "coefficients of exploitation" (rates of work and payment) in each section, set the optimum number of shops and of workers in each shop, determine job allocations from top to bottom, and take charge of the financial relations of the factory.

Other commissions of the Factory Committee were to deal with reconversion from war production, the supply of raw materials, and the supply of fuel. The commissions were "entitled to invite the attendance of technicians and others in a consultative capacity." Since no factory is an isolated unit, the *Manual* announced the intention of grouping the Factory Committees into regional federations and these into an All-Russia Federation. "Workers' control of industry, as a part of workers' control of the totality of economic life," must be seen, it declared, "as the workers moving into fields previously dominated by others. Control should merge into management." [9]

Such a development was completely against the intentions of the Bolshevik Party, which had seized state power, controlled the soviets, and to a considerable extent the unions, and now desired to centralize the economy under its own direction. Far from wanting workers to take over the factories, Lenin shortly before taking power had called for a "compulsory syndicalization" of industry which "does not in the least affect conditions of ownership and does not deprive the proprietor of a single penny of his money." [10] "Socialism," he added, "is nothing else than a capitalistic State monopoly worked in the interests of the whole nation and therefore no longer a capitalist monopoly." [11] But, as Arthur Rosenberg wrote in his *History of Bolshevism*,

> Armed workmen intoxicated by their revolutionary victory were not to be kept within the bounds of such a moderate scheme of reform. Instead they took possession themselves of the factories and drove out their employers.
>
> It is clear . . . that the Bolsheviks did not expropriate Russian employers but that it was accomplished as the result of spontaneous action on the part of the workers and against the will of the Bolsheviks. [12]

Before seizing power, the Bolshevik Party had supported the Factory Committees and their demands for workers' control as a way to undermine the old regime, but now it saw them as a threat to its own authority and attempted to bring them under its control by making them responsible to an All-Russia Council of Workers Control run from above, of which less than one-quarter of the memers were to come from the Factory Committees and most of the rest from party-controlled organizations. As E.H. Carr wrote of this move, "Those who had paid most lip service to workers' control and purported to 'expand' it were in fact engaged in a skillful attempt to make it orderly and innocuous by turning it into a large-scale, centralized, public institution." [13]

The trade unions played a central role in this process. According to Trotsky's biographer, Isaac Deutscher, a few weeks after the October Revolution—

he Factory Committees attempted to form *their own* national organization, which was to secure their virtual economic dictatorship. The Bolsheviks now called upon the unions to render a special service to the nascent Soviet State and to discipline the Factory Committees. The unions came out firmly against the attempt of the Factory Committees to form a national organization of their own. They prevented the convocation of a planned All-Russian Congress of Factory Committees and demanded total subordination on the part of the Committees. [14]

Once the Bolshevik state thus seized the initiative in industry, it established a Supreme Economic Council, attached to the "Council of People's Commissars"—the Bolshevik cabinet—with power over all existing economic authorities. Through its appointees and organs, the Bolshevik Party succeeded in establishing its control over the factories, sending in its own representatives as managers. As Lenin put it soon after, "we passed from workers' control to the creation of the Supreme Council of National Economy." [15]

The movement toward workers' self-management was defeated in Russia for several reasons. First, a large proportion of the workers accepted the idea that the Bolshevik Party represented their interests and that its seizure of power meant control by the workers. Second, the Bolshevik Party possessed a powerful organization prepared to defend its power by ruthlessly suppressing all opposition to it. Third, it was widely felt that a powerful centralized organization was necessary and the only alternative to chaos. The workers represented only a tiny part of the population of Russia, and could not rule the vast peasantry by themselves. Neither did they believe they could cope with the collapse of the economy and underdevelopment of the country.

Another interesting case of a mass strike developing into a direct attempt by workers to take charge of production occurred in the Italian factory occupations of 1920. Despite a substantial increase in real wages [16] from 1918 to 1920, the working classes of Italy were in continuous turmoil. Membership in the dominant union federation, the C.G.L., increased from 250,000 to 2,200,000.[17] In 1919, 1,000,000 industrial workers and 500,000 peasants struck [18] in 1920, the figures were 1,200,000 and 1,000,000.[19] In late June and July, 1919, riots against the high cost of living swept through the entire country, with crowds sacking hundreds of shops in dozens of cities and proprietors handing over their warehouse keys to the unions to distribute their goods. "The authorities often found it useless to invoke the aid of troops on a large scale because the soldiers fraternized with the mobs." [20] In the countryside, peasants began seizing land that had been promised them during the war

The year 1920 began with strikes of state postal, telegraph and railroad workers — C.G.L. officials had to discourage constituent organizations from joining local strikes in solidarity with the railroad workers. Textile, sulphur and metalworkers struck in February. In March there was a general strike in Milan protesting the killing of a streetcar worker. In Turin in April a general strike raged over union powers, triggered by a conflict over daylight saving time. Workers had occupied and in some cases run factories in various parts of Italy, without this yet developing into a concerted movement.

Out of the mass strike workers developed a determination centered in the auto city of Turin, to take direction of production The process started with the metalworkers union's demand for recognition of plant grievance committees (*commissioni interne*) which would discuss with management questions of wages and the distribution of work. They were recognized by the Turin employers in early 1919, and until August were seen essentially as agencies for decentralized union activity with specific, limited functions agreed on by union and management. The committees were under great pressure from the rank and file; one union official complained that within fifteen days or so after a grievance committee was elected, the workers would send it packing, accusing its members of betrayal and collusion with management.[21]

Toward summer, revolutionary discussion groups developed in the Turin factories around the idea of transforming the grievance committees into factory councils through which workers would develop the power and capacity to take control of the factories. At the Fiat plant in August, 1919, the workers threw out the old grievance committee and the new one held elections to establish a factory council of commissioners selected by the work-teams in each department of the plant. All workers could vote regardless of union and political affiliation, and commissioners were removable by referendum at any moment. By October, nearly all Turin metalworking shops had factory commissions, with the commissioners from different factories meeting on a city-wide basis. By the end of the year, 150,000 Turinese were organized in councils.[22] The union leaders tried to gain control of the councils by demanding that the voters and commissioners be union members, but won only the latter.

In August, 1920, metalworkers' union wage demands were turned down. The unions were broke and unwilling to risk a protracted strike, so they called a "working by the book" slowdown. The employers began to respond with lockouts, and the union called for factory occupations September 1st to forestall them. Workers held hundreds of plants in Milan, as well as others throughout Italy, including most of the country's heavy industry. In Turin, vortex of the movement, the factory councils took over management and started up production under their own direction, while protecting the plants from counter-attack. At Fiat-Centro, production of around thirty-seven cars per day was maintained, compared to sixty-eight in normal times, despite the desertion of technicians and white-collar workers.[23] "It seemed to most Italians that the revolution had begun." [24]

The C.G.L. on September 5th listed the three courses available: to confine the movement to the metalworkers; to spread it throughout Italy; or to transform the factory occupations into a revolution. The unions opposed immediate revolution. The Socialist Party thereupon offered to take charge of the movement—but instead of choosing one course or another, it merely called for the Parliament, then in recess, to convene. With this, workers gave up the initiative. The Prime Minister, who "knew socialist leaders too well to fear any revolution of their making," [25] stalled until the movement lost momentum, then negotiated a settlement based on a wage increase, holidays and severance pay. Between September 25th and 30th, the occupations ended.

The Italian factory occupations of 1920 illustrate how the sense of power workers develop in the course of mass strikes, combined with the inability of the existing authorities to meet their demands, leads naturally to the idea of workers taking over production for themselves. It also illustrates the fundamental conflict that has arisen again and again at such moments between organizations developed to adapt workers to existing society (such as unions and political parties) and those which aim to win workers' complete control over society—workers councils, soviets, and the like. Waiting for the unions and the Italian Socialist Party led inevitably to loss of the power the workers had already won. The result was disastrous. The Turin socialists had warned several months before,

The present phase of the class struggle in Italy is the one which precedes

300 *either* the conquest of power by the revolutionary proletariat . . . *or* a terrible reaction on the part of the property-owning class and the government caste. No form of violence will be spared in their effort to subjugate the industrial and agricultural proletariat; they will endeavour to smash once and for all the workers' organs of political struggle (the Socialist Party) and to incorporate the workers' organs of economic power (trade unions and co-operatives) into the machinery of the bourgeois State.[26]

Within two years, Mussolini's Fascist movement had indeed taken power, after informing the leaders of Italian industry that "the aim of the imminent fascist action is the restoration of discipline, especially in the factories." [27]

Perhaps the most impressive example of workers' management of production occurred in Catalonia during the first stage of the Spanish Civil War. Nearly half of the industrial workers in Spain were in Catalonia. They possessed strong anarchist and syndicalist traditions and a powerful belief that in the event of revolution the workers and not the state would take over society. In the months before the Civil War, the national congress of the C.N.T., the dominant union federation in Catalonia, laid out a revolutionary program expressing this belief:

Once the violent aspect of the revolution is finished, the following are declared abolished: private property, the state, the principles of authority and, as a consequence, the classes which divide men into exploiters and exploited, oppressed and oppressors.

Within each community elected committees would deal with agriculture, hygiene, culture, discipline, production, and statistics.

All these functions will have no executive or bureaucratic character. Apart from those who discharge technical functions . . . the rest will perform their duties as producers, meeting in sessions at the end of the day to discuss the questions of detail which do not require the approval of the communal assembles.

The communes were to be based on free associations of workers in their syndicates (unions), producing and exchanging the necessities of life, and linked in "regional and national federations for the realization of their general objectives." [28] The C.N.T.'s structure was adapted to this goal.

The C.N.T. had a number of prominent leaders, but the real power rested not in a bureaucracy of paid union officials — there were none — but in local assemblies of workers in the various trades who formulated their own policies and were free to take action on their own. They sent delegates, mandated and with circumscribed authority, to local committees and national congresses, which were

essentially coordinating bodies with no authority over the local   301
groups.

The months between February and July, 1936, were ones of
extreme labor unrest in the young Spanish Republic. According to
one estimate there were 110 general strikes [29] as well as numerous
uprisings and other outbreaks; a right-wing military revolt was anticipated at any time. On July 18th, the revolt broke out, led by General Francisco Franco, who expected to occupy most of the country
within a few days. The Republican government was largely unprepared to meet it and had few loyal troops of its own, but the workers in large parts of Spain demanded and received arms, counter-
attacked, and defeated the rebellion in perhaps half of the country.
The result was that "the government . . . lost all authority. The
workers, through their party and trade union organizations, became the real rulers of the country and the organizers of the war."[30]
Throughout much of Spain the Socialist and Communist unions
and parties merely extended state control and left private production intact, but in Catalonia the story was different.

After the workers of Barcelona, the main city of Catalonia, defeated the military rising in two days of street fighting, they were

Wide World Photos

Revolt of Franco's troops was initially crippled by resistance of Spanish workers.
But attempts at workers' control of industry were defeated by the Republican
government itself before Franco's final victory.

302 the only real social force. The upper classes fled, went into hiding, or were killed. Companys, head of the middle-class Catalonian government, told the anarchist leaders, "Now you are masters of the city and of Catalonia. . . . You have conquered and everything is in your power." [31]

The Catalonian workers thereupon began organizing society for themselves. They took over the railroads, busses, trams, and subways, the petroleum companies, the automobile industries, the steamship companies, the hospitals, electricity, gas and water systems, the large stores, the munitions plants, the theater and movie houses, with the workers in each responsible for production. General meetings of the workers elected councils in which all activities of the workplace — production, administration, technical services, etc. — were represented. Collectives of barbers, bakers, shopkeepers and the like regulated small trade. Coordination was largely carried on through the unions. The evidence indicates that the life of the city was at least as well run as before the revolution, despite the crisis conditions. The Austrian historian Franz Borkenau arrived three weeks after the rising and recorded in his diary that —

> The amount of expropriation in the first few days since 19 July is almost incredible. In many respects, however, life was much less disturbed than I expected it to be after newspaper reports abroad. Tramways and buses were running, water and light functioning. [32]

Borkenau visited a collectivized bus factory and reported that

> Only three weeks after the beginning of the civil war, two weeks after the end of the general strike, it seems to run as smoothly as if nothing had happened. I visited the men at their machines. The rooms looked tidy, the work was done in a regular manner. Since socialization, this factory has repaired two busses, finished one which had been under construction and constructed a completely new one. The latter wore the inscription "constructed under workers' control." It had been completed, the management claimed, in five days, as against an average of seven days under the previous management. Complete success, then.
>
> It is a large factory, and things could not have been made to look nice for the benefit of a visitor, had they really been in a bad muddle. Nor do I think that any preparations were made for my visit . . .
>
> But if it would be hasty to generalize from the very favourable impression made by this particular factory, one fact remains: it is an extraordinary achievement for a group of workers to take over one factory, under however favourable conditions, and within a few days to make it run with complete regularity. [33]

Wages and money were not abolished, but profits were eliminated, wages were levelled upwards, and equalized between men and women, skilled and unskilled, adults and juveniles, increased for those with families, and reduced for directors. In some cases food was made available by food supply workers not on the basis of money but of tickets showing the holders had been working.

These extraordinary developments were made possible in large part because Spanish workers had planned and discussed them for years. A contemporary observer in Spain, Gaston Leval, later recalled —

For decades, anarchist papers and reviews and pamphlets had been forming in militants a habit of acting individually, of taking initiative. They were not taught to wait for directives from above. They had always thought and acted for themselves—sometimes well, sometimes badly. Reading the paper, the review, the pamphlet, the book, each developed and enlarged his own personality. They were never given a dogma of a safe, uniform line of action. In the study of concrete problems, in the critique of economic and political ideas, clear ideas of revolution had gradually matured.

For some time, the problems of social reconstruction had been the order of the day . . . A great number of the 60,000 readers of the libertarian review *Studi* followed with interest the detailed articles on the problems a revolution faces, in food supply, fuel, or agriculture. Many syndicalists groupings did likewise . . . I knew many syndicalist committee members who understood the problems of revolution and economic organization very clearly. They spoke intelligently about raw materials, imports, the need to improve or eliminate this or that branch of industry, the armed defence, and other matters.[34]

Workers' militias were organized at the same time. George Orwell, himself a volunteer in a militia unit from Catalonia, described them in *Homage to Catalonia:*

In the early days of Franco's revolt the militias had been hurriedly raised by the various trade unions and political parties; each was essentially a political organization, owing allegiance to its party as much as to the central government . . . The essential point of the system was social equality between officers and men. Everyone from general to private drew the same pay, ate the same food, wore the same clothes, and mingled on terms of complete equality. If you wanted to slap the general commanding the division on the back and ask him for a cigarette, you could do so, and no one thought it curious. In theory at any rate each militia was a democracy, and not a hierarchy. It was understood that orders had to be obeyed, but it was also understood that when you gave an order you gave it as comrade to comrade and not as superior to inferior. There were officers and N.C.O.'s, but there was no military rank in the ordinary sense; no titles, no badges, no heel-clicking and saluting. They had attempted to produce within the militias a sort of temporary working model of the classless society. Of course, there was not perfect equality, but there was a nearer approach to it than I had ever seen or than I would have thought conceivable in time of war.[35]

Workers similarly replaced the police force in patrolling the streets

304   and borders. For practical purposes, they were society.

The Catalonian government, with no power of its own, endorsed the workers' action, and the leaders of the C.N.T. supported it in turn. A Central Committee of Anti-Fascist Militias of Catalonia coordinated activities connected with the war effort, in cooperation with the government. Gradually, the government, which C.N.T. leaders had joined, asserted more and more authority over the situation. For example, on October 24th, it passed a collectivization decree which recognized the workers' seizure of the factories but set up machinery for governmental coordination and supervision which eventually developed into the means of government control. Thus began a process in which, as the *New York Times* put it somewhat later, "The principle of State intervention and control of business and industry, as against workers' control of them in the guise of collectivization, is gradually being established . . ." [36] Even Companys complained that production had fallen off owing to the prodigious bureaucratization set up by the government; an army of inspectors and directors had descended on the factories, and the workers had been demoralized, Companys said.[37]

Similarly, the Republican government gradually broke up the various militia units, whose proud cry had been "Militiamen of freedom, never soldiers!" and dissolved them into its new army, in which traditional divisions of rank and authority were reestablished.

This gradual retreat of the revolution must be explained on several levels. First, the workers succeeded in maintaining production, but they did not build up a system of coordination under their own control. Since the need for coordination was strongly felt, this function passed first to the union and party leaderships, then to the government. This problem was aggravated by the isolation of the revolution; the central government used its control of materials needed by the Catalonians to force them to accept its authority. This became even more decisive as Russia became the prime supplier of war material and used its position to build up the previously insignificant Communist Party and to destroy the anarchists and their allies. Finally, Italian and German military support made a Franco victory always probable, so that the Catalonian workers were under constant pressure to submit to government demands for coordination and unity or face extermination. Even anarchist leaders, pledged to eternal hostility to any state, joined the Republican government and refrained from attacking it.

The final suppression of the revolution came in May, 1937, and it came not at the hands of Franco, but of the Republican government. Two months before, the government had dissolved the revolutionary patrols in Catalonia and established a unified police force, much to the resentment of the C.N.T. workers. Newspaper attacks capped by murders of leaders on both sides brought tensions to a fever pitch. On May 3rd, the Catalonian police launched an attack on the telephone exchange, which had been run by the workers for ten months, after which street fighting broke out throughout the city. The government in Madrid took advantage of this situation to send 4,000 soldiers to occupy Barcelona, even though a truce had been reached, finally establishing its authority there until the time of its defeat by General Franco.

The actual course of events which leads from a mass strike to a revolution is of course unique in each case. But certain common elements can be seen in each of the examples we have discussed.

1) In the course of a long period of conflict, workers form the goal of taking over production themselves. This goal develops as a response to two conditions that an escalating workers' movement eventually produces. First, the workers reach the limit of what they can gain without taking power. This limit is generally experienced in the intransigence or counter-attack of the old rulers, expressed through lockouts, *coups d'etat* and the like. The obvious solution that presents itself, therefore, is removing the old rulers from power. Second, the workers discover through their own actions their real power and ability, and therefore realize that taking over management is possible for them. The goal of a dual power over management which we have seen in American, Russian and Italian mass strikes then passes over into a desire for unilateral control.

2) At some point, workers take over the productive apparatus through occupations, street action or both. In Russia and Catalonia, this occurred through brief barricade battles; in Italy through occupations. Both of course are normal aspects of the mass strike itself, but are here put to a further purpose.

3) Workers have to find means to defend themselves against the counter-attacks of the old rulers. In both Russia and Spain, counter-revolution took the form of civil war backed by foreign powers. In Italy it took the form of armed bands. In each case, workers formed guards or militia units based on the factories. Their greatest strength, however, lay not in warfare but in their overwhelming numbers, their control of production, and the justice and popular support of their cause.

4) Workers start producing for themselves. This begins as part of the struggle itself—provisioning the population, providing

306   needed equipment, etc. But it has a further significance: it is the
vital tip-point in the social balance of power, showing that society
can and is going on without the old rulers. At first, production can
be resumed on the basis left by capitalism; the machines are still
there, the workers already know how to run them, and all that is
necessary is to start them up. Similarly, the links between different
units of production already exist in the form of order departments
and transportation facilities; initially these can be used to assure
the flow of raw materials and products where they are needed.

5)   In each of the cases we have examined, we can see the
competition between two types of organization. In one, power
moves from the top down. The activity of great numbers of people
is directed by a special group. This is the case under capitalism. It
is likewise the case in the forms of state control into which the Russian and Spanish revolutions evolved. In the other, power moves
from the bottom up. The basic cell-unit of decision is simply those
who work together at a particular task. They decide what they will
do, and themselves coordinate their activity with others. This form
of organization can be observed in the factory committees and
councils we have seen develop in Russia, Italy and Spain—as well
as in numerous other cases we have not examined here, such as
Germany after World War I and Hungary in 1956. These organizations start out simply as means to coordinate the struggle of groups
acting in solidarity with each other. But because they follow the organization of the productive system itself, their structure is excel-
lently adapted to taking up the coordination of work.

As we have seen, the work-groups are the cell-units of mass
strikes. The principles under which they could govern their own
activity can be seen in the self-organization of the sitdown strikers
in Flint in 1937. All those who worked together simply met in assembly and made the decisions that affected their common activity,
and all were responsible for doing their share of carrying the decisions out. As our foreign examples have shown, they could have
run not only the sitdown but the factory itself in this way. Certain
experts such as engineers and chemists might sometimes be needed, but the foremen and the rest of management would be completely unnecessary.

Since society is not composed of isolated units, workers
would face the problem of coordinating from below an enormous
range of social activities. For if those who do the work do not coordinate their activity, someone else will and thereby gain power
over them—as we have seen in our Russian and Catalonian examples. The coordinating councils and committees we have described in this chapter give an imperfect but useful idea of how work

groups can coordinate their activities from below. Different groups can be tied together by liaison committees of many types, weaving "a variegated net of collaborating bodies through society."[38] Just what forms of coordination would be necessary cannot be predicted, but it is clear that each group would need at least to coordinate with its suppliers, with others doing the same work, with those who use their product, and with others in the same community. Such an organization would allow the entire life of society to be brought under human control while realizing the principles of cooperation and self-directed activity which underlie the mass strike.

This conception of the revolutionary process is of course far different from the model of insurrection familiar from the eighteenth and nineteenth centuries. It is this very difference, in fact, that makes possible an outcome different from past revolutions. In the past, a special minority has seized state power and then directed the reorganization of society, thereby retaining the real power in its own hands. But mass strikes are actions of the people themselves. In directing their own activity the people themselves possess the real social power, and unless they give it up to someone else they can retain it in the new society.

Of course, in any such situation there will always be individuals and groups who would like to establish themselves as the ruling power, governing in the name of the people and the workers. This, indeed, is just what defeated such past revolutions as that of Russia in 1917, where the Bolshevik Party seized power in the name and under the guise of the soviets of workers, peasants and soldiers, in order to establish their own control. In any revolutionary situation there will undoubtedly be numerous such parties and groups clamoring for power. They may even sincerely believe they are serving the revolution. They will undoubtedly put themselves forward as the champions of whatever ideas are popular at the time — just as the Bolsheviks embraced workers' control and the anarchistic soviets when they really meant to centralize power in the hands of the party. Leaders will try to entrench themselves in every position of power from the shop to the most central organs of the revolution.

Nor is it only in such organized parties and groups that the seeds of a new ruling minority lurk. There is a natural tendency for responsibility to re-centralize in the hands of a few individuals, accepted leaders, who then come to do more and more of the movement's thinking and deciding for it. This occurred to a considerable extent in Catalonia. Such people, if entrenched for a long

308 enough time in the various coordinating bodies, could gradually develop into a separate class of decision-makers who would come to rule.

There can be no guarantee in advance against these possibilities. Only the will to keep in their own hands the power they have taken can protect ordinary people from losing it. As long as the real responsibilities and initiative remains with the work-groups themselves, coordinating organs cannot become a new separate ruling group. Their power can be circumscribed by giving them no authority or means to impose their will on those they represent; limiting their role to particular questions; mandating or rotating delegates, with recall of those defying mandates; keeping all activities public; and giving coordinating bodies no means to execute decisions save the activity of those they represent. Under such circumstances, workers can prevent the development of a new ruling group simply by refusing to work for anyone but themselves.

Past mass strikes have ended in the restoration of control from above. But what would happen if ordinary workers succeeded in holding power themselves? Can the continuing life of society be organized by those who actually do the work? Since no such cases have arisen to date, we can only try to visualize what might happen —using what has happened so far as a guide.

In order to survive, the workers must promptly restore the production of life's necessities. Unless this is done, social panic inevitably results. It can be done by the already existing work groups themselves. All that is necessary is to reactivate the existing agricultural, energy, transportation, and other systems. We have seen this happen in Catalonia. The different units which form a chain of production can coordinate their action initially through simple liaison committees.

In each workplace, everything that happens in the production process can be recorded — what machinery and labor is used in each step, how much time is put in by each worker, how much is produced. On the basis of this information, workers can understand and therefore manage production — compare the advantages of different machines and techniques, allocate work responsibilities, and make similar decisions. The same information can be calculated for each group of related enterprises, each branch of production and each community and region. Through their coordinating organs the workers can decide what to produce, how much to produce, how much to put aside for new equipment and the like. The level at which each of these decisions is made depends on how wide a range of people is affected by them. In short, a new and readily intelligible system of accounting is called for, which will reveal rather than conceal the actual flow of work and materials — and which will thereby make possible effective control from below.

In contrast to the present system, this allows production to be planned to meet human needs. To produce the necessities and amenities of life for everyone, a great expansion is required in just those areas which the present system has failed to provide — housing, medicine, nutritious foods, community facilities and the like. No doubt, many aspects of consumption become more collective than at present, with community meals, housing, transportation, medicine and the like expanding the range of possible life styles. New life styles give rise to new needs; the workers and their coordinating organs have to meet them as they come to be felt.

An enormous amount of labor currently goes into waste and destruction. The making of nuclear weapons, Cadillacs, advertising, and polutants simply has to be stopped. The state, military, and other bureaucratic establishments pose a threat to popular rule until disbanded. Whatever useful functions they perform, such as health care and construction, can be taken over by the workers who previously performed them. A great many commodities produced today serve needs deliberately generated by the present system through advertising, emulation, and other forms of social con-

Steve Bohrer

The calling in of the repressive power of the state against student actions generated a broad base for student resistance during the late 1960's. Cops on campus became a hated symbol.

trol. Their production naturally tapers off as these pressures cease and manipulated forms of consumption decline.

The large numbers of workers engaged in wasteful and destructive activities such as military production, sales promotion and management, can shift to productive work. Blacks, women, the unemployed, and others hitherto largely excluded from production can join the work groups. At the same time, a great many activities not presently organized as jobs, such as housework and child care, can come to be considered as valued forms of social labor. Everyone able to work takes up his or her share with an equal responsibility, not only for performing it, but for planning and controlling it. With the elimination of waste production and the increase in productive workers, the time each person has to work can be reduced to a fraction of the present work time.

The new workers coming into production generally lack the skills necessary for the work. Even those doing familiar work are handicapped in their knowledge because they have been limited to one particular function. All are victims of a carefully fostered ignorance of how the different parts of the work are integrated. In order to understand the workplace they will have to manage, each one has to teach his own knowledge to the others. Through job rotation, the work can be kept interesting and such inequalities as that between skilled and unskilled workers dissolved. This requires apprenticeship training, especially for those members previously denied the opportunity to learn special skills. This rotation can include such work as child care and housekeeping, which come to be viewed like any other work; men must be trained in this work by women, so that the latter can gain equal participation in other activities.

Young people can receive much of their education through participation in various work-groups rather than through educational institutions separate from life. Indeed, the division between life and learning breaks down, as work becomes a constant expansion of skills and capacities. The constant discussion, decision, and application of one's own plans become in themselves an education in social management. In short, an enormous growth of education is one of the main features of this as of other post-revolutionary societies; but here education is a process of teaching each other, not of inculcation by the state. All such teaching and learning are considered, like other work, part of meeting society's needs.

The production plant which the workers inherit has been centralized with a view to profit-making and bureaucratic control. Enormous populations have been concentrated in urban belts while vast regions have been farmed without regard to the natural qualities of the terrain. Entire cities and regions have specialized in the production of coal, steel, cars and the like. This has unbalanced the natural environment of every region and restricted the people of each area to limited forms of life. By controlling production from below, workers are able in many cases to make the units of production smaller and better adapted to the local environment and needs — even while improving the coordination among the various units. This process of decentralization not only helps restore ecological balance, but allows a much greater social diversity, in which local units can experiment with new forms, and in which everyone can experience many kinds of work. It also allows more economic independence for local communities and regions, thus providing another barrier to any group trying to seize central social power.

The inherited means of production are organized to reduce the necessary amount of labor only when profits are thereby increased. Nor do they aim to maximize the freedom and pleasure of work. Workers can eliminate a great part of the more boring, repetitive and degrading jobs through automation. At the same time, they can recover the pleasure of personal creativity found in craftsmanship — craftsmanship now based on an advanced technology.

At this point the opportunity for an infinite range of experimentation opens up. In some cases work can be altogether removed from a factory context, an individual doing his share at home whenever he feels like it — a virtual return to cottage industry. In other cases, the whole community can participate with pleasure in such activities as harvesting. Since necessary work time is minimal, most of people's time is free for whatever they desire. With the principle of cooperative self-direction spreading to all social activities there even ceases to be a special realm of "work" or any reason to think of people as "workers." They are simply people doing the things they need in order to live as they want to.

The basic idea underlying such a society is simply that the individuals who make it up are working together to meet each other's needs. Each working group must take responsibility for meeting society's needs in its area of work, knowing that others are working in turn to produce for its various needs.

Simple and obvious as this idea is, the thought that people could live by it immediately comes in conflict with our conventional image of "human nature." Aren't people too irresponsible and selfish for it to work? We live in a society where "nice guys finish last" and where people have to be cutthroat to "make it." Hence people's potential for selfishness and irresponsibility is maxi-

312   mized and their cooperative feelings repressed. But even in contemporary society, we see behavior which contradicts this. For example, the overwhelming majority of fathers support their families, and rare is the mother who does not take responsibility for her young children. Is this "merely biological"? It may be considered biological in the sense that people have an inborn capacity for taking responsibility to meet needs beyond their own. But this capacity need not apply just to the immediate family; when we examine different cultures we find that each has its own pattern of mutual responsibilities.

It is true that the kind of society we have projected will require a change from selfishness to cooperation and from passivity to responsibility. Indeed, this transformation is the inner content of revolution, the necessary corollary when people take control over their own lives.

It is just this transformation which we see beginning in the mass strike.

Chapter 9: Footnotes

1. E.H. Carr, *The Bolshevik Revolution, A History of Soviet Russia, 1917-1923,* Vol. 2 (Baltimore: Penguin Books, 1966), p. 63.
2. *Ibid.*
3. A.M. Pankratova, Fabzovkomy Rossii v borbe za sotsialisticheskuyv Fabriky [Russian Factory Committees in the struggle for the socialist factory] (Moscow: 1923), p. 9, cited in Maurice Brinton, *The Bolsheviks and Workers' Control 1917-1921* (London: Solidarity, 1970), p. 10.
4. Brinton, pp. 8-9.
5. Carr, pp. 69-70.
6. *Ibid.,* p. 72.
7. R.V. Daniels, *The Conscience of the Revolution* (Harvard University Press, 1960), p. 83, cited in Brinton, p. 5.
8. A. Pankratova, p. 36, cited in Brinton, pp. 10-11.
9. Brinton, pp. 25-6.
10. Arthur Rosenberg, *A History of Bolshevism* (Garden City, N.Y.: Anchor Books, Doubleday & Co., Inc., 1967), pp. 115-6.
11. *Ibid.*
12. *Ibid.,* pp. 124, 126.
13. Carr, p. 75.
14. I. Deutscher, *Soviet Trade Unions* (London: Royal Institute of International Affairs, 1950), p. 17, cited in Brinton, p. 19.
15. V.I. Lenin, *Sochineniya XXII,* p. 215, cited in Brinton, p. 22.
16. Neufield, *Italy,* p. 368
17. *Ibid.*
18. *Ibid.,* p. 370.
19. *Ibid.,* p. 379.
20. *Ibid.,* p. 371.
21. *Ibid.,* p. 372.
22. "Introduction to Gramsci, 1919-1920," in *New Left Review,* No. 51.

23. Giuseppe Fiori, "Antonio Gramsci" (*NLB,* London, 1970), p. 138.
24. Neufield, p. 379.
25. *Ibid.,* p. 380.
26. Fiori, *op. cit.,* p. 128
27. Fiori, *op. cit.,* p. 158.
28. James Joll, *The Anarchists* (N.Y.: Grosset & Dunlap, 1966), pp. 252-3.
29. Wilfred H. Crook, *Communism and the General Strike* (Hamden, Conn.: Shoe String Press, Inc., 1960), p. 294.
30. Gerald Brenan, *The Spanish Labyrinth* (N.Y.: Cambridge University Press, 1967), p. 317.
31. Joll, p. 255.
32. Franz Borkenau, *The Spanish Cockpit* (1937) cited in George Woodcock, *Anarchism, a history of libertarian ideas and movements* (Cleveland: Meridian Books, World Publishing Co., 1967), p. 395.
33. *Ibid.,* pp. 395-6.
34. Gaston Leval, "Some Conclusions on the Spanish Collectives, *Anarchy,* No. 5 (July 1961), p. 154.
35. George Orwell, *Homage to Catalonia* (N.Y.: Harcourt, Brace & World, Inc., Harvest Book ed., 1952), p. 27.
36. *New York Times,* February 1938, cited in *Living Marxism,* Vol. IV, No. 6 (April 1939), p. 172.
37. Brenan, p. 321.
38. Anton Pannekoek, "Workers Councils" (*Root and Branch* Pamphlet 1, 1970), p. 54.

Afterword:
A Challenge to Historians

"If there is any one paramount characteristic of books on American history, it is that they are not histories of the people. Histories of the generals, the diplomats, and the politicos there are plenty; histories of the people—the plain people—there are few.

"This is no accident. It is part of the great conspiracy which consists in drawing an iron curtain between the people and their past. The generals, the diplomats, and the politicos learned long ago that history is more than a record of the past; it is, as well, a source from which may be drawn a sense of strength and direction for the future. At all costs, that sense of strength and direction and purpose must be denied to the millions of men and women who labor for their living. Hence, the record of their past achievements is deliberately obscured in order to dull their aspirations for the future." [1]

These words are as true today as when they were written a quarter of a century ago. The very memory of revolt is a subversive force. Societies, like individuals, are adept at forgetting those aspects of their past which do not fit their present self-image. For it is just those aspects of the past which preserve the threat—and the promise—of possibilities different from the present. Historians, far from preserving those memories, have generally served as a filter by means of which they are screened.

For most of that quarter century, American history has been dominated by the so-called consensus school. Its basic argument, as David Donald summarized it, is that "most Americans throughout our history have been contented participants in the capitalist system." [2] Such a view can be maintained only by systematically ignoring the events described in this book. Even when the verbally expressed values of ordinary working people seem to bear out such a view, the actual history of working-class action proves it absurd. The "consensus school" turns out to be nothing but the purveyor of a conservative myth which we have seen dating back to 1888, when James Bryce wrote that in America, "There are no struggles between privileged and unprivileged orders, not even that perpetual strife of rich and poor . . ." [3]

It is more surprising to find similar views expressed among the so-called New Left historians who have emerged as the critics of the "consensus school." Yet so far they have done little to reveal the actual history of working-class action in America. For example, not a single paper in *Toward a New Past: Dissenting Essays in American History*—a collection of self-styled "New Left" historical writings published recently—dealt with workers' own action. The only paper dealing with the industrial working class was entitled "Urbanization, Migration and Social Mobility in Late 19th Century America." It concluded, without the slightest discussion of the three great mass strikes within that period, that—

> For all the brutality and rapacity which marked the American scene in the years in which the new urban industrial order came into being, what stands out most is the relative absence of collective working-class protest aimed at reshaping capitalist society.[4]

Such assumptions both grow from and contribute to the widespread New Left belief that the working class today is simply "part of the system."

But what about the few historians who specialize in labor history? On the whole, they have ignored the initiative and self-directed action of ordinary workers. Where they have been unable to ignore it, they have treated it as an irrational aberration, an inability to relate to the reality of the existing system of society. They have generally assumed that the significance of labor history lay in the development of large-scale, centralized, bureaucratic labor organizations.

Traditionally, labor history has tended to deal almost exclusively with the development of trade unions, implying that the workers had no history but that of the unions. This is much the same as considering the history of a nation as identical with the acts of its government. Recently, labor history has begun to develop a less restrictive focus. Thus, for example, David Brody wrote in the preface to his *Steelworkers in America,* "The steelworkers themselves have been the focus, not one or another of the institutions or events of which they were a part." [5] Similarly, Irving Bernstein wrote in the Preface to *The Lean Years,* the book "begins with the worker rather than with the trade union."[6]

But this approach seems to be largely accompanied by an assumption that, except for unionism, workers are passive victims of circumstances and events, not active human beings trying to shape their lives against overwhelming forces. Thus, Brody continued—

My aim has been to study the process by which their working lives in America's steel mills were shaped . . .[7]

And similarly, Bernstein wrote—

I am, of course, concerned about the worker when he is organized and

316   devote considerable attention to the manner in which his union bargains
for him. But this is not all. I am interested in him when he is unorganized,
in his legal status, in his political behavior, in his social and cultural activities, and in how the employer and the state treat him.[8]

Bernstein's "political behavior" and "social and cultural activities"
hardly suggest the large-scale, spontaneous, and self-directed action independent of trade union direction, in which we have observed workers engaged decade after decade.

Historians of American trade unionism since John R. Commons have rightly emphasized the evolutionary adaptation of trade
unions to the existing structure of American society. As they have
pointed out, the success of trade unions as institutions within the
present economic system has depended on their sloughing off aspirations that could not be achieved within that framework. This
is often portrayed as an expression of American "pragmatism."

This powerful evolutionary perspective, however, is applied
one-sidedly. It generally ignores the repeated breakdown of this
trade union adaptation on behalf of the working class. In periods of
crisis, trade unions have either collapsed altogether, or have at the
very least lost the power to maintain workers' standard of life at a
currently acceptable level. (Standard of life, of course, includes not
only wage rates but security, level of misery in work, environmental conditions, war, peace, repression, and everything else that affects individuals' lives as well.) With this breakdown of adaptation,
a new evolutionary process starts up as workers search experimen-
tally for new forms of organization and action based on their own
power rather than that of the system. Indeed, mass strikes are essentially the result of the breakdown of existing modes of adaptation and the attempt to find new ones. Thus they are not "utopian"
but "pragmatic"—even when the power toward which they tend
would mean dissolving the existing organization of society rather
than adjusting to it.

The fault in most labor history does not lie with "pragmatism"
per se, but with too narrow an interpretation of it. For one thing,
pragmatism as a philosophy envisions adaptation not simply as an
acceptance of the status quo, but as a tranformation of it. For another, trade unionism's tactics must be judged a failure of adaptation insofar as their result has been to leave workers virtually powerless over their lives. An approach to history based on pragmatism
requires that past action be evaluated in terms of its contribution to
problems we have not yet solved.

Historical debate about radicalism in the American working
class has generally centered around the question: Why did the U.S.
not follow the European pattern of a socialist party supported by

socialist trade unions? This formulation of the question presupposes that the development of organizations holding socialist ideals is the key index of the radical or conservative nature of the working class. This assumption, however, is undermined by the experience of the past fifty years, in which the official Left organizations—whether liberal, socialist, or Communist—have consistently blocked the efforts of workers to take direct power over production. The European model of socialist parties and unions turns out not to be a revolutionary model at all, for when European workers acted in a revolutionary manner, they did so *against* these organizations. Therefore, in judging the American working class it is the action of the workers themselves that must form the starting point of analysis, not the ideology of the organizations that developed to regulate their place in society. If that action challenged by force the right of owners to manage their property as they saw fit—and it has for the past century—then it is anti-capitalist in essence and revolutionary in trajectory.

Two strategies have helped historians to discount mass strikes. The first is to write them off as aberrations, unimportant because they do not reflect the normal functioning of American society. But as Charles Walker wrote,

Frequently more can be learned of the character of an individual, a class or a community in a few hours of crisis than in a lifetime of routine living.[9]

It is at such times that the veil of stasis is rent and the opposing forces maintaining and undermining the existing form of society revealed.

The second strategy is to treat various strikes and movements as separate, virtually unrelated events. Thus there is a book on the Homestead strike and a book on the Pullman boycott, a book on the Seattle general strike and a number on the steel strike of the same year, but I have found only one book dealing with a period of mass strike as a whole.

By ignoring the most serious challenges to the status quo, historians are enabled to ignore the central role of repression in American society. The threat—and employment—of private, police, and military armed force has been a constant factor moulding the so-called American consensus. Control by violence, as Marcus Raskin has pointed out, is often hardly visible but it is "the central fact of human relations in American society. It dictates the contours of the political structure and announces that no social contract exists."[10] The assumption that American society is based on consent may be attractive, but it hardly fits the facts. Instead, we find that the realm of protected liberties is a small, circumscribed sector of

318 society, surrounded by vast hierarchical institutions based on command and backed by force. Repression is absent from American history only where the status quo is unchallenged.

These various attitudes have led historians to ignore vast areas of class conflict in the United States. Historians—even labor historians—pass over in a paragraph or two strikes involving hundreds of thousands of people, accompanied by armed conflict on a substantial scale, simply because they made no contribution to the development of collective bargaining. Even in those strikes about which entire books have been written, the action of workers outside of formal organized channels is usually largely ignored.

A change of perspective by historians would lead to a large-scale investigation of this material, similar to the outpouring of research on black history which has recently begun to compensate for centuries of neglect. In preparing this book, I found that hardly a single aspect of class conflict in America has been adequately studied. I can assure anyone considering research in this area that large bodies of data untapped in the past and only rapidly surveyed here lie waiting to be explored.

A change in perspective by historians should be reflected also in their relation to contemporary material. Millions of dollars today are spent preserving the records of the Presidents and other "elite" figures, but great mass events like the 1970 student strike and the postal and Teamster wildcats will be as written on water, traceable only in newspaper clippings a dozen years hence. When historians recognize the significance of popular movements, academic history departments will begin to turn their resources—including the recently developed technology of oral history—to preserving data on the mass struggles that are going on all around us today. If professional historians fail to perform this task, those outside the club will have to undertake it themselves—for it is they who need the knowledge it will provide.

It is not only the subjects covered or the techniques employed which has tended to make history serve a conservative myth. Even more, it is the assumption that the past is significant only as it has contributed to the present form of society. This in turn is based upon the assumption that the future will be essentially a continuation of the present—that historical change, in short, has stopped.

But as E.H. Carr put it in *What Is History?*, the historian must not only ask the question "why?," but also the question "whither?" [11] The culmination of the past—that which gives it significance—is not the present, but the future. The historian's work—as opposed to the mere antiquarian's—is important because it contributes to what we need to know to cope with the practical problems of the future.

Of course, if the future is simply a continuation of the present, then the "lost causes" of the past are indeed lost forever. But the long-term continuation of the present structure of human society is almost inconceivable today. The new threats of nuclear and ecological disaster, combined with the more traditional effects of economic, social, and military crisis, mean that humanity—if it survives at all—will do so only through fundamental changes of its way of life. But even if the present organization of society remains viable, is its continuation to be desired when it serves at every turn to block the potential for human freedom, creativity, and well-being which society itself has created?

The focus of the historian must change if he is to contribute to human survival and liberation. His responsibility is to find those social processes and structures which promise an alternative to the ones now dominant. He must show what factors advance and retard their development. He must clarify the weaknesses, faults, and limitations of the dominant structures which lead people to develop alternatives to them. In short, he must show what forces might prefigure a movement by the underlying population to assert their will over society.

Afterword: Footnotes

1. George F. Addes and R.J. Thomas, in introduction to Henry Kraus, *The Many and the Few* (Los Angeles: Plantin Press, 1947).
2. David Donald, *New York Times Book Review*, July 19, 1970.
3. James Bryce, quoted in Henry David, *The History of the Haymarket Affair, A Study in the American Social-Revolutionary and Labor Movements* (N.Y.: Collier Books, 1963), p. 39.
4. Stephen Thernstrom, "Urbanization, Migration, and Social Mobility in Late Nineteenth-Century Amerca," in *Toward a New Past: Dissenting Essays in American History,* Barton J. Bernstein, ed. (N.Y.: Vintage Books, Random House, 1969), pp. 172-3.
5. David Brody, *Steelworkers in America, The Non-Union Era* (N.Y.: Harper Torchbooks, Harper & Row, 1969), p. ix.
6. Irving Bernstein, *The Lean Years, A History of the American Workers 1920-1933* (Baltimore: Penguin Books, 1966), p. ix.
7. Brody, p. ix.
8. Bernstein, p. ix.
9. Charles R. Walker, *American City, a Rank-and-File History* (N.Y.: Farrar & Rhinehart, 1937), p. xiii.
10. Marcus Raskin, *Being and Doing* (N.Y.: Random House, 1971), p. xv.
11. Edward H. Carr, *What Is History?* (N.Y.: Random House, Vintage Books, 1967), p. 143.

Index

329

Book designed by Virginia Clive-Smith.
Production: Jon Goodchild, Tom Hardy, Vickie Jackson
Carol Raskin, Dian Aziza Ooka.
Index: Chet Roaman